Into that
Darkness

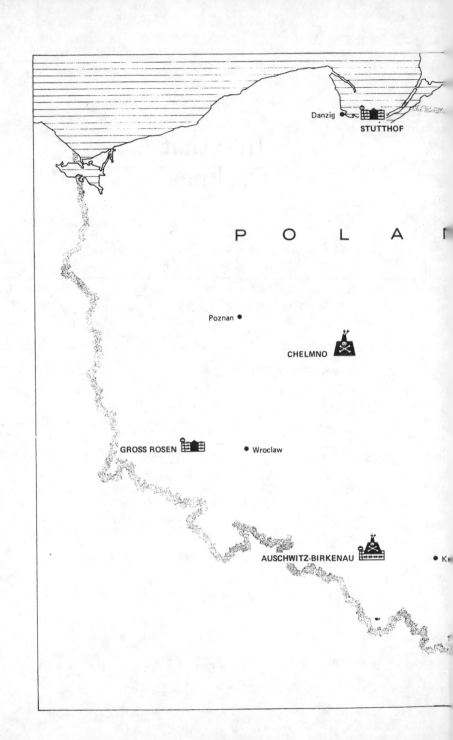

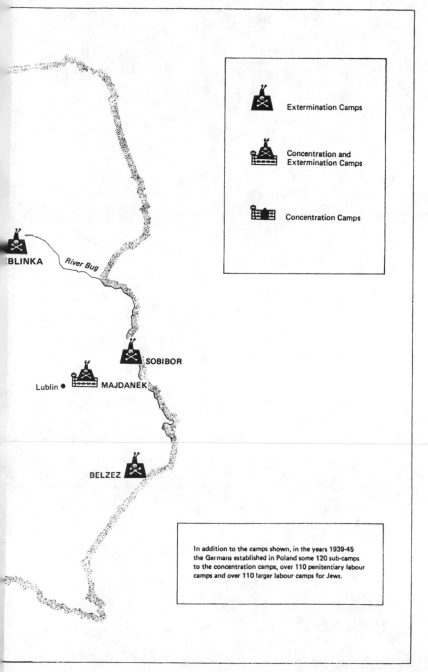

Extermination Camps

Concentration and
Extermination Camps

Concentration Camps

BLINKA · River Bug

SOBIBOR

Lublin ● · MAJDANEK

BELZEZ

In addition to the camps shown, in the years 1939-45
the Germans established in Poland some 120 sub-camps
to the concentration camps, over 110 penitentiary labour
camps and over 110 larger labour camps for Jews.

Gitta Sereny

Into that Darkness

An Examination
of Conscience

Vintage Books
A Division of Random House
New York

First Vintage Books Edition, January 1983
Copyright © 1974 by Gitta Sereny
Published in the United States
by Random House, Inc., New York. Originally published in
England by Andre Deutsch Limited, London, and in the
United States by McGraw-Hill, Inc., New York, 1974.

Library of Congress Cataloging in Publication Data
Sereny, Gitta.
Into that darkness.
Originally published: London : Deutsch, 1974.
Bibliography: p.
Includes index.
1. World War, 1939-1945—Prisoners and prisons, German.
2. Concentration camps—Europe.
3. Stangl, Franz.
I. Title.
D805.G3S456 1982   940.54′72′4304355   82-40049
ISBN 0-394-71035-5   AACR2

Manufactured in the United States of America

3579C864

To Don
and to our children Mandy and Chris,
and to Elaine

Everywhere the human soul stands
between a hemisphere of light and
another of darkness . . .

Thomas Carlyle (1795–1881)

The power of choosing between good
and evil is within the reach of all.

Origen (c185–254)

Contents

Acknowledgments

I am indebted to many people and organizations for their help in the preparation of this book.

Of the latter I must thank first and foremost the German judicial authorities who gave me access to Düsseldorf prison and Franz Stangl, and particularly the Governor of the prison, Herr Eberhard Mies and his wife, for their kindness throughout those strenuous weeks. I am grateful too to the Polish authorities for their help in Poland, and the Austrian Ministries of the Interior and Justice for their assistance in Vienna.

Chief Prosecutor Adalbert Rückerl, Director of the Central Authority for Investigation into Nazi Crime, in Ludwigsburg, and his colleagues have spared no effort to assist me ever since my first research into this subject for a series of articles on the Nazi crime trials for the *Daily Telegraph Magazine* in 1967.

The Institute for Contemporary History in Munich, and in particular Dr Lothar Gruchmann from whose work on Euthanasia in the Third Reich I quote in this book, provided a wealth of documentary material. I also thank the West German Bundesarchiv in Koblenz.

I am particularly indebted to the Wiener Library in London and to their extraordinarily knowledgeable staff. I don't think any serious book on National Socialism could be undertaken without the help of this unique institution.

The two men in West Germany who I believe know more than anyone else now about specific Nazi crimes are Chief Prosecutors Alfred Spiess and Kurt Tegge. Kurt Tegge has spent years on the Einsatzgruppen trials in Hamburg, and Alfred Spiess prosecuted both in the Treblinka trial and the Stangl trial in Düsseldorf. I am grateful to both of them for so liberally sharing their knowledge with me. No formal expression of gratitude could possibly do justice to the amount of practical help and advice I had from Alfred Spiess. Neither of these men, of course, necessarily share my

9

opinions or my evaluation of the individuals I discuss in this book.

I thank Count Eduard Raczynski, former Foreign Minister of the Polish Government in Exile; Mr Adam Ciolkosz, former Socialist Member of Parliament in Poland; and M. Kazimierz Papée, former Polish Ambassador to the Holy See, for their interest in this book and for their considerable help. Equally I thank Vienna City Counsellor Herr Hubert Pfoch for allowing me to quote his extraordinary wartime diary and the use of the photographs he took as a courageous young man in Poland.

A special word of thanks to Horst Münzberger who permitted me to gain insight, and briefly to share with him, a staggering human conflict.

I also want to thank in this particular section of the acknowledgments a number of men and women who consented to talk to me but asked not to be quoted, or for whom it would obviously have been damaging to be named.

I owe thanks to many of my friends for their concern for me during the years I worked on this book.

Above all perhaps to Ruth Alice and Klaus von Bismarck and their (many) children and young relatives. Theirs is the new Germany which I love and trust: it is my luck to have them as my friends.

To Catherine Valabregue for sunny breaks in France and for our home from home in Paris. To Mädi and Hansibert Törring for their ever-open door and the lovely peace of Seefeld on so many occasions. To Sally and Philip Dowson for the constant reassurance of their friendship. To Ronald Preston for his unstinting help. To Amador Aguiar in Brazil, whose interest reinforced my belief in the universal application of the problems this book is concerned with.

My gratitude (again) to John Anstey, Editor of the *Daily Telegraph Magazine*, for his unfailing receptiveness to complex and often controversial ideas.

To Nina van Pallandt and to Enrique Arias for their encouragement after ploughing through a rough draft; and to Paul Neuburg at the same stage for his particularly valuable criticisms, every one of which was justified.

To Alice Hammerstein Mathias for her research in poetry – and for finding exactly the right words in Carlyle and – above all – Origen.

I want to thank my old and dear friend Paul Palmer for his faith in a very young writer years ago: this, I think, may be the book he meant.

Diana Athill edited *Into That Darkness*. She has lent it – and me – her warmth, her intelligence, her literary fluency, and a quality of involvement I had little right to expect. I am grateful that she has become my friend. And I also thank my American editor, Berenice Hoffman, whose perspicacity saved me from serious blunders.

The stability of both my children in the face of considerable odds, and the gaiety and happiness of my daughter Mandy throughout, were my most valuable support during the past three years.

And, above all, I thank my husband, Don Honeyman, who has contributed to and is part of every aspect of the work on this book.

Gitta Sereny Honeyman

London, June 1973

The photographs of Franz Stangl in prison and talking to the author are by Don Honeyman. The photograph of Treblinka now is from the collection of Alexander Bernfes.

Preface

My dialogues with Franz Stangl, Kommandant of Sobibor and Treblinka, which were published in an abbreviated version in October 1971 in the *Daily Telegraph Magazine* in England (and subsequently in magazines throughout the world), represent the framework upon which this book is constructed: its focus. But they are finally only a small part of it.

I originally conceived the idea of talking with Stangl when, attending his trial in Germany in 1970 (as, in the course of journalistic work, I had attended other Nazi crime trials), I realized that whatever else he might have been, he was, unlike many others I had observed under similar circumstances, an individual of some intelligence.

He was the only Kommandant of an *extermination* camp who had been brought to trial. There were, extraordinarily enough, only four men who specifically filled that function: one is dead, and two have managed to disappear from sight. I had felt for many years that, despite the great number of books and films on the Nazi era, there was a whole dimension of reactions and behaviour we had never yet understood and which yet is deeply relevant to the pressures and perils which beset us now and may threaten us in the future.

I thought it essential, before it became too late, to try at least once, as far as possible unemotionally and with an open mind, to penetrate the personality of a man who had been intimately involved with the most total evil our age has produced. It was important, I thought, to assess the circumstances which led up to his involvement, for once not from our point of view, but from *his*. It was a chance, I felt, to evaluate, through examining his motivations and reactions as he described them rather than as we wished or prejudged them to be, whether evil is created by circumstances or by birth, and to what extent it is determined by the individual himself, or by his environment. Stangl was the last and ultimately the only man of that particular calibre with whom such an experiment could be attempted.

The seventy hours I talked with him – in German – provided a beginning of the answers I sought. But others were needed to complete the picture; not only because his words – those of a profoundly troubled man who frequently revealed extraordinary manifestations of a dual personality – needed to be evaluated against the historical records and the memory of others who had known him, but also because – I came to recognize – no man's actions can be judged in isolation from the external elements that shape and influence his life.

I spent another eighteen months studying records, and seeking out men and women in several corners of the world who were involved in one way or another with the story Stangl told. Some were intimately involved, like his family in Brazil who continue to love him; some appallingly, like the ss personnel who worked under him and who are now back in society after serving prison sentences, and like high Nazi officials, at one time his administrative superiors; some tragically, like the camp survivors who, after miraculously escaping, have now remade their lives in different countries; some marginally, as diplomatic observers, or as innocent witnesses to the catastrophes in German-occupied Poland. And lastly there were the priests who helped people like Stangl escape from Europe after the Third Reich ceased to exist.

My talks with such priests, and others who were bent on justifying the actions of Pope Pius XII and his advisors, faced me with a disconcerting moral conflict, for I am very conscious of the value to society of the continuity – the stability – which the churches provide, and of their present vulnerability. In the final analysis, however, despite my reluctance to add to the polemics about the record of the Vatican and Pope Pius XII during the Nazi period, the sombre facts, previously unpublished, which emerged during my research could not be ignored. It seemed essential to pinpoint responsibility, if for no other reason than to demonstrate how many men of the Church did *not* share the Vatican's attitude.

As far as it is possible for any thinking individual who was intensely involved, like most young people in Europe at the time, in the events of World War II, I approached the research for this book with a minimum of prejudice and with determination to question but not to hurt.

14

The truth is however, that most of the men and women who agreed to relate and examine, with extraordinary honesty and at considerable sacrifice to their peace of mind, the most intense experiences of their lives, ended by revealing themselves deeply, not really for this book but out of their own need to explore the past. I have deleted a few things which appeared likely either to distress them, or cause damage to third persons. None the less, the journey between self-discovery at this level of intensity, and seeing one's thoughts and anguish reproduced in print is a long one, and unfamiliar to most people. I can only hope that the book will contribute to the understanding of all those who helped it come into being, and not cause them embarrassment or pain.

It is through all of them that the theme of this book evolved and crystallized. It is not intended to be primarily an account of horror, though horror is unavoidable, nor is it only an effort to understand one man who was uniquely implicated in the greatest tragedy of our time. It is a demonstration of the fatal interdependence of all human actions, and an affirmation of man's responsibility for his own acts and their consequences.

The People Who Speak

While researching this book I talked with many more people than those I quote. Here, for the reader's convenience, I list under six headings only those whose words provide a major contribution to the actual text.

The main story.

FRANZ STANGL, Police Superintendent of the Euthanasia Institute, Schloss Hartheim, November 1940 – February 1942; Kommandant of Sobibor, March 1942 – September 1942; Kommandant of Treblinka, September 1942 – August 1943. Interviewed in Düsseldorf Remand Prison where he was awaiting the result of appeal against a life sentence, in April and June 1971.

THERESA STANGL, his wife, interviewed at her home in São Bernardo do Campo, Brazil.

HELENE EIDENBÖCK, his sister-in-law, interviewed at her home in Vienna.

Former SS men who worked with Stangl.

FRANZ SUCHOMEL, who worked in the Euthanasia Programme – photographic section – 1940–2, and later at Treblinka. Interviewed at his home in Altotting, Bavaria.

OTTO HORN, who worked in the Euthanasia Programme in 1941, then in Russia and as of September 1942, in Treblinka. Interviewed at his home in West Berlin.

GUSTAV MÜNZBERGER, who worked in the Euthanasia Programme and as of August 1942 at Treblinka. Interviewed at his son's home in Unterammergau, Bavaria.

Survivors of the extermination camps Sobibor and Treblinka.

STANISLAW SZMAJZNER, who was at Sobibor, to whom I talked in Goiania, Brazil, where he is an executive in a paper factory.

RICHARD GLAZAR, who was at Treblinka, to whom I talked at his home near Berne, in Switzerland, where he works in an engineering firm.

SAMUEL RAJZMAN, who was at Treblinka, to whom I talked in Montreal, where he runs his own lumber company.

BEREK ROJZMAN, who was at Treblinka, to whom I talked in Warsaw where he works in a factory. He is the only Treblinka survivor still living in Poland, and he accompanied me when I visited the camp-site.

JOSEPH SIEDLECKI, who was at Treblinka, to whom I talked at his home in Upper New York State where he is *maître d'hotel* at a large resort.

External witnesses of events connected with Sobibor and Treblinka.

WLADIMIR GERUNG AND HIS WIFE. Wladimir Gerung is chief forester of Sobibor and custodian of the camp-site. His wife lived within twenty miles of the camp while it was in operation.

HORST MÜNZBERGER AND HIS WIFE. Horst is the son of Gustav Münzberger and helped me understand what it is like to be the son of a man who was in charge of the gas chambers at Treblinka.

HUBERT PFOCH, now a Vienna City Councillor, who as a young soldier in transit, on August 21, 1942, witnessed the arrival of a transport at Treblinka and who has kindly allowed me to quote from the diary he kept at the time, and to reproduce photographs he took.

FRANCISZEK ZABECKI, who was traffic controller at Treblinka (town) station from May 1941 until after the camp was demolished. A member of the Home Army (the Polish resistance), his undercover job was reporting German troop movements, but it enabled him to keep a detailed – and unique – record of all the transports coming through his station on the way into Treblinka camp.

In connection with the Euthanasia Programme.

DIETER ALLERS AND HIS WIFE. Dieter Allers is a lawyer who in December 1940 was appointed chief administrative officer of T4, which administered the "General Foundation for Institutional Care" (the euphemism for the Euthanasia Programme), and later – although Herr Allers contests this – the "Final Solution". Sentenced to two years' imprisonment in a recent euthanasia trial, he is now back home in Hamburg where I spoke to him and his wife. Frau Allers did her war service as a secretary for 'T4' (and briefly at the Euthanasia "Institute", Schloss Hartheim). She and her husband met and married during that period.

ALBERT HARTL, who left the Roman Catholic priesthood in 1934, joined the SS (Sturmbannführer – Major), and in 1935 was appointed Chief of Church Information at the Reich Security Office: a position enabling him to be uniquely well informed on the relationship between the National Socialists and the Churches with reference to the Euthanasia Programme.

In connection with the escape network provided by the Catholic Church in Rome, and the relationship between the Vatican and Nazi Germany.

MONSIGNOR KARL BAYER, Director of the International Caritas in Vienna, who held a similar position in Rome during the period discussed in my book.

DR EUGEN DOLLMANN, who was Hitler's interpreter in Rome and now lives in Munich.

MADAME GERTRUDE DUPUIS, who has held an impoitant position in the International Red Cross in Rome since before World War II.

HIS EXCELLENCY, MONSIEUR KAZIMIERZ PAPÉE, Polish Ambassador to the Holy See from July 14, 1939, to December 1948, who still lives in Rome.

FATHER ANTON WEBER, a Palatine priest at the St Raphael Society in Rome, who was closely concerned with providing aid for refugees and escapees.

BISHOP JAKOB WEINBACHER, Auxiliary Bishop of Vienna, who in 1952 took over as Rector of the Anima in Rome from Bishop Alois Hudal (now dead) from whom Stangl obtained a Red Cross passport and funds to enable him to escape to Syria.

FATHER BURKHART SCHNEIDER, SJ, head of the team of Jesuit historians working on the Vatican publication *Actes et Documents du Saint Siège relatif à la Seconde Guerre Mondiale.*

Part I

I

I FIRST met Franz Stangl on the morning of Friday, April 2, 1971, in a little room which was ordinarily used as a waiting and rest room for lawyers visiting the Düsseldorf remand prison. The room was the same size as the cells in the prison's modern block, the block in which Stangl was detained. It had the same barred windows, the same dreary view of the paved inside yard, and the same kind of minimal furnishings in blond polished pine. It was impersonal, neutral, with nothing in it to please or edify, but equally nothing to distract the eye or mind: the right place for the particular seventy hours I was to spend with this particular man.

When, on December 22, 1970, the Düsseldorf court sentenced Stangl to life imprisonment for co-responsibility in the murder of 900,000 people during his tenure as Kommandant of Treblinka, "Nazi-hunter" Simon Wiesenthal, who had played a part in his capture, told reporters that Stangl's conviction by the Germans was at least as important as Adolf Eichmann's by the Israelis. "The Stangl case", he said, "provided West Germany with their most significant criminal case of the century. If I had done nothing else in my life but get this evil man, I would not have lived in vain."

It was difficult to associate the quiet, courteous man the prison governor presented to me that morning, with that description.

Sixty-three years old, Franz Stangl was tall, well built, with receding grey hair, a deeply lined face and red-rimmed eyes. He was wearing grey flannel trousers, a white shirt, a tie and a neat grey sweater. When I met him he had been in prison four years and two weeks, virtually all of this time in solitary confinement. During the three years of the preparations for the trial, the prison also accommodated several of his former subordinates and the strictest precautions were taken to prevent them from communicating with one another. But even after these men, their sentences confirmed, were moved to a penal institution, he remained in isolation in his

21

six- by twelve-foot cell because several young prisoners had muttered threats against his life. Only a few days before I met him, his increasing depression had decided the prison authorities to allow him a daily period of exercise in the prison yard and some contact with selected prisoners. "But even now he hardly talks to anyone," one of the prison officers told me later. "He is a loner." Most of his day was spent in his cell reading and listening to the radio, his prison possessions arranged around him in pristine symmetry.

Despite his totally sedentary life Stangl was muscular, straight-backed and to all appearances both relaxed and controlled.

He and the prison governor, Herr Eberhard Mies, a former lawyer, shook hands and bowed to each other. Presented to me, Stangl bowed again – both times it was a gesture of courtesy, not deference or even respect. Herr Mies inquired after his health. Speaking quietly and conversationally in the soft German of his native Austria, in the semi-formal way it is taught in Austrian provincial schools, Stangl replied that he was feeling better. "I have signed up for the chess club," he said, "and I think I'll attend some classes when they start again after Easter. Literature, I think; it will be interesting. They are going to have them twice a week, aren't they?" Unexpectedly, it seemed an encounter between equals. Stangl, very different from the "small man" I had been told I would find, gave the disquieting impression of an imposing and dominant personality in full control of himself and his environment.

This impression persisted up to a point, and despite his obvious apprehension about our impending talks, throughout that first morning. After we had been left alone, he immediately began to rebut various accusations made during his trial. The arguments, the phraseology, the very words he used were gratingly familiar from his and other trials for Nazi crimes: he had done nothing wrong; there had always been others above him; he had never done anything but obey orders; he had never hurt a single human being. What had happened was a tragedy of war and – sadly – there were tragedies of war everywhere: "Look at Katyn," he said, "look at Dresden, Hiroshima and now Vietnam." He was sorry, yes sorry for that young American lieutenant who, like him, had done no more than obey orders in Mai Lai and was now having to carry the can.

I listened to him all morning, almost without interrupting. His

22

sentence was on appeal and it was clear that he had been advised, or had convinced himself, that these "interviews" would enable him – he may even have thought they were intended to enable him – to state his case once more in the only way the cases of people like himself had ever been stated. The precedent had been established at Nuremberg where the arguments proposed by the defence for some of the accused were sometimes close enough to a kind of truth to throw at least some doubt on the *quality* of their guilt. It was a technique which, for want of anything better, had subsequently been adopted by all who followed the Nuremberg accused into the dock, whatever their standing, whatever their past involvement. But polemics was not what I had come for.

Shortly before breaking off for lunch – when, I had been told, I would have to give him as much time as he wanted for his meal and rest – I told him that having listened to him for two and a half hours I thought I had better explain what I really wanted. He could then think about it and let me know after lunch whether he wanted to go on. I said that I knew inside out all the things he had said that morning; all of them had been said before by any number of people. And I didn't wish to argue the right or wrong of any of this; I felt it was pointless. What I had come for was something quite different: I wanted him really to talk to me; to tell me about himself as a child, a boy, a youth, a man; to tell me about his father, his mother, his friends, his wife and his children; tell me not what he did or did not do but what he loved and what he hated and what he felt about the things in his life which had eventually brought him to where he was sitting now. If he didn't want to do this, but preferred to go on in the vein of that morning's recital, then I would listen to him, I said, to the end of that afternoon, go back to England, write a little something about the interview, and that would be the end of it. But if, after thinking about it, he decided to help me delve deeper into the past (*his* past, because things had happened to and inside him which had happened to hardly anyone else, ever) then perhaps we could find some truth together; some new truth which would contribute to the under-standing of things that had never yet been understood. If this could be done I would be prepared to stay in Düsseldorf as long as he liked; days or even weeks. I told him, too, that he had to know from the start that I abhorred everything the Nazis had stood for and done, but that I would promise him to write down exactly what he said, whatever it would be, and that I would try – my own feelings notwithstanding – to understand without prejudice.

When I'd finished he didn't say anything, only nodded. And when a moment later the guard came to take him back to his cell, he left the room with nothing but a small formal bow. I was not at all sure I'd see him again.

I lunched that day in the canteen and talked to several members of the prison staff. It was evident at once that they *liked* Stangl. "If only they were all like Stangl," they said, "our life would be a bed of roses." Some of them said "like *Herr* Stangl". I remarked on that "Herr" to one of the older guards, who shrugged and said, "That's what we are supposed to call them now. 'Herr' indeed!"

Prison staff in West Germany are well trained (including 200 hours of lectures on psychology), and almost all the officers I spoke with that day, and in the ensuing weeks, appeared to me to be articulate and compassionate men who were intensely interested in what my conversations with Stangl would produce. They spoke freely about the complicated conflicts his presence in the prison brought to their minds. Many of them questioned – as do most people in Germany – the continuation of the Nazi crime trials so many years after the events, and several of them brought up the same worn-out arguments: nobody in Germany had known anything of the horrors, and no one who had not lived under a dictatorship could understand or presume to judge. At the same time almost all of them – though there were exceptions – agreed unhappily that as long as any of the men who were involved in these terrible deeds were alive, it would be immoral to do nothing. One of the men I spoke with on that first day was twenty-four – he hadn't even been born at the time of Treblinka. "Stangl", he said thoughtfully, "impresses us like a *man* – you know what I mean? An intelligent human being, not a brute like Franz." (Kurt Franz, a former cook, was Stangl's notoriously brutal adjutant, who briefly commanded and then liquidated Treblinka after Stangl was relieved, and is now serving a life sentence in West Germany.) "Perhaps . . . " he went on, "now at long last one of them is going to have the courage to explain to my generation how any human being with mind and heart and brain could . . . not even 'do' what was done – it isn't our function to say whether a man is 'guilty as charged' or not – but even see it being done, and consent to remain alive."

Stangl looked indefinably different when he was brought back to the little room on the second floor at 2 p.m. He had taken off his tie and unbuttoned the top button of his shirt, but he still looked spruce – that wasn't it. He was as well shaved as he had been in the morning – had probably shaved again – yet he no longer looked quite clean-shaven, nor was his skin as taut and young-looking as before. Earlier I had noticed and been slightly surprised by his broad red hands because they had seemed so much in contrast to the rest of his appearance and bearing, but now it flashed through my mind that they fitted him, or at least some part of him.

"I've thought about what you said," he told me at once, his voice slightly unsteady. "I hadn't understood before – I hadn't understood what you wanted. I think I understand now . . . I want to do it. I want to try to do it. . . ."

There were tears in his eyes before we even began to speak of his childhood. "I thought you just wanted – you know – an 'interview'," he said, emphasizing that loaded term. I had some English cigarettes and he took one – he was, I soon saw, a chain-smoker. "My childhood," he began, shaking his head several times, "I'll tell you. . . ."

He was born in Altmünster, a small town in Austria, on March 26, 1908. His only sister was then ten, his mother still young and pretty, but his father was already an ageing man.

"He was a nightwatchman by the time I was born, but all he could ever think or talk about were his days in the Dragoons [one of the Austro-Hungarian Imperial élite regiments]. His dragoon uniform, always carefully brushed and pressed, hung in the wardrobe. I was so sick of it, I got to hate uniforms. I knew since I was very small, I don't remember exactly when, that my father hadn't really wanted me. I heard them talk. He thought I wasn't really his. He thought my mother . . . you know. . . ."

"Even so, was he kind to you?"

He laughed without mirth. "He was a Dragoon. Our lives were run on regimental lines. I was scared to death of him. I remember one day – I was about four or five and I'd just been given new slippers. It was a cold winter morning. The people next door to us were moving. The moving van had come – a horse-drawn carriage then, of course. The driver had gone into the house to help get the furniture and there was this wonderful carriage and no one about.

"I ran out through the snow, new slippers and all. The snow came half-way up my legs but I didn't care. I climbed up and I sat in the driver's seat, high above the ground. Everything as far as I could see was quiet and white and still. Only far in the distance there was a black spot moving in the whiteness of the new snow. I watched it but I couldn't recognize what it was until suddenly I realized it was my father coming home. I got down as fast as I could and raced back through the deep snow into the kitchen and hid behind my mother. But he got there almost as fast as I. 'Where is the boy?' he asked, and I had to come out. He put me over his knees and leathered me. He had cut his finger some days before and wore a bandage. He thrashed me so hard, his cut opened and blood poured out. I heard my mother scream, 'Stop it, you are splashing blood all over the clean walls.'"

He said that when he was eight, two years after the beginning of World War I, his father died of malnutrition. "He was thin as a rake; he looked like a ghost, a skeleton."

A year later his mother married a widower who also had two children. "One was a boy exactly my age: we became inseparable. He was killed, in 1942."

"Did your stepfather treat you like his own son?"

"He was all right" – he paused. "Well, of course I wasn't his son, was I?" He paused again. "I remember, sometimes I felt jealous of my stepbrother."

When the two boys were fourteen, Stangl's stepfather wanted them to leave school and go to work in the local steel mill where he worked himself. "He wanted us to earn money – he always thought of money. Wolfgang – my stepbrother – he didn't mind: he was very happy-go-lucky; he didn't mind anything. But I had my eye on working for the nearby textile mill – that's what I always wanted to do, and for that I had to be fifteen. So I got my mother and the school principal to say I had to stay in school another year."

"Did you have many friends?"

"No, but I had taught myself to play the zither and I joined the zither club." He began to cry quietly and wiped his eyes with the back of his hand. "Excuse me. . . ."

He left school at fifteen and became an apprentice weaver.

"I finished my apprenticeship in three years," he said. "When I was eighteen and a half I did my exams and became the youngest

master-weaver in Austria." He was still proud of this achievement.
"I worked in the mill and only two years later I had fifteen workers
under me. I earned two hundred schillings a month, and gave
four-fifths of it to my parents."

"Is that all you kept for yourself? At twenty, was that enough?"

He smiled. "I was making twice that by giving zither lessons at
night."

"Did you have more friends by then?"

"No. But I had the zither. On Sundays I built myself a Taunus –
a sailboat." Again he began to cry and continued for a long time.
"Excuse me. . . ."

"What is it that makes you cry when you remember this?"

"It was my happiest time." He shook his head again and again
with a gesture of helplessness.

By 1931 – at twenty-three – five years after becoming a master-
weaver, he had come to realize that he was at a dead end. "Without
higher education I couldn't get further promotion. But to go on
doing all my life what I was doing then? Around me I saw men of
thirty-five who had started at the same age as I and who were now
old men. The work was too unhealthy. The dust got into your
lungs – the noise. . . . I had often looked at young policemen in
the streets: they looked so healthy, so secure – you know what I
mean. And so clean and spruce in their uniforms. . . ."

"But you hated uniforms?"

He looked surprised. "That – that was different."

Looking back at Austria during the early thirties, when following
the years of depression there was violent conflict between the
Socialists and the Austrian Nationalist – and devoutly Catholic –
Chancellor Dollfuss, I could see that there might be something in
this "difference". It was a place of constant turbulence, alarming
headlines, hostile crowds, street fighting, police sirens, shootings,
barriers; and, perhaps in contrast to the anarchy in the air – I
remembered from my own childhood memories – uniforms *did*
seem attractive.

Stangl applied to join the police and went for an interview. "It
was quite difficult," he said, "quite an exam, you know."

Several months later, when he had already more or less given up
hope, he was notified that he was to report within days to the
Kaplanhof – the police training barracks in Linz – for basic
training.

"I went to see the owner of the mill and explained why I had made that decision. He said, 'Why didn't you come and talk to me about it rather than do it secretly? I intended to send you to school, in Vienna.'" He cried again.

"Couldn't you have changed your plans when he told you that?"
He shook his head. "He didn't ask me."

The Austrian police training was tough. "They called it the 'Vienna School'," he said. "They were a sadistic lot. They drilled the feeling into us that everyone was against us: that all men were rotten."

He stayed at the school for a year, then became a "rookie". Working first as a traffic policeman and then on the riot squad, he graduated in 1933. "Even then we had to go on living in barracks. But it didn't matter to me: my girl friend, who I had met in '31, had gone to Florence to work as a nanny for the Duca di Corsini. I had nothing to do except work. So I volunteered for special duties, evenings and weekends."

"What sort of special duties?"
He laughed, "Oh, you know, just flushing out villains here and there. It was all good experience and I knew it wouldn't hurt my record. During the Socialist uprisings in February 1934 there were terrific street battles in Linz. In one of them the Socialists entrenched themselves at the Central Cinema and we had to fight for hours to get them out. I was the one who flushed the last ones out that night at 11 p.m. – after well over twelve hours. I got the silver Service Medal for it."

Through the weeks to come, however terrible the stories he was telling, Stangl was constantly to fall back into police jargon. *"Der war ein Strolch"* – "he was a villain" – he would say, applying this almost affectionate description indiscriminately to a whole range of people across the years: first Austrian politicians and crooks, then Germans and Poles, Christians and Jews.

In July 1934 the Austrian Chancellor, Dollfuss, was assassinated. "Of *course* the Nazis killed him," Stangl said, in a tone which made it quite clear that, as an Austrian police officer, he had automatically condemned such an act. A few days after the assassination, Stangl found a Nazi arms cache in a forest; a feat which three months later earned him a decoration – the Austrian Eagle with green-white ribbon – and a posting to the CID school.

"That was the beginning," he said grimly. This medal and the reason for it, he said, hung over him like a sword of Damocles for years. The training at the CID school was "fantastically intensive", he said. "Twenty-one lecturers for nineteen students. But for me, I know this now," he said heavily, "it was the first step on the road to catastrophe."

In the autumn of 1935 he was transferred to the political division of the CID in the town of Wels, thirty minutes by train from Linz (the capital of the province), and at that time, three years prior to the Austrian Anschluss – the German annexation of Austria in March 1938 – a hotbed of illegal Nazi activities. "I was just getting married," he said. "Wels was a very nice place to live. And the assignment was considered a great plum for a man not yet thirty."

"What were your duties in your new assignment?"

"Well, you know what Austria was like then. We had to ferret out anti-government activities by anyone: Social Democrats, Communists *and* Nazis." As a Kriminalbeamter – a CID officer – he wore civilian clothes.

"But perhaps seeing it was Wels, and the way many of you felt privately about the Nazis, perhaps you acted a little less severely, did you, against the Nazis than the others? A little differently in your manners?"

"Among the eighteen men in that department there were certainly some who favoured the Nazis," he answered in a reasonable tone of voice. "But in general, you know, the Austrian police was very professional. Our job was to uphold the law of the land. And on the whole that's what we did, never mind who was involved."

"But surely, for an intelligent man, in the midst of the political turmoil of Austria at that time, it was impossible not to form his own ideas? What did you yourself feel about the Nazis then?"

Stangl had a curious habit, which was to become very familiar as our talks went on, of changing from the semi-formal German he usually spoke to the popular vernacular of his childhood whenever he had to deal with questions he found difficult to answer. This was manifestly not a conscious act; nor did it necessarily mean that at those moments he was lying. In fact it was often, on the contrary, when he was telling a very difficult truth that he took this instinctive refuge in the "cosy" language and mannerisms of his childhood.

"You know," he said, "outside, of course, of doing my job

properly, I wasn't really very interested. You see, I had just got married. I had, for the first time, a home of my own. All I wanted was just to close the door of my house and be alone with my wife. I was mad about her. I really wasn't political you see. I know it sounds now as if I should – or must – have been. But I wasn't. I was just a police officer doing a job."

"But a job you liked?"

"Oh yes, I liked it. But there was nothing heinous or even very dramatic about it then. It was just a job one tried to do as correctly – as kindly, if you like – as possible. Though, it is true, the *way* one did one's job could not be quite isolated from circumstances."

"Circumstances?"

"Well, you see, until early 1937, the Minister of the Interior was a confirmed anti-Nazi, Dr Bayer. But in the early spring of 1937 – just a year before the Anschluss – he was sacked and there were changes all the way down the line. Our new Director of Police was a man called Rubisch and he let it be known immediately – at the very first meeting all of us attended – that from that moment on the attitude of the police towards the Nazis had to change. And of course a year later, in March 1938, everything changed."

"Had you known in advance that the Germans were coming in on that day?"

"Oh no," he replied immediately. "I suppose there were people amongst our lot who knew. But I didn't. You have no idea, though, how organized they were, nor how frightened we became at once."

In his account of these times, Stangl manifested a prodigious memory. By the time he had reached the Socialist uprisings of February 1934 he had mentioned sixteen names, mostly of people who had only briefly crossed his path. By noon of the third day, my list of names he had remembered had grown to fifty-four, and I stopped counting.

"What affected us a lot though," he went on, "was Cardinal Innitzer's call to Catholics to co-operate. And of course the fact that Schuschnigg [who succeeded Dollfuss as Chancellor] threw in the sponge at once. What *I* felt above all was fear. You remember that medal I'd been given – the Eagle? Well, five people had received that at that time. The Nazis took over on March 13; on the 14th they arrested two of those five and a few days later a third. That left only my friend Ludwig Werner and myself. Meanwhile in Linz they had shot two of the chiefs of our department. People we'd seen just a few days before. No trial, nothing – just shot them. Another one, also a friend of mine, was arrested too. And Dr Bayer – the former minister – he was sent to a concentration camp. I helped to get him out of Buchenwald later.* One of our chiefs used to make open remarks against the Nazis. We all used to wonder amongst ourselves how we could stop him. But how could we take it upon ourselves to warn a superior? I remember, one of the other men in my section – his name was Schlammer – he said to me, 'You'd better let your Eagle fly out of the window'.† Ludwig Werner and I were becoming frantic. We had all been given a questionnaire to fill out. One of the questions – the most important one, we thought – was whether we had been illegal Nazi Party members. Werner said we had to *do* something – we couldn't just sit and wait for them to take us. We decided that the first thing to do was to get rid of our file cards; we had this index, you know, with an annotated card for each person in our district who had been suspected of Nazi, Sozi [Socialist] or Communist sympathies. So the first thing we did was to flush the cards down the lavatory."

"*All the cards?*"

"No, just the ones referring to Nazis. And then Werner remembered a lawyer who had been an illegal Nazi and whom he, I and another colleague had helped a bit not long before. . . ."

"*What do you mean helped?*"

"It's the sort of thing one was able to do at times before '38 – just warn someone who was under suspicion to watch his step."

"*Nazis?*"

"Not necessarily. Anybody nice – decent, you know."

This was not a very likely explanation. But I had felt from the beginning that, except on the rarest occasions, it would be essential to let him develop his story in his own way, without showing obvious scepticism or interrupting with critical comments.

"Werner thought," he said, "that we could ask this lawyer – Dr Bruno Wille was his name – to say that he knew we had been illegal members."

"*Did it work?*"

"Yes. Werner went to see him and he said he'd arrange for our names to appear on the illegal Party lists for the previous two years.

* I have been unable to confirm this claim. G.S.

† After Stangl's death I found a piece of paper in his cell on which he had noted a correction: the man's name was not Schlammer, but Hermann Treidl.

31

So after that we filled out the questionnaire and said that we'd been Party members since 1936."

"*And that wasn't true?*"

He shook his head. "No."

The question of whether or not he had been an illegal Party member had been the subject of considerable discussion at Stangl's trial; and what was particularly discussed was the prosecution's contention that before the Anschluss he had contributed to a fund for the aid of Nazi detainees, and that this went a long way to prove his illegal Party membership.

"*How about these contributions you are supposed to have paid to a Nazi aid-fund?*"

"Well yes, I did contribute to an aid-fund. The first week I was transferred into the CID the chief came around one day with a young girl and introduced her to Werner and me as someone who was collecting for the relatives of political prisoners."

Ludwig Werner, questioned in Austria in 1968, shortly before he died of natural causes, was evasive regarding the extent of his "friendship" with Stangl and his knowledge of his opinions or actions. He himself, he said, had been relieved of his duties on October 22, 1939, and was arrested on November 14 and accused of being an opponent of the Nazi Party and of having had illegal financial dealings with a Jew. He was sent to Sachsenhausen concentration camp and kept there until April 1941, when he and his family (as was the custom for political unreliables) were compulsorily moved to Bohemia where he worked in a civilian job until he was called up in 1943 for service on the Eastern front. He was a prisoner of war in Russia from 1944 until 1948, after which he again worked as a CID officer in Leoben, Austria, until his retirement in 1965. He would not say that he had been a friend of Stangl's, but neither had they been enemies. He had no memory whether he and Stangl had ever discussed political matters. Therefore he couldn't say what Stangl's attitude towards National Socialism had been. "All of us, though," he said, "at that time – just before the Anschluss – sympathized with the Nazi Party. I don't mean just the participants of that police course, but the population in general."

Regarding the questionnaire, many officials, he said, "wrote more than was strictly true. Because one was afraid of being sacked." Yes, he remembered Dr Bruno Wille. "He was a member of a legal firm," he said tersely, and refused to be drawn beyond that. Regarding the aid-fund, he couldn't say whether Stangl had paid contributions to such a fund. Nor did he even remember if such a fund had existed, so he was unable to comment on whether or not it was for the purpose of supporting political detainees who were Nazis, or detainees of other political persuasions.

"I went home that day after we got that business organized with Dr Wille," Stangl said, "you know, terrifically relieved. I was so grateful to Ludwig Werner for finding that solution – you have no idea. Anyway, the moment I got home, I told my wife: I thought she'd be as relieved as I. . . ." Suddenly he began to cry again, but differently this time: the deep sobs of a man reliving a pain long suppressed.

"What happened?"

"She hated them you see," he finally went on. "We are Catholics of course, and she is very devout, always was. She was so terribly, terribly angry. 'You betrayed me with these swine,' she said, and I suddenly realized that she didn't believe me. She thought I really had been an illegal Nazi. Oh my God. . . ." He went on crying for many minutes.

"Did you end up by convincing her?"

"A long time – it took a long time." It was clear he was still not sure that he had ever convinced her.

And he had not. It was not only the Düsseldorf court thirty-two years after the event who disbelieved Stangl's assurance that he had not been an "illegal" Nazi. Months after I had first seen Stangl, his wife, in Brazil, was to repeat to me that she had not believed him.

"No, of course I didn't tell them that when I had to testify at his trial – how could I have?" she said. "If my husband hadn't told you about it himself, perhaps I wouldn't have admitted it to you either. But as it is, *because* he told you – and the way he told you – today is the very first time that I feel perhaps he did tell me the truth then – perhaps he wasn't an illegal after all." And she too cried.

Frau Stangl's sister, Helene Eidenböck, who lives in Vienna, had no doubts. "Oh yes," she said, "I think he was an 'illegal' – they all were, you know, in that part of Austria. If he hadn't been, he

33

wouldn't have got on so fast. And that's what they wanted, both of them – to get on."

And former ss Franz Suchomel, who worked under Stangl at Treblinka, and now, after four years in prison, lives in southern Germany, said, "Stangl told me himself that he had been an 'illegal'. He wore on his uniform jacket the chevron of the 'Old Fighters', which wasn't that easy to obtain."

Neither of these last two opinions is necessarily proof that Stangl was lying, since obviously if his story to me was true, the fact that his name had been entered on the "illegal" list would have allowed him to establish his membership as part of his record and would thus automatically have given him the privileges that went with such a record; while he could conceivably have told Suchomel that he had been an "illegal" because he wanted to secure his position by getting this piece of information around. What it does prove, however, is that both his family and his "troops" had believed him to be not a "conscripted" but a "voluntary" Nazi.

The deeper he went into his story, the clearer emerged the picture of the fatal fusion between his own character, and the sequence of events.

"What," I asked, *"was your first specific contact with the Jewish situation in Austria after the Anschluss?"*

"At that time they said that what they wanted was to force the Jews to emigrate – you know, just to leave."

"That's what you thought the policy was?"

"It *was* the policy. They had set up a special section of the Gestapo for 'Jewish Action' – Section IIB2 – where they established a register of Jews and their property." (In Vienna this department was headed by Eichmann. All the research into this subject tends to confirm that the 'Final Solution' – the physical extermination of the Jews – was not proposed, and probably not even considered except, possibly, in private conversations between Hitler and Heydrich, until 1940.)

"What did you have to do with Section IIB2?"

"In principle nothing. I was in the political section, 2C. But you see, I think they knew how I felt. You know, that I wasn't *really* with them. Because after the Austrian Kristallnacht* the

---

* The "Night of Broken Glass" in the autumn of 1938 when Jewish shops all over Germany were smashed and synagogues were burnt.

Gauleiter – Eigruber – called me in and advised me to keep my mouth shut and help IIB2 whenever I was asked."

"Didn't that sound sufficiently ominous to you to indicate that this was the moment to get out?"

"But you see, it wasn't ominous then, and it wasn't a question of 'getting out': if it had only been as simple as that! By this time we heard every day of this one and that one being arrested, sent to a KZ [concentration camp], shot. It wasn't a matter of choosing to stay or not stay in our profession. What it had already become, so quickly, was a question of survival."

"So what finally was your first direct contact with whatever it was they were doing about the Jews?"

"It was after the Sudeten thing:* I was ordered to accompany the chairman of the Jewish Council to Bohemia. They wanted us to check how many Jews were still living there and what they owned in property. Four of us went: myself and one of my juniors, Hirschfeld the chairman – a very nice fellow – and his secretary, a young chap called Hunger."

"How did you travel?"

"Oh, by car."

"But presumably you had to stay somewhere overnight. How was that organized?"

"We stayed together, in a hotel. We ate together. How can I explain? It was all quite ordinary and friendly. As I said, Hirschfeld was a nice man. He had a very difficult job. You see, every Jew who wanted to emigrate forfeited his property. But they also each had to pay a certain sum – it was called a 'tax' – in order to get the exit permit. It was Hirschfeld who had to find this money for poorer Jews who didn't have enough. On that trip he told me lots of stories of the trouble he was having getting rich people to give him money for poorer ones. After that trip, for a long time he'd always come to me when he needed help, because he knew I'd do what I could."

"Do you know what happened to him later?"

"I am not sure," he said vaguely. "I think somebody said he'd gone to America."

---

* October 1938, when the Germans marched into the Czech border province, the Sudetenland.

Max Hirschfeld, it is true, went to America in December 1939, and lives in San Francisco. He refused to come to Germany to testify at Stangl's trial and his testimony was taken in San Francisco (this happened in several cases when a witness was unable or unwilling to go to Germany). Mr Hirschfeld confirmed the car trip to Bohemia; or rather, he said there were two such trips, each of them lasting only one day. "We all had lunch together," he said. "I paid the bill for everybody without being asked." Mr Hirschfeld denied that he had visited Stangl in his office. He said that Stangl was subordinate to two other officials, Botke and Greil, and that Greil had also been along on the trips to Bohemia. Stangl himself, said Mr Hirschfeld, had no authority, but received his orders from these two. "His office was next to Botke; it was he I went to see and Stangl could hear what I discussed with him."

It was suggested by the defence that Mr Hirschfeld had written Stangl a postcard from the USA, but Mr Hirschfeld said that was not true, although he *had* sent a postcard to Greil with whom he "had good contact" and who had repeatedly helped him. He also said, however, that "Stangl was not impolite to me. He addressed me as 'Hirschfeld', but that was the custom; he said neither '*du*' nor 'Jew' to me. Eichmann was different – he always addressed me in the third person. . . . To describe my relationship with Stangl as 'amicable' is certainly exaggerated. I would say, however, that I could converse with him more freely than with other officials of that department."

In January 1939, shortly after the political, i.e. security, branch of the police had been absorbed into the Gestapo, that section of the Wels police department was transferred to Gestapo HQ in the provincial capital, Linz. "But we had our lovely flat in Wels," Stangl said, "so I commuted every day. Our chief now was a German, a terrible reactionary from Munich, Georg Prohaska. I hated him at once. Soon after we were transferred, some man came from Berlin and 'in the name of the Führer' [he said it derisively] read out our new ranks. Me, 'in the name of the Führer', they appointed Kriminalassistent. But I wasn't having it: that was a demotion, not a promotion. In Austria a Kriminalbeamter – which is what I had been – is a permanent position; it gives you the right to a pension. A Kriminalassistent in the German police hierarchy is nothing – just a temporary."

"Was this ever rectified?"

"Oh yes, a few weeks later. They acknowledged they'd made a mistake and confirmed my status of *Beamter auf Lebenszeit* [established civil servant]. And they promoted me to Kriminal-oberassistent, the German equivalent of what my next promotion would have been in Austria.* But Prohaska," he continued, "had found out that I wasn't somebody who'd allow himself to be pushed around, and he hated me from that moment on and made my life a misery. It was only very shortly after this that I was ordered to sign a paper certifying that I was prepared to give up my religion."

"What exactly did it say on the paper?"

"It said that I affirmed that I was a *Gottgläubiger* [believer in God] but agreed to break my affiliation to the Church."

"How did you feel about signing that? How strongly did you feel about the Church?"

"Well . . . of course I've always been a Catholic. . . ."

"But?" He didn't answer. *"Were you a regular church-goer?"*

"My wife and children always go."

"Yes, but you?"

"No," he finally said. "I always went at Christmas, of course, and Easter. . . ."

"So signing this document wasn't really all that difficult, was it?"

"I didn't like to."

For a man of Stangl's character, whatever his religious attitude, the Church has a tremendous significance as a symbol of respectability and status. Equally, any official document is something of the greatest import. There is no doubt therefore that signing this document was a decisive step in the gradual process of his corruption. Frau Stangl was later to confirm its importance.

I asked Stangl whether he had seen it as a compromise he had to make in order to keep his job.

"Not just my job," he said. "Much more than that – as I told you before. By then I had heard that I had originally been on a list of officials to be shot after the Anschluss. And not only that; at that very moment, a disciplinary action had been started against me because I had approved the arrest of a poacher who turned out to be a high Party member."

* This would appear to indicate that the rank they had originally given him *was* in fact the equivalent of his Austrian rank at the time, and it is interesting to note that in spite of this, his protest was effective.

"How did that come within the province of the political police?"

"Because the local police of Güsen – that was the place – had informed the State police that a number of people in the town had accused this area leader of large-scale poaching, and that, as he was a Party member, they didn't feel competent to act against him. What they meant of course was that they were scared stiff. Anyway, I went over to talk to him and have a look around his house and I found all the paraphernalia – you know, traps and all that: so I arrested him. And immediately found myself in hot water over it with Prohaska in Linz. He had me on the carpet: how dare I accuse a Party member? I told him that for me a villain was a villain, whoever he was. And so they started this disciplinary action against me. It was all Prohaska – he hated my guts. . . ." He often left sentences incomplete, allowing his tone of voice to indicate his feelings.

Substantiating evidence for the key role attributed to Prohaska by Stangl is meagre. Frau Stangl clearly remembers that "in Linz there was, of course, right away this Prohaska with whom he had trouble from the word go"; but Stangl's "friend" and colleague, Ludwig Werner, while saying that he had disliked Prohaska, who was "a coarse, rough Bavarian", could not recall whether he had harassed Stangl. A witness for the defence at Stangl's trial – a woman called Helene de Lorenzo who, when in trouble with the Nazi authorities in Linz in 1938–9, had found Stangl helpful – had formed "the best impression" of him, and *was* aware that Prohaska was known in Linz as a particularly dreaded member of the Gestapo. Prohaska himself, who at the time of the trial was working in Munich as a commercial traveller, had a (not uncommon) partial failure of memory, and would only say, "I cannot state with certainty today whether the accused was my subordinate in the police. I know I didn't like him because he was unreliable."

"After we moved to Linz," Stangl said, "the whole atmosphere in our offices and in all relationships changed."

"What was it? Distrust of one another? Jealousy?"

"All that and more. Constant alarmist rumours. Always 'this one has been arrested, that one shot, this one put on the black list, that one's walking a tight-rope'. I myself was absolutely certain that they were still plotting against me because of the Eagle. And then – the way people talked, it was – it had become . . ." he floundered. "How can I explain it to you . . . ?"

38

"Well, how did it differ from the way they had talked before?"

"Differ? It was like. . . ." Words failed him. "Before, we had been civil servants and we talked and spoke like civilized people. Now, with the arrival of all these *Piefkes* [Austrian slang equivalent of *Krauts*] all one heard was the gutter language of the barracks. And you see, the people they would discuss in those terms weren't criminals; they were men we had looked up to, respected. And now, suddenly . . ." he still sounded bewildered about this ". . . they were dirt. There was one time I remember, they were talking about Dr Berlinger, one of our chiefs before the Anschluss [later he was to say he wasn't sure of this name]; they'd arrested him and one of them – in the duty-room – was describing how he'd been interrogated. . . ." He stopped, embarrassed.

"They hurt him?"

He looked away from me. "They laughed and said, 'He pissed all over himself.'" He turned back to me. "Imagine, *Dr Berlinger*. I hate . . . I hate the Germans," he suddenly burst out with passion, "for what they pulled me into. I should have killed myself in 1938." There was nothing maudlin about the way this was said; he was merely stating a fact. "That's when it started for me. I must acknowledge my guilt."

This, on the second day of our talks, was the only time Stangl acknowledged guilt in a direct way until almost the end. In his mind the later events in his life – which we were approaching – were inseparable from these beginnings. When he volunteered an acknowledgment of guilt for his comparatively harmless failings at this stage of his life, it was – I felt – because he wanted and needed to say "I am guilty" but could not pronounce the words when speaking of the murder of 400,000, 750,000, 900,000, or 1,200,000 people (both official and unofficial figures vary, depending on the source). Thus he sought to find an acceptable substitute for which he could afford to admit guilt. Except for a monster, no man who *actually participated* in such events (rather than "merely" organized from far away) can concede guilt and yet, as the young prison officer in Düsseldorf put it, "consent to remain alive".

CAN ANY man – or his deeds – be understood in isolation from his childhood, his youth and manhood, from the people who loved or didn't love him, and from the people he loved or needed? Stangl had said that "all he wanted" was to be alone with his wife; and his first deep tears came when he recalled their first serious discord, when she thought he had deceived her about joining the "illegal" Nazi Party. After this, any mention of his wife – and there were many – brought on helpless tears. There can be no doubt whatever of his deep love for her and need for her love and approbation in return; no doubt at all that he, whatever he became, was capable of love.

Theresa Stangl is small, blonde and attractive. She was sixty-four years old when I visited her in Brazil but looked far younger; her figure had widened a bit but was still trim. She speaks "proper" Austrian-German rather than the colloquial language of her province. It is the speech of a considerably "better than ordinary" provincial school. My first visit to her, on October 7, 1971, coincided with her thirty-sixth wedding anniversary, and her house in Sao Bernardo do Campo, about thirty kilometres from São Paulo, was full of roses which her children – three girls – had given her that morning.

São Bernardo, a tiny Detroit, is Brazil's automobile town. Mercedes, Rolls-Royce Parts and several other plants are there, but above all Volkswagen SA – it is their biggest factory outside Germany, and the place where Stangl worked during part of the time he spent in Brazil before his capture.

Despite the rich industries it houses, and full employment, São Bernardo is shabby and still has the air of a pioneering town. The Stangls' little pseudo-villa, which they built with their own hands and which is perhaps slightly more solid than most of its neighbours, is one of thirty-odd such houses on a virtually unpaved street. In this working-class neighbourhood, where people range in colour from black through coffee, yellow and cinnamon to white, Frau Stangl – I watched her repeatedly talking with her neighbours – is obviously popular and considered a good neighbour.

The house has three and a half small bedrooms, a narrow living room, a primitive but functional bathroom, a dining room and a kitchenette. The loft of a small building across the courtyard, which Stangl built as a weaving workshop, has been made into a little flat where Renate, the middle daughter, sleeps. The house, pink and white, with bright flowers in the yard, is incongruously reminiscent of the Austrian countryside, and the life the Stangls live in it is simple. They cook with butane gas, purify their water by means of a filter installed on the roof, heat both house and water with difficulty, and their furniture is no more than adequate. There is a television set and two radios, and half a dozen shelves housing about two hundred books. Some of these are in Portuguese, which Frau Stangl and her daughters speak fluently, but most of them are good conventional reading in German: Dumas, Lawrence's *The Seven Pillars of Wisdom*, Sonderström, Thomas Mann. There are no political books, although Frau Stangl was to tell me that her husband "was always reading all the books that have been written about camps and all that. He read everything." There are a number of German magazines on a coffee table in the living room. There is a silver-framed photograph of Stangl there, and another, taken in prison a week before he died, for the *Daily Telegraph Magazine*, in Frau Stangl's bedroom. In front of both pictures are flowers and candles. On the wall of the living room hangs a pleasant painting of an Austrian landscape; on the TV stands a vase of dried Alpine flowers. Most of the furniture, carpets and books stem from "home". But aside from a small baroque gold-framed mirror there are no objects of value. It is a well cared-for but frugal upper-working-class household – the house of their beginnings in Brazil.

Theresa Stangl, born Eidenböck in 1907, was the oldest of five children, three boys and two girls, whose parents at the time of her birth ran a well established family business – a *Parfümerie* – in Steyr, a beautiful town in the province of Upper Austria (Oberösterreich). "The shop had always done very well," Frau Stangl said, "but my father soon ran it into the ground."

Thea (as her husband called her – she was "Resl" to her family) was closest to her eldest brother Heine, four years her junior. Her sister Helene, two years younger than she, was "different" from her, she said. And her two younger brothers came much later – in 1920 and 1922. "My father was a very good-looking man," she said. "He took after his French grandfather. But he was a dreamer, a megalomaniac; he 'invented' things, took out patents for

41

innumerable ideas none of which ever worked. He didn't have the technical qualifications ever really to work out any problems. He began to drink heavily. And one day, in a drunken stupor, he signed papers selling the business. By this time he had already sold part of our big house and we lived in the back. Drink turned him into a brute: he was unspeakable to my mother. When he came home drunk, she had to kneel down and ask him to forgive her, God knows for what – *she* never knew – and then he cuffed her into bed. He beat me too."

After a while his only earnings were from selling cards, sewing thread and that sort of thing "from inn to inn". Even so, there must have been a little money left, because Thea's mother, feeling that her eldest daughter was particularly gifted, entered her as a pupil in the Ursuline convent in Linz. "My upbringing was mainly influenced by this exclusive boarding-school and by my grandmother – a wonderfully distinguished woman." It would appear, however, that she did not remain at this school for the customary length of time, up to matriculation at eighteen. By the time she was seventeen she had already graduated from a commercial college, had a secretarial post at the Steyr car-works and was helping to support the family.

"It was a very cold winter," she recalled. "Father had been off on one of his dates with one of his many paramours. I had bought myself an anorak. He came home from his fling in the middle of the night and saw the anorak hanging on a peg in the hall, so he realized that I hadn't handed over all my money. He dragged me out of bed in my night-clothes, stood me up in front of a window and lunged at me with a bayonet he was always fooling around with. Thank goodness, by that time terrified, I had dropped to the floor, and he was so drunk, he wasn't steady on his feet: he went through the window with his bayonet and wounded himself. I ran away, out into the icy night in my night-dress and ran to our neighbours. They were shoemakers and their daughter was a schoolfriend. He beat up my mother instead of me, till she was black and blue, but I never went back. I rented a room in Steyr and continued to work at the Steyr works until I was twenty. In 1927 I went to Vienna and got a job at the patent office. I was theatre-crazy; I spent all my money on theatre tickets rather than food or clothes. And I sang in the church choir.

"Weaknesses? Yes, I had weaknesses, but it's only now I

realize what they were: I was proud of being clever in school, of always having the best marks; the teacher used to say to my mother, 'I can't measure her by the class average – it doesn't apply to her.' Aside from that, already in school I sang and acted – my mother paraded me around and showed me off to everybody."

Frau Stangl's sister Heli – Frau Helene Eidenböck, whom I visited, unannounced, in Vienna in 1972 – was obviously equally aware of the "differences" between the two of them. A woman of transparent integrity and great charm, her answers to questions are simple and direct; there is no doubt that in her time she has felt bitter about her sister – not to speak of her sister's husband – and she certainly remembers this pain. But later she said that they are closer now – better friends than they had been.

Heli Eidenböck worked for many years as a cook in a big restaurant near Vienna's City Hall. Her husband – of rather late years – a construction engineer who died in 1968, was a Jew. "My mother doted on Resl and my eldest brother," she said. "I and the younger boys were closer to our father. Yes, perhaps he *was* rough on Resl sometimes: I think he was fed up with my mother's mooning over her. She was given all kinds of opportunities we never had. My mother thought she was so clever, so pretty. She went to boarding-school you know, a convent. She really became quite different to the rest of us. We had nothing to say to each other. . . ."

"After two years in Vienna," said Frau Stangl, "in 1928, it was the beginning of the Depression and people were being sacked everywhere. But I had felt anyway for some time that I must do something else, something I could get *involved* in, and I had thought of social work. I applied to the School of Social Work in Linz and they took up my references. People in Steyr said the school would be mad to take me; that I didn't have a thought in my head except dancing and theatre. But the principal called me in for an interview and she said she didn't believe it and that I was to take a test. That was the first 'test' I took, the first time I heard that word. It took all day, but I sailed through and they accepted me. I went to the school for two years, from March 1930 on, and I loved it. We had terrific fun and learned so much: it was a wonderful course.

"One of the things we had to study was midwifery. And one day, in the door of the Women's Clinic in Linz, my friend Anna

Vockenhuber introduced her cousin Franz to me, a tall handsome man. The moment I saw him I said to myself, here is someone I like. I liked his looks, his manners, just everything about him. Though when we got talking, although I fell in love with him, I think I felt as much compassion or pity for him as love: he told me about his awful childhood; how alone he had been; his terrible father; his jealousy of his stepbrother Wolfgang – it was sad.

"By the time I met him he was already doing well in the police and I thought it was wonderful how hard he worked. We saw a lot of each other. Whenever he had a free moment he came up to see me at the Riesenhof [her school]. We went to concerts, theatres and wine-cellars – it was a glorious time.

"When I graduated in 1932, the principal called me in and told me that the princely family of Corsini in Florence were looking for a governess. She said she couldn't think of anyone she was willing to recommend as highly as me, and did I want to go. Well, I told Paul – I always called him Paul – and he was very upset. But I thought to myself, we can't marry yet and what shall I do? I must admit, it was *very* tempting anyway. I so much wanted to see something of the world before I settled down, and I was dying to get to know the 'princely' life. So I went, in the early summer of 1932. It was wonderful, just wonderful. They were wonderful to me. They had two little girls of four and six. There were of course staff who did everything domestic; a nursery maid to do their laundry and all that, and servants to do the cleaning. I was only there to speak German and some French to them and to do their 'nursery-kindergarten' work with them. The Corsinis had castles all over the place; I travelled with them wherever they went. And whenever I could I haunted the Florence museums. They used to send a man-servant to look after me, wherever I went. I ran the poor man off his feet. I stayed with them for two and a half years. Paul wrote to me every day, or almost every day. I wrote him once a week."

Later it turned out that at that time Frau Stangl still called her husband Franz, not Paul. This emerged when she showed me a wooden jewellery box he had carved for her while he was in the SS internment camp after World War II: it was inscribed *In lieber Treue und stiller Sehnsucht, Dein Franzl.* "That's what I called him in my first love," she said then. "Later I told him that everybody around where we lived was called Franz – 'I'll call you Paul'. And that's what I remember him as: Paul."

There is a split in Frau Stangl's attitude to her husband; on the one hand she "stands by him" romantically, honourably and conventionally. On the other hand, she seeks *small* ways to emphasize her individuality, her separateness from him. Her renaming of him is in some subtle way connected with this. At the time when she changed from Franz to Paul, the split was not so marked, but she probably felt even then, perhaps unconsciously, a need to emphasize her intellectual and moral superiority over her husband. If, for example, she says now, "He wrote to me every day, or almost every day; I wrote him once a week", this, one may infer, is a way of indicating that she is and always was a separate and different kind of person, more needed by him than he was needed by her. How, indeed, in the context of the present, *could* she allow herself to be seen as needing him (as in a human way she doubtlessly does), considering what he became?

"After two and a half years," she continued, "Paul wrote he couldn't stand my being away any more, so I went back – in May or June 1935. He had a flat in Linz then, where I stayed. He stayed at the police barrack," she added quickly. They had not slept together during their courtship, she said. "We got married in Wels, in October 1935 – it wasn't a formal wedding; the verger was our witness. Paul had borrowed a motorbike and we went on a short honeymoon to Mittenwald." After that they moved into a flat they had prepared – the one Stangl was later to describe nostalgically as "my first real home". Later they moved to another one, just as small, but with a garden, at Weiradenhausstrasse 4 in Wels. And that remained their home until Frau Stangl joined him in Syria in 1949.

"The flat at Roseggerstrasse," she said, "was very small, but nice. I got pregnant at once and I was completely concentrated on Paul, my home and the baby I was carrying. The only people we ever saw socially were one other young couple in the same house, but even them very rarely: we were sufficient to ourselves." She met none of his colleagues in the police and knew little about his work except that he was constantly being promoted, praised and even decorated for this and that achievement. "I was very proud of him."

She said she was soon aware of his wild ambition. "It lasted until the end of the war." But it is likely that she didn't learn to understand until much later that this ambition was a weakness in him rather than – as it seemed first – a sign of strength.

"Was he vain?" I asked.

"Vain? No, I never thought of him as vain – just incredibly tidy."

In our discussions Frau Stangl's memories of the pre-Anschluss time in Austria were mostly of this warm married life; obviously a refuge for both these young people with unhappy childhood backgrounds. But in letters a year after our talks she wrote slightly differently about her childhood – after this passage of time she sought safety, perhaps, in clichés: "My father was a prosperous man from a highly reputable and distinguished family," she now said. "At that time Austria was beset by severe economic crises and he had to sell his business and began to drink. As he had no head for alcohol, he was at that time often drunk. But he took himself in hand later and was a wonderfully good father to me then and loved by everyone."

It was not only about her own childhood that she changed the emphasis upon reflection. "I don't think that my husband's difficult childhood had any influence on his development," she wrote in the same letter. "You see, the boy was only eight years old when his hard old jealous dragoon of a father died. And he had his young incredibly industrious and loving mother who one year later, married again. And his stepfather, who still today at ninety-four or ninety-six I think, is going strong, was an exemplary, good and much loved father to him. . . . "

In São Bernardo, at the time when we met, Frau Stangl remembered vividly the day, very soon after the Anschluss, when her husband came home from work and, the moment he entered the house, said, "It's all right now – I've fixed it – we don't have to worry any more: they can't do anything to us now."

"I asked him what he had done," she said. "I had of course known how worried he had been – with all those people being arrested, shot. . . ." Oddly enough, however, she does not appear to have known in detail about the *Adler* – the "Eagle" decoration he had received before the Anschluss and on which, in his talks with me, he blamed so much of what he subsequently did or submitted to. Nor does she appear to have known about his having been on "a blacklist of police officials due to be executed" as he told me.

"He told me then," she said, "that his friend Ludwig Werner had 'organized' with Dr Bruno Wille so that Paul's and Werner's

46

names would be inserted into a list of illegal Nazi Party members. I remember very well that this Dr Wille was a *friend* of Werner's. . . ." But she didn't believe her husband's story. "It was a terrible blow to me," she said. "It was as if this man I had so respected, so admired, suddenly fell off the pedestal I had put him on. 'You betrayed me with these swine, these gangsters,' I told him. 'You who I thought an honourable man, working for his country.'" And these were the very same words Stangl had used to describe this incident to me. Certainly they would not have been in communication about this specific question between the time he told the story to me in Düsseldorf prison, and the time he died – nineteen hours after I saw him last – when in fact he had no idea that I would go to see his wife in Brazil.

I asked Frau Stangl why she had said this to him, why she hadn't believed his story.

"I've always had a feeling for truth," she said, "a kind of hunch if you like, even about future events. I just knew that day that he wasn't telling me the truth. And the thought that he had lied to me all this time, he who I had believed incapable of lying, was terrible for me. There were so many factors involved: how can I put it? You see, I was an Austrian, with all my heart and soul. And then, I was devout – I always have been. What I believed in happened to be the Catholic Church; it was the Church of my country and I was brought up in it. But mainly I just believed in God. And to think – oh, it was a terrible blow, just a terrible blow. My man . . . a Nazi. . . . It was our first real conflict – more than a fight. It went deep. I couldn't . . . you know . . . be near him, for weeks, and we had always been so close; this had always been so important between us. Life became very difficult."

Even though the way her husband had told *me* about this, caused her to waver for a moment while I was there, it is clear that although she heard him tell this story and testify about it many times, she never really believed him. But none the less, she also said that he never gave the impression of being a Nazi, never even showed the slightest sympathy for them. "And he never said anything against Jews," she said. "I never heard him say a word like that. There were *always* people coming to our house who knew he was in the police and wanted to ask him for help. I even said to him once, I remember, 'Can't you see them somewhere else, a café or something?' But he said, how could he. . . ." (There is no evidence that

47

any Jews ever came to Stangl's house, and he himself did not claim it.)

She remembered well his telling her about the chairman of the Jewish Council in Linz, Herr Hirschfeld. "He said", she recalled, "that he was glad Hirschfeld himself was going to be able to get out. And then one day he came home and said Hirschfeld had told him something extraordinary. He'd said he was going to go to Australia if he could; because if he went anywhere closer, like the US, there'd be Jews, and wherever there were groups of Jews there would be pogroms. He said Hirschfeld said that the character and personality of Jewish group-living made that almost inevitable. I remember Paul saying, 'Isn't it extraordinary that he should say that about his own people?'

"Very soon after that, his whole department was moved to Linz but he still came home to Wels every night – oh, he wouldn't have stayed away. And in Linz, of course, there was at once this Prohaska with whom he had trouble from the very beginning.

"I remember the day he came home with that form and said, 'Now they want me to sign this,' and it said on it – I can't quite recall the exact wording, but something about his affirming that he was a 'believer' but that he renounced his allegiance to the Catholic Church. I said, 'Of course you aren't going to sign it.' That was the second awful blow for me: finally we couldn't talk about it any more, he wouldn't talk about it: and in the end I never knew whether he had signed it or not, but I really thought he hadn't. Are you sure he did? This was when he began to say from time to time that he wanted to get out of the police. But then you see, the war started and he was given an 'indispensable' rating and then, of course, he had to stay. . . . "

3

In NOVEMBER 1940 Stangl, by now again promoted, was ordered to report to Berlin for instructions.

"The order was signed by Himmler," he said, a tone of awe in his voice even now. "It said I was transferred to the General Foundation for Institutional Care (Gemeinnützige Stiftung für Heil und Anstaltspflege) and that I was to report to Kriminalrath

Werner at the Reichskriminalpolizeiamt Berlin, Werd'scher Markt 5. Kriminalrath Werner told me", he continued, "that it had been decided to confide to me the very difficult and demanding job of police superintendent of a special institute which was administered by this Foundation, the HQ of which was Tiergartenstrasse 4 in Berlin."

"Did you know then what Tiergartenstrasse 4 was?"

"I had no idea. I had heard it vaguely referred to now and then as T4, but I didn't know what their specific function was."

This was no doubt true at that time. For Tiergartenstrasse 4 was the hub of what was for years the most secret operation in the Third Reich: the administration first of the "mercy-killing" of the mentally and physically handicapped in Germany and Austria, and later of the "Final Solution": the extermination of the Jews.

The building which housed T4 – as it was called for camouflage purposes – was an inconspicuous villa in Berlin-Charlottenburg, one of Berlin's exclusive suburbs. The planning and orders came from the Führer Chancellery in the building of the Reichs Chancellery in the centre of Berlin, a special department Hitler had created to administer his private affairs and consider petitions addressed to him personally. The Führer Chancellery was a comparatively small and very exclusive organization headed by Philip Bouhler whom Gerald Reitlinger has described as the most "shadowy figure the National Socialist hierarchy produced", and who exerted considerable influence on Hitler's thinking and actions.

Men like Bouhler, Brack and Blankenburg* (now dead) and a few others, and the medical "luminaries" who eventually lent their names to these activities, particularly the psychiatrists Professors Nitsche, Heyde and Dr Mennecke, were the so-called "desk-murderers". None of them, nor their staff in the offices of T4, ever actually committed murder. And some of them – at least

---

* Philip Bouhler, Reichsleiter NSDAP, head of the Führer Chancellery, died, believed suicide, in prison camp at Emmerich, Bavaria, between May 18 and 21, 1945 (according to death certificate).
Viktor Brack, SS Oberführer, Chief of Section II of the Führer Chancellery, executed at Landsberg, June 2, 1948.
Werner Blankenburg, SA Oberführer, Brack's second-in-command; escaped prosecution by changing his name to Bielecke; died in Stuttgart in November 1957.

at the start of these appalling events – seem to have believed sincerely that a "merciful" Euthanasia Programme was justified: a belief shared by the many perfectly honourable people who today propose legalizing euthanasia on demand. But once the euthanasia "institutes" came into being, no one either in the Führer Chancellery or T4 could continue to harbour illusions; it was abundantly clear that what was happening was not "assisted suicide", or the "mercy-killing of grievously suffering patients upon their own or their relatives' request on therapeutic grounds", but legalized murder, undertaken for starkly economic – and later political – reasons ... and even at that, its "legality" was only a pseudo-legality. The Führer-order on which the programme was launched was never officially recognized by the Reich Ministry of Justice, which in fact, within the limitations imposed by its members' fear of the consequences, opposed Hitler's order in this instance all along as "unconstitutional".

The planners and administrators of these "programmes" were, of course, mainly bureaucrats functioning in offices hundreds of miles away from where their ideas and orders were put into practice. During the first and decisive years, 1938 and 1939, they were physically, and therefore psychologically, far removed from the terrifying reality of their activities. They were thus enabled to convince themselves – as all those who lived to testify in trials were to claim – that they were simply administering the "public health" of the nation and were in no way directly concerned with violence or horror.

But for those who were actively involved it was very different.

When Stangl, in his conversations with me, began to speak of his transfer to the Euthanasia Programme, I noticed for the first time an alarming change come over his face: it coarsened and became slack and suffused. The veins stood out, he began to sweat, and the lines in his cheeks and forehead deepened. This was to happen repeatedly in the days and weeks to come when he had to speak about a new and terrible phase in his life.

"Kriminalrath Werner said that both Russia and America had for some considerable time had a law which permitted them to carry out euthanasia – 'mercy-killings' – on people who were hopelessly insane or monstrously deformed. He said this law was going to be passed in Germany – as everywhere else in the civilized world – in the near future. But that, to protect the sensibilities of the population, *they* were going to do it very slowly, only after a great deal of psychological preparation. But that, in the meantime, the difficult task had begun, under the cloak of absolute secrecy. He explained that the only patients affected were those who after the most careful examination – a series of four tests carried out by at least two physicians – were considered absolutely incurable so that, he assured me, a totally painless death represented a real release from what, more often than not, was an intolerable life.''*

"What was your first reaction, your first thought when Kriminal-rather Werner said these things?"

"I . . . I was speechless. And then I finally said I didn't really feel I was suited for this assignment. He was, you know, very friendly, very sympathetic when I said that. He said he understood well that that would be my first reaction but that I had to remember that my being asked to take this job showed proof of their exceptional trust in me. It was a most difficult task – they fully recognized it – but that I myself would have nothing whatever to do with the actual operation; this was carried out entirely by doctors and nurses. I was merely to be responsible for law and order."

"Did he specify what he meant by law and order?"

"Yes. I would be responsible for maintaining the maximum security provisions. But the way he put it, almost my main responsibility would be to ascertain that the protective regulations regarding the eligibility of patients would be adhered to, to the letter."

"But the way you are telling about it, now, you were obviously not ordered to do this. You were given a choice. Your own immediate reaction, quite properly, was horror. What made you agree to do it?"

"Several times during this talk, he mentioned – sort of by the

* Although the "medical commission" did travel to some institutions, such careful medical examinations were by no means the rule. Most decisions of life or death were much more routinely made at T4, purely on the basis of a questionnaire which had been sent out by "Amt IVg" – subsection for institutional care – of the Ministry of the Interior to all mental institutions, asking for details on all patients who were senile, retarded or suffering a variety of other mental debilities: criminally insane, under care for five years or more, of foreign or racially impure extraction, incapable of work or capable of only routine mechanical tasks such as peeling vegetables. This was sent out on the pretext of gathering information to assist in economic planning (and apparently only two men in the Ministry were informed of the real purpose) but photocopies were then turned over to T4 "medical staff", who marked each case with a plus or minus sign: Life or Death.

way – that he had heard I wasn't altogether happy in Linz. And then, he said, there was this disciplinary action pending against me. That would of course be suspended if I accepted this transfer. He also said I could choose either to go to an institute in Saxonia, or one in Austria. But that, on the other hand, if I chose to refuse the assignment, no doubt my present chief in Linz – Prohaska – would find something else for me to do."

"*And that decided you, did it?*"

"The combination of things did; the way he had presented it; it was already being done by law in America and Russia; the fact that doctors and nurses were involved; the careful examination of the patients; the concern for the feelings of the population. And then, it is true, for months I had felt myself to be in the greatest danger in Linz from Prohaska. After all, I already knew since March 13, 1938, that it was simpler to be dead in Germany than anywhere else. I was just so glad to get away from Linz."

"*So what happened?*"

"I reported to Tiergartenstrasse 4, I think to SS Oberführer Brack who explained what my specific police duties would be." (When Stangl said this, and for some time after, it seemed significant that he, at that point a police officer of comparatively minor formal rank, should have been interviewed and instructed by SS Oberführer Victor Brack, who was one of the top officials of the Führer Chancellery. Since then, however, I have learned from Dieter Allers, former chief administrative officer of T4, that Brack interviewed and instructed personally *all* personnel assigned to T4 – "He even interviewed the chars," said Allers.)

"I said I'd try to do it, and that I would like to stay in Austria where I would be nearer my family. He said that, to be effective in my new job, I had to be superior in rank to the local police chief of the nearest police authority, Alkoven – it was a man called Hartmann – and I would therefore be transferred to the uniformed branch with the rank of lieutenant."

"*Were you to wear uniform?*"

"Yes, the green police uniform [which he continued to wear until Christmas 1942, when – in Poland – he became assimilated to the SS and was given the grey SS field uniform worn by all German SS at Treblinka]. He gave me the name of a village not too far from Linz, and a telephone number; I remember, it was Alkoven 913. I was to return to Linz, pack and tell nobody where I was going.

I was to go to an inn on the outskirts of Linz – the Gasthaus Drei Kronen it was, on the Landstrasse – and phone that number. And I'd be given instructions."

("Yes, of course I remember when he was first called to Berlin," said Frau Stangl thirty-one years later in Brazil. "He told me he had to report to Tiergartenstrasse 4. He said, 'I wonder what *that* is.'")

"I only stayed at home for a day, I think," Stangl continued, "and then did what they had told me to do: you know, I went to the Drei Kronen and called Alkoven 913. A man answered, I told him my name and he said, 'I'll come and get you' – and about an hour later a kind of delivery van drove up – the driver was in civvies, a grey suit. When I asked him where we were going he wouldn't say – he just said, 'In the direction of Everding.' And after an hour we got to Schloss Hartheim."

"How did it look?"

"Oh, it was big you know, with a courtyard and archways and all that. It hadn't been a private residence for some time: they'd had an orphanage in it I think, and later a hospital. Almost the first person I saw – it was such a relief – was a friend: a colleague from the police, Franz Reichleitner."

It would appear that Reichleitner,* whose subsequent career paralleled Stangl's, if on a slightly lower level, was equally glad to see him. "He said they'd told him I was coming and he'd been waiting for me near the entrance. He had arranged for us to share a room. He'd show me around later, he said, but first he had to take me to meet the doctors in charge and Hauptmann [Captain] Wirth."

This was the first appearance of Stangl's next *bête noire*, the notorious Christian Wirth – the "savage Christian", as he was to be called. It was Wirth who carried out the first gassing of Germans certified incurably insane, in December 1939 or January 1940 at Brandenburg an der Havel. According to Reitlinger's *The Final Solution*, "Wirth's name does not occur in any of the surviving correspondence concerning euthanasia." It would now appear from Stangl's account, which is confirmed by one of his former subalterns, Franz Suchomel, that in mid-1940 Wirth was appointed as a kind of roving director or inspector of the dozen or so institutions of this kind in "Greater Germany". Suchomel says that he came to Hartheim as a *"Läuterungs-Kommissar* because the place

---

* Killed by partisans in Trieste in 1944.

was an undisciplined pigsty". A little over a year later he was appointed Kommandant of Belsec, the first of the three principal extermination camps to be installed in occupied Poland between March and May 1942. And later again–according to surviving documents–in August 1942 he was designated supervising "Inspector" of these three camps, Belsec, Sobibor and the largest–Treblinka.§ This sequence of appointments reconfirms the preparatory role played by the Euthanasia Programme for the "Final Solution". (In practice, if apparently not, as has also been claimed, as a formal training.)

"Wirth was a gross and florid man," Stangl said. "My heart sank when I met him. He stayed at Hartheim for several days that time, and came back often. Whenever he was there, he addressed us daily at lunch. And here it was again, this awful verbal crudity: when he spoke about the necessity for this euthanasia operation, he wasn't speaking in humane or scientific terms, the way Dr Werner had described it to me. He laughed. He spoke of 'doing away with useless mouths' and said that 'sentimental slobber' about such people made him 'puke'."

"What about the other people there? What were they like?"

"There were the two chief medical officers: Dr Renno* and Dr Lohnauer.† And fourteen nurses; seven men and seven women. Dr Lohnauer was a rather aloof sort of man, but very correct. Dr Renno was very nice, friendly."

"In the weeks and months to come, did they ever talk to you about what was being done there?"

"Often, very often, especially Dr Renno. You know . . . " he suddenly said, sadly, "you have no idea what the patients were like who were brought there. I had never known there *were* such people. Oh my God – the children. . . ." (Dieter Allers said later that he couldn't understand this reference to children: "No children were killed at Hartheim," he said. "There were special places for that"; and the Ludwigsburg Central (judiciary) Authority for Nazi Crimes confirmed that if there were children who were killed at Hartheim, it could only have been isolated cases.)‡

§See pages *85-86* for additional history of the camps in Poland and 111 for Stangl's description, which contradicts the August date in the documents.

* Excused from euthanasia trial because of ill health; now living in the Black Forest.

† Committed suicide.

‡ "Child-euthanasia" was, on the whole, a separate programme, which began earlier and ended long after the general euthanasia *Aktion*.

It was claimed by various defendants in euthanasia trials – and Dieter Allers repeated

54

"But didn't it ever occur to you to think 'what if my mother or my child were in this position'?"

"Ah," he answered at once, "but they had told us immediately that there were four groups who were exempt: the senile; those who had served in the armed forces; those who had been decorated with the *Mutterkreuz* [a decoration for women designed to glorify motherhood], *and* relatives of Euthanasia Aktion staff. Of course, they had to do that."

"But aside from that then, did you have any more scruples?"

"For a long time. After the first two or three days I told Reichleitner that I didn't think I could stand it. By then I'd heard that the police official who'd had the job before me had been relieved upon his request because he had stomach trouble. I too couldn't eat – you know, one just couldn't."

"Then it was possible to ask to be relieved?"

"Yes. But Franz Reichleitner said, 'What do you think will happen if you do the same? Just remember Ludwig Werner.' He knew of course about my friend Werner's being sent to the KZ.* No, I had very little doubt of what would happen to me if I returned to Linz and Prohaska."

"You say you saw your wife quite frequently: it must have become obvious to her that you were under strain – it must have shown up somehow. Didn't she ever ask you again what you were doing? That's very unlike a wife, isn't it?"

"She asked, but only casually you know. She was used to my not being able to discuss service matters."

"Do you think the patients at Hartheim knew what was going to happen to them?"

---

this to me – that "parents were asked to authorize 'mercy-death'" for their children. What actually happened was that parents were informed that *Kinderfachabteilungen* – Special Sections for children – were being established all over the country. They were asked to sign an authorization for their severely disabled children to be transferred to these wards and were told that, as these were in fact intensive-care units where highly advanced experiments would be carried out, this represented a unique chance for their children's possible recovery. *This* was how the Nazis obtained authorizing signatures – which were subsequently paraded in the trials. Eleven Special Sections were involved; each of them had between twenty and thirty beds. What *is* true, however, is that – unlike the adults – children were kept in these wards for a period of observation lasting between four to eight weeks. But none of my informants was able to recall any case of a child who was returned to an ordinary hospital, or to its parents, once it had been taken to a "Special Section". The children were "put to sleep" with injections and, from all accounts, were not aware of their fate.

* Werner was sent to a concentration camp, the legal record shows, not for asking to be relieved but for "having had financial dealings with a Jew".

"No," he said immediately, with assurance. "It was run as a hospital. After they arrived they were again examined you know. Their temperatures were taken and all that. . . ."

"Why would anybody want to take the temperature of people who were mentally sick?"

"I don't know. But that's what they did. They had two tables in a sort of hall the patients were taken to when they arrived; at one of them sat the doctors and at the other nurses. And each arriving patient was examined."

"For how long?"

"Oh, it varied; some just a minute, others a bit longer."

"One has read of patients in these 'institutes' trying to run away in terror, with nurses or guards pursuing them along the corridors. . . ."

"I don't think that ever happened," he said, sounding genuinely surprised. "I have certainly never heard of such a thing. You see, even Wirth said, 'The people must not be allowed to realize that they are going to die. They have to feel at ease. Nothing must be done to frighten them.'"

"Were there any wards? Did it ever happen that any of them stayed – a night, or more?"

"Oh no, never."

That patients were sent to these institutions only to die without delay was confirmed by Franz Suchomel. He, a Sudeten German, was mobilized into the SS – he says he doesn't know why (Dieter Allers was to tell me later more about the method of recruiting for T4), and was first sent to the "institute" at Hadamar as an assistant in the photographic laboratory. Or so he said at our first meeting: later, in one of several letters replying to specific additional questions, he changed this and said that he had been assigned to work at T4 in Berlin. (The truth is that he worked in both these places.) "The institutes", he said, "were designated from A to F. Hartheim was C; Hadamar was E; Sonnenstein, also called *die Sonne*, was F. They gave me a dark-room and told me to develop photos for the archives. In the four institutes where gassings took place patients never stayed for more than a few short hours. Certainly nobody ever got out." (There were in fact six where gassing took place, but only four were operational at any one time. And this does not take into account the eleven "special" hospitals where children were "put to sleep" by injections.)

Suchomel said at his first meeting with me that the psychiatrist

Professor Heyde had his office next to his dark-room at Hadamar. This man, who was sentenced to death *in absentia* by a German court in 1946, escaped and practised in Flensburg in Germany under the name of Sawade until 1959, when he gave himself up. He committed a slightly mysterious suicide: he was found strangled, lying on the floor, with a noose attached to the central heating pipes – in Limburg prison in 1963. According to Suchomel, "He was the head of the whole thing, he developed it." In a subsequent letter he says, "Heide [*sic*] had a flat at Tiergartenstrasse 4, next to my office. He was the top expert in the mercy-killing business. He only stayed at his flat when he had official business in Berlin. He was, I was told, an authority in his field. . . . I know that there was a research institute into mental illness in Strasburg; he may have run that. That's where the brains of selected mental patients were sent for research purposes." And Dieter Allers too talked a great deal about the scientific purposes of the Euthanasia Programme. "People have completely misunderstood: now it is constantly being misinterpreted. Just look at the world now: don't you think something very much like this will have to happen?"

Stangl was in fact intellectually and emotionally considerably more affected by the whole euthanasia issue than the other people I have talked to who were directly involved with the programme.

"You were speaking earlier about having many doubts and many discussions about the rights and wrongs of the euthanasia programme. Can you elaborate a little on this?" I asked him.

"Strangely enough," he said, "you see there was somehow more freedom to talk there than I had had in Linz. Of course, we couldn't talk to anyone outside, but amongst ourselves we discussed the fors and againsts all the time."

"And did you get to the point where you convinced yourself you were involved in something that was right?"

"Of course, I wasn't 'involved' in that sense," he said quickly. "Not in the operational sense."

I reformulated my question. *"Did you get to the point where you convinced yourself that what was being done was right?"*

"One day," he said, "I had to make a duty visit to an institution for severely handicapped children run by nuns. . . ." ("What the devil," said Allers, "was he doing going to a place like that? He had no business going to any of the hospitals: his job was death certificates.") "It was part of my function," said Stangl, "to see

57

that the families of patients – afterwards – received their effects: clothes and all that, and identity papers, certificates, you know. I was responsible for everything being correctly done."

"What do you mean by 'correctly done'? How were the families notified?"

"Well, they were told the patient had died of a heart attack or something like that. And they received a little urn with the ashes. But for our records, as I told you, we always had to have these four attestations, otherwise it . . . it couldn't be carried out. Well, in this case the mother of a child who had been brought from that particular institution had written to say that she hadn't received a candle she had sent the child as a present shortly before it died. That's why I had to go there: to find the candle. When I arrived, the Mother Superior, who I had to see, was up in a ward with the priest and they took me up to see her.

"We talked for a moment and then she pointed to a child – well, it looked like a small child – lying in a basket. 'Do you know how old he is?' she asked me. I said no, how old was he? 'Sixteen,' she said. 'He looks like five, doesn't he? He'll never change, ever. But they rejected him.' [The nun was referring to the medical commission.] 'How could they not accept him?' she said. And the priest who stood next to her nodded fervently. 'Just look at him,' she went on. 'No good to himself or anyone else. How could they refuse to deliver him from this miserable life?' This really shook me," said Stangl. "Here was a Catholic nun, a Mother Superior, and a priest. And they thought it was right. Who was I then, to doubt what was being done?"

"If these people in this mental hospital for children knew what was happening to their patients, then others must have known too: it was known, wasn't it?"

"This was the only time I heard anyone 'outside' speak of it," he said stiffly.

According to a letter dated May 16, 1941, from the County Court in Frankfurt to the Minister of Justice, Gürtner (actually to his deputy), the Euthanasia Programme had become common knowledge. The children of Hadamar, where one of the "institutes" was located, were in the habit of shouting after the blacked-out buses, "Here are some more coming to be gassed." "The patients are taken to the gas chamber in paper shirts," the letter continues.

"The corpses enter the furnace on a conveyor belt, and the smoke from the crematorium chimney is visible for miles. At night, Wirth's experts, picked by the Berlin Gestapo . . . drink themselves to oblivion in the little Hadamar Gasthof where the regular customers take care to avoid them."

Frau Stangl too – on the whole a woman of exemplary honesty – confirms that she had been aware of what was going on. "I read – or I may have heard in Church – Graf Galen's sermon, and I remember even talking to my husband about it when he came on leave. But at that time of course, I neither knew he was stationed at Hartheim, nor, even if I had known, would it have meant anything to me. I never knew that Schloss Hartheim was one of those places until after the war. I can't remember what my husband replied when I discussed Graf Galen's sermon with him, though I can recall that he never initiated any talk about that. But then, of course, he wouldn't have; it was simply part of his personality, his discipline, never to discuss at home things to do with the service. After the war he told me what he told you too now; about the nun, the priest, and the poor little sixteen-year-old idiot boy in the little basket."

We cannot possibly know now how many nuns and priests, perhaps particularly affected by the sadness and hopelessness *many* people feel who work continuously in mental institutions, came at that time to agree – quite possibly in an agonizing conflict of morals – that euthanasia represented a release, the chance of an eternal and far happier life for these particular patients. But we do know now that at least some of their superiors did not share the attitude of the nun and priest Stangl had met. The protests of various Protestant and Catholic bishops in 1940 and 1941 reached a climax in the Galen sermon on August 3, 1941, at the St Lambert Church in Münster.

It was during that summer too that Hitler, in the course of a trip through Hof, near Nuremberg, where his train was held up when some mental patients were loaded on to trucks, is said to have had the novel experience of being jeered at by an outraged crowd. Whatever the reason, on August 24, 1941, Dr Karl Brandt (as he was to testify later) received verbal instructions from Hitler at his HQ to stop the Euthanasia Programme. There is no written record of the order. Brandt transmitted it to Philip Bouhler by telephone.

4

To UNDERSTAND how the Euthanasia Programme was practicable in a theoretically Christian country in the twentieth century, we must further examine the history of its development. We must also at least consider a disturbing story which has never been publicly aired and which rests on personal and circumstantial evidence. This evidence, however, has a disconcerting relevance because, if, as I believe, it is to be trusted, it would appear to prove that the Catholic Church, including the Vatican, knew of Hitler's euthanasia plans before the programme ever began.

According to a careful analysis, *Euthanasia and Justice in the Third Reich* by Lothar Gruchmann, political scientist at the Munich Institute for Contemporary History, the question of euthanasia – the "destruction of unworthy life" – arose as early as 1933, in the course of government discussions regarding the proposed changes in the German criminal code. At that time the German Catholic Church declared uncompromisingly that any kind of legally sanctioned euthanasia was incompatible with Christian morality. Two years later, in 1935, Dr Franz Gürtner, Reich Minister of Justice, was to reject outright a proposal for legal sanction of euthanasia made by the Prussian Ministry of Justice. But a first compromise could be sensed in the *formulation* of his rejection: his report (on the work of the criminal law commission) said that "a (judicial) sanction of the destruction of unworthy life was out of the question", but that the National Socialist State was "already providing against these degenerations in the nation's body by measures such as the law for the prevention of hereditary disease in coming generations, which means that these degenerations are in effect in the process of decrease."

The draft law Gürtner was referring to, for compulsory sterilization of men and women suffering from hereditary diseases, was originally discussed in a meeting of the Reich cabinet on July 14, 1933 – six days prior to the projected signing on July 20 of the Concordat between the Nazi government and the Holy See which was negotiated by Cardinal Pacelli and signed by Pius XI. On this occasion the then Vice-Chancellor, Franz von Papen, objected to the draft law as proposed, on the grounds that Catholic dogma opposed sterilization. The compromise he suggested was that sterilization should only be authorized upon the voluntary decision of a patient or, as an alternative, the "detention" of such patients might be considered. Hitler however opted for the original draft, but agreed that the publication of the law should be delayed until after the signing of the Concordat on July 20, 1933. The law accordingly was made public on July 25 and immediate reactions from a number of Catholic clergy were to prove that von Papen's anxiety about the reaction of the Catholic Church was well founded.

Father Robert Leiber, sj, Father Confessor and long-time friend of Eugenio Pacelli (Papal Nuncio in Germany 1917–1929; Cardinal Secretary of State at the Vatican 1930–1939; and Pope Pius XII 1939–1959), addressed a long letter to Cardinal Pacelli on August 17, 1933, in which he expressed his deep disquiet over many facets of the National Socialist government.

In view of the many doubts raised during and since World War II over Pope Pius XII's attitude toward the Nazis (which necessarily figures in many places in this book) Father Leiber's well-known anti-Nazi convictions must in all fairness be registered, particularly as there is documented proof* that Eugenio Pacelli, at least in the earlier years, fully shared these apprehensions.

In the August 17, 1933, letter, Father Leiber said that he was "particularly anxious over the ideological confusion that had been brought into the minds of German Catholics. The National Socialists", he said, "are doing everything they can to convince the Catholic population that an ideological agreement has [also] been reached between the Nazis and the Church. Already for six months now, Catholic authorities no longer dare (nor are given the opportunity) to expose and emphasize the ideological differences between the Party and the Church. Indeed," he continued, "a number of professors at Catholic theological faculties have already come around to that point of view and are teaching that it is not the function of the State to serve the people, but the people to serve the State." He continued to say that these particular theologians were attributing Catholic origins to the principles of the totalitarian state, and were using out-of-context quotations from, among others, Thomas Aquinas to substantiate their claim; and even that falsely,

* For instance, a letter from Ivone Kirkpatrick, British Minister to the Holy See, to Robert Vansittart, Under Secretary of State to the Foreign Office, August 19, 1933.

said Father Leiber, as the quotations were in fact from Aristotle, whose "concept of the relationship between man and State was totally antique-heathenish".

Father Leiber went on to say that although the final clause of the Concordat assured the Catholic Church the right freely to disseminate its ideology, he had found no one in Germany who believed that this privilege could in fact be exercised. Already, he said, it was impossible to get ideas or articles contrary to the opinion of the Party into even *Catholic* publications. If they included such an item, the Catholic editor was removed and replaced with a National Socialist, but the publication continued to appear as if under Catholic auspices (thereby obviously lulling the reader into a false security). Amongst several examples he cited, Father Leiber enclosed a cutting of a case in point from the magazine *Germania* (published by von Papen) of Sunday August 13, 1933, with an article by Professor Dr Josef Mayer, professor in moral theology at the University of Paderborn.

Professor Mayer (who in 1927 had already published a highly controversial work on the sterilization of the insane) was here, said Father Leiber, cleverly propagandizing the new German law on eugenics on the pretext of interpreting the formal Catholic point of view. "Such articles," wrote Father Leiber, "are even more harmful than openly advocating this law." (The mention here of Professor Josef Mayer is, as will be seen shortly, of great relevance to later events.)

The 1933 law for compulsory sterilization of those suffering from hereditary disease was followed two years later, on October 8, 1935, by the *Erbgesundheitsgesetz* – the law to "safeguard the hereditary health of the German people". This expanded the original law by legalizing abortion in cases of pregnancy where either of the partners suffered from hereditary disease.*

Reichskommissar for Health and Hitler's personal physician, Dr Karl Brandt,† testified at Nuremberg that euthanasia had long been on Hitler's mind. As early as 1935 he had told the then Minister of Health, Gerhard Wagner, a notorious advocate of euthanasia, that "if war came, he would take up and resolve this question, because it would be easier to do so in wartime when the Church would not be able to put up the expected resistance".

* Separate from the Nuremberg law enacted a week later, directed against the Jews.
† Condemned to death on August 28, 1947.

So Hitler and those around him, at least in these early years, were well aware of the fundamental opposition of the Catholic Church to euthanasia. Equally, there can be no doubt whatever that Hitler – nothing if not realistic – was, and in fact remained until the very end, perfectly aware of the power of the Catholic Church in Germany. If he had not been so aware of it, he would not have felt it necessary to exercise such stringent controls, particularly on the educational activities of the Church and – as Father Leiber pointed out – on the dissemination of its ideology.

And yet, despite this well justified misgiving regarding the potential reaction (and influence on the population) of the Catholic Church, Hitler, in the early autumn of 1939, took the fateful step towards "legalized" murder. A signed note from Hitler to Philip Bouhler was found after the war in the files of the Ministry of Justice. It bears no date, but according to the testimony of Dr Karl Brandt, it was made a secret decree at the end of October 1939 and was backdated to September 1. "Reichsleiter Bouhler and Dr Brandt are charged with the responsibility for expanding the authority of physicians who are to be designated by name, to the end that patients who are considered incurable in the best available human judgment after critical evaluation of their condition can be granted mercy-killing."

It is true that the war had begun, providing the camouflage under which Hitler had predicted in 1935 he would "resolve this question". But even the war could not have been considered sufficient to deflect the attention of the Churches from this dark undertaking which could not in the long run remain hidden. And indeed, as it turns out, the Nazis quite realistically *didn't* think they could hide it and therefore took the only step open to them: they sought out ways to "feel the pulse" of the Churches and then acted in accordance with what they found.

I have discussed the evolution of the Euthanasia Programme with a number of people in Germany who were involved in it (and others who deplored it); particularly with two men who were disastrously and closely connected with it at different periods and in different functions, but both at a high level.

One of them is Herr Dieter Allers who, as a young lawyer, on January 1, 1941 (a relatively late stage of the operation – two months after Stangl was assigned to T4) became chief administrative officer of T4 and who, after having been convicted of "psychological

63

collaboration" in a recent euthanasia trial in Frankfurt, was sentenced to two years' prison (considered served while awaiting trial). He is now back home, living with his family in Hamburg. Herr Allers – and incidentally his wife, who also worked at T4 – gave me information on a variety of administrative points which appears in relevant places throughout this book. And in an attempt to explain his own feeling about the acceptability of euthanasia, he advised me to see Herr Albert Hartl who, he said, would be able to tell me about an extraordinary sequence of events in which he had been involved.

The story told to me subsequently by Albert Hartl concerns one short and specific period of vital importance to the evolution of the Euthanasia Programme: between March 1938, when Hitler moved into Austria, one of the traditional strongholds of the Catholic Church in Central Europe, and the autumn of 1939 when war began, and Hitler signed his secret decree which enabled the murder of the mentally and physically handicapped to commence.

I met Albert Hartl in the small town on Lake Constance where he teaches the history of art in a girls' school, and lives with his wife, also a teacher, in a charming flat full of modern paintings and ancient pottery. He was then sixty-six. As a young man of twenty-one – son and grandson of teachers – Hartl became a priest. He had severe doubts even then about his vocation and about the dogma of the Catholic Church. "Just before I was ordained," he said, "I went to see a Jesuit *Domkapitular* I much admired and told him of my doubts. This old and venerable priest knelt down, took my hand in both of his and said, 'Believe me, my son, you are meant to be a priest: all of us have these doubts; they always come; but they will pass. Once you are ordained, once you wear the cloak of the Church – they will pass.' And so I became a priest."

He remained a priest for five years, most of that time teaching at a Catholic boarding-school in Freising. "My doubts were never resolved; on the contrary, they increased and strengthened. My whole concept of morality – my whole philosophy of life, as it developed, was inconsistent with the dogma. So, after five years, around 1933–4, I left the priesthood, and the Church."

Before he took this step, Hartl, presumably searching for other ideals, had joined the National Socialist Party. He had been instrumental – however haplessly, as he now says – in the arrest and conviction for anti-Nazi statements of the headmaster of his school, a man called Rossberger. Hartl was a witness for the prosecution when Rossberger was tried and sentenced to three months in prison.

After leaving the Church, Hartl joined the SS and in 1935 was given the job of Chief of Church Information at the Berlin head-quarters of the SD – the Reich Security Services.* It is not entirely clear what his functions were, but he has always maintained – and was never shaken during years of interrogation, first by the Americans, then by German courts – that his role was always in "intelligence" and was never "operational" – or executive. His position as head of one of the most important SD intelligence depart-ments was, nevertheless, one of unique significance. And the fact that, despite these years of interrogation, he was never charged with any crime and in all the trials he took part in, was only heard as a witness, must speak for itself, and for the authenticity of the things he now says.

Regarding the beginning of the Euthanasia Programme, he says that in the second half of 1938, he received an order from Heydrich to report to Brack in the Führer Chancellery for a meeting involving a secret matter of State. Brack told him that many requests had been reaching the Führer Chancellery from near relatives of people with incurable mental diseases, asking Hitler to permit the mercy-deaths of these patients. It was therefore being considered, said Brack, whether the State should take action in this matter. But Hitler was opposed to it for the time being, especially because, having just received considerable support from the Catholic Church in Austria on the occasion of the Anschluss, he did not wish to provoke any conflict with them now. For this reason Brack wanted to have the question cleared up whether in fact there was or would be fundamental opposition from the Church to euthanasia of the incurably insane by the State.

Hartl says that Brack asked *him* to write an Opinion on this question, but that he refused, on the grounds that he did not feel competent to do this. In his view, he had told Brack, such an

* The SD, headed by Heydrich, was composed of the Security Police, which included the Gestapo or SIPO – or Secret Political Police; the KRIPO – the criminal investigation department; and the information branches. The SS, which began as Hitler's bodyguard, became over the years a vast empire within the State, served by its own troops and headed by Himmler. After the death of Heydrich in 1942, the SD was assimilated into the SS, but even prior to this the two organizations complemented each other with exchanges of personnel and information.

65

Opinion had to be written by a practising priest who understood something of Catholic moral doctrine. Instructed to find such a man, he addressed himself first to the canon of the St Kajetan Church in Munich, Dr August Wilhelm Patin. Hartl does not deny that one of the reasons why he first went to Dr Patin was that Patin – a practising priest at the time – was Himmler's cousin. "But Dr Patin," said Hartl, "finally seemed to me to take this matter much too lightly: he just said he didn't think there would be fundamental opposition and gave some primitive reasons for his opinion. It was useless. That's what finally made me suggest to Brack that we should commission a professor of moral theology to write a real expert Opinion.

"The man I was thinking of was Professor Dr Josef Mayer, who was teaching moral theology at the Catholic philosophical-theological University of Paderborn, of which he had, in fact, been Rector for a time. He was therefore a man of considerable standing and, having produced a substantial work on the sterilization of the insane in 1927, was already known to be concerned with, and open to argument about, these questions.

"I went to see Professor Mayer, I think it was in the beginning of 1939 – but I can't remember the exact date. I told him exactly what Brack had told me: that Hitler wanted an Opinion on the attitude of the Catholic Church towards euthanasia. I don't think I knew Professor Mayer before this meeting – although I saw him repeatedly in later years: we travelled to Rome together in 1944; we stayed at the Hotel Felipe Neri . . . our trip then was for the purpose of finding out what possibilities there might be to change the course of the war at the last moment; to establish contact through the Vatican with the Western powers and join with them against the Bolsheviks. But that was much later. . . .

"In 1939, as I say, I don't think I knew him personally. Yes, I had warned him of my coming – not through someone else: I did it myself. I was always very careful when seeing theologians or priests. And I never met them in uniform: it would have been embarrassing for them. I visited the professor two or three times I think, in his flat: it was in a university annexe. I think I saw two rooms, everything full of books. I ate with him, but I never stayed overnight. On that day, when I went the first time, I told Professor Mayer he would be paid a fee, obviously not depending in any way on what he said. What was required was a real expert Opinion. All he was going to be paid for was his time and expenses. Professor Mayer accepted the commission and, as I recall, worked on it for at least half a year."

Hartl says that at the end of that period, he himself went to pick up the paper in Paderborn. "I remember I went to the flat, and something or other – typing or correction – wasn't quite done. The secretary still had it or something like that. Anyway, he finally brought it to me, to the train."

The Opinion, says Herr Hartl, consisted of approximately one hundred pages, typewritten, on thin manuscript paper, average size and double-spaced. There were five copies of it, each bound in a blue folder. He left Paderborn on an afternoon train, spent the five hours of the journey reading, reached Berlin in the late evening and finished reading the manuscript that night.

Professor Mayer's Opinion, he says, was an academic paper: but there *was* a feeling, there were indications, that he himself was sympathetic to euthanasia. Going at great length into historical precedents and quoting a number of moral arguments for and against, Professor Mayer suggested that the whole problem of the mentally ill suffered under the error of Christ that the mentally ill were possessed by the devil. It was because of this that, particularly in the Middle Ages, they were whipped, tortured and burned. He said that a subsequent period of relative enlightenment led to more humane treatment and the setting up, at least in some places, of asylums. But these times did not last and there was a return to the medieval practices and superstitions. Only in relatively modern times, Professor Mayer wrote, had a large number of theologians totally rejected euthanasia of the mentally ill, and even they not unanimously. These objections could not, therefore, be considered a categorical moral condemnation. As proof of this lack of decisive unanimity, Professor Mayer cited the Jesuit moral system of probability (*Probabilismus*). This system, he said, claims that "there are few moral decisions which are from the outset unequivocally good or bad. Most moral decisions are dubious. In cases of such dubious decisions, if there are reasonable grounds and reasonable 'authorities' in support of personal opinion, then such personal opinion can become decisive even if there are other 'reasonable' grounds and 'authorities' opposing it." Mayer referred specifically to Thomas Aquinas and finally, concerning the killing of the incurably mentally ill, presented his conclusion: as there were reasonable grounds and authorities both for and against it, euthanasia of the mentally ill could be considered "defensible".

Albert Hartl says he brought the five copies of the Opinion to Brack at the Führer Chancellery the next day. "About four weeks later Brack called me in and told me that, since the Opinion indicated clearly that a unanimous and unequivocal opposition from the two Churches was not to be expected, Hitler had withdrawn his objections and had ordered the Euthanasia Programme to be started."

Hartl says, however, that even then *he* was not convinced. "I suggested to Brack that considering what was at stake, I thought we should inform the representatives of both Churches of what the Opinion said, and of Hitler's decision." Brack, it appears, agreed and Hartl was told to inform Josef Roth, a former – and officially never lapsed – priest who was in charge of the Catholic section of the Reich Church Ministry.* Reichsleiter Bouhler himself, Brack said, would inform Bishop Wienken, the official liaison man between the Fulda Bishops' Conference (the German Episcopate) and the government.

Hartl says he informed Josef Roth – who then received a copy of the Opinion from Brack – and that he asked Roth to inform the Papal Nuncio, Cesare Orsenigo, as well as the Archbishop of Osnabrück, Bishop Berning, who was very influential in Prussia. "When I told Roth, he didn't voice any objection," Hartl says. "He just listened. He told me later that he had informed both Berning and Orsenigo." Berning apparently commented that "some pages of this Opinion" were "highly embarrassing to the Church", while Orsenigo, Roth claimed, had apparently pointedly withheld all comment and merely remarked that he took "informal" cognizance of the information." (In diplomatic language, this would mean that while an *official* acceptance of information would have entailed an official transmission of the information to the Vatican, *informally* accepted information entailed no such official obligation – in a situation like this, one would think, a pointless diplomatic distinction, as there could surely be no doubt what the Nuncio's obligation was.)

Brack apparently told Hartl that Bishop Wienken had expressed "considerable understanding for the planned measures" but had remarked that "one had to realize there were some 'hotspurs'

* Joseph Roth died, in the summer of 1942, ostensibly by drowning in the River Inn.

amongst the German Bishops who were likely to use this matter to deepen the controversy between Church and State."

Hartl claims that on the Protestant side, the Pastor von Bodelschwingh – especially suitable as he was head of an institution for the mentally ill – was informed. Here again, Brack is quoted as saying that von Bodelschwingh said neither yes nor no, but merely insisted that his own institution was to be exempted. (According to Lothar Gruchmann's *Euthanasia and Justice in the Third Reich* the Pastor von Bodelschwingh, together with Pastor Braune, another high-ranking Protestant minister, also director of an institution for the mentally sick, became particularly articulate in their protests *against* euthanasia, certainly as of the spring of 1940.)

Hartl says that shortly after these initial steps, he was instructed to meet with a small group of doctors and lawyers – about eight to ten people – and tell them about the Opinion. Later he was to address two more such groups. The first one included the psychiatrist Professor Werner Heyde who was to become the medical director of the programme. "I talked for about half an hour," said Hartl. "There were no questions afterwards, and no discussion. They were quiet."

If this account, as given by Hartl, is true it opens yet another dimension to the already existing doubts about the moral leadership of the Holy See during the period of the Nazi rule in Germany.

The credibility of this whole sequence of events seemed at first to depend to a large degree on the personality and motivations of this one man, Albert Hartl.

I was – to be blunt – originally disposed to distrust him: a priest who had given away to the Gestapo another cleric to whom, at the very least, he owed professional loyalty; a man who upon leaving the priesthood joined the SS and whose functions, furthermore, seemed to presuppose a readiness to deliver to the Nazis former brothers in faith; and a man who had eventually (as I learned from him) been sent to serve in Russia and had later been imprisoned in Nuremberg while under interrogation for his possible part in the *Einsatzgruppen* murders.* (He was in fact cleared of this in 1949.) It did not seem to me, initially, that this was a man whose word one could accept on an issue of such magnitude, without corroboration.

---

* The *Einsatzgruppen* – action groups of the Security Police – were employed for killing civilians in occupied Eastern territory.

In addition, this was such an extraordinary – in journalistic terms such a sensational – story; how was it, how indeed *could* it be that no newspaper, no magazine had ever picked it up, even when it was apparently finally aired in Germany at two euthanasia trials, first in 1965 and then again in 1967? Indeed, why had it never been brought up in Nuremberg when Brack, after all, was on trial for his life, and when surely proof that the Churches had known about euthanasia before it began and had tacitly sanctioned it – by calculated silence – would have helped his case?*

The fact that Herr Dieter Allers told me that Brack had told him, too, about Professor Mayer's Opinion when he first met him in January 1940, and that he had added that the "Vatican knew about it too" did not necessarily add to my faith in the authenticity of this story.

But then, in anticipation of meeting Herr Hartl, I obtained records and transcripts of a Frankfurt euthanasia trial in March 1967 at which not only Albert Hartl, but also Professor Josef Mayer had appeared as witnesses. And simultaneously I received a copy of a circular sent on March 6, 1967, by Johann Neuhäusler, Auxiliary Bishop of Munich, to all archepiscopal and episcopal authorities in Germany, Austria and all countries formerly occupied by the Germans. I also received two more photocopies: one a brief extract, in Latin, from the *Diocesan Gazette* for the Württemberg Diocese of Rottenburg dated March 24, 1941; the other a copy of a circularized Pastoral letter, *Mystici Corporis*, from Pope Pius XII, dated *June 29, 1943*.

Important though Herr Hartl's personality was to start with, it now became almost irrelevant, and so did any other doubts. The documents speak for themselves.

In the 1967 Frankfurt euthanasia trial, the transcripts show, Herr Hartl told his story – just as, according to another transcript he had done in 1965 and as he was to do again, in 1973, when talking to me – without hesitation and remaining totally unruffled despite an obvious atmosphere of scepticism in the court, and aggressive cross-examination. He spoke briefly, clearly, factually

---

* A possible answer to this legitimate question was provided by Herr Hartl, who told me in 1973 that Brack, apologizing for his silence, had told him while in prison in Nuremberg that he had returned to the Catholic faith in anticipation of the death sentence. "He said," claimed Herr Hartl, "that in return for his silence the Church had promised to look after his family."

and without any attempt to magnify or for that matter to justify his own part in the events.

Professor Josef Mayer, for whom – even reading the transcript – one could feel instant compassion since he was eighty-one years old and very obviously under desperate strain,* denied at first all knowledge of Herr Hartl, and an Opinion such as he had described. In the course of cross-examination however, every one of his denials and arguments collapsed and what emerged in the end was that Professor Mayer *had* been commissioned by Hartl to write the Opinion, *had* done this work in full knowledge of "all his friends and colleagues" (and one must remember that he was, in 1938-9, professor at a Catholic university and thereby under the eyes and the authority of the Church), *had* had the Opinion typed by a secretary and *had* delivered the copies himself to Hartl at the railway station. It would take too much space to reprint here the details of this testimony. But in essence Professor Mayer thus confirmed every claim Hartl had made. This is particularly important as every trace of this document has disappeared; it has never been produced at any of the euthanasia trials; all Catholic authorities in Germany deny ever having seen it; the superbly equipped Institute for Contemporary History in Munich and the Ludwigsburg Central Authority (for the prosecution of Nazi crime) searched all its relevant files without finding a copy, or even a mention of it in any documents of the period. And the West German *Bundesarchiv* in Koblenz which now houses the more or less complete documentation of the period including the documents recently returned by the National Archives in Washington, although aware of its existence, was also unable to find it. It is impossible to avoid the conclusion that the total disappearance of this historical document is probably more indicative of the importance assigned to it by those most closely affected by its content and significance, than would have been its ready availability for inspection.†

Professor Mayer also presented to the Frankfurt court upon request, the letter circularized by Bishop Neuhäusler.

* He died later that year.
† Subsequent to the original English publication of this book – and before its announced publication in three predominantly Catholic countries – Father Robert A. Graham S.J., one of the four editors of *Les Actes et Documents du Saint Siège relatif à la Seconde Guerre Mondiale*, acknowledged – if grudgingly – in the March 1975 issue of *Civilta Cattolica* that the Mayer Opinion, the existence of which had heretofore been denied by all Catholic authorities, was in fact written.

In this letter the Bishop (an inveterate opponent of the Nazis who spent most of the war years in Dachau concentration camp, and whose own political integrity is beyond question) requested all those to whom it was addressed to search in their pastoral archives for evidence of pronouncements by the Church on the question of euthanasia, be it in pastoral letters, sermons by bishops, protests to any authorities whatever or directions to the clergy or to Catholic (medical) institutions.

After describing, with asperity, the personality and record of Albert Hartl, and implying that the persons who were allegedly informed of the planned euthanasia were all, or nearly all, lapsed priests,* Bishop Neuhäusler wrote that Professor Mayer totally denied that he had ever pronounced himself in favour of euthanasia. In a tone bordering on despair, he then cited all the German bishops who had spoken up against euthanasia. Beginning with Cardinal Bertram and Cardinal Faulhaber in 1934 – both of whom he quoted at length *verbatim* – he went on to Archbishop Gröber in 1937. He next mentioned, briefly, the Vatican's correspondence with the German government as reported in the Vatican "White Books" of 1934 and 1935 – when the Vatican "already rejected sharply the small evil of sterilization. Unfortunately there were no more 'White Books' in the following years, and we cannot ascertain at present," the Bishop's letter continues, significantly enough, "whether the Holy See pronounced itself on the subject, when large-scale euthanasia began in 1939. We are requesting information from the Vatican about this today."

Bishop Neuhäusler then returns to the further protests from German bishops... after a long and fatal pause of three years: Cardinals Bertram and Faulhaber in August and November 1940; Archbishop Gröber and Bishop Bornewasser von Trier, the Bishop of Limburg and of course the infinitely courageous Bishop of Münster, Count Galen – all in 1941; and finally a pastoral letter from all the German bishops, dated September 12, 1943, and certainly remarkable for the period, in which the bishops protest not only against euthanasia but against the murder of "innocent hostages, prisoners of war or penal institutions, and human beings of foreign race or extraction".

* Incorrect: Drs Josef Roth and Wilhelm Patin were still priests when these events occurred and the people allegedly "informed" included a number of bishops and at least one cardinal.

"After this flood [of proof] of protests by the bishops against euthanasia," wrote Bishop Neuhäusler, "I was asked by one of the defending counsel [present at a meeting on March 3, 1967, when the Bishop was consulted for five hours about the attitude of the Catholic Church towards euthanasia during the relevant period] why the bishops had been silent for so long after their initial protests in 1934. I was able to say that, after all, one could not shoot at rabbits which were either not there or at the very least not visible. There was no destruction of unworthy life in 1938 to 1939, at least not on a large scale, certainly not with knowledge of the public." He was, however, to add (a remark of sad significance) "I myself made an effort to 'bring light into this darkness' by sending, around 1939, a *Domkapitular* to the two places at which one suspected euthanasia was being carried out: Grafeneck and Hartheim: both in vain. No one around these towns knew anything or dared to say anything. It was only when whole buses of patients were fetched at night from hospitals and asylums [in 1940] that one had grounds for protest."

This is a valid argument only if protest by the Churches against acts incompatible with morality or human rights is to be determined by the extent to which these acts are *public knowledge*. Although – Bishop Neuhäusler is right – these appear to be the standards that have been applied, at least during the 1939–45 period we are concerned with in this book, it is difficult to see how they can be justified on any moral grounds.

The argument has been made to me that the Mayer Opinion, even if it was presented to the Papal Nuncio and several bishops, was merely taken "cognizance of", not "approved"; and that this in no way committed the Catholic Church to Mayer's interpretation of doctrine or attitude. This is of course true; there is no proof that either Bishop Wienken, Bishop Berning, Cardinal Orsenigo, or even Drs Roth or Patin necessarily agreed with all or any part of Professor Mayer's Opinion. But this argument by-passes the crucial point: that this Opinion was commissioned and then made known to these authorities for one specific purpose: to find out if the Church would *actively* oppose a Euthanasia Programme by the State. The answer was clear enough to Hitler; there would be no immediate and concerted action. And indeed there *was* none. The record is deplorably clear; the killing of mentally – and incidentally,

73

physically – sick German and Austrian children began in the late summer of 1939, even before the infamous Hitler order was signed. And by October the complete programme was in full swing.

According to all the evidence now on hand, whether knowledge was official or unofficial, obtained through fair means or foul, transmitted through practising or lapsed priests, it was literally impossible for the Church – which has what has been called the "best information service in the world" at its disposal – to have been in ignorance. And whichever way one looks at it there is that appalling hiatus between the summer of 1939 and the spring of 1940 when no one in the German Churches raised their voice.

The first to speak up was the Protestant Bishop of Württemberg, Theophil Wurm, who on March 19, 1940, addressed an outraged letter of protest to the Minister of the Interior, Dr Frick. Even then – and by this time tens of thousands must have been dead – the Vatican did not speak. (The Pope was merely to refer months later, on December 15, 1940, to "the courageous letter from Württemberg" in a letter to Konrad von Preysing, Bishop of Berlin. Nor was the Holy Father heard from when his own German cardinals, Bertram and Faulhaber, at last protested in letters to Reich Minister of Justice Gürtner, in August and November 1940.)

On November 27, 1940, one year and two months after the official beginning of the Euthanasia Programme, the Holy Office met in conclave and made its first official statement on the subject of euthanasia. But even this, the mildest of pronouncements, stating that the "extinction of unworthy life by public mandate [was] incompatible with natural and divine law", was only mentioned once, in Latin, on the Vatican radio (December 2), and in the *Osservatore Romano* (December 6), equally in Latin, of course. It remained virtually unheard in Germany.

"Virtually" because, extraordinarily enough, one German bishop, Preysing, Bishop of Berlin, on March 9, 1941, read it from the pulpit of St Hedwig's Cathedral in Berlin.

It has always seemed puzzling to me that, while the famous sermon of the Bishop of Münster, Count Galen, on August 3, 1941, has generally been credited with forcing Hitler to stop the Euthanasia Programme, not a single book I have read has mentioned this sermon delivered by the Bishop of Berlin.* Even the "Letters to

* Nor did Bishop Neuhäusler mention him in his circular naming those who protested.

74

the German Bishops", Volume II of the six volumes published so far by the Vatican of documents and letters pertaining to World War II, only mentions this remarkable sermon in a long footnote.*

- "With the same devotion to principles," said Bishop Preysing, "with which the Church protects matrimony, the moral focus of the people, she also protects the individual's right to life. We know that nowadays exceptions are claimed in theory and practice, to the holy right of the innocent to life and protection. These exceptions are being justified on medical, economic, yes even eugenic grounds. . . . The law of God proclaims that no earthly power, including the State, has the right to take the life of the innocent. This divine law is irrevocable. . . ." The Bishop continued to say that the Pope had "very recently" decreed that the law of the Church which states that "there is no justification and no excuse to take the life of the sick and weak for any reason whatever . . . be once again confirmed." † Following which the Bishop read out the Holy Office pronouncement.

The occasion for this sermon was a mass in commemoration of the coronation of Pius XII. The Pope's only reaction to this sermon – which subsequently was so mysteriously fated to be forgotten by all historians – was to thank the Bishop (on March 19, 1941) for his letters – "of 10, 11, and 17 January; 8, 15 and 22 February, as well as of 6 March [in which the Bishop had included a draft of the sermon] of which We have taken careful cognizance, especially too of your sermon on the occasion of the coronation mass at St Hedwig's. We welcome every honest word with which you bishops defend the right of God and of the Holy Church in public. . . ."

("Nobody cared about what those fellows said in church," said Dieter Allers, when I asked him how the population reacted to the sermons by Preysing, Galen and others. "Hardly anybody went to church anyway," he said. "All we cared about was our crust of bread and getting the war over and done with." I believe that Herr Allers underrates the effectiveness of word-of-mouth information. Nevertheless, he may of course be right; in which case one would have thought that it was even more essential – now that the Churches had begun to admit to the knowledge about euthanasia –

* Page 208, Vol. II, *Actes et Documents du Saint Siège relatif à la Seconde Guerre Mondiale.*

† Subsequent to the English language publication of this book, the author learned that Bishop Preysing's sermon was quoted on page 270 of *The Nazi Persecution of the Churches* by John S. Conway (Weidenfeld & Nicolson, 1968).

that their information, and particularly the stand finally taken by the Holy Office, be disseminated in print, whatever the risk.)

The only place in Germany, however, where the pronouncement of the Holy Office was seen in print, was in one single paper, the little *Diocesan Gazette* of the little town of Rottenburg, in Württemberg (significant, if one remembers that the first church-man to speak out was the Protestant Bishop of Württemberg) on March 24, 1941 – in Latin. By now the Euthanasia Programme had become a public scandal and courageous Churchmen all over Germany did protest against it. Five months later, whatever the reason, Hitler ordered it stopped.

Pope Pius XII himself only spoke out against euthanasia – clearly and succinctly – in his Pastoral Letter *Mystici Corporis* which appeared on June 29, 1943. By then it was irrelevant to the 60,000–80,000 children and adults, many of them no doubt incurably insane, many others merely handicapped, with illnesses for which cures have since been found, who had been murdered.

For many years now the general assumption has been that Hitler's order to stop the Euthanasia Programme was a direct result of pressure by the Churches and the public.

But Dieter Allers was to tell me that when Brack and Blanken-burg discussed his new assignment with him, which was to begin as of January 1, 1941, they said specifically that it was "*for half a year*". "We expect to finish by latest July," Allers quotes Brack as saying.

A similarly puzzling remark was made to me by a spokesman for the Vatican, Father Burkhart Schneider, SJ – a historian of considerable reputation – who, commenting on the Galen sermon, said that it was of negligible importance.* "The Programme was almost finished anyway," he said, "they had more or less killed all those they had intended to kill. And in some respects, in fact, it continued. . . ."

What Professor Schneider was referring to here was what was done in several of the euthanasia institutes *after* the Programme was "officially" stopped, when under the code name "14 f 13", thousands of concentration-camp prisoners, politicals, "habitual"

* Father Schneider, introduced to the author through the good offices of a Bishop in the Vatican Secretariat of State as the Editor in Chief of the team compiling *Les Actes et Documents du Saint Siège relatif à la Seconde Guerre Mondiale* and a "spokesman for the Vatican in this matter", now wishes it to be known that he is not the Editor in Chief and that he is not and never was a spokesman for the Vatican.

criminals and Jews were certified as "incurable" (in German: *invalid*–literal translation–patient) and gassed.* Every one of the former T4 people I discussed this development with professed to deplore it now, but to have been in total ignorance of it at the time.

5

"AT HARTHEIM," Stangl said, "the winding up process ran very smoothly, but not everywhere." In October 1941 he was sent to Bernburg near Hanover, an 'institute' where the doctor in charge was Dr Eberl (another figure, like Wirth, who was to reappear soon afterwards in Poland, and in Stangl's life).

"There were all kinds of things which had to be settled properly in the institutes," Stangl said rather vaguely about his "tour" at Bernburg. "I had to look after property rights, insurance and that sort of thing. After all, some of those who died left children who had to be properly provided for. Bernburg was a *mess*."

Perhaps: but according to the records it was Bernburg as well as Hartheim which, from November 1941, were used for the gassing of political prisoners whose "eligibility" for euthanasia was certified on the "14 f 13" forms issued by a committee of psychiatrists, primarily Professors Heyde and Nitsche and Dr Fritz Mennecke – all now dead.

"*You had no idea,*" I asked Stangl, "*that political prisoners from concentration camps were being gassed in the institutes by then?*"

"No, not within my experience. At least I never knew this."

Franz Suchomel, however, did know it; of course, as he was then stationed at T4 in Berlin, he can better afford to admit knowing it. "Hartheim existed until the end of the war," he said. "They brought people there from Mauthausen; I don't know whether from other places too. But I have even heard tell that they were still gassing at 'C' [Hartheim] when the 'Amis' [Americans] were already on the Rhine."

In view of these facts on record regarding events at Bernburg and Schloss Hartheim while Stangl was still there, his assertion that he knew nothing about them certainly throws doubt on his veracity in this instance. It is, however, just possible – and not out of keeping with his personality – that, as he rarely actually *saw* the victims but limited himself to his function of checking the

* This development is fully described in Reitlinger's *The Final Solution*, page 141.

"lunacy certificates" issued by the commission, it may not have occurred to him to question the signatures on certificates of eminent specialists such as Heyde, Nitsche and Mennecke. He could conceivably have accepted these papers as genuine and never have realized that these particular patients were in fact healthy men and women.

While I remain sceptical on this point, I am convinced that Stangl managed to keep his wife in complete ignorance of what he was involved in at Schloss Hartheim. It was not only the secrecy rule that would have prevented him from telling her; it was also because he was profoundly dependent on her approval of him as a husband, a father, a provider, a professional success – and also as a man. Even if he persuaded himself that the Euthanasia Programme was justifiable (*all* of these men did) and even if an occasional remark she made (as she did later to me) could have given him reason to think that at least theoretically she might not totally disagree with this opinion, he could not possibly be sure that she would react with anything but horror to the idea that he himself was actively involved, and he would certainly not have risked the consequences of such a reaction.

"Yes," Frau Stangl said to me in Brazil. "Of course I remember when he was called to Berlin. He didn't know [what T4 was]; certainly it seemed to me at the time that he had no idea what was wanted of him. When he came back he merely said he'd been transferred to a special job, but not far away and that he would be able to see us quite often. He said that his assignment was an official secret, and that he couldn't say anything, so I didn't ask further. I did see him every two weeks after that: I saw no change in him during that time. But then, when he came home, he only stayed for a few hours, a night perhaps. No, I had no idea there was anything wrong – I suspected nothing."

In February 1942, after "cleaning up the mess in Bernburg", Stangl returned briefly to Schloss Hartheim, "really only to say goodbye and collect the rest of my gear. It was all over with there: the staff was still there, but everything was empty and quiet – no patients. I was told to report to T4 in Berlin to get new orders. I went and my briefing was very short; I was told that I could either return to Linz and put myself at the disposal of Prohaska, or, alternatively, I could elect a posting east, to Lublin." ("He left, I think in March," said Frau Stangl, "from Linz. I remember I went to the station in Wels when he came through – we must have prearranged my coming to the station, though I don't remember doing that. But I remember, there were other people on the train who knew him. And I remember he got off the train and hugged me very hard. He didn't say where he was going except to get his marching orders in Berlin. All I had was his APO number.")

"What did they tell you you'd be doing in Lublin?" I asked Stangl.

"Something was murmured about the difficult situation of the army in Russia, and anti-partisan action, but this was never elaborated on. Anyway, for me it wasn't a difficult decision: I was prepared to fight partisans any day rather than Prohaska in Linz. I was told to proceed to Lublin and to report to the SS Polizeiführer, Brigadeführer Globocnik."

6

THE QUESTION of the role of the Euthanasia Programme as a preliminary to the extermination of the Jews, and of how the people who operated both came to be selected, has never been fully developed.

I believe this to be a point of primary importance in relation to evaluating individual responsibility. And it was largely to discuss this question that I sought out Dieter Allers.

When World War II broke out, Herr Allers – a young lawyer – was working in the department of education of the Reich Ministry of the Interior. Mobilized, he was sent to Poland as a sergeant training recruits. "I was scheduled to go to officer's training school," he said, "but then, in November 1940, my mother met Werner Blankenburg in the street in Berlin. When she told him what I was doing he said, 'That's ridiculous. There is an opening in my department for a lawyer. I'll fix it.' And that's how I got into T4. When Brack and Blankenburg instructed me about my job a month later," he continued, "they said specifically that the assignment would be for about half a year. I thought I'd be a soldier again in July or August."

"Of course they told you what it was about; how did you yourself feel about the moral side of it?"

"Well, as far as I myself was concerned, the idea of euthanasia

79

was not new to me; I had read quite a lot about it. Good heavens, it's been discussed, and on the cards, for centuries. What was intended at the time has been completely distorted since."

Herr Allers, like so many others who held high position in the Nazi administration, is an intelligent man. Intelligence, of course, is not necessarily equated to morality; indeed can become perilous if applied to nefarious purposes. My four talks with Herr Allers and his wife – who was always present – were amongst the most difficult I had in the course of preparing this book. As a man and a German, Herr Allers is totally unrepentant. While one can have an inverted kind of respect for someone who has the courage, or stubbornness, to admit to ideals which many others so rapidly disclaimed after the Nazi defeat, it is at the same time frightening when a man of intelligence is so blind to the reality of the past.

"You ask how did people generally get into T4," he said; "not the administrators, but those who then worked in the institutes and so on. Well, I was always of the opinion that most people got in through connections. They would hear of the job as being 'attached to the Führer Chancellery' and that sounded good. Then of course these jobs carried extra pay; and it meant not having to go to the front."

"That's right," said Frau Allers. "After all, that's how I got into it." She, like her husband, was in T4 until the end. "I was working in a fashion boutique and I was desperate to do something more useful for my country. A friend told me she thought she might be able to help me get into the Führer Chancellery where she was working as a secretary. 'Secret work,' she said. Well, that sounded very exciting, so I went. And got in. I had no idea what it was until I was in there."

"There was this tailor from Bohemia," said Herr Allers, "let's not mention names. But he suddenly wound up in T4 as a photographer. The way that happened, no doubt at all, was because he had a pal from his home-town who was already in there as a photographer and they fixed it between them." (Franz Suchomel, who told me he had "no idea how I came to be posted to T4".)

"On the other hand," Herr Allers continued, "you have somebody like Christian Wirth. Everybody now is on about how he was the arch-villain, how awful he was. . . ."

"He *was* awful," Frau Allers interrupted; she did a short tour of duty – six weeks – as a secretary at Schloss Hartheim. "After that I asked to be transferred back to Berlin," she said. "I couldn't stand it. But Wirth was awful to the men; he was a vulgar horrible person."

"He is dead," said her husband, "so it's easy to say that now. . . ."

"You didn't see him with his men: he *was* horrible. . . ."

"He was an officer in World War I [non-commissioned]. He was decorated with the very rare golden Military Cross. He was a good soldier. When this business here started, he was a police officer in Württemberg. You don't know the Württembergers," he said both to his wife and to me. "They *are* like that: a rough lot who use coarse gestures and language. But I am sure that when Grafeneck [the first euthanasia institute] was opened up and they needed a couple of police officers to put in charge, whoever was the chief of police in that district simply said 'You and you' – and one of them was Wirth. Perhaps it was because he was a tough sort of man his superiors thought capable of doing a difficult job; but it wasn't a matter of careful or scientific selection of these people. Stangl, for instance – I think he got into it because he had connections; how do *I* know with whom? Perhaps Eigruber, the Gauleiter. A lot of Austrians were in it, as you know. Anyway, somebody from down there recommended him. It certainly wasn't that he was known in Berlin; how would *they* have known him? His story of being interviewed by Ministerialrath Werner," he said, "that's phoney for a start. Ministerialrath Werner was the second-highest ranking official of the Reichssicherheitsamt; you don't think a man like that would have bothered to see a mere Kriminalassistent, do you? Oh yes, Brack saw him, that's for sure; he saw everybody, including the chars."

As it happens, I looked into this with some care and according to the records it was indeed Kriminalrath Paul Werner (later promoted, now retired) who instructed Stangl.

We discussed at some length the claim made by Simon Wiesenthal in his book *The Murderers Are Among Us*,* that the euthanasia institutes, in particular Hartheim, Hadamar, Sonnenstein and Grafeneck were used as formal "schools for murder". ("Hartheim," Herr Wiesenthal writes, "was organized like a medical school – except that the 'students' were not taught to save human life but to destroy it, as efficiently as possible.")

The fact that not only Herr Allers, but four of the ss men I

* Heinemann, London, 1967.

81

discussed these infamous places with at great length were all rather nonplussed at this idea, and all said that they certainly hadn't been "schools" is not of decisive importance: the statements of former SS personnel who administered, or worked in these places, and later in the extermination camps in Poland, must be taken with the utmost caution. However willing they may be now to speak with relative frankness, there must always be an element of self-protection. But what *is* important is that it is hard to see in this instance what they have to gain by denying that they had been "schooled" for murder at the euthanasia institutes, if that in fact was what happened. They would surely appear in a slightly less terrible light if they could claim that they had been scientifically conditioned – brainwashed – to death-camp work, rather than assigned to it because their natures seemed particularly suited to such activity.

"I'd give anything to understand," said Horst Münzberger, whose father was in charge of driving people into the gas chambers in Treblinka. "If I could only know why they chose just him, just my father."

Gustav Münzberger, who when I talked with him in 1972, was sixty-eight and just out of prison after serving a twelve-year sentence for his part in the murders of Treblinka was loth to discuss anything to do with Treblinka but had little hesitation in talking about his time at Sonnenstein. But the idea of the place being used as a "training centre, with students" seemed genuinely new to him. Shedding for a moment the pose of senility which he affected for most of our conversation, he became reasonably alert and articulate. "I can't think that it was," he said in the tone of someone having a stimulating intellectual discussion. "If it had been, we in the kitchen would have known" – he was on kitchen duty throughout, he says – "because of the rations, you see. One time there was a big meeting, with doctors from everywhere and officials from Berlin. We catered for that – I remember that very distinctly. But students – no, there weren't any; no outsiders at all, just the permanent staff."

And the permanent staff, according to Stangl, Franz Suchomel and all remaining documentation, was very small. Simon Wiesenthal in his book had quoted an Austrian photographer as admitting having taken photographs of the victims in their death agony.

All the former SS men agree that photographs were taken. "I don't think, though," said Suchomel, who seemed sincerely interested in clearing up this point, "that there were ever any photographs taken of people actually being killed. You see I would have seen them; because later my work included filing all the photographic material. And as for 'schooling' or 'training' – what would they have taught anybody? What is true, of course, is that the people who were involved in the actual killing process in the institutes, those who worked in the crematoria – we called them *die Brenner* [the burners] – became calloused, inured to feeling. And they were the ones who were afterwards the first to be sent to Poland." This sounds to me convincing – except for the attempt to limit the conditioned callousness to a few. There *was* no need for training in the sense of formal schooling for anything. What indeed could they have been taught? But the work at the euthanasia institutes, as Suchomel says, did "inure" *all* of them to feeling and thus prepare them for the next phase.

"The photographs," Herr Allers said, "were taken for the record – for each patient's file. This was usually done in the Zwischeninstituten [intermediate institutes] most of them were sent to for a while."* He shook his head. "This is all part of the distortion I mentioned before: all this was really just the beginning of a very wide and long-term research programme to improve the public health of the nation."

"One thing I can testify to personally," said Frau Allers, "and you can quote me: as far as Schloss Hartheim was concerned, there wasn't any possibility of taking photographs of people while they were dying. There was nothing in the door but a tiny peep-hole, like one has on a front door. You put one eye to it to see, but you couldn't take a photograph through it."

"You saw this tiny peep-hole yourself?"

"Yes, I did."

"That was just there to allow the doctors to confirm when it was over," said her husband. "There *was* one person who was sent to Hartheim for a week or two to see how it worked, I remember that; that was Dr Gorgass who later worked at Hadamar. But as far as I know, that was the only time that happened."

* The method of "intermediate institutes" was adopted for camouflage purposes when the public first began to be suspicious about the destination of the blacked-out buses which fetched patients from mental hospitals.

I asked Herr Allers whether the personnel files at T4 showed evidence that the psychiatrist Professor Heyde had a hand in evaluating the T4 personnel. He said there *were* no personnel files at T4; he claimed the men's records were kept at their home-stations. (This is not true: T4 personnel were paid, either entirely or certainly their supplements, by the T4 office. When pressed on this point, Herr Allers conceded that there might have been "file cards" for each man, for "administrative purposes", but no personnel files.) He also said that as far as he knew, Professor Heyde had nothing to do with the evaluation of personnel.

He then came back once more to how people got into T4. "None of them, except those they later called the burners, could have got in without their own doing," he said again. "You mentioned Münzberger: for heaven's sake, he was a *carpenter*; why on earth should anybody recruit just *him* for this work – unless, as he no doubt did, he put in a request for what sounded like a cushy job, just like all of them did. Except the burners – that was perhaps different; they were strictly the troops. They were ordered there, by numbers. Some sergeant picked them out 'you and you and you'. And you can take my word for it that the sergeant didn't know what he was picking them out for. When the Euthanasia Programme finished . . . " he said, and I interrupted.

"But of course, it didn't *really* finish then, did it? Then came '14 f 13', didn't it?"

"Up to now," he said angrily, "we have talked sensibly; if you are now going to bring that up, there is no use in continuing." However, he did continue. "I don't know much about this – only what I've read. But I do know one thing from following the 'doctors' trials': as far as I can remember, Professor Nitsche, who was a wonderful old man ["A lovely man," said his wife] only went to Dachau once; he testified about that in his trial; he had not found anyone there he considered mentally ill, and he had said so at the time. I can't say the same about Professor Heyde, or Dr Mennecke; they and some others were ss medical officers; they may have had to go there more often. But certainly both Nitsche and Heyde believed in euthanasia, not as Nazis, but as responsible physicians.

"What I was going to say: when the Euthanasia Programme ended, almost all of the personnel – don't forget, there were four hundred of them – were sent to Russia. You tell me now that

Wirth and a group went to Chelmno-Kulmhof:* well, I promise you, this is the first I've heard of it. I know Dr Eberl went to Russia for a while as a medic and I certainly always thought all of them did.

"They all had a piece of red paper in their paybooks signed by the OKW (Oberkommando der Wehrmacht)," continued Herr Allers, "saying they were not to be employed at the front. This was a Führer command: he didn't want any of them caught by the Russians." (The same notation was in the paybook of all members of the *Einsatzgruppe* 1005.)

The fact that Herr Allers claims – I believe in good faith – that he didn't know until now "that Wirth and a group" had gone to Chelmno, is not as surprising as one might think. The extent of interdepartmental intrigues and personality feuds in the Reich administration was quite extraordinary and often resulted in people who were theoretically closely involved with events, in practice not knowing anything about them. The apparently minor point Herr Allers has raised here is in fact an interesting and significant illustration of these conditions, and his information about the transfer of the T4 personnel to Russia may possibly allow a new view of the famous letter Dr Fritz Mennecke wrote to his wife on January 12, 1942. "Since the day before yesterday," he said, "a large delegation from our organization, headed by Herr Brack, is on the battlefields of the East to help in saving our wounded in the ice and snow. They include doctors, clerks, nurses and male nurses from Hadamar and Sonnenstein, a whole detachment of twenty to thirty persons. *This is a top secret.* Only those persons who could not be spared were excluded. Professor Nitsche regrets that the staff of our institution at Eichberg had to be taken away so soon."

This letter–quoted in all histories of the period–has always been interpreted as referring to the transfer of euthanasia personnel to *Poland* for the extermination programme. It had seemed to me for some time that neither the description of this group, nor the dates, fitted this description; Chelmno *was* set up–by Wirth–but in the early summer of 1941, several months *before* this particular group went 'East'. And what's more: for reasons which remain

---

* Chelmno was the first of the "death-camps" to be set up in occupied Poland but appears to have been originally intended as a euthanasia institute. On May 1, 1942, the Gauleiter Artur Greiser proposed to Himmler that 25,000 tubercular Poles from the "Warthegau" should be admitted to Chelmno for "special treatment".

obscure, Chelmno did not come under the authority of T4 but was always under the immediate supervision of RSHA (*Reichsicherheitshauptamt*). However, as it was originally planned as a euthanasia institute, it may well at first have been staffed with doctors and nurses. But when Chelmno, in December 1941, became the first of the extermination camps for Jews—at that point possibly only intended for the Jews of the new (Germanized) province "Warthegau"*—there can be little doubt that the medical staff would have been withdrawn. Except for the terrible Dr Eberl who was first director of the Bernburg institute and later briefly commanded Treblinka, no SS doctors or SS *female* nurses are known to have worked in any of the extermination camps in Poland. So it is indeed possible, and even probable, that "most of the four hundred personnel from T4" *were* sent to Russia, to be used as medical personnel behind the front lines while being kept in reserve for the expanded Euthanasia Programme already in the planning stage for the rest of Europe. Only ninety-six of them—the sum total of German SS to be actively involved—were picked out of these four hundred to run the three camps of the *Aktion Reinhard*: the extermination of the Jews in Poland.

One might well be sceptical of Herr Allers' opinion – though he should know – that none of these men were chosen on the basis of specific qualities or qualifications; that in fact they either volunteered or were assigned to these tasks by chance. And disbelief appears to be supported by the case of Otto Horn, an SS man at Treblinka who was acquitted at the Treblinka trial in Düsseldorf but who, none the less, appears to me particularly significant from the point of view of establishing whether or not these people were simply assigned because they happened to be available, or whether they were carefully selected.

The details of Horn's story are presented somewhat differently by him and by his former colleague at Treblinka, Suchomel. Both versions, however, point to a definite pattern of selection.

Horn, a professional male nurse originally from eastern Germany, who says his war-record has prevented him from ever getting a job since, is a small man with white hair, a firm trim body and a smooth and rested face. He lives by himself in a neat first-

*See Martin Broszat *Hitler und die Genesis der Endlösung* in the *Vierteljahreshefte fur Zeitgeschichte*, 4/1977.

floor flat in a pleasant, generously heated block on a tree-lined street in the centre of Berlin. The living room is well furnished, with silver, glass, knick-knacks and a beautiful radio-record player; it is the home of a comfortably established man.

Horn became a nurse as a very young man, working mostly in mental hospitals. "Until I was called up," he said, "in 1939. Then of course they put me in the medical corps. Political? No, I wasn't ever political. When it [the Nazis] started, I just ignored it. I had an interesting profession – what did I care about their politics? But, of course, in Germany nurses are civil servants – and because of that, later on I had to join the Party, otherwise I couldn't have kept my job. But it was only a formality. And then, when we were called up, what did *we* know of what they were doing in Berlin? I was in Kiev when I was suddenly told I was transferred. Those things happened – one didn't ask why – one just went. In fact, it was funny because I was actually discharged; I had my discharge papers and was told to go home and report to my unit in Dresden. At my home station later I was notified to report to – I think Berlin. And then they sent me to Sonnenstein (the institute at Pirna) and then to Poland.

"I stayed only a few days at Pirna," he said. "Four, I think. I don't know what they wanted of me there. I wondered too. By that time – September 1942 – there was nothing and nobody left there – just a few men...." He then mentioned some names of other euthanasia and Treblinka men. "And oh yes, I met a friend from home, also a medic and we just stuck together. We didn't do anything there – exercises, I think, and otherwise we just lay about – for eight or fourteen days [he had forgotten that he had earlier said 'four']. No, they didn't tell us anything.... Oh well, yes, we did hear that they had killed people there. What did I think? Well – that that won't do..." the sentence trailed off. "No, we didn't talk about it much. My chum and I, we said something now and then, but on the whole we didn't discuss it.

"And then we went to Poland – twenty of us. No, nobody told us where we were going and why – oh yes, finally somebody said it was a resettlement camp for Jews...."

Franz Suchomel's version is so different that it requires mentioning: "Horn," he says, "was at the *Sonne* much earlier. It was from there he came to the photo-section in Berlin [where he was himself] in the early winter of 1941. [That would have been around

November.] And from there he was sent to Russia as part of the *OT-Einsatz* – a purely T4 organization. Then he came back to Berlin to the photo-section, and then to Poland." Suchomel adds that Horn had the reputation in Treblinka of being a decent man who never hurt anyone, and this was in fact confirmed by a number of survivors.

None the less, Horn's transfers – it emerges clearly both from his own evasions, and from Suchomel's quite precise account – were by no means as haphazard or casual as he (and Herr Allers) claim. When telling me his story, he made a very special point of his having travelled back from Russia by himself. "Oh yes," he said, "I had travel orders and all that. But nobody had given me any schedule: they just said, 'Go on home.' "

This already points to a very exceptional position; as we know, the German army didn't operate this casually.

What emerges from these two accounts is: Otto Horn, a young male nurse, a citizen of Silesia, in Germany proper – i.e. the *Altreich* – was recruited, or assigned, we cannot know which unless he (or Herr Allers) tells us the truth, to T4 probably in early 1940 when he was sent to the euthanasia institute Sonnenstein. From there – presumably when the Euthanasia Programme officially ended – he was temporarily transferred to the photo-section at T4 in Berlin (also rather mysterious, for what was a nurse doing in a photo-section?) and was then sent to Russia, probably as part of the general transfer of T4 personnel that Herr Allers spoke of. The significant point however is that, according to his own description, he – by himself – was "suddenly told" in Kiev that he was transferred back to Germany. Why, out of several hundred personnel, would *one* man, who had already been sent all the way East, to the Ukraine, be picked out to go back to Germany, in order – as he claims, although Suchomel's story differs – to be sent back East again, to Poland, just a few weeks later?

The only convincing explanation is, in fact, that Otto Horn – and all the others who were picked for the *Aktion Reinhard* – were individually selected on the basis of evaluation of their previous record in the Euthanasia Programme.

Herr Allers claims to know very little about individuals attached to T4, or indeed about the expansion of the Euthanasia Programme into the *Aktion Reinhard*. However, this personnel, wherever they

88

were, and whatever their assignments, were administered from the offices of T4 in Berlin. Herr Allers continued as administrative director until May 1944, when a high-powered administration in Berlin obviously became superfluous and he was transferred to Trieste – incidentally, to take the place of Wirth who had been killed. (This information comes from judiciary authorities in Germany, not from Herr Allers himself.) Considering his situation, Herr Allers and his wife showed some courage in talking with me at all; but considering the extent of his unique knowledge of matters we know far too little about, and on which all records have disappeared, one could wish that he had shown even more.

Although prepared up to a point to discuss euthanasia, Herr and Frau Allers were less ready to talk about T4 and the Jews.

"When did you first hear about what was happening to the Jews in Poland?" I asked, and there was a long silence.

"Oh, some time in '43," Frau Allers finally said.

"Is that what you remember too?" I asked her husband. By 1943 millions of Jews had already been killed, and the SS men who directed the killing were paid, issued papers and sent on frequent leave by the Berlin T4 office which also, as Herr Allers was to concede later, looked after a special leave-centre on the Attersee in Austria, for T4 personnel and their families.

"How would we have known?" he said.

"Well, how did you feel about it when you *did* hear?"

"Can you ask us that?" Frau Allers said. "Can you sit here, in this room with us, and ask us that question?"

"Well, yes I can," I answered. "You were there; you didn't leave T4 when the Euthanasia Programme in Germany ended. You stayed. You knew."

"Well of course terrible, awful," she said. "We had nothing against Jews. I used to go to school with Jews. Only the other day I found a photo of myself in a Jewish kindergarten in Berlin. . . ."

"Yes," added Herr Allers, "when I went to school, there were fifty boys in my class, forty of them Jews. That wasn't right, was it – in Charlottenburg . . . But how did we feel? How could we feel? It goes without saying – terrible. But what could one do? . . .

"But, this whole miserable business about the Jews," he said later. "Do you know the *real* history of it? Nobody here thought of extermination; if you had said to somebody in Germany, a man in the street *or* an SS officer 'We are going to kill the Jews', he would have said 'The man is mad: have him locked up!' Originally what they wanted to do was put into practice an old Polish plan. You can find it outlined in one of Pilsudksi's books; one-third to be killed; one-third re-settled somewhere; and one-third to be allowed to assimilate. According to this they first planned to create a Jewish state in Madagascar. It was to be included in the treaty with the French. And when that didn't work out they thought of establishing it in the province of Lublin. I think it was only when nothing else worked out that they decided. . . ." He stopped.

"Are you sorry about it now? Do you regret what was done?"

"Well yes, that goes without saying. But, on the other hand, if one realizes what the situation was in Germany in the early 1930s: I remember when I said I wanted to study law, somebody in my family took me to the Ministry of Justice in Berlin. We walked along a corridor and he told me to read the names on the office doors we passed. Almost all of them were Jews. And it was the same for the press, the banks, business; in Berlin all of it was in the hands of Jews. That wasn't right. There should have been *some* Germans."

"Of course, they *were* Germans, weren't they?"

"Well yes, but you know what I mean. . . . I was thinking some more," he said later, "about what Stangl said to you, remember? About when he came to T4 and was given the choice of either going East, or back to his home station; I've never wanted to harm those people who went to Poland, so I've never said this: I think it is quite possible that Stangl – as he told you – and others too, did not know what they were going to do in Poland. But, if they had any suspicions [Stangl said he had learned later that "some of the men knew"] then, after all, they didn't *have* to go; just like Stangl, they *were* asked. There *was* an element of choice. . . ."

Part II

I

HISTORICAL RECORDS in the public domain prove beyond any doubt that the Nazi extermination of the Jews, and concurrently of large numbers of gypsies, was intended as only the first step in a gigantic programme of genocide of all the so-called "inferior races" of Europe. A beginning was made both in Russia, where the Nazis are said to have killed about seven million civilians between 1941 and 1944, and in Poland where the reported figures vary, depending on the source, from between 800,000 to 2,400,000 Poles other than Jews.

In view of these monstrous figures, and of the fact that genocide in one form or another has existed as long as human history is recorded – not least in our time, and also perpetrated by nations other than the Germans – it is not altogether surprising that the question "What is so different about the Nazi murder of the Jews?" has been asked time and again, and often by enlightened people.

Perhaps because so much has been written, over so many years, about the highly emotive subject of the Nazis and the Jews, many people now manifest a weary – and wary – resistance to it. Hard facts have become blurred and some indeed have never been accepted.

Using – or misusing – the perspective of history, some chroniclers of the time will have us believe that the extermination of the Jews was almost an accidental development, somehow forced upon the Nazis by circumstances. Dieter Allers' "Nobody here thought of extermination" has been said to me dozens of times in Germany, and by people far less implicated than Herr Allers.

But the truth is that the record does not bear out that defence. The ways and means towards achieving this enormous act of murder only evolved with time, but the intention was there almost from the start. On January 30, 1939, Hitler said in the course of a speech to the Reichstag: "Today I will once more be a prophet. If

93

SOBIBOR EXTERMINATION CAMP
as remembered by Stanislaw Szmajzner

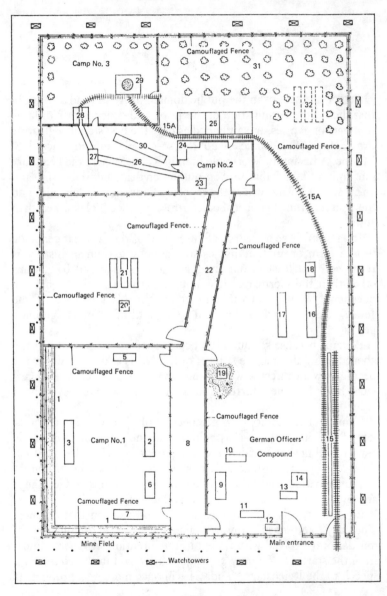

1. Anti-escape trench
2. Barracks housing the shoe-maker, tailor, jeweller, and hat-maker (exclusively for German Officers); also living quarters for workers
3. Barracks for all workers in Camps 1 and 2
5. Tailor and shoe-maker for Ukrainian guards; bakery, painters
6. Machine-shop and blacksmith
7. Carpentry shop
8. Area for selections
9. Officers' recreation room
10. Officers' baths and barber
11. Officers' quarters, "The Birds' Nest"
12. Sentry box
13. Garage
14. Two-storey building for officers
15. Railway platform
15A. Small rail line to Camps 2 and 3
16 and 17. Living quarters for Ukrainian guards
18. Kitchen stores, Ukrainian guards
19. Water-tank, with garden round it
20. Wooden observation tower
21. Victims' belongings
22. Communication corridor with Camp 2
23. Deposit for gold and valuables
24. Electrical workshop, stables, depository for tinned goods
25. Store-rooms for clothes, utensils, etc
26. "Himmelstrasse" – access to "baths" and hair-cutting
27. Hair-cutting
28. Gas chamber
29. Crematorium, and quarters for workers
31. Woods
32. Munitions deposit for material from the Russian front (sorting and repair)

the international Jewish financiers inside and outside Europe should again succeed in plunging the nations into a world war, the result will not be the bolshevization of the world and thus the victory of Jewry, but the annihilation [*Vernichtung*] of the Jewish race throughout Europe."

It is true that the so-called "Madagascar Plan" – conceived by the Poles in 1937 and briefly considered by the French as a solution to the voluntary resettlement of 10,000 of the many thousands of Jewish refugees who had been given sanctuary in France between 1936 and 1938 – was taken quite seriously by at least some of Nazi leadership for a short time. Eichmann is said to have been busy for a year working out the details. When the idea of eventually shipping four million people to Madagascar was defeated by its own lack of realism, the same faction of Nazi administrators who had entertained it as a possibility turned to the idea of setting up a Jewish reservation in the province of Lublin (Lublinland, it was to be called). But these were only pipe-dreams, quite possibly encouraged by those few really in Hitler's confidence in an effort to mislead the others.

On March 13, 1941, an ambiguous Führer order was communicated to the army command in Russia. "By order of the Führer, the Reichsführer SS has been given special tasks, arising from the conclusive and decisive struggle between the two opposing political systems. Within the limits of the set tasks, the Reichsführer SS acts independently upon his own responsibility." The fact that this Führer order, which was to cover the execution of a wide category of "undesirable elements" in conquered Eastern territories, referred primarily to the Jews was never to be put into words, or on paper.*

The Nazi plans for the "Final Solution" in terms of mass murder had crystallized as the plans for invading Russia were made. The armies advancing into Russian territory in June 1941 were closely followed by the infamous *Einsatzgruppen* (Action Groups) who carried out faithfully the Führer order for the execution of "Jews, gypsies, racial inferiors, asocials and Soviet political commissars".

One of the SS signals concerning these "actions" was found amongst *Einsatzgruppen* records after the war. Addressed to the security police, Riga, from the commander of the security police (and SD) Eastern zone, and entitled "Executions", it requests "im-

* As Reitlinger says in *The Final Solution*, page 84, "Even those to whom it was passed were not all informed at the same time."

mediate information regarding number of executions categorized as *(a)* Jews; *(b)* Communists; *(c)* Partisans; *(d)* Mentally ill; *(e)* Others. (The signal also requested the information: "Of the total, how many women and children?")

The reply, addressed to Group A in Riga, states that executions up to February 1, 1942 were: *(a)* Jews, 136,421; *(b)* Communists, 1,064 (amongst them 1 Kommissar, 1 Oberpolitruck, 5 Politruck–presumably Communist Party titles); *(c)* Partisans, 56; *(d)* Mentally ill, 653; *(e)* Poles, 44; Russian POWs, 28; gypsies, 5; Armenian, 1. Total: 138,272; of which, women, 55,556; children, 34,464.§

By early 1942, behind the front from Riga and Miusk to Kiev and the Crimea, they had killed well over 500,000 Jews – two-thirds of them, as we can see from the signal, women and children, and nearly all by shooting in previously dug mass graves.

Albert Hartl, the former chief of the Church Information Service at the Reich Security Office, who had been sent to Russia in January 1942 with a commission from Heydrich to "report on the cultural and spiritual condition of the population", told me of the day he was invited to dine at the *dacha* – the weekend villa outside Kiev – of Brigadeführer (Major-General) Max Thomas, the higher SS and police leader who was his nominal superior. "I was going with Standartenführer (Colonel) Blobel," he said. "I hardly knew him but he was invited to dinner too, so we went together. It was evening and just getting dark. At one moment – we were driving past a long ravine. I noticed strange movements of the earth: clumps of earth rose into the air as if by their own propulsion – and there was smoke: it was like a low-toned volcano; as if there was burning lava just beneath the earth. Blobel laughed, made a gesture with his arm, pointing back along the road and ahead of us, all along the ravine – the ravine of Babi Yar – and said, "Here lie my 30,000 Jews."* (Hartl, a few months after that, had, or faked, a nervous breakdown, was first hospitalized in Kiev and then sent for six months to a convalescent home in the country. After this he was returned to Germany and, by request, invalided

§A further document, from the same source, now establishes that *Einsatzgruppe* 3 (EK 3, for *Einsatzkommando*, in official language) began their executions on July 4, 1941, and, carefully listing places, dates and number of victims, allows the conclusion that this one killing-command murdered at least these 138,272 people in seven months.

* The movement of the earth was caused by the thaw releasing the gases from the corpses.

out of active, including administrative, service with the SS.)†

But in spite of its hideous effectiveness in Russia, shooting was soon rejected as inefficient for what Himmler was to call "the enormous task ahead" in Poland. It was also too dangerous, in that too many German soldiers from the ranks of the Wehrmacht as well as from the SS had to be involved. New techniques were called for, and here the euthanasia personnel (some of whom had already been involved in the "work" in Russia) found a new role.

What was different, and of unprecedented horror, in the Nazi genocide of the Jews as it now developed, was the concept and organization of the "extermination camps". Even today there is still widespread misunderstanding about the nature of these very special installations of which there were only four,* all of them on occupied Polish territory and all of them existing for only a short time.

Ever since the end of World War II these extermination camps have been confused in people's minds with "concentration camps", of which there were literally dozens, spread all over Greater Germany and occupied Europe, and which have been the primary subject of descriptions in fiction and films.

There are two main reasons for the persistent confusion between these two kinds of Nazi installations; the first is that appallingly few people survived the extermination camps, and those who did are neither necessarily particularly articulate, nor anxious to relive their horrifying experiences. The second reason – far more subtle – is a universal reluctance to face the fact that these places really existed.

There is a somewhat similar confusion – in the sense of one concept being marginally more acceptable than the other – between "War Crimes" and "Nazi Crimes". (Although the misinterpretation, or misapplication, of *these* two terms is far more deliberate and politically motivated.) For the truth is that "Nazi Crimes" ("NS Crimes" in Germany), although their perpetration was facilitated by war, had in their origins nothing whatever to do with the war.

In *Mein Kampf*, written in 1923, Hitler had already committed himself to a concept of a new Europe based on racial theories according to which the whole of Eastern Europe was to become a

† "Anybody who really wanted to, could get out by faking a nervous breakdown," Hartl told me.

* Five if we include Birkenau, the extermination section of Auschwitz – which, however, also functioned partly as a labour camp. See map at front of book.

"service population" for the benefit of the "superior races" (in addition to Germany: Scandinavia, Holland, some of France, and Britain). Even if there had been no war, or if Germany had won the war after the fall of France in 1940, the conditions under which this programme could have been implemented would have had to be created. It would still have been found necessary to kill, or at best sterilize, all those in Eastern Europe most likely to resist: the intellectuals and the social and religious élite. Racially "pure" children would still have been shipped to Germany in infancy and brought up by German foster-parents or in German institutions. (A beginning to this particular phase was in fact made during the war, when 200,000 Polish infants were forcibly removed from their parents. A large number of them were returned to Poland through the efforts of UNRRA in 1945-6, but by no means all of them were found.)*

Hitler's new Europe was entirely based on this concept of superior and inferior peoples. Whether by annexation or by war, he was determined to create machinery for putting into practice the decimation of Eastern Europe. Equally, war or no war, as no other practical solution offered itself, he would eventually have had to find ways of physically exterminating the Jews; the only logical conclusion of the psychological defamation campaign on which most of his programme was built.

The "concentration" camps were originally set up as extended prison services to deal with those resisting the New Order, and to eliminate them, with bogus legality, as "traitors" or "spies" if their "re-education" proved impossible. From 1941, most of these camps became vast slave-labour markets, but even then they still varied a good deal in severity, largely depending on the nationality of the prisoners they catered for. And even in the worst of them, however terrible the conditions, they offered at least a slim chance of survival.

The "extermination" camps offered no such chance. They were created for the sole purpose of exterminating primarily the Jews of Europe, and also the Gypsies. There were four of these installations, planned *exclusively* for extermination; first, and as a testing ground, Chelmno (Kulmhof), set up in December 1941. Then, following the Wannsee Conference of January 1942 which, chaired by Rein-

* When working as a child-tracing officer for UNRRA in Germany in 1945-6, I found that numerous German foster-parents were honestly unaware that their adopted children had been stolen from Poland as infants.

hard Heydrich, put the official seal of approval on the extermination programme, Belsec (March 1942), Sobibor (May 1942), and the largest of them, Treblinka (June 1942). All were within a two-hundred-mile radius of Warsaw.

The decision to place all of them on Polish soil has been attributed widely to the well-known anti-Semitism of large segments of the Polish population. Although this fact may have marginally influenced the choice, it is more reasonable to assume that it was mainly prompted by tactical considerations. Poland's railway system covered all of the country, with stations in even the smallest towns; while large tracts of the Polish countryside, densely forested and very thinly populated, made isolation possible. In this sense – and this sense only – the war did contribute to making this huge and sinister operation possible, for it is unlikely that it could have been attempted in any other region of Europe.

None of the extermination camps existed for longer than seventeen months when, one after the other, they were totally obliterated by the SS. The official Polish estimate – the most conservative, and not universally accepted – is that approximately 2,000,000 Jews and 52,000 gypsies (children made up at least one-third of this total) were killed in these four camps during that period.

The concentration camps too had gas-vans, gas chambers, crematoriums and mass graves. In them too people were shot, given lethal injections, gassed, and apart from being murdered, hundreds of thousands died of exhaustion, starvation and disease. But – even in Birkenau, the extermination section of Auschwitz (where 860,000 Jews are believed to have been killed) * – there was in all of them a chance of life.

In the extermination camps, the only people who retained this chance from day to day were the pitifully few who were kept as "work-Jews" to operate the camps. Eighty-seven people – no children among them – survived the four Nazi death-camps in Poland.

But it was not only the policy behind the Nazi murder of the Jews which distinguished it from other instances of genocide. The methods employed, too, were unique and uniquely calculated. The killings were organized systematically to achieve the maximum

* Reitlinger, *The Final Solution*, pages 500–501, estimates that of the approximately 851,200 Jews deported to Auschwitz, probably some 700,000 were gassed and cremated in Birkenau.

humiliation and dehumanization of the victims before they died. This pattern was dictated by a distinct and careful purpose, not by "mere" cruelty or indifference: the crammed airless freight-cars without sanitary provisions, food or drink, far worse than any cattle-transport; the whipped-up (literally so) hysteria of arrival; the immediate and always violent separation of men, women and children; the public undressing; the incredibly crude internal physical examinations for hidden valuables; the hair-cutting and shaving of the women; and finally the naked run to the gas chamber, under the lash of the whips.

"What did you think at the time was the reason for the extermination of the Jews?" I was to ask Stangl.

"They wanted their money," he replied at once. "Have you any idea of the fantastic sums that were involved? That's how the steel was bought, in Sweden."

Perhaps he really did believe this, but I doubt it. Globocnik's final accounting disclosed that the *Aktion Reinhard* (named after Heydrich) netted the Third Reich DM 178,745,960. To one man, in relation to his monthly wage, this may seem a lot of money. But what is it in the context of a nation's normal income and expenditure, in war or in peace? It is a trivial sum.

"Why," I asked Stangl, *"if they were going to kill them anyway, what was the point of all the humiliation, why the cruelty?"*

"To condition those who actually had to carry out the policies," he said. "To make it possible for them to do what they did." And this, I believe, was true.

To achieve the extermination of these millions of men, women and children, the Nazis committed not only physical but spiritual murder: on those they killed, on those who did the killing, on those who knew the killing was being done, and also, to some extent, for evermore, on all of us, who were alive and thinking beings at that time.

2

WE BEGAN on the Polish part of Franz Stangl's story on the morning of the fourth day. Everything he had told me up to now had led up to this moment. His description of his childhood and youth had frequently been interrupted by deep emotion and tears, so the prospect of having to begin the account of his work in the

Nazi death-camps would, I was sure, be even more daunting to his spirits. I too was apprehensive about the coming hours.

I waited for him outside the door and watched him walk down the long corridor towards me. He smiled from far away and the closer he came the more noticeable was a subtle – and yet not all that subtle – change in his bearing; where before there had been a mixture of eagerness and slight diffidence in his morning greeting, there was now a curious kind of bland composure, and when he bowed from the waist, an overdone *bonhomie*.

When seated at the table, he began instantly, without being urged or requestioned, to talk about his arrival in Poland in the early spring of 1942. He sounded brisk and confident, speaking like an objective observer who can describe macabre and terrifying events with feeling and yet fluency and detachment.

"There were twenty of us travelling together," he said, "all from the Foundation. I was put in charge."

"And none of you knew what awaited you in Poland?"

"Later I found out that three or four of them had known, but at the time they said nothing – they didn't let on.

"I reported to the SS HQ Lublin," he went on, "as soon as I arrived. It was very strange. The SS HQ was in the Julius Schreck Kaserne – a kind of palace surrounded by a large park. When I gave my name at the gate, I was taken through the building into the park. They said the general would meet me there." (This was Gruppenführer (Lieutenant-General) Odilo Globocnik, who directed the extermination of the Jews in Poland and who was to commit suicide on June 6, 1945, when about to be arrested by a British patrol in Carinthia.)

"It was a beautiful spring day," Stangl remembered. "The grass was very green, the trees in bud and there were new flowers everywhere. I came upon Globocnik sitting by himself on a bench about ten metres away from – and with his back to – the building. There was a lovely view across lawns and trees to buildings far away.

"The general greeted me warmly. 'Sit down,' he said, patting the space next to him. 'Tell me all about yourself.' [Once again Stangl had fallen into the provincial Austrian vernacular which from then on, except when talking about his wife, he was to use whenever he quoted conversations or described particularly disturbing events.] He wanted to know all about my training in the police, my career, my family – everything. I realized that this was in the nature of a 'test' to ascertain whether I was really suitable for whatever assignment I was to have."

"*You mentioned, of course, your work in the Euthanasia Programme?*"

"I said that I had been attached to the 'Foundation for Institutional Care'," he said tersely.

"*Who else was there?*"

"I saw no one at all. The park seemed empty too. It was very quiet and very beautiful. When I finished he said that no doubt I knew that the army had just had some major setbacks in the East. The SS was going to have to help. It had been decided, he told me, to open a number of supply camps from which the troops at the front could be re-equipped. He said that he intended confiding to me the construction of a camp called Sobibor. He called an aide – who must have lurked somewhere nearby – and told him to bring the plans."

"*To the bench?*"

"Yes," he shook his head. "It really was very odd. The plans arrived and he spread them out on the bench between us and on the ground in front of us. They showed a design for a camp: barracks, railway tracks, fences, gates. Some of the buildings – bunkers they were – were crossed out with red ink. 'Don't worry about those,' he said, 'concentrate on getting the rest done first. It has been started but they've got Poles working there. It's going so slowly I think they must be asleep. What the place needs is someone to organize it properly and I think you are the man to do it.' And then he said he'd arrange for me to leave for Sobibor the next day – that was all."

"*How long did this conversation last?*"

"About three hours."

"*And during those three hours – all on that bench in the park – did he ever hint at what the real purpose of Sobibor was? Did he mention the Jews?*"

"Not with one word. I had no idea whatever. He did ask me whether I'd like to go and visit Christian Wirth. But I said, 'Brigadeführer, excuse me for saying so, but Wirth and I don't exactly see eye to eye. I'd just as soon not see him any more than necessary.'"

"*Did he say where Wirth was and what he was doing?*"

"No, only that he was stationed not far away."

There appeared to me to be two improbabilities raised by this story: first, was it likely that a comparatively junior officer would have been received so informally by the general, and second, would Stangl still have been left in ignorance of the purpose of the work to which he was being assigned (given that he *was* ignorant) at this stage?

On the first point Franz Suchomel, who read my conversations with Stangl in the German newspaper *Die Zeit*, was highly sceptical. He wrote me saying, "It sounds like a fairy tale. Globocnik was *General of the Police* and *SS Obergruppenführer* [his emphasis] – there could never have been such a comradely tone between them except possibly during a drinking session." On the other hand, Dieter Allers, better qualified, I think, to evaluate this encounter, sees the interview as "quite possible". Since, however humble Stangl's rank then was, he was being appointed to a key job at the start of a very difficult operation, it was, he thought, not unreasonable to assume that the man in charge would want to assess his calibre personally (just as Brack had previously done with all new T4 personnel).

In March 1972 I succeeded in finding the building in Lublin Stangl had described to me. It is now being used as a school for domestic science. Although it has none of the style and grandeur of "a palace", it is a big place and could well have looked imposing to him. The young headmistress sent for older colleagues likely to be better informed about that period than herself, and they confirmed that during the occupation the whole neighbourhood had been strictly off-limits to anyone but the SS; and three of them, who had lived nearby at the time, said that the building was definitely "Governor Globocnik's seat". They said that the garden used to be quite big and that thirty years ago the view from near the house over a vista of trees and lawns was probably unimpeded. And near the house, at just the distance described by Stangl, there *was* a wooden bench, facing away from the house, which looked as though it could have been there for decades. My visit coincided with the time of year of Stangl's interview with Globocnik, and it seemed far too cold for sitting out of doors; but my informants said that the coming of spring in that part of Poland varies a great deal from year to year, and that it was perfectly possible that in 1942 (which was to turn into one of the hottest summers on record) the trees could have been in bud and flowers could have been in bloom.

Suchomel's scepticism, significantly enough, referred to the "comradely" tone of the interview, and not to the other points of doubt: Stangl's description of where this conversation had taken place and his claim that he was not told the true purpose of the camp he was to construct. The Düsseldorf court certainly did not believe Stangl on this, but I consider it at least possible that he was telling the truth, and not only because I questioned him about it closely and repeatedly, and found him always consistent in his replies however I turned and changed the questions.

In the early spring of 1942 the planned physical extermination of the Jews was known to comparatively few people even amongst the highest party echelons, and the population of Germany – there can be no doubt of this whatever now – was at that time, though not later, in total ignorance of these intentions. Victor Brack testified at his trial in Nuremberg that when he was originally requested to send euthanasia personnel to Lublin and put it at the disposal of Globocnik, neither he nor Bouhler had "any idea" that they were to be used in the mass extermination of Jews. He claimed that it was only in June 1942 that Globocnik took Philip Bouhler (chief of the Führer Chancellery) into his confidence, whereupon, according to Brack, Bouhler protested that if his men worked on "*such an inconceivable assignment*" they would not be fit to be employed subsequently in mercy-killing.

Brack, according to the record, was involved in the planning of the death-camps in the East as early as the autumn of 1941, so it is unlikely that his denial of knowledge on behalf of himself and Bouhler corresponds to the truth. But Bouhler's expression of anxiety as to the effect of the work on the "staff", as he quoted it, rings true as an indication of the nervousness felt by those administering the extermination programme. There must have been considerable uncertainty about the men; even for the Nazis there must have been an enormous difference between the – as they claimed – carefully controlled mercy-killing of the incurably and often miserably sick, and the systematic and brutal murder of thousands upon thousands of healthy men, women and children. There must inevitably have been some doubt as to whether the men sent to Poland to launch the project would, when it came to it, be capable of carrying it through. And such doubts may well have suggested that a policy of gradual initiation – or perhaps sudden initiation, but *at their actual place of work* – would be wiser than giving them full information from the start. There was also the very real danger of leaks. No one who has gone into these matters can continue to believe that SS men never told their wives about their activities.

One example of this is Gustav Münzberger, who was at the Sonnenstein euthanasia institute before he went to Treblinka. "Well," Frau Münzberger told me, "I knew after a while what he was doing. He wasn't supposed to say of course, but you know what women are," and she smiled comfortably. "I probed and probed and finally he told me. It was awful of course," she added, just as comfortably, "but what could *we* do?" The fact is that by no means all German women would have been so accommodating, particularly not if they had known the nature of their husband's work *before* they were involved in it. For the Nazi hierarchy the spreading of information in this way could have been a very real danger. And the possibility that wives would stop their husbands from accepting such assignments was another.

There is the further point that the administration needed to have a strong hold over these men. To order a man to some nebulous "strictly secret duty" in the East was one thing; to keep him at it once he realized what was involved was possibly quite another. I do not believe that these particular men were not carefully evaluated before they – just *they* out of the 400 T4 personnel – were offered the assignment to Lublin. But it is quite likely that it was decided to keep the majority of them in relative ignorance of exactly what this assignment entailed until they actually reached their final destination, *saw* what it was, and by seeing became implicated and aware of the danger their knowledge represented.

I did not readily believe Stangl's account of his introduction to his death-camp commands; I shall always have my doubts about it. But like many other things which would not have happened under normal conditions and to normal people – it is not impossible that it was true.

Stangl told me about his first visit to the Sobibor site on two occasions, a month apart. During our second series of talks I repeated several questions (all on matters about which I had doubts). His story started the same way both times, but differed slightly in some respects later on.

"I spent that first night in an officers' billets in Lublin," he said.

"Did you go sightseeing?"

"No, I was tired. I was going to make an early start the next day and went to bed early. The next morning a car with a driver picked me up and we drove first to Cholm [Chelm – but he always called it either Cholm or Colm] where Globocnik had said I was to introduce myself to the surveyor, Baurath Moser, who was in charge of the materials I would need for Sobibor."

"Did this Baurath Moser tell you anything about Sobibor's ultimate purpose?"

"No. But then, I didn't ask him; it never occurred to me. Globocnik's instructions had been quite clear: Sobibor was a supply camp for the army. The surveyor and I only discussed materials."

"How far was Chelm from Sobibor? And Sobibor from Lublin?"

"Colm was about thirty kilometres from Sobibor: Sobibor about 110 kilometres from Lublin [about forty-five and 160 in fact]. Baurath Moser suggested we make a round of the camps he supplied in the district. The first camp I saw was about half-way between Colm and Sobibor, a farm called Griechhof [this camp was actually called Kirchhof]. It employed two to three hundred Jewish women, mostly German or at least German-speaking. I went in there to look around. There was nothing – you know – sinister about it: they were quite free, if you like; it was just a farm where the women worked under the supervision of Jewish guards."

"What do you mean by 'Jewish guards'?"

"Well, I suppose you could call them Jewish police. As I say, I looked around and the women seemed quite cheerful – they seemed healthy. They were just working, you know."

"Were these 'guards' armed?"

"They were armed with *weissen Schlagmitteln* [a really extraordinary word, in literal translation meaning 'white implements for beating']."

"What do you mean by that? Clubs? Whips?"

He shrugged his shoulders: it was a question he wouldn't answer. "We got to the village of Sobibor around supper-time. In the middle of the village there was another work camp. The man in charge carried a gun and wore a blue uniform I wasn't familiar with; he took me to a barrack where we had supper – Jewish girls served us. During the meal he described the work that was being done there: it was mostly drainage."

"And who was doing the work?"

"Jewish prisoners."

"Well, had you expected to find all this? Or did you now begin to ask questions?"

"No, I didn't. It was just a work camp in the middle of a Polish village using Jewish labour. There wasn't anything special about this: foreign labourers were being used everywhere." It was confirmed to me in Poland that these two camps were indeed labour camps for Jewish women, mostly from Czechoslovakia and Austria, who apparently lived there under comparatively humane conditions and worked on drainage projects.

From this point on, for reasons I never quite understood, Stangl presented two different versions of his first sight of Sobibor camp.

"I asked where the Sobibor camp-site was," he said on the first occasion, "and they wouldn't tell me, they just said it was too late to go there that night and that we would spend the night in the village. We went the next morning – it turned out to be only six kilometres away."

During our second series of talks he mumbled something about a bridge having come down and a river flooding, and said they went back to Chelm for the night and he returned to Lublin in the morning, going to Sobibor three days later with six other men including his friend Michel, who had been stationed with him at Hartheim. He told me later that Michel – about whom he gave me three different stories – had fled to Egypt at the end of the war and was presumably still there.

"What did the camp look like when you got there?"

"It was just the Sobibor railway station. The station building and across from it the forester's hut and a barn, that's all; just those three wooden buildings."

"And who did you find at Sobibor?"

"That was a surprise for me," he said the first time, "because there were several people there I already knew: they'd been in the .... you know ... the Euthanasia Programme. Especially one – Michel, he'd been the head nurse at Hartheim."

(He repeated this answer on a second occasion, but when I asked him the same question yet again, six weeks later, he suddenly said that Michel had actually travelled to Sobibor with him.)

"Weren't you a bit surprised to see Michel there? What did you think a nurse was doing at this supply camp site?"

"Well, I didn't really think about it. I knew of course that as the *Aktion* was over, the staff had become available – *something* had to be done with them. Also, it was very nice for me to have a friend there."

It was of course quite clear at the time that the story of his beginnings in Poland and of some of the euthanasia phase, was at least partly fabrication, partly rationalization and partly evasion. But having pressed him about this repeatedly – on each occasion when we went through it again – I hoped that if I didn't press him too hard, he would find it possible later on to revert to telling me the truth about the rest of it, however difficult.

He went on to describe the Polish workers, whom he found a "lackadaisical lot". "They lived in the neighbourhood and went home at night – no doubt to get drunk on their *slivowitz*. Anyway, they always arrived late in the morning."

Within two or three days he obtained a Jewish "work-com-mando" of twenty-five men, he said, and some Ukrainian guards from a nearby training camp, Trawniki. "At that time we really had nothing, no amenities for anybody," he said. "Those first weeks we all bunked in together."

"What do you mean 'all together'? The German staff, the Ukrainian guards and the Jews?"

"At first we just used one hut while we were working on the others: *we* slept on the floor in the kitchen, and the others in the loft. Everything had to be built from scratch."

"When did you first find out what the camp was really for?"

"Two things happened: when we'd been there about three days, I think, Michel came running one day and said he'd found a funny building back in the woods. 'I think there is something fishy going on here,' he said. 'Come and see what it reminds you of.' "

"What did he mean, 'in the woods'?"

"It was about ten or even fifteen minutes' walk away from the railway station where we were building the main camp. It was a new brick building with three rooms, three metres by four. The moment I saw it I knew what Michel meant: it looked exactly like the gas chamber at Schloss Hartheim."

"But who had built this? How could you possibly not have noticed it before? Or seen it on the plans?"

"The Poles had built it – they didn't know what it was to be. Neither Michel nor I had had any time yet to go for walks in the woods. We were very busy. Yes – it was on the plans, but so were lots of other buildings . . . " the sentence trailed off.

"All right, you hadn't known: but now you knew. What did you do?"

His face had gone red. I didn't know whether because he had been caught out in a lie or because of what he was about to say next; it was much more usual for him to blush in advance than in retrospect.

"The second thing I mentioned happened almost simultaneously: a transport officer, a sergeant, arrived from Lublin – he was drunk – and said, to *me* [he sounded angry even now] that Globocnik was dissatisfied with the progress of the camp and had said to tell me that 'If these Jews don't work properly, just kill them off and we'll get others'."

"What did that indicate to you?"

"I went the very next day to Lublin to see Globocnik. He received me at once. I said to him, 'How can this sergeant be permitted to give *me* such a message? And anyway, I am a police officer: how can I be expected to do anything like that?' Globocnik was very friendly. He said I had misunderstood: I was just overwrought. He said, 'We'd better get you some leave. You just go back for the moment and get on with the building. You are doing fine.' And then he said, 'Perhaps we can arrange to have your family come out for a bit.' So I went back. What else could I do?"

"Did you ask Globocnik about the gas chambers?"

"There was no opportunity," he said firmly. "I went back to Sobibor and talked it over with Michel. We decided that somehow we had to get out. But the very next day Wirth came. He told me to assemble the German personnel and made a speech – just as awful, just as vulgar as his speeches had been at Hartheim. He said that any Jews who didn't work properly here would be 'eliminated'. 'If any of you don't like that,' he said to us, 'you can leave. But under the earth,' – that was his idea of being humorous – 'not over it.' And then he left. I went back to Lublin the next morning. Sturmbannführer (Major) Höfle,* Globocnik's aide then, kept me waiting in the office all day, and again the next morning. Then he finally told me that the General would not be available for me. I went back to Sobibor. Four days later a courier came from Lublin with a formal letter from Globocnik informing

---

* Hans Höfle, Deputy Director of the *Aktion Reinhard*, hanged himself in the Vienna remand prison in August 1962 while awaiting trial.

me – in ice-cold language – that Wirth had been appointed inspector of camps and that I was to report to him at Belsec forthwith."§

Wirth had by then commanded both Chelmno and Belsec, a much larger establishment. At Chelmno it was found that the method of gas-vans was impracticable for the huge task on hand, and he claimed to have invented the Jewish *Sonderkommandos** (probably falsely, as this idea, reverting to the legend of the Pharaonic tombs, seems more likely to have emanated from Heydrich's fertile intellectual brain). At Belsec the first large-scale exterminations with engine exhaust gas in gas chambers were begun in March 1942.

"I can't describe to you what it was like," Stangl said; he spoke slowly now, in his more formal German, his face strained and grim. He passed his hand over his eyes and rubbed his forehead. "I went there by car. As one arrived, one first reached Belsec railway station, on the left side of the road. The camp was on the same side, but up a hill. The Kommandantur was 200 metres away, on the other side of the road. It was a one-storey building. The smell . . . " he said, "Oh God, the smell. It was everywhere. Wirth wasn't in his office. I remember, they took me to him . . . he was standing on a hill, next to the pits . . . the pits . . . full . . . they were full. I can't tell you; not hundreds, thousands, thousands of corpses . . . oh God. That's where Wirth told me – he said that was what Sobibor was for. And that he was putting me officially in charge."

Although I have never doubted that Stangl's first experience of a death-camp in operation was – as he claimed – that day in Belsec, he did give me, here too, two versions of this experience, although they were only marginally different. (His giving different versions of events is not too important from the point of view of facts. It is, however, of psychological relevance, for the gradual decrease in evasions, embellishments, and anxiety to project a favourable image of himself reflects significantly and accurately the intensity of his emotion, and possibly the psychological changes these conversations produced in him.)

The second time I asked him to tell me this story, he said:

§The timing reported here by Stangl is contradicted by documents on record, in particular Christian Wirth's personnel file which states that he was Kommandant of Belsec until August 1942, when he was appointed *Inspektor* for the Sonderkommando (special command) *Einsatz Reinhard*.

* The system of forcing physically stronger Jews to despoil and bury their own people before they in turn were killed.

"Wirth wasn't in his office; they said he was up in the camp. I asked whether I should go up there and they said, 'I wouldn't if I were you – he's mad with fury. It isn't healthy to go near him.' I asked what was the matter. The man I was talking to said that one of the pits had overflowed. They had put too many corpses in it and putrefaction had progressed too fast, so that the liquid underneath had pushed the bodies on top up and over and the corpses had rolled down the hill. I saw some of them – oh God, it was awful. A bit later Wirth came down. And that's when he told me...."

The historical record provides a number of horrifyingly graphic descriptions of Wirth's Belsec where the installations constantly broke down, causing unimaginable suffering to the deportees who were either left waiting, naked and without food or water, in the open, sometimes for days, or else were crammed into railway cars the floors of which had been covered with lime and were left to suffocate on sidings only a few hundred metres from the camp. These conditions – the beginnings of which Stangl obviously saw in April 1942 – have been described by Jan Karski in *The Story of a Secret State*,* and by Kurt Gerstein. Both men visited Belsec. Gerstein did so in his official capacity as Obersturmführer (Lieutenant) in the SS Health Department and his description of the gas chambers is probably the most terrible that has emerged from approximately that period. Gerstein's somewhat ambiguous but undoubtedly tortured personality has been amply described in the literature (although his death, in Fresnes prison on July 17, 1945, remains clouded in mystery). Karski (now professor at Georgetown University in Washington, D.C.) who was an indomitable courier for the Polish government in exile, spent a day at Belsec disguised as a Ukrainian guard. Karski's description of the extermination of the Jews in Poland reached London and Washington as early as October 1942 (presumably, at least through the diplomatic post, also the Vatican in Rome). Although the fact of the physical extermination of the Jews in Poland was by then thoroughly known to the Allies – and to the Vatican – Karski's detailed description to the world press, MPs, Members of Congress and religious leaders in London and Washington, and his meetings with Anthony Eden and President Roosevelt, provided the first testimony of an eye-witness. If previously there had been any

* Hodder, London, 1945.

doubt, after meeting Karski or reading his report, the Allied leaders knew precisely what was happening in Poland.

I had no doubt whatever of Stangl's sincerity when he described his reaction to Belsec. Nor could one doubt that this was the real moment of decision for him: the time when he might have braved what he certainly considered the deadly dangers of taking a stand ... and didn't because it wasn't in him to do so.

"I said [to Wirth] I couldn't do it," he said. "I simply wasn't up to such an assignment. There wasn't any argument or discussion. Wirth just said my reply would be reported to HQ and I was to go back to Sobibor. In fact I went to Lublin, tried again to see Globocnik, again in vain: he wouldn't see me. When I got back to Sobibor, Michel and I talked and talked about it. We agreed that what they were doing was a crime. We considered deserting – we discussed it for a long time. But how? Where could we go? What about our families?" He stopped. He stopped at that point, when he told me about it, just as he and Michel must have stopped talking about it at that point; because, if there was nothing they could or dared *do* – there was nothing else to say.

"But you knew that day that what was being done was wrong?"

"Yes, I knew. Michel knew. But we also knew what had happened in the past to other people who had said no. The only way out that we could see was to keep trying in various and devious ways to get a transfer. The direct way was impossible. As Wirth had said, that led 'under the earth'. Wirth came to Sobibor the next day. He ignored me; he stayed several days and organized everything. Half the workers were detailed to finish the gas chambers."

"While Wirth was organizing, what were you doing?"

"I just went on with other construction work," he said wearily. "And then one afternoon Wirth's aide, Oberhauser, came to get me.* I was to come to the gas chamber. When I got there, Wirth stood in front of the building wiping the sweat off his cap and fuming. Michel told me later that he'd suddenly appeared, looked around the gas chambers on which they were still working and said, 'Right, we'll try it out right now with those twenty-five work-Jews: get them up here.' They marched our twenty-five Jews up

*Josef Oberhauser was sentenced on January 21, 1965 in Munich, to 4½ years of imprisonment. Following his release, he was said to be working in a Munich wine cellar where my request for information about him, however, met with blank refusal.

there and just pushed them in, and gassed them. Michel said Wirth behaved like a lunatic, hit out at his own staff with his whip to drive them on. And then he was livid because the doors hadn't worked properly."

"What did he say to you?"

"Oh, he just screamed and raved and said the doors had to be changed. After that he left."

"And after he was gone, what did you do?"

"The same thing; I continued the construction of the camp. Michel had been put in charge of the gassings."

"Put in charge by whom?"

"By Wirth."

"So now the exterminations had really started; it was happening right in front of you. How did you feel?"

"At Sobibor one could avoid seeing almost all of it – it all happened so far away from the camp-buildings. All I could think of was that I wanted to get out. I schemed and schemed and planned and planned. I heard there was a new police unit at Mogilev. I went again to Lublin and filled out an application form for transfer. I asked Höfle to help me get Globocnik's agreement. He said he would do what he could, but I never heard of it again. Two months later – in June – my wife wrote that she had been requested to supply details about the children's ages: they were going to be granted a visit to Poland."

3

THE EXACT date on which Sobibor became fully operational is not quite certain; it was either May 16 or May 18, 1942. It is certain, however, that in the first two months, the period when Stangl was administering the camp, about 100,000 people were killed there. Soon after that, the machinery broke down for a while and exterminations did not recommence until October.

I drove to Sobibor by way of Lublin on a cold Friday in March 1972, and we passed the camp-site before we realized what it was. It is marked by a light-brown stone monument, ten feet tall, on which are engraved the words: "In this place from May 1942 until October 1943 there existed a Hitler extermination camp. At this camp 250,000 Russian, Polish, Jewish and Gypsy prisoners were murdered.* On the 14th of October 1943 an armed rebellion took place, with several hundred prisoners taking part who, after a battle with the Hitler guards, escaped." Facing the monument is Sobibor railway station. The station building has probably been improved, but the forester's cottage – built of timber and painted green and dark brown – in which Stangl lived, appears to be unchanged. It is now inhabited by the families of two foresters, and the little room in which Stangl worked and slept is still a bedroom. It overlooks the railway track, which was known in the camp as "the ramp". Transports may have halted slightly further back rather than directly opposite his window, but it would still have been impossible for Stangl to avoid seeing them.

The site – about 160 acres of forest – is quiet. The big clumps of pines and other trees are thick enough even in March to hide all open spaces. It is dark in the woods, with a musty, damp smell. "In Sobibor," Franz Suchomel had said, "one couldn't do any killing after the snow thawed because it was all under water. It was very damp at the best of times, but then it became a lake."

There is a road about thirty feet wide, still in good condition, stretching from the railway track into the woods. It was constructed under either Stangl or his successor Reichleitner, and the SS called it the *Himmelfahrtsstrasse* – the Road to Heaven. The area adjoining the disembarkation ramp, no larger than a medium-sized football ground, was called Camp II. Cunningly divided by means of blind fences into squares and corridors, with many narrow "doors" from one square into another, it allowed the systematic separation of the arriving deportees, usually without arousing their suspicion. From the arrival point at the ramp, all that was visible were the fences, tightly camouflaged with evergreen branches, the distant trees, and – to the left – the small cluster of barracks (now a bare and open space) known as Camp I where the SS staff, the Ukrainian guards and the "work-Jews" lived and worked. This was all the 250,000† who were killed in Sobibor ever saw.

I walked along the road they had to take – except that now there

* In *They Fought Back* (survivors' recollections edited by Ury Suhl, Crown, New York, 1967) Alexander Pechersky, a Russian prisoner at Sobibor and former officer in the Soviet army who led the October rising, contested this figure. He said that more than half a million people were murdered at Sobibor between May 1942 and October 1943. Accounts by survivors also deny that any non-Jewish Poles were killed there.

† The official Polish figure.

was complete solitude and silence. After perhaps half a mile it ends in a large tract of open land. In the centre, facing the road, is a huge mound of earth, an artificial hill thirty feet high, the bottom half of which is faced with glass laid over millions of tiny pebbles. Inset in the middle is a small square filled with dried wild flowers. This mound, now overgrown with grass and bushes, marks the place where the three gas chambers stood and symbolizes the grave of those who died there.

The air is clear and clean. There is the sound of birds, the occasional whistle and clatter of a train, the far-away clucking of chickens; familiar sounds which, thirty years ago, must have offered momentary illusions of reassurance. But the earth round the mound is dark and terribly fine while the soil over the rest of Sobibor is a light brown sand which gives underfoot. And one is jolted out of any effort at detachment by the sickening shock at realizing that – even these three decades later – one must be walking on ashes.

The custodian of the site is Wladzimier Gerung, head forester of the region, who lives with his wife in a new house on the other side of the railway, about twenty-five yards from the station. We went to see them, unannounced. The Gerungs, tall, easy-moving people with open faces and quietly courteous manners, came to Sobibor eighteen years ago. But as a girl, throughout the war, Pani Gerung lived near Chelm. "Oh yes," she said, "people in Chelm knew what was going on in Sobibor – how could they not? They could smell it – the air was rancid even though it was twenty miles away. And the sky lit up in the night with their terrible fires."

I asked whether she and the people who lived around her had feelings against the Jews. She shook her head. "No – it was just . . . there was nothing one could do. Except, I think sometimes, what our neighbours did."

The neighbours – farmers – had taken in two children of a Jewish pedlar when their parents were put into a ghetto; a girl of five and a boy of fourteen. The boy, on hearing that his parents and all the rest of the ghetto "had been taken away", had disappeared, but the farmer adopted the girl legally and kept her as his own child. The little girl, said Pani Gerung, looked very Jewish, and to start with both children had to be passed from one house to another to keep them hidden: "Relatives and friends, everyone took them," said Pani Gerung. "The little girl's name was Elisabetta. In 1947 relations turned up and took her to Israel. She wrote to the farmers for several years. Then the letters stopped. Now they are old and deaf. They missed her terribly."

Any Pole who, during the occupation, was found assisting or hiding a Jew was summarily shot; the *Sondergerichte* – special courts – who tried such people accepted no pleas in defence. The penalty was automatic. None the less, in spite of the strong anti-Semitism of large sections of the population, there are a number of documented examples of families – like the one quoted by Pani Gerung – who did extend such help. And there were also some Jewish children who were hidden by nuns in convents although the Catholic Church in Poland was immeasurably more pressured than anywhere else in Europe; ninety-five per cent of the priests held in concentration camps were Poles. In the government-sponsored *History of Help to the Jews In Occupied Poland*, the Polish writer Wladyslaw Bartoszewski (who is by no means only wedded to the party-line) cites a number of examples; the account he gives is, perhaps, made all the more convincing because the figure he finally has to cite for the number of Polish Jews actually rescued by his compatriots is so pitifully small that it heavily underlines the heroism of the relatively few who were willing or felt able to take the risk.

It was difficult to remember Polish anti-Semitism when talking to these two people who belonged to the very region – the extreme east of Poland – where it was most rampant. Their manner of speaking, their caring for the Sobibor Memorial and their protectiveness of the mementos they have collected (two flags, some documents, a map of the camp, and the visitors' book with its pathetically few signatures) has a reverent, tender quality.

At Stangl's trial, his activities at Sobibor were, for administrative reasons, not included in the prosecution's case. But even so, his behaviour and attitude while there became part of the trial record and one of the matters brought up by each of the few Sobibor survivors who came to Düsseldorf as witnesses, was the fact that he often attended the unloading of transports "dressed in white riding clothes". It was when he tried to explain this to me that I became aware for the first time of how he had lived – and was still living when we spoke – on two levels of consciousness, and conscience.

"When I came to Poland," he said, "I had very few clothes:

one complete uniform, a coat, an extra pair of trousers and shoes, and an indoor jacket – that's all. I remember, during the very first week I was there, I was walking from the forester's hut – my quarters – to one of the construction sites and suddenly I began to itch all over. I thought I was going crazy – it was awful; I couldn't even reach everywhere at once to scratch. Michel said, 'Didn't anybody warn you? It's sandflies, they are all over the place. You shouldn't have come out without boots.' [This would appear to indicate that Michel *was* there ahead of him.] I rushed back to my room and took everything off – I remember just handing all the stuff to somebody out of the door, and they boiled and disinfected everything. My clothes and almost every inch of me was covered with the things; they attach themselves to all the hair on your body. I had water brought in and bathed and bathed."

It was difficult at that point not to recall that in these camps the prisoners retained as "work-Jews" had to stand at rigid attention, caps off, whenever a German passed. Anyone who moved, for any reason whatever – cramps, itches or anything else – was more likely than not to be hit or beaten with a whip, and the consequences of being struck could go far beyond momentary pain: any prisoner who, at the daily roll-call, was found to be – as they called it – "marked" or "stamped", was a candidate for immediate gassing.

"These sandflies must have been an awful problem for the prisoners, weren't they?" I asked.

"Not everyone was as sensitive to them as I. They just liked me," he said, and smiled. "Anyway, what I wanted to tell you, with all this wear and tear, and the heat – it was very hot you know – my clothes fell apart. Well, one day, in a small town not far away, I found a weaving mill; I was interested in it because, you remember, that had been my profession once. So I went in. They were making very nice linen – off-white. I asked whether they'd sell me some. And that's how I got the white material; I had a jacket made right away and a little later jodhpurs and a coat."

"But even so, how could you go into the camp in this get-up?"

"The roads were very bad," he explained blankly. "Riding was the best mode of transport."

I tried once more: "Yes, but to attend the unloading of these people who were about to die, in white riding clothes . . . ?"

"It was hot," he said.

4

OF ALL the survivors of Treblinka and Sobibor who were brought to Germany by the prosecution (or defence) to testify at Stangl's trial, perhaps the only one Stangl really identified – who he remembered clearly as an individual and whose testimony, as he said to me, "hurt him deeply", was Stanislaw Szmajzner, like the Stangls an immigrant to Brazil. Stangl appeared almost to feel that Szmajzner had betrayed him.

"My family," Stangl said to me, "were never anti-Semitic: remarks against Jews were unknown in our house. But after Szmajzner's testimony, first to the police in Brazilia, to the Brazilian press, then his book – he wrote forty pages about me – and then in Düsseldorf at the trial, they did feel rather bitter." (Actually there are only two pages directly concerning Stangl in Stanislaw Szmajzner's book *Hell in Sobibor: the Tragedy of a Jewish Adolescent.**)

Frau Stangl, too, always emphasized to me how friendly she and the girls felt about the Jews – and indeed, how friendly Jews had been to them, in Brazil. At one moment during the week I spent with her, she pointed at some particularly splendid flowers that had arrived that morning, orchids I believe, on the table in her living room – this was the day after her family had celebrated her thirty-sixth wedding anniversary – and said, "These were sent to us by Jews." And she, too, repeatedly referred bitterly to Szmajzner.

Stan Szmajzner, slight in build, with an expressive face, firm wiry hands, intelligent eyes and a warm smile, lives now in Goiania, a thriving industrial town in Central Brazil. He was a boy of fifteen when he broke out of Sobibor in October 1943; so he was still only forty-three when we met. (It was the second uprising in a death-camp, just as extraordinary as the first one, in August in Treblinka. Four hundred to five hundred people managed to get out but only thirty-two survived.) Stan Szmajzner has succeeded in creating for himself a new life on a new continent, in a new language and amongst people who could not possibly be further removed from

* Edicion Bloch, Brazil, 1968.

his native environment but have accepted him as one of their own. He has married a Brazilian, has a child, and his closest friends, almost his adoptive parents, are one of the best-known liberal families in Brazil. Senator Pedro Ludovico was Governor of the province of Goiás until a fairly recent government change, and founded the city of Goiania. My meeting with Stan Szmajzner was at the Senator's house; the Senator referred to Szmajzner at lunch repeatedly as his "extra son", and Stan works, in a position approaching that of a partner, in a paper factory owned by the Senator's son. Stan's book, with a preface by Senator Ludovico, sold 10,000 copies – a considerable achievement in a country so far removed from Europe's troubles.

The reason why Stangl remembered Stanislaw Szmajzner so well is that, fourteen years old at the time and looking even younger, Stan had worked in Sobibor as a goldsmith. "I went almost every day to watch him work," Stangl said. "He was a wonderful goldsmith and a nice boy."

Szmajzner was born in Pulawy on the Vistula in Poland, the middle child of a prosperous orthodox Jewish family. His father was a fruit exporter, dealing principally in the export of strawberries to, surprisingly enough, Germany. Stanislaw went to a Hebrew school.

For a child from an orthodox Polish Jewish family, he appears to have been exceptionally independent from a very early age. "I didn't really like school very much," he told me. "It worried my parents a lot because in our family boys were traditionally good scholars. But school work bored me. What fascinated me, from very early on, was the craft of working with gold. There was a remarkable master-goldsmith in Pulawy – his name was Herzl – and I used to watch him whenever I could. When I was ten, I made a bargain with my father: I said that if he would allow me to take lessons from Pan Herzl, I would promise in return to work hard at school. Well, he said, all right, it was a deal, and that's how I became a qualified goldsmith by the time I was twelve – the year the Germans invaded Poland. It saved my life."

For two and a half years after the German invasion of Poland, the Szmajzner family moved from one town to another in an effort to ameliorate their lot. Six months after the invasion, Stan, his brother-in-law, Josef, and the goldsmith Herzl slipped across the Russian frontier in the hope of greater safety in Soviet territory; but the Hitler-Stalin pact was still in force and the Russians promptly shipped all Polish Jews back to the Germans in Poland. A second attempt was more successful. Josef decided to stay in Russia; Herzl and Stan worked for a while at their craft until home-sickness and anxiety about his family drove Stan back to Pulawy.

Although still only thirteen years old, Stan often took the initiative, not only in trying to save himself but also in advising his parents how to cope; unlike most of the Jews in this part of the world, he appears to have felt instinctively that safety lay in individual and unconventional action, not in remaining with the "group". None the less, circumstances always forced them back into the ghettos. "For a whole family, it was impossible to do otherwise," said Stan. "By the autumn of 1941 we were living in the ghetto of Wolwonice. Conditions had deteriorated to the point where people were literally dying of hunger and my father decided to try to 'pass' as a Catholic and beg for food in the streets 'in the name of Jesus'. But it brought him more shame than food; he cried every night because he had been driven to commit such sacrilege. And the greatest risk was being found out by a Pole; they were always ready to denounce Jews to the Germans. Even in these terrible times – terrible for the Christian Poles too – anti-Semitism was so virulent, the Jews were as afraid of the Poles as they were of the Germans. My young brother, Moize, volunteered to work for the Germans as a servant, in our old home town, Pulawy, because my father wanted to know what had happened to our belongings; he had left everything in the care of Polish neighbours. [Polish Jews always refer to non-Jewish Poles as "Poles" and to themselves as "we" or "Jews".] Moize went to see them and they told him that every single thing we owned had been taken by the Germans and that there was nothing left. But it wasn't true; it was they who had taken everything and there was nothing we could do about it, nothing at all."

While the family, especially Stan, Moize and their little nephew Jankus went from ghetto to ghetto, always trying to make them-selves as useful to the Germans as possible, the deportation (or "resettlement" as it was called) of the Jewish population proceeded. Their turn came half-way through 1942. I have listened in many places around the world to men and women speaking of these awful memories. But in no place, perhaps, was it quite so extraordinary as this hot October day in a pioneering town ten thousand miles away from Poland's pine forests in the middle of Brazil.

"After a night in a barbed-wire enclosure near the station at Malenzow," Stan said, "early next morning they put us on a freight train, a hundred or a hundred and fifty in each car; so many that we had to stand up one against another. There were no windows, no sanitary facilities, there was no light, no air. People urinated, defecated and vomited. A few, the weakest, died standing up and had to stay standing up – there was no room to do anything else with them."

Stanislaw, his parents, his twelve-year-old brother, Moize, his older sister and her eleven-year-old son, Jankus, a cousin aged twenty and several more distant relatives arrived in Sobibor on May 24, 1942.

"When the door of our car was pushed open," he said, "all we could think of was to get out into the air. What I saw first was two guards with whips – later we found out they were Ukrainian ss. They immediately began to shout, '*Raus, raus*,' and hit out blindly at those who stood in front. Of course, this made everyone move quickly; those in the back pushed towards the front, and those in front, the immediate target of the Ukrainians' whips, jumped off as quickly as they could. It was all perfectly planned to get us out of the cars with no delay. They only opened three cars at a time – that, too, was part of the system. When I jumped down with my family, I immediately caught hold of my brother's and little nephew's hands. I even shouted 'We must stick together'. My older cousin also managed to stay with us but we immediately lost sight of my father. We looked around desperately, but the hurry, the noise, the fear and confusion were indescribable; it was impossible to find anyone once one lost them from sight. About twenty metres away, across the 'square', I saw a line of ss officers and they were shooting. I especially noticed Stangl," Stanislaw said, "because he wore a white jacket – it stuck out. He was shooting too. I can't say whether he killed anyone, or in fact whether anyone *was* killed by these shots or not, but they were certainly shooting. No, I can't say whether Stangl shot into the crowd or above it – they were all shooting. The purpose was to get us all to run in one direction; through a gate and a kind of corridor into yet another square."

Stanislaw Szmajzner is as impressive a man now as he was without doubt a remarkable boy at fourteen. His testimony – very nearly the only one that linked Stangl directly to a personal act of violence – weighed heavily at Stangl's trial. There is no doubt that SS officers in the camps carried guns. ("German officers and enlisted men carried the same arms," said Franz Suchomel. "German 'Walther' pistols, for which there was never enough ammunition; and 'Nagans' from Russian stocks, with lots of ammunition, and aside from that each enlisted man had an infantry rifle for emergencies. Non-commissioned officers also had submachine-guns for emergencies, but neither of these last were carried ordinarily. The Ukrainians were first issued looted guns but later they were also given German rifles. To be honest, all guns were of Czech origin, Mausers – Model 24 – with the stamp of the Slovak army. The submachine-guns were Finnish, because they too were better than the German ones. The German staff *had* to carry whips – I myself was often taken to task by Franz and Küttner for not having one. For Stangl the Jews made a small riding-crop, but he rarely carried it. When transports arrived the Ukrainian guards had whips too. Amongst the Jews, the Kapos and the 'camp elders' had whips, and also the men from the 'Blue Command' [who assisted at the arrival of transports]. The whips were made of leather, but they didn't have anything 'in' them as has now been claimed. . . .")

And Richard Glazar, a highly intelligent Czech survivor of Treblinka, who has even less reason than Suchomel to defend Stangl, says, "They all carried guns and whips [at Treblinka] except for Stangl. He only carried a small riding-crop."

In the final analysis it is, of course, irrelevant whether or not Stangl carried a gun, and indeed – considering everything else he stood for in these camps – whether or not he actually used it. Even so, as a matter of principle, in this evaluation of what he said to me – and he maintained throughout, and throughout his trial, that he never shot into any crowds – one must at least pose the question: is it possible that time and memory can have played a not uncommon trick and blurred an impression of many years ago? *Could* a small boy, in the horror of this arrival, intent on keeping hold of his even younger relatives, trying to see what was happening to his mother and sister and desperately searching the crowds for his father – could this youngster really see over or through a tight-packed crowd of jostling, gesticulating people, which SS officer, twenty metres away and whether wearing a white jacket or not, was actually holding and using a gun? Stan Szmajzner, I know, will be the first to understand the motives of this question and to know that it is not in the slightest degree meant to reflect on his integrity.

Stangl, insisting that he had never shot into a crowd of people, appeared to be more indignant about this accusation than about anything else, and to find irrelevant the fact that, whether he shot into the group or not, these very same people died anyway, less than two hours later, through actions ultimately under his control.

This may appear to be a marginal matter, but I believe it to be peculiarly significant in representing a profoundly mistaken emphasis accepted – perhaps of necessity – by the courts, and also by the public and by the individuals involved: a concept whereby responsibility has been limited to momentary and often isolated actions, and to a few individuals. It is, I think, because of this universal acceptance of a false concept of responsibility that Stangl himself (until just before he died), his family and – in a wider but equally, if not even more, important sense – countless other people in Germany and outside it, have felt for years that what is decisive in law, and therefore in the whole conduct of human affairs, is what a man *does* on isolated occasions rather than what he *is*.

To Stanislaw Szmajzner, the shooting incident was merely a tiny part of an enormous and horrendous panorama of memories. He seemed almost surprised at the importance ascribed to it. And he and many other survivors – far more than people who were only later or indirectly involved in these matters – came much closer to evaluating men like Stangl for what they *were* rather than for what they *did* on isolated occasions. The detached humanity and wisdom of some of the survivors is perhaps the most astounding thing to evolve out of these events.

"At the exit of the corridor into the second square," Stan continued his story, "two more Ukrainians divided the arrivals into two groups: women and small children to the right, men and boys to the left. The women were immediately lined up in rows of four – my mother and sister too – and marched off through another gate at the right, we had no idea where to. Then they lined us up in fours too. That's when I first saw Gustav Wagner, a very tall man, slightly malformed, who walked with a looped sort of movement of his body. He bellowed, 'Carpenters, tailors, mechanics – step out.' This was when we became certain it was a labour camp. I still don't know today what made me step forward. But I got out of the line, stepped up to him and said – in German of course – 'Don't you need a goldsmith?' Well, of course, I was just a little boy – he looked down at me and said, 'You? Are you telling me you are a goldsmith?' I said yes, I was, and so were my two brothers and my cousin, and I pointed at them. Of course they weren't, but I just said they were because it seemed the thing to do. I quickly opened my rucksack and brought out some of my tools – that's all I had in there – and showed them to him and also showed him something I had made. God knows what inspiration had made me bring it. Well, he told us to step out of the line and waved us to a corner. 'Go and sit there,' he said, and a bit later he sent another boy – a sign-painter he was. And we sat there, for hours I think, until everyone else from the transport had gone through that same gate on the right – we still didn't know where. And then he came back and took us to yet a third courtyard in which there was an old wooden hut which he unlocked and pushed us into. It was empty except for an older man who rushed towards us and asked whether we were Jews. He said he was a sign-painter too, and had arrived the day before and that he had been put in that hut with ink and brushes and told to paint signs 'Camp I, Camp II, Camp III'.

"We waited a long time – it was already dark when the door was unlocked again and Wagner told my brother and me to bring along a tin that was standing there, to fetch coffee and bread from another hut. When we got back we realized that the tin had contained petrol before and we couldn't drink the coffee. But we had the bread. And afterwards we lay down on the ground and slept. The very next morning Wagner came with Stangl. So I was a goldsmith, they said. I sat down then and there and made something for them from a little bit of metal I had brought. They watched for a while and later I gave them what I had made. But anyway, that was the beginning. They brought me gold to work with that very afternoon."

In his book Szmajzner described this first meeting with Stangl in greater detail: "He dressed impeccably and appeared vain although his eyes seemed kind. He had a soft voice, good manners and was extremely polite. He looked like a young university professor..." and he went on to say that Stangl had said repeatedly that he was amazed to find a boy of his age capable of making good jewellery.

"Stangl seemed so friendly when they brought the gold in the afternoon," he told me. "I felt encouraged to ask about my father. I told him that I'd like to go and see my father. 'Where is he, please?' I asked. 'You are much better off here,' Stangl answered in a very friendly way. 'This is a much better place to work. Don't worry about him. He is all right.'

"They assigned my brother to work with me; my little nephew was eventually made bootboy for the officers; he also had to run their baths and that sort of thing. And my twenty-year-old cousin was appointed Platzmeister: he had to tidy up the square where transports arrived – organize the belongings into lots and so on. [The Szmajzner family obviously arrived before the camp was completed and the work organized. Later the workers were grouped into Kommandos, each performing different functions.]

"We still had no idea what happened to all the people. The six of us – us four and the two sign-painters – were the only people in Camp I for several days. Wagner was responsible for us and we saw Stangl every day – he appeared to come just because he enjoyed watching me. Every time he came I'd ask him about my father, and he always said the same thing: not to worry, just to work and that I'd be all right. The Ukrainians were not allowed to enter the 'gold-hut', but other SS officers came, of course, as soon as they realized we were working there, and all of them ordered things.

"It was on the seventh day after we arrived that a Ukrainian guard came [presumably to the window of the hut] and said he had a message for me, which he would give to me if I gave him some gold. I said I'd give him the gold the next day. The note was from another cousin who was – he wrote – in Camp III [the gassing and burial camp]. He wrote that I was to say the *kaddish* for my father. 'Here no one remains alive,' he said. 'Pray for them.'

"Then we knew. And we learned too that out of every transport they kept fifty strong men and boys and made them clean up after a transport had been killed. The corpses weren't burnt then – they were buried in lime-pits. And when they had finished cleaning up, they too were killed. This happened every day in the beginning. It was only later that semi-permanent Kommandos were formed who did this work for weeks, months and – a few of them –

throughout the whole existence of the camp. But from that moment on the awareness of the proximity of death never left me. Though – it is true – deep inside me I never believed that I – I – would die.

"I still saw Stangl every day. He seemed fascinated by my work. And he talked to me; you know – he chatted, almost as if we were normal people, I the craftsman, he the customer.

"For a long time after I had received the note from my cousin in Camp III I didn't ask him any more about my father. But one day, just to see what he would say, I said again, 'How is my father?' This was weeks later, but he said again, 'He is fine; don't worry about him: just do your work.'

"I knew that work was the only security we had. I worked day and night. The trick was to make oneself indispensable. And they *all* wanted gold things. Oh yes, I am sure I made things for Stangl. I can't remember what, but all of them ordered things; like decorations or monograms for handbags for their wives and girl friends. There was *so* much gold, so much money, so many things: we lacked nothing for our day-to-day life. As long as the rich transports arrived, we had all the food in the world, everything we could imagine.

"One day, fairly early on, we were told to stay in our barracks; if we showed ourselves outside, we'd be shot on sight. There was great commotion and from the window we could see a line of cars arrive. Later we found out that it was Himmler; and he came again some months afterwards. The very day after his visit, construction was stepped up and only too soon afterwards there were new buildings, new facilities, and the number of transports and people being killed increased tenfold.

"Soon we had company in our barrack: three young women, Eda, Esther and Bagle, who came to work as cooks. Then two shoemakers, two bakers, five tailors, one milliner – more and more arrived and finally they split us up into groups living in different barracks. I was made 'block-eldest' of my group, which included laundresses, cooks, bricklayers, bakers and us goldsmiths."

In his book Stan tells of a short love-affair with the cook, Bagle. She had arrived at the camp with her husband, who was killed at once. "I had made love once before," Stan wrote, "to a young girl of about fifteen in the ghetto at Wolwonice where we were all sleeping very cramped. But I felt terribly inexperienced. I liked

Bagle. One day I went to the kitchen. She said Eda and Esther, who worked there with her, were out having a wash. I thought the opportunity right and kissed her face and told her I wanted her. She smiled and said I was too young for her. 'Esther is nearer your age,' she said. But I told her I didn't like Esther – I liked *her*. And I told her I'd never had an apple, and didn't like to experiment with a green one. And then I saw she was actually proud that I wanted her instead of the younger girl, and she came to me."

One of the things on which I questioned Stan Szmajzner closely was a matter he had testified about to the Brazilian police and later at the trial: a great deal had been made of it in the press in Brazil. He said that Stangl was in the habit of bringing him sausages on Friday night and that he would call loudly, "Here's some sausage for you to celebrate the Sabbath." The implication was clearly that Stangl, in a particularly outrageous way, was tormenting this young boy from an orthodox Jewish background by tempting him, when he was presumably starving, to eat pork. In October 1970 I was present on the last day of Stangl's trial when Stan testified to this effect, and certainly I – like the court, the newspapers and before this, the Brazilians – gained the impression that this was what he was intending to convey.

Stangl, in his conversations with me, was to refer repeatedly and bitterly to this part of Szmajzner's testimony. "That business with the sausage," he said, "was deliberately misinterpreted. . . . It's true I used to bring him food and probably there was sausage. But it wasn't to taunt him with pork; I brought him other things too. It was because we received our food allocations on Fridays and – there was a great deal of food in the camp much of the time – we had food left over. I *liked* the boy. . . . He testified in Brazil – and you should have seen how the papers there *ate* it up, what they made of it – that I used to stand in front of the window of the barrack where he worked and shout tauntingly, holding up the sausage. But I never did such a thing. . . . I don't *know* what the sausages – if sausages there were – were made of. But you know, during the war pork sausage was a luxury; I honestly don't think it could even have been pork; it was most probably a mixture of beef and breadcrumbs."

In Brazil Stan told me that he hadn't really meant to convey that Stangl had taunted him, and that he himself didn't know what the sausages were made of. I asked him whether he realized the interpretation that had been given to what he had said – he had re-

128

peated the same thing three times and it was interpreted three times the same way.

"I don't know that I did know," he said. "I didn't really mean it that way, though; I think he *was* perhaps just doing me a good turn; it's perfectly true that he seemed to like me; that he made a sort of pet of me. Perhaps he really did want to help me. Still," he added thoughtfully, "it was funny, wasn't it, that he always brought it on a Friday evening?"

I am not absolutely convinced that Stangl was incapable of this sort of playful cruelty; it is just possible, in the context of the change that (as we will see later) came over him quite soon after his arrival in Sobibor. And it is equally possible that, if he did do it, he would deny it later not only to others but to himself. As our talks progressed, it became clear that what he was most concerned about (until the last two days) were what one might call the lesser manifestations of moral corruption in himself; once again, what he *did* rather than what he *was*. It was his "deeds" – his relatively mild deeds – he was at great pains to deny or rationalize rather than his total personality change.

Stan Szmajzner also said in court, and to me, that Stangl had ordered him to make a monogram for a handbag. On re-examination in court he had also said that whether for a whip, handbag or ring, he was sure that he had made *something* for Stangl. He explained that on Wagner's and Stangl's orders he made rings for all the SS men – silver ones with germanic symbols – *Runen* – inset in gold: 🌱 stood for life and 🔻 for death, both of which, as Wagner told him, the SS controlled.* Stangl, he said, had no need to make a secret of bringing him small quantities of gold to melt down. "All of them brought gold – later it was gold fillings with the flesh and blood still on them, the way they had been torn out of people's mouths.... Stangl," he testified, "was always cheerful and treated me with kindness. I didn't have the impression from him – of being in a camp. [But] I certainly thought that the gold he brought was for his personal use. He had no need to send other people, or to hide."

*These same symbols were used by *Lebensborn*, the Nazi breeding institutes for racial improvement, where thousands of "racially superior" young girls were mated with members of the SS and where their offspring – property of the state, without parents – were then brought up. An indeterminate number of such small children were found in these institutes, or places connected with them, at the end of World War II, quietly removed and discreetly placed with fosterparents.

In court Stangl insisted that he had never told Szmajzner or anyone else to melt down gold. "I merely watched him work," he said. "I told him once to cut the oakleaves out of a silver one-Mark coin and to insert my monogram in gold and silver – that's all."

"Szmajzner's testimony," Frau Stangl told me, "was obviously very important to us because he lives here [in Brazil] as we do. When he testified before the police in Brazilia, it was all over the papers – it did Paul a lot of harm. He was very hurt by it, he told me, because Szmajzner was just a boy in Sobibor and Paul really liked him."

Szmajzner allowed press photographers to take pictures of him with Frau Stangl after the hearing ended in Düsseldorf. I remember being amazed at seeing this survivor of Sobibor pose with Stangl's wife for smiling pictures, and I asked Stan about it in Goiania. "I agreed to it," he said "because I had nothing against Stangl's family and I was aware of how hard all this was on them. I thought if I showed my own goodwill towards them by posing for pictures with Frau Stangl for the Brazilian press, this might reflect on the public attitude here towards Stangl's family."

Throughout our long conversation Stan Szmajzner was fair and tolerant. Indeed, I felt, almost too anxious to give credit where he could, to a man whose family "who had nothing to do with all this", was also living in *his* chosen country. This was in sharp contrast to his attitude on hearing from me that Gustav Wagner was still alive and was probably in Brazil, information which I had from Stangl. On hearing this, Stan cried. "It is the worst, the most terrible shock you could have given me," he said. "That man. Here in Brazil. To think that I am now breathing the same air as he – it makes me feel terribly, terribly ill. . . . I would not know how to find words to describe to you what a terrible – a truly terrible man that is. Stangl – he is good by comparison, very good. But Wagner – he should be dead. . . ." He begged me to find out where Wagner was, because, he kept on repeating, "I must do something." It took most of the day, off and on, to calm him and persuade him that vengeance ought not to be his.

I asked Stan Szmajzner how it was, in his own opinion, that he had managed to survive. What sort of person did you have to be, to survive these camps? What were the special qualities needed?

"I understand your question," he said. "Yes, we too were corrupted, of course: life was everything. I remember how furious we used to be when the transports came from the East rather than the West. Those coming from Germany, Holland, Austria, Hungary – they brought clothes and above all, food; we could go and choose anything we liked. The ones from Poland and points east had nothing, and then we went comparatively hungry. It is true, you see, if there hadn't been gold, we wouldn't have lived. So, in a sense, their death meant our life.

"I never saw Stangl hurt anyone," he said at the end. "What was special about him was his arrogance. And his obvious pleasure in his work and his situation. None of the others – although they were, in different ways, so much worse than he – showed this to such an extent. He had this perpetual smile on his face. . . . No, I don't think it was a nervous smile; it was just that he was happy."

5

"Did you want your family to come to visit you in Poland?" I asked Stangl.

"I wanted to see them, of course. But don't you see what the fact that they were allowed to come meant? Globocnik had said to me, months before, that I needed leave. But they weren't going to let me go home, like other people. I was in danger, it was quite obvious. And they were making damn sure I knew about it."

Stangl's wife and two little girls, six and four, arrived very soon after his wife had written to tell him of the forms she had filled out, and they all went to stay with the surveyor, Baurath Moser, in Chelm, twenty miles or so from the camp.

"Were you officially on leave then, or did you have to go to Sobibor during that time?"

"While we were in Colm, I was on leave."

"Did your wife ask you what you were doing in Sobibor? What sort of camp it was?"

"Very little then: as I told you she was used to my not being able to speak to her of service matters. And we were so glad just to be together. The funny thing was, though, that I heard nothing from Lublin, or from Wirth. I didn't have any official instructions how long my leave was to be, how long the family would be allowed to stay, or anything. After about three weeks I went to see Höfle and asked him. He said, 'Why make waves? If nobody's said anything to you, why not just keep them here for a while? Find a place to stay nearby, and don't worry'."

"What did you think that meant?"

"I was so glad to have them there, you know; it was such a relief, I just decided not to think, just to enjoy it. I found rooms for us on an estate just a few kilometres from Sobibor camp, near the village. It was a fish-hatchery belonging to Count Chelmicki [he said 'Karminsky', but Frau Stangl corrected this later]."

"How far exactly was that from the camp?"

"Five kilometres."

Pan Gerung, the custodian of Sobibor, remembered the fish-hatchery well thirty years later; it had been demolished a year before I visited Poland. But he and his wife were dubious about the Stangl family having stayed there. "You are probably confusing it with a big white house the Germans built as a kind of country club for their officers, on the other side of the lake. They used to go there for weekends, for the fishing – and other days too, in the evenings. An enormous amount of drinking went on there, and other things. Poles weren't allowed in."

I replied that I was sure it was the fish-hatchery the Stangls had stayed at – no doubt they had requisitioned rooms there because the other place was unsuitable for small children.

"But the fish-hatchery was four kilometres from the camp, through the woods," said Pan Gerung. "If he really rode through these woods, on his own – why, anyone could have shot him, any time." This Polish inhabitant of a different Sobibor, in a different age, sounded honestly puzzled, even amazed. And what he said was true: everyone in those parts knew what Sobibor was; everyone knew Stangl was the camp's Kommandant; anyone – if for no other reason than a gesture – could have shot him on those almost daily rides through the woods. But no one did.

"The Chelmickis," I said to Stangl, *"must have known or guessed what was going on at Sobibor. However secret an operation it was, there must have been rumours. Did your wife still not know?"*

"The Chelmickis were very nice. But I don't think they would have dared to talk about it even if they had heard rumours." (" . . . The Jews who worked in the fish-hatchery," Frau Stangl was to write to me later, "were all treated very well. And so was I. . . .")

"But my wife *did* find out, though not from them," Stangl said. "One of the non-coms, Unterscharführer Ludwig, came by once while I was out. He had been drinking and he told her about

132

Sobibor. When I got back she was waiting for me. She was terribly upset. She said, 'Ludwig has been here. He told me. My God, what are you doing in that place?' I said, 'Now, child, this is a service matter and you know I can't discuss it. All I can tell you, and you must believe me: whatever is wrong – *I* have nothing to do with it.' "

"*Did she believe this, without further questions or arguments?*"

He shrugged. "She spoke of it sometimes. But what else could I say to her? It did make me feel, though, that I wanted her away from there. I wanted them to go home. The school term was about to start for the older of the girls anyway. . . ." the sentence trailed off.

"*It was too difficult having them there now that she knew. Wasn't that it?*"

He shrugged his shoulders again and for a moment buried his face in his hands. "Just about then I had a message that I was to come to Warsaw to see Globocnik – by this time he had two offices, one in Warsaw, the other in Lublin. Now it seemed even more urgent to me to get the family home. I got hold of Michel and said that I entrusted my family to him; for him to get them out as quickly as possible. Then I said goodbye to my wife and children and went to Warsaw."

"*When did they leave?*"

"Later I found that Michel got them out in four days. But I only found that out after they had gone. And I didn't know what awaited me in Warsaw. I thought that this was probably it – that I was finally for it. But when I got to Globocnik's office, he was nearly as friendly as he'd been the first time we met. I couldn't understand it. He said, almost as soon as I came in, 'I have a job for you; it is strictly a police assignment.' I knew right away there was something wrong with it, but I didn't know what. He said, 'You are going to Treblinka. We've already sent a hundred thousand Jews up there and nothing has arrived here in money or materials. I want you to find out what's happening to the stuff; where it is disappearing to.' "

"*But this time you knew where you were being sent; you knew all about Treblinka and that it was the biggest extermination camp. Here was your chance, here you were, face to face with him at last. Why didn't you say right there and then that you couldn't go on with this work?*"

133

"Don't you see? He had me just where he wanted me; I had no idea where my family was. Had Michel got them out? Or had they perhaps stopped them? Were they holding them as hostages? And even if they were out, the alternative was still the same: Prohaska was still in Linz. Can you imagine what would have happened to me if I had returned there under these circumstances? No, he had me flat: I was a prisoner."

"But even so – even admitting there was danger. Wasn't anything preferable by now to going on with this work in Poland?"

"Yes, that's what we know now, what we can say now. But then?"

"Well, in point of fact, we know now, don't we, that they did not automatically kill men who asked to be relieved from this type of job. You knew this yourself, didn't you, at the time?"

"I knew it *could* happen that they wouldn't shoot someone. But I also knew that more often they *did* shoot them, or send them to concentration camps. How could I know which would apply to me?"

This argument, of course, runs through all of Stangl's story; it is the most essential question at which, over and over, I found myself stopped when talking with him. I didn't know when I spoke with him and I don't know now at which point one human being can make the moral decision for another that he should have the courage to risk death.

However, my reactions to some of the things Stangl said in this part of his account changed slightly subsequently, as a result of my conversations with his wife. These demonstrated very clearly that – if nothing else – he had manipulated events, or his memory of events, to suit his need to rationalize his guilt, his awareness of his guilt or (at that point in our talks) his need to avoid facing it.

"He had written to me soon after he got to Poland saying he was 'constructing'," said Frau Stangl, "but he didn't say what. And all I could think of was how glad I was he wasn't at the front. And then, when he'd been there for a long time without leave [it was interesting that she considered two months 'a long time'], he wrote to say that they were going to let us come to visit him as he was not going to be allowed on leave away from the East at all. And shortly afterwards a Wehrmacht officer arrived with travel papers for us.

"The two children and I travelled out in June. I remember we missed the connection in Cracow; you can imagine what it was like travelling with two small girls in the middle of the war.

"No, I knew nothing – nothing whatever. He met us off the train, and, of course, we hadn't seen him in months, it was just wonderful to see him again. Once again, that was all I could think of. We went to stay in Chelm in the house of the chief surveyor, Baurath Moser. In a way I suppose that was the first time I came into contact with anything to do with Jews [in Poland] because he had two young Jewish girls there, as domestic servants. They were called the two *Zäuseln** – I don't really know why. They were nice girls, helped me with the children and all that. Although I hadn't any notion of the true situation, there were things that made me wonder: you see, the walls of the house were very thin and I would hear Baurath Moser in the room next to ours when I was in bed. He had both the girls – the *Zauseln* – in there and . . . well . . . he did things to them, you know. It would start every night with his telling them what to take off first and then what next and what to do and so on . . . it . . . it was very embarrassing. And I didn't like what he did to the girls; but, you know, I mainly asked myself, 'Why do they do it? Why don't they just give notice?' That's how little I knew." (Later, in a letter, Frau Stangl mentioned these girls again – and this time slightly differently: "The two *Zäuseln* in Chelm," she wrote, "were always merry, had good food, and were very neat.")

"But I was very glad when Paul told me he had arranged for us to move to the fish-hatchery – it would be better for all of us, and I was glad to get the children away from that house. No, while we were in Chelm, Paul was on leave; it was when we moved to the fish-hatchery that he had to go back to work.

"And one day while he was at work – I still thought constructing, or working at an army supply base – Ludwig came with several other men, to buy fish or something. They brought schnapps, and sat in the garden drinking. Ludwig came up to me – I was in the garden too, with the children – and started to tell me about his wife and kids; he went on and on. I was pretty fed up, especially as he stank of alcohol and became more and more maudlin. But I thought, here he is, so lonely – I must at least listen. And then he suddenly said, '*Fürchterlich* – dreadful, it is just dreadful, you have

* Probably best translated as "tousle-heads".

135

no idea how dreadful it is.' I asked him 'What is dreadful?' –
'Don't you know?' he asked. 'Don't you know what is being done
out there?' – 'No,' I said, 'What?' – 'The Jews,' he answered.
'The Jews are being done away with.' – 'Done away with?' I
asked. 'How? What do you mean?' – 'With gas,' he said. 'Fantastic
numbers of them [*Unheimliche Mengen*].'

"He went on about how awful it was and then he said, in that
same maudlin way he had, 'But we are doing it for our Führer.
For him we sacrifice ourselves to do this – we obey his orders.'
And then he said, too, 'Can you imagine what would happen if
the Jews ever got hold of *us*?'

"Then I told him to go away. I could hardly think. I was already
crying. I took the children into the house. I sat there, staring,
staring into an abyss – that's what I saw; *my* husband, my man,
my good man, how could he be in this? Was it possible that he
actually saw these things being done? I knew about Wirth – Paul
had talked about him from the moment I arrived, even at the
station – but that wasn't what I was thinking of then. . . . My
thoughts were in a whirl; what I needed above all was to confront
him, to talk to him, to see what he had to say, how he could
explain. . . ."

She left the children playing in their room and went out along
the path in the forest she knew he would have to take to ride home.
"I walked for a long time and sat down on a tree-trunk to wait for
him. When he rode up and saw me from afar, his face lit up – I
could see it. It always did – his face always showed his joy the
moment he saw me. He jumped off his horse and stepped over – I
suppose to put his arm around me. But then he saw at once how
distraught I was. 'What's happened?' he asked. 'The children?'

"I said, 'I know what you are doing in Sobibor. My God,
how can they? What are *you* doing in this? What is your part
in it?' First he asked me how I'd found out, but I just cried and
cried; and then he said, 'Look, little one, please calm down, please.
You must believe me, I have nothing to do with any of this.' I
said, 'How can you *be* there and have nothing to do with it?' And
he answered, 'My work is purely administrative and I am there to
build – to supervise construction, that's all.' – 'You mean you
don't see it happen?' I asked. 'Oh yes,' he answered. 'I see it. But
I don't *do* anything to anybody.'

"Of course, I didn't know he was the Kommandant: I never

knew that. He told me he was the *Höchste Charge*. I asked him what that meant and he said again he was in charge of construction and that he enjoyed the work. I thought, 'My God.'

"We walked back to the house, me crying and arguing and begging him over and over to tell me how he could be in such a place, how he could have allowed himself to get into such a situation. I am sure I made no sense – I hardly knew any more what I was saying. All he did, over and over, was reassure me – or try. That night, I couldn't bear him to touch me – it was like that day in 1938 when I had kept away from him for weeks . . . weeks and weeks, until I finally felt sorry for him . . . but that night in Sobibor-Salovoce he seemed to understand. He just kept stroking me softly and trying to quiet me. Even so, it was several days before I . . . let him again. And that was only just before he was called to Lublin to see Globocnik. I finally allowed myself to be convinced that his role in this camp was purely administrative – of course I *wanted* to be convinced, didn't I? But anyway – I can't quite remember the sequence of events, but I know I wouldn't have parted from him in anger.

"We were rowing on the lake with the children that day when Michel arrived on the shore. This was the only time I saw him. No, *he* never did anything for us after Paul left. I don't know what Paul meant when he told you it was Michel who 'got us out'. Michel called to us across the lake and said that a message had come through to say that Paul was to report to Globocnik. We rowed back to the shore and Michel said, 'They mean now, at once; you have to come with me right away.'

"We went back to the house and I remember, I helped him get changed and then he left.

"After he had gone that day I got terribly depressed: you see, although I had allowed him to convince me that he wasn't really part of what was happening, I couldn't forget it; how could I have? That night Countess Chelmicki found me crying. In my terrible need to talk to somebody I told her what I had found out.

" 'Don't you think we know?' she asked. 'We've known about it since the beginning. But you must calm yourself; it is dreadful, but there is nothing to be done. We are convinced that your husband is a decent man.' She really cared. She spoke to me – you know – like a friend, intimately and warmly. I was very comforted by her kindness.

"The next day Paul came back, just for a day, or even less. He said he was being transferred, to Treblinka – a place, he said, that was in a terrible mess, where the worst *Schweinereien* were being done, and where it was necessary to make a clean sweep with an iron broom. I said, 'My God, I hope not another place like this one here,' and he said no, he didn't think so – for me not to worry. I said I wanted to go home."

I asked Frau Stangl whether it had not been her husband who told *her* he wanted them to go home.

"No, I told *him*. And, well ... then he left. I'd told him I wanted to leave as quickly as possible – I didn't want to impose on the Chelmickis a moment longer than necessary. Anyway, the next day Reichleitner came to the fish-hatchery."

Franz Reichleitner, who had been with Stangl at Hartheim, took over as Kommandant of Sobibor after Stangl left. "He said he wanted to have a look around the fish-hatchery," Frau Stangl continued. "Well, of course I knew him, you know, because he had married my friend Anna Baumgartner from Steyr and so I felt I had something in common with him; I trusted him you know, so I said, 'You know, if I thought that my Paul had anything to do with the awful things which are being done at Sobibor, I wouldn't stay with him another day.'

"He answered quite spontaneously, you know, not thinking it over at all. He said right away, 'My God, Frau Stangl,' he said, 'but your husband has absolutely *nothing* to do with that. That's all Wirth. You don't think, do you, that he would allow anyone to rob him of the pleasure of doing away with the Jews? You know how he hates them. Your husband's part in this is purely administrative.'" (Before Frau Stangl told me this, she had already testified at the trial, that after the war, in Brazil, Gustav Wagner had also told her that her husband had had nothing to do with the extermination of the Jews in Sobibor.) "Well," she went on, "to be truthful, that really did relieve my mind and lighten my spirits. After all, unless Paul and Reichleitner had carefully planned it together – and to tell the truth, the possibility did occur to me – the fact that they told me exactly the same thing, in the same words, had to mean it was true. Why otherwise should Reichleitner have bothered to tell me?"

It didn't occur to Frau Stangl then or now that Reichleitner, who had just taken the job over from Stangl, could have found

138

this conversation with his friend's wife awkward on his own account, and might conceivably have been indirectly stating, or justifying, his own case.

"I left a very few days after that," she said. "I think it was Reichleitner who brought me the travel documents signed by Globocnik – it may have been just two or three days after Paul left. I think Reichleitner also drove us to the train in Chelm. And so I went home. I had a letter from Paul soon after, but it said nothing about Treblinka; he had told me I must *never* mention Treblinka nor anything about it, or make any of my 'remarks' in my letters – he knew me so well – as all letters were censored. . . . I didn't see him after that for months. . . ."

"Resl and the two girls came to stay with me overnight on their way back from Poland," said Helene Eidenböck in Vienna. "I went to meet them at the East Station. No, she didn't seem very depressed, not that I remember. She said they'd been staying at a fish-hatchery and I saw all their photographs . . . was it then or later, I am not sure – of him too, yes, in that white jacket, with the children, and a big dog too I remember. . . . Later, of course, when we read what he was – I thought of that photo and thought, 'It only needed the riding crop and there he was, just as they described him at the trial. . . .' "

6

By THE time Stangl left Sobibor a lot of information about the Nazi death-camps in Poland was beginning to reach the outside world.

In July 1942 the Polish government in exile in London, in an officially released report from underground sources, had detailed the massacre of 700,000 Jews since the German invasion, including the use of gas-vans at Chelmno. Szmul Zygielbojm, a leader in the Jewish Socialist Bund, who escaped from Poland after his wife and children had been killed and after fighting in the defence of Warsaw, broadcast on the BBC, world-wide, to bear witness to the awful facts and to beg the world, "to ponder over the undiluted horror of the planned extermination of a whole people. . . . The governments of Great Britain and America," he said, "must be compelled to put an end to this mass murder. For if we do not try to find a means of stopping it, we shall bear part of the moral responsibility for what is happening."

On July 17 the Berlin radio announced the round-up of 18,000 Jews in Paris, saying they would "all be deported to the East, as previously announced". German radio, throughout the war, was minutely monitored by the Allies and this announcement must certainly have been noted. On July 22 began the "resettlement" of the 380,000 Jews in the Warsaw ghetto, and again the Allied Governments were informed by the Polish Government in exile.

A detailed account of American and British reaction to these events has been given by Arthur D. Morse in *While Six Million Died*.* Here there is only space to mention that on August 1, 1942, Gerhart Riegner, in Switzerland for the World Jewish Congress, learned from a leading German industrialist with access to Hitler's immediate circle that many months earlier Hitler had ordered the extermination of all the Jews in Europe. Mr Riegner sent a cable to Rabbi Wise in the United States, via the US State Department: "Received alarming report . . . plan all Jews in countries occupied or controlled by Germany numbering from three and a half to four million excluding Jews in the Soviet Union [a significant sentence showing the extent of the informant's knowledge] should after deportation and concentration in East be exterminated at one blow to resolve once and for all the Jewish question in Europe. . . ."

This cable was apparently suppressed by the State Department – the first of many similar political decisions – and only reached Rabbi Wise, via the British Foreign Office and the London branch of the World Jewish Congress, on August 28. And Dr Wise was persuaded by Sumner Welles to refrain from any public announcement of the extermination order until "official confirmation" could be obtained. Myron Taylor, the President's Special Envoy to the Holy See, was asked to check these allegations with the Vatican.

Between August 4 and September 14 the governments of Brazil (who initiated this step), Great Britain, Belgium, Poland, Uruguay, Yugoslavia and the United States all sent notes to the Vatican Secretary of State calling the attention of the Holy See to the "cruel and inhuman treatment by the Hitler forces of the civil population in areas occupied by the Germans", and suggesting that "a

* Secker and Warburg, 1968.

similar condemnation of these atrocities by the Holy Father would have . . . a helpful effect . . . in bringing about some check on the unbridled and uncalled-for actions of the forces of the Nazi regime."

This – in line with diplomatic custom – was still in fairly general terms. On September 26 Myron Taylor delivered a far more explicit note to Cardinal Maglione, communicating information received by the Geneva office of the Jewish Agency for Palestine from "two reliable eye-witnesses (Aryans),"* one of whom came on August 14 from Poland:

> "(1) Liquidation of the Warsaw ghetto is taking place. Without any distinction all Jews, irrespective of age or sex, are being removed from the ghetto in groups and shot. Their corpses are utilized for making fats and their bones for the manufacture of fertilizer. Corpses are even being exhumed for these purposes. †
>
> "(2) These mass executions take place, not in Warsaw, but in specially prepared camps for the purpose, one of which is stated to be in Belsec. . . ."

The letter ends, after making three more points, by asking for any confirmation or additional information the Vatican might have, and for suggestions "as to any practical manner in which the forces of civilized public opinion would be utilized in order to prevent a continuation of these barbarities".

This communication was not to be answered until October 10 when Harold Tittman, the American Representative at the Holy See, transmitted the following reply to the State Department:

> "Holy See replied today to Mr Taylor's letter regarding the *predicament* of the Jews in Poland in an informal and unsigned statement handed me by the Cardinal Secretary of State. After thanking Ambassador Taylor for bringing the matter to the attention of the Holy See, the statement says that reports of *severe measures* taken against non-Aryans also reached the Holy See from other sources but that, up to the present time, it has not been possible to verify

---

* Myron Taylor's brackets; as other US and British documents of the time prove, information obtained from Jews was considered unreliable.

† This information was not exact in detail. They were, as we know, not "shot"; and the universally accepted story that the corpses were used to make soap and fertilizer is finally refuted by the generally very reliable Ludwigsburg Central Authority for Investigation into Nazi Crimes. The Authority has found after considerable research that only one experiment was made, with "a few corpses from a concentration camp. When it proved impractical the idea was apparently abandoned."

the accuracy there. However, the statement adds, it is well known that the Holy See is taking advantage of every opportunity offered in order to mitigate the sufferings of *non-Aryans*...."*

Late October finally saw the formation of a War Crimes Commission in the United States; but the official statement announcing it included the President's exemption from guilt of all but the Nazi leadership.

This was followed on December 17 by an official condemnation by all the Allied nations of the extermination of the Jews by the Nazis. The Allies served notice that those responsible would not escape punishment, reaffirming "their solemn resolution to insure that those responsible for these crimes shall not escape retribution and to press on with the necessary practical measures to this end."

On Christmas Eve, 1942 – when what Richard Glazar was to call the "peak period" of the extermination of the Jews in Poland was already past and more than a million had been killed in the four extermination camps in Poland – Mr Tittman sent Secretary of State Hull another cable. He had had – no doubt at one of the Vatican's Christmas receptions – another conversation with the Cardinal Secretary of State in which Cardinal Maglione, with reference to the mass extermination of the Jews, said that "although deploring the cruelties that have come to his attention, the Holy See was unable to verify Allied reports as to the number of Jews exterminated...."†

---

* Author's italics.
† The extent of the Vatican's knowledge of the facts by December 1942 is documented on pages 328–33.

Part III

I

THE MAIN impression I had carried away from Sobibor was one of beauty: the quiet, the loneliness, above all the vastness of the place, which left everything to the imagination. Treblinka was different.

The Poles have spared no effort to reconstruct the whole of the camp as a national monument which, while adequately portraying the horror, can also leave one with some feeling of human dignity. But it doesn't work. All one can think of is the terrible smallness of the place.

We *know* that more than a million human beings were killed and lie buried in these few acres, but it cannot be believed. The main reason why it is so difficult to visualize lies in nature itself: where there used to be huts, barbed wire, tank traps and watch-towers, there are now hundreds of bushes and young pine trees which the Germans planted to camouflage the site when, having accomplished what they set out to do, they obliterated the camp at the end of 1943. The trees have grown to a respectable height and lend a misleading air of normalcy and space. There were, of course, some trees while the camp was in operation – carefully left standing where they could deceive the eye, or decorate the staff's living quarters. But, unlike Sobibor with its massive forests, in Treblinka the means of camouflage were mostly man-made: tall fences of barbed wire interwoven with branches of pine and evergreen which shut off the four sub-sections of the camp from view, but certainly not from hearing. What they called "the tube" which led from the "undressing barracks" in the lower camp – Camp I – to the gas chambers in the upper camp – Camp II – was a fenced-off path no more than a hundred yards long, with a right-angled turn near the end. And the earthen wall and ten-foot fence between the two main parts of the camp again created only a visual barrier – no more than that. Not a single soul in the place could have been oblivious of the monstrous carnage which took place here most mornings of that year.

TREBLINKA EXTERMINATION CAMP

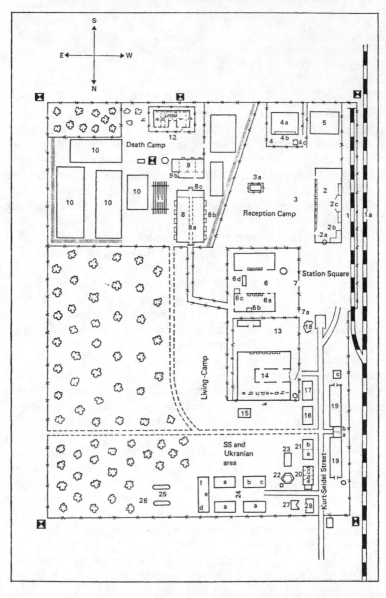

RECEPTION CAMP

(1) The ramp (station platform) where "Blue Command" worked. (1a) Line to Treblinka Labour Camp, about 2 kilometres away – a separate installation, its prisoners mostly Christian Poles, not Jews

(2) Large sorting barracks for goods, eventually disguised (on side facing railway) as a station, with (2a) fake clock and (2b) fake ticket windows. (2c) Sliding doors used only after victims had been removed

(3) Sorting Square, where "Sorting Command" worked. (3a) Latrine

(4) *Lazarett* (fake hospital). (4a) Pit for burning bodies, (4b) low earth bank, and (4c) shelter for guard

(5) Pit for corpses from transports

(6) Undressing barracks, where "Red Command" worked, for men and (6a) women. (6b) Cash-desk, (6c) hair-cutters, (6d) notice-board displaying instructions

(7) Main entrance. (7a) Entrance for guards. (7b) Gate leading to (7e) "The Tube". (7d) Storage for bottles, pots, pans etc.

DEATH-CAMP

(8) "The Tube" led directly to (8), new gas chambers, entered through small doors (8a) from a central passage, emptied of bodies through larger doors (8b). The engine room (8c) supplied carbon monoxide exhaust fumes

(9) Old gas chambers. (9a) Engine room

(10) Burial pits, first used with lime, then emptied and refilled with ashes, the bodies having been burnt on "the Roast".

(11) "The Roast". (11a) Pit used for burning experiments. (11b) Unused pit

(12) Living quarters for Jews working in Death-camp. (12a) Women, (b) doctors, (c) Kapo, (d) showers, (e) latrine, (f) men, (g) kitchen and (h) outside laundry

LIVING CAMP

(13) *Appelplatz* (square for roll-call)

(14) Living quarters for work-Jews. (14a) Gold-Jews, (b) women, (c) joiners, (d) tailors, (e) shoemakers, (f) Kapos, (g) sick-bay, (h) laundry, (i) kitchen, (j) sleeping quarters, (k) barred windows, and (l) latrine

(15) Stables

(16) Textile store

(17) Bakery

(18) Coal pile

SS AND UKRAINIAN AREA

(19) Living quarters and mess for SS. (19a) Munitions, (b) showers, and (c) petrol pump

(20) Building containing (a) air-raid shelter, (b) sick-bay, (c) dentist, and (d) barber

(21) Domestic staff, (a) Polish girls, and (b) Ukrainian girls

(22) Zoo

(23) Building which became workroom for Gold-Jews

(24) "Max Bielas Barracks" – living quarters for Ukrainian guards. (24a) Sleeping quarters, (b) doctor, (c) barber, (d) kitchen, (e) mess and (f) day-room

(25) Potato cellars

(26) Exercise area for Ukrainians

(27) Cellar, use unknown

(28) Kommandant's quarters

The camp was surrounded by an inner fence of barbed wire camouflaged with branches, 3–4 metres high, a space with tank obstacles, 40–50 metres wide, and an outer fence of barbed wire.

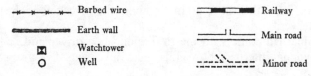

—x—x—x—x— Barbed wire		▬▬▬▬▬ Railway
━━━━━━━ Earth wall		⌐┘ ┕ Main road
▣ Watchtower		⌐‾‾‾ Minor road
O Well		

The single railway track laid from Treblinka town station into the camp is now represented by great beams of wood laid along its course. I walked along it, trying to visualize what the people in the freight-cars would have seen. The snow from the night before had frozen on the ground and on the trees; it was not unlike the approach to a ski resort, quiet, clean, green and white. Of course, most of the trains had no windows, but there would have been cracks between doors, or holes in walls. Did the view reassure them? Did they allow themselves to believe that this little track, running between these lovely trees – for here the trees were left standing – couldn't lead to anything too bad?

Whether their illusion of reassurance (if they felt it) was prolonged or destroyed upon reaching the 'ramp' – the arrival platform – depended on when they arrived and who they were.

If they were Western Europeans, their arrival was at no time grossly alarming; and after the ramp had been disguised as a railway station complete with flower-beds, in the second half of the year, it became even more deceptive. Richard Glazar, a survivor who was one of a preferential Czech transport and came on a passenger train, said, "We all crowded to look out of the windows. I saw a green fence, barracks, and I heard what sounded like a farm tractor. I was delighted." Medical orderlies were lined up to "care for" the old and sick; polite voices bade them disembark at their leisure, but in an orderly fashion, please; and, except by an oversight, there was not a whip to be seen – a whole macabre fakery. These people might well have been confirmed in the belief that they had reached a resettlement centre where they could rest before being assigned to places of work and residence.

But if they were Eastern Europeans, whether during the first or the second half of the year, then the moment the train stopped they saw the Ukrainian guards with their whips lining the platform, the SS drawn up behind them; all this deliberate, to provoke instant dread and foreboding. They were literally whipped out of the trains, and hurried and harried until the moment of their death.

These were the images which pressed on the mind when I entered what had been the camp proper and began to walk along the path to the gas chambers – the tube; as in Sobibor, the SS called it the "Road to Heaven".

Four people had come with me to Treblinka; a driver and an intelligent young interpreter, Wanda Jakubiuk; sixty-five-year-old Francizek Zabecki, former member of the Home Army* and traffic superintendent of Treblinka (village) railway station, and Berek Rojzman, sixty years old, who lost his whole family in Treblinka and is the only survivor of the camp still living in Poland.

It was a bitingly cold day – in spite of fur-lined boots my feet were soon freezing. After thirty minutes or so of walking around on our own Wanda and I came face to face among the trees. "The children," she burst out, with exactly the words which were dominant in my mind: "Oh my God, the children, naked, in this terrible cold." We stood for a long moment, silent, where they used to stand waiting for those ahead to be dead, waiting their turn. Often, I had been told, their naked feet had frozen into the ground, so that when the Ukrainians' whips on both sides of the path began to drive them on, their mothers had to tear them loose. . . . Standing there, it was unbearable to remember, yet both Wanda and I felt that this deliberate effort to visualize the reality of a hell none of us can really share was what we had to do – it was the least we had to do.

The memorial built by the Poles on the site of the death-camp is a fine one: thousands of granite slabs, the different sizes representing the number of people killed from different cities and towns in Europe. The natural rock is scattered in what seems to be a random way, stones representing tiny villages next to larger ones standing for towns and cities, and all of them dwarfed by the huge rugged rock which stands for the more than three hundred thousand people from Warsaw who died here.

Franciszek Zabecki's work during the war as traffic supervisor of Treblinka station – an important junction for German military traffic to the East – and as a vital informant for the Polish underground, makes him a unique personality from the historical point of view: the only trained observer to be on the spot throughout the whole existence of Treblinka camp. He was placed there originally to report on the movement of troops and equipment. He lived with his wife and their three-year-old son in the first-floor flat of the station building. His duties were the registration of all trains and way-bills and the counting of the carriages of all military trains, carried out round the clock with the help of an assistant

* Underground organization directed by the Polish government in exile in London.

149

traffic-controller also working for the Home Army. He was thus a witness of all the transports that passed through the station on their way into the camp.

Pan Zabecki began working for the railway in 1925, when he was eighteen. After a brief spell as a prisoner of war in 1939, he was manœuvred by the underground into the vacant job at Treblinka station in May 1941. He spent the first year consolidating his position in the district, collecting the required data for the underground on the Germans' development of the important line between Kossov, near Treblinka, and Malkinia, a staging-point for troops and material travelling east, and making contacts, including some with German railway personnel.

In the early spring of 1942 the Germans established a small labour camp for Poles near a stone quarry deep in the woods, about four kilometres from the station. "The first inkling we had that something more was being planned in Treblinka," Pan Zabecki said, "was in May 1942, when some SS men arrived with a man called Ernst Grauss who – we found out from the German railway workers – was the chief surveyor at the German District HQ. They spent the day looking around and the very next day all fit male Jews from the neighbourhood – about a hundred of them – were brought in and started work on clearing the land. At the same time they shipped in a first lot of Ukrainian guards."

This whole eastern district of Poland – in a triangle of which were placed three of the four extermination camps – lies very close to the Russian border.

"Many of the Ukrainians had friends near here in the village closest to Treblinka, a hamlet of two hundred inhabitants called Wolga-Oknaglik. It's a tiny place, no school or church – the children go to school six kilometres away in Kossov. But it was from there we began to hear rumours. We heard that a large area of wooded land had been fenced in and some of it was being cleared; a barrack was being built, we were told, for German personnel, and another for the workers. And a well had been sunk for water. Within an incredibly short time we heard that not only had a camp been set up, but we also saw them lay tracks from our main line into the fenced-off area.

"It is difficult to describe to you now the atmosphere of that time. When I say we heard rumours, I mean a whole series of unconnected and contradictory wild-sounding interpretations

150

of events. Some things, of course, we saw for ourselves. Others we felt sure were only guesses or inventions about what went on behind those fences.

"It was said that it was to be another labour camp; a camp for Jews who would work on damming the River Bug; a military installation; a staging or control area for a new secret military weapon. And finally, German railways workers said it was going to be an extermination camp. But nobody believed them – except me."

The extermination camps at Belsec and Sobibor had by then been functioning for some time, "But we hadn't heard of them at all," said Zabecki. "You see, from the point of view of the Home Army, for instance, Sobibor was in the district of Lublin; each district was autonomously administered and there was no communication between the districts. However, I had vaguely heard of Auschwitz – I didn't really know *what* went on there, but I told my colleagues that *I* believed what the German railway workers said. [There was no extermination installation at Auschwitz at that time, so it was indeed rumours he had heard.] Of course one had no conception of what 'extermination camp' really meant. I mean, it was beyond – not just experience, but imagination, wasn't it?

"On July 23, 1942," he continued, "my colleague, Josef Pogonzelski, was traffic superintendent for the day. The day before we had had a telegram announcing the arrival of 'shuttle trains' from Warsaw with 'resettlers'. This wire was followed by a letter-telegram giving a schedule for the daily arrival of these shuttle trains as of the following day, July 23. We were waiting for them as of the early morning, wondering what they were. At one moment two ss men came – from the camp I think – and asked 'Where is the train?' They had been informed by Warsaw that it should already have arrived, but it hadn't. Then a tender came in – the sort called a railway-taxi – with two German engineers, one was called Blechschmied, the other, his assistant, Teufel. They had been sent ahead to guide the first trains along the new track, into the camp.

"When the first train arrived – it was 9.30 a.m. – we could hear it from far away. Not because of the noise of the train, but because of the cries of the people, and the shooting.

"There were guards sitting on the roofs of the cars, with their sleeves rolled up, holding guns. They looked as if they had killed; as if they had had their hands in blood and then washed before arriving. The train was very full – incredibly full it seemed. It was a hot day but, bewildering to us, the difference in temperature between inside the cars and out was obviously such that a kind of fog came out and surrounded the train. There were chalked figures on each car – you know the Germans with their methodical ways – that's why I know exactly how many people were killed in Treblinka. The figures on each car varied between 150 and 180. We didn't know what was happening, but we began to note down the figures that very first day, and we never stopped for a year, until it was over. The train had left Warsaw the night before – it had travelled almost twelve hours . . . at least that's how long the people had been in there – the trip ordinarily only takes about two hours.

"The people called out of the trains that they were being taken to work on farms or in factories, but we didn't think so. We drew our own conclusions; a transport this carefully guarded, with so much shooting. . . .

"We had been told that the track to the camp could only take twenty cars at a time. One train usually had at least twenty cars, and sometimes in the weeks and months to come, three trains would arrive together. So everything except twenty cars would just stay in our station until they finished with each lot of twenty.

"But that first day – as I said before, it happened I was not on duty, and I wanted to know what was going on. We had been warned that the approaches to the camp were strictly off-limits and guarded. But actually there was a road of sorts that passed the perimeter of the camp – you see, there were fields all around it belonging to peasants who . . . oh yes . . . continued to work their fields throughout the existence of the camp. So it wasn't as off-limits, or as guarded as all that – ever."

("Oh yes," said Berek Rojzman, "they worked there all right." – "But then, they saw everything that was going on?" I asked. Both he and Pan Zabecki seemed surprised at my surprise. "Of course they did," they answered. "They were there all day.")

"Anyway," Zabecki went on, "I took a bicycle and cycled a stretch up the road and then got off, pretending that my chain had slipped, in case somebody saw me. I heard machine-guns, and I heard people screaming, praying to God and – yes – to the Holy Virgin. . . . I cycled back and I wrote a message to my [Home Army] section chief – we used to leave our messages under the arms in the statue of the saint in the square in Kossov – I informed my chiefs that some disaster was happening in my district. . . .

152

"After that the trains arrived every day. Within two weeks people began to try to escape, sometimes as many as one hundred out of one transport. There were times when whole cars arrived empty – at that initial period there were three specific occasions when this happened, and on each of these the guards were executed. The Germans who worked at the station told us that there was a punishment cellar in the camp: that's where the [Ukrainian] guards were taken."

(The day before, in Sobibor, Pan Gerung, the forester, had taken me to see a brick construction, not much larger than a pill-box, three or four yards away from the old forester's cottage which had been Stangl's billet and office. "You look at it," he had said. "We don't know what it was for. Tell me what you think." The door opened on to about eighteen steps leading down into total darkness. It smelled dank and mouldy and something – indefinable – else. At the bottom was a small room, about six foot square, ventilated by two tiny slits almost at ceiling level. The floor was earth, the thick walls and the ceiling of rough reddish stone. And into the ceiling were driven four huge hooks. Stangl had never mentioned this room to me. Whatever its purpose, it was a place of horror.)

At the time of my visit to Poland, in 1972, everyone I met officially was very reluctant to discuss the question of past or present anti-Semitism, and Pan Zabecki, although a transparently honest man, was no exception to this rule. Except that – because he was so honest – his evasions were the more obvious.

"No," he said, looking embarrassed, "I don't think one can say that people around here were anti-Semitic. The Germans had set up ghettos in all the towns and I remember that in the smaller places the people took food to the ghettos and gave it to the Jews."

It is certain as I have already said that many people in Poland, on many occasions and at tremendous risk to themselves, did try to help Jews. But other informants, less inhibited by official presences, told me that if Christian Poles took food to Jews, particularly in Eastern Poland, it was more often than not in order to sell it. "In the barbed-wire enclosure near Malenzow," said Stanislaw Szmajzner, "we had no food or drink, and a few Poles came and offered water in exchange for gold rings or money. Nobody had much left, but whoever did, gave these traders their valuables to get a sip of water." And Richard Glazar said " . . . the going rate for two white rolls, three-quarters of an ounce of sausage and a third of a litre of vodka was between ten and twenty US dollars – often more."

None the less, some of the details Pan Zabecki gave from his own experience did confirm the existence of individual acts of compassion such as that described by Pan Gerung in Sobibor.

"When people realized that not only adults but babies were being killed," Pan Zabecki said, "they felt pity. It manifested itself first by their bringing water to the trains. It really is very difficult to describe adequately what it was like and what we all felt," he said again. "I myself couldn't do anything – I couldn't allow myself to be seen exchanging one word with people on the transports or make one gesture towards them; it would have jeopardized the work I was doing for the underground. It is difficult to show to you in words how pitiful it was, the kind of compassion people felt, and yet the little – the terribly little they *could* do: you see, even the German railway workers tried at first to help – the engineer in charge ordered the huge canisters from the engine to be used to shuttle drinking water to the trains as they stood in our station. And at first the train supervisors allowed this. But after a few days it was stopped. But even then, people continued to bring water, until the Germans began to shoot to keep them away from the trains.

"The population was horrified – not only because of what they saw; they were paralysed with fear and horror, and then quite soon they became physically ill from the terrible smell that began to emanate from the camp. But then too, you see, everybody became terrified for themselves; they were *seeing* all this and one became more and more convinced that anyone who witnessed these unspeakable horrors would have to be eliminated too.

"There was a railway family sharing our accommodation in the station house, and they had children of ten and twelve. For days these children went with their parents to take water to the Jews; but the children reacted so strongly, the parents became afraid they were being made ill by it, and they sent them away, to relatives in Pruszukow. My wife, too, had been taking water to the Jews every day and I finally said to her, 'You mustn't go any more: you have a small child, I don't want you to risk it.' Anguish on behalf of the Jews," he said, "turned very quickly into this

154

sharp fear for ourselves. But, you must imagine what it was like living here: every day, as of the early morning, these hours of horror when the trains arrived, and all the time – after the very first days – this odour, this dark foggy cloud that hung over us, that covered the sky in that hot and beautiful summer, even on the most brilliant days – not a rain-cloud promising relief from the heat, but an almost sulphuric darkness bringing with it this pestilential smell.

"There was a period – in the beginning – when my wife could no longer function at all; she could no longer do anything around the house; she couldn't cook, she couldn't play with the boy, she couldn't eat and hardly slept. She had a sort of complete nervous breakdown. When I was a POW she had managed, but now she broke down completely. This extreme condition she was in lasted for about three weeks, then she became pathologically indifferent; she did her work, moved, ate, slept, talked – but all of it like an automaton. . . .

"Of course there was no question of a normal sexual life; we felt we lived in a cemetery; how could one feel joy there?

"Of course, for many of us men it was different – we had more of a purpose; we were so involved in our activities for the 'Conspiracy'*, it gave us an outlet for our emotions, for our hate. We were very very busy, you know – we not only did our ordinary jobs, and collected and delivered information, but we also did partisan training in the woods. For us, in the final analysis, it was a very full life. But I could see that my friends' wives reacted just like my wife did.

"I know a great deal has been said about the brutality of the Ukrainians," he said, "but actually the Lithuanians who mostly guarded the trains were much worse than the Ukrainians; they really were sadists; they used to shoot at people, blind, through the windows of the cars, when they begged for doctors, water and to be allowed to relieve themselves. They did it as a sport – they laughed and joked and bet while they did it. Amongst the Ukrainians there were several who we knew wanted to get away. But you see, that too was dangerous; they were in just as much danger as everybody else. One of the Ukrainian guards did escape, with the help of his Polish girl friend from that little village near us. Stangl himself came to the village then and asked the village chief – the mayor I

* The Polish Resistance.

suppose you'd call him – who this Ukrainian had visited. First he refused to say but then they beat him and he told. Then they went to the father of this girl and took him to the camp. His old mother hanged herself that night; actually the man was allowed back home the next day.

"And then there was the other side of the coin: the Ukrainians began to have a great deal of money. And they wanted more and more women. One farmer forced his twelve-year-old daughter to sleep with Ukrainians. The Conspiracy learned of this and a group went one night and beat him up. Then there was the case of two Polish girls who came from somewhere, got a room and 'received' Ukrainians; the Conspiracy shaved the head of one of them and executed the other.

"As time went on there were more and more violent incidents of one sort or another and people were more and more afraid. One of my colleagues at the station, an engineer who was helping me count cars, Tadeuz Kancakowski, was seen by the Germans putting a note with figures on a spike; two German civilians came and took him to an office in Malkinia. He was sent to Majdanek [the concentration camp near Lublin] and never returned. And in the autumn, we suddenly heard that twenty cars were being readied for something in our own station. People became absolutely frantic – they thought that now it was our turn. About two hundred people packed up that very night and left; that was about the time, too, when all the children, and most of the women went away. After that there were almost only men left in the region.

"No," he said, "I didn't consider sending my wife and boy away. I was too busy; I didn't want to stay by myself – the cooking and everything – it would have been impossible. I convinced her that she had to bear it just as I had to. After that she slowly became better...."

2

I HAVE already mentioned the extraordinary metamorphosis in Stangl's face, which I first saw when he began to speak about his work in the Euthanasia Programme, and which had recurred whenever we reached a point in his story which was really intolerable. He underwent this change again when we began to speak of what he found when he arrived at Treblinka. His voice became slurred and again his face thickened, coarsened and turned dark red.

"I drove there, with an SS driver," he said. "We could smell it kilometres away. The road ran alongside the railway. When we were about fifteen, twenty minutes' drive from Treblinka, we began to see corpses by the line, first just two or three, then more, and as we drove into Treblinka station, there were what looked like hundreds of them – just lying there – they'd obviously been there for days, in the heat. In the station was a train full of Jews, some dead, some still alive . . . that too, looked as if it had been there for days."

"But all this was nothing new to you? You had seen these transports constantly, in Sobibor?"

"Nothing like *this*. And in Sobibor – I told you – unless one was actually working in the forest, one could live without actually seeing; most of us never saw anybody dying or dead. Treblinka that day was the most awful thing I saw during all of the Third Reich" – he buried his face in his hands – "it was Dante's Inferno," he said through his fingers. "It was Dante come to life. When I entered the camp and got out of the car on the square [the *Sortierungsplatz*] I stepped knee-deep into money; I didn't know which way to turn, where to go. I waded in notes, currency, precious stones, jewellery, clothes. They were everywhere, strewn all over the square. The smell was indescribable; the hundreds, no, the thousands of bodies everywhere, decomposing, putrefying. Across the square, in the woods, just a few hundred yards away on the other side of the barbed-wire fence and all around the perimeter of the camp, there were tents and open fires with groups of Ukrainian guards and girls – whores, I found out later, from all over the countryside – weaving drunk, dancing, singing, playing music. . . ."

I was given a somewhat different account by SS sergeant Franz Suchomel who was posted to Treblinka before Stangl, on August 20. I spent a day talking to him at his house in Bavaria, and after that we communicated by letter because he suffers from a heart condition and said it was too taxing for him to *talk* about it (he did in fact have a second heart attack some time later). After reading the Stangl interviews in the German newspaper *Die Zeit* he wrote to say that it was not true that there were corpses outside the camp, or tents nearby with whores. "It's true there was a lot of garbage lying about, possibly also paper money, but never gold, diamonds, etc. True enough, thousands of stacked corpses. . . ."

Against this, however, there is the extraordinary eye-witness account recorded at the time by Hubert Pfoch, then a member of the illegal Austrian Socialist Youth Organization, and now president of the Vienna City Council. As a young soldier moving up to the Eastern front, he saw a transport to Treblinka on August 21, 1942. The photographs he took—at considerable danger to himself (see pages 4 and 5 of illustrations)—were part of the evidence at the trial of ten former Treblinka guards in Düsseldorf in 1964.

"Our infantry company is en route from Vienna to Russia, via Mährisch Ostrau, Kattowitz, through the Upper Silesian industrial region to Radom, Lukow and Siedlce where we arrive in the evening and are given soup," he wrote (he gave me photocopied pages from his wartime diary). "From time to time we can hear shooting, and when I got out to see what was going on, I saw, a little distance from our track, a loading platform with a huge crowd of people – I estimated about 7,000 men, women and children.

"All of them were squatting or lying on the ground and whenever anyone tried to get up, the guards began to shoot.

"The night was sultry, the air sticky and we slept badly.

"Early next morning – August 22 – our train was shunted on to another track, just next to the loading platform, and this was when we heard the rumour that these people were a Jewish transport. They call out to us that they have been travelling without food or water for two days. And then, when they are being loaded into cattle cars, we become witnesses of the most ghastly scenes. The corpses of those killed the night before were thrown by Jewish auxiliary police on to a lorry that came and went four times. The guards – Ukrainian volunteer SS, some of them drunk – cram 180 people into each car ["I counted," Herr Pfoch told me] parents into one, children into another, they didn't care how they separated families. They scream at them, shoot and hit them so viciously that some of their rifle-butts break. When all of them are finally loaded there are cries from all cars – 'Water,' they plead, 'my gold ring for water.' Others offered us 5,000 zloty [2,500 Reichsmark] for a cup of water. When some of them manage to climb out through the ventilating holes, they are shot the moment they reach the ground – a massacre that made us sick to our souls, a blood-bath such as I never dreamed of. A mother jumps down with her baby and calmly looks into a pointing gun-barrel – a moment later we hear the guard who shot them boast to his fellows that he managed to 'do' them both with one shot through both their heads."

Hubert Pfoch told me when I met him in Vienna in 1972 that he and his friends asked their officer – a young first lieutenant – to intervene with the SS officer in charge.

"He agreed to do it," said Herr Pfoch, "but when he suggested to the SS officer that this outrageous spectacle was unworthy of Germany and German honour, the SS bellowed that if our officer and the rest of us 'Ostmarkler' (*Ostmark* was the Nazi term for Austria as a province of the Third Reich) didn't like it and didn't shut up about it, he'd be glad to 'add a special car to the train for us, and we could join the Jews and warmongers and get to know Treblinka.' " The next part of the entry in the young Pfoch's diary would seem to prove Stangl's memory quite correct.

"When at last our train leaves the station," Pfoch wrote, "at least fifty dead, women, men and children, some of them totally naked, lie along the track. We saw the Jewish police remove them – all kinds of valuables disappeared into their pockets, too. Eventually our train followed the other train and we continued to see corpses on both sides of the track – children and others. They say Treblinka is a 'delousing camp'. When we reach Treblinka station the train is next to us again – there is such an awful smell of decomposing corpses in the station, some of us vomit. The begging for water intensifies, the indiscriminate shooting by the guards continues. . . . Three hundred thousand have been assembled here," Pfoch continued [and we must remember that this diary was written in *August 1942*]: "Every day ten or fifteen thousand are gassed and burned. Any comment is totally superfluous. . . ." And then he adds, obviously in a mild attempt to make his diary a trifle less perilous if found: "They say that arms were found in the ghettos and that is the reason for these counter-measures."

Commenting to me on the photograph on page 5 of the illustrations, Herr Pfoch said that seconds after he had taken it, the tall Ukrainian soldier in the background hit out so hard at the children who were "slow to move" that he split the butt of his rifle in two.

159

Stangl told me that on that first visit to Treblinka he was shown round the camp by Dr Eberl, the Kommandant. "There was shooting everywhere . . . I asked him what was happening to the valuables, why weren't they being sent to HQ. He said – he said in the face of all the stuff we were wading through – 'The transports are ransacked before they ever leave Warsaw.'

"I went straight back to Warsaw and told Globocnik that it was impossible: no order such as he had given me could be carried out in that place. 'It's the end of the world,' I said to him, and told him about the thousands of rotting corpses. He said, 'It's supposed to be the end of the world for them.' And he told me to stay in Warsaw that night, that he would call Wirth in for a meeting. . . .

"I had heard that the new police chief of Warsaw was a man from my wife's home town in Austria. I went to see him as soon as I left Globocnik and I begged him to help me get a transfer."

"Did you tell him about Treblinka?"

"No, no, you don't understand: it would have been madness; the secrecy regulations were absolute."

This was, of course, ridiculous when, as he had put it "whores from Warsaw" had congregated around the camp, not to speak of what we have learned since. But equally, there *is* ample evidence in the records of rigorous, if obviously fairly futile, security regulations.

"But he said anyway he'd help; he'd try to get me into an anti-partisan unit. He wrote everything down – I really thought this time it would work. But it didn't. I never heard from him again. Of course, any transfer required Globocnik's signature – without that it couldn't be done. And I know now it was stupid of me ever to hope. Globocnik could never have let me go. . . .

"Wirth came the next morning. And after his meeting with Globocnik we went back to Treblinka. We went into a long meeting with Eberl as soon as we arrived. I went to the mess for some coffee and talked to some of the officers. They said they had great fun; shooting was 'sport'; there was more money and stuff around than one could dream of, all there for the taking; all one had to do was help oneself. In the evening, they said, Eberl had naked Jewesses dance for them, on the tables. Disgusting – it was all disgusting."

Suchomel, who is nothing if not a meticulous witness and always eager to – as it were – "defend" the Jews, had his own comments to make on this. "There were never nude Jewesses dancing on tables," he said, "that's untrue. What is true is that once Eberl, when he was drunk, made a dancer dance naked in the kitchen. He ordered her to undress – which she did most unwillingly. When Wirth heard of this later, he had the poor girl shot. August Hengst had played the pimp on that occasion."

Suchomel had another remark to make about Stangl's arrival in Treblinka. "The first suggestion I heard Stangl make after he arrived," he said, "was to put buckets in the tube for the women. They all defecated you know, while they ran, or stood there, waiting. Stangl said he had put buckets in the tube in Sobibor and it had proved helpful. Wirth answered 'I don't care a damn what you did with the shit in Sobibor. Let them beshit themselves. It can be cleaned up afterwards.'" Apparently two men were then assigned to "cleaning up" the road to the gas chambers between transports.

"That night at dinner," Stangl continued, "Wirth announced that Eberl and four of his staff had been recalled for an important mission and that he, Wirth, would be staying for a while. Eberl and the others left the next morning. Wirth stayed for two weeks or so and reorganized the camp. He tidied it up – I will say that for him. He rang Warsaw and stopped all transports until the place could be cleaned up."

This whole timetable, as Stangl described it to me, is open to doubt, and not merely because of the slight discrepancy between how his wife remembered the sequence of events, and how he did. The trial evidence appears to prove that Globocnik had been made aware of the breakdown situation at Treblinka "some time in August" – well before the time Stangl describes – and had gone there himself with his aide Oberhauser, who testified to this effect at the trial, and Wirth. According to this account, Globocnik relieved Eberl then and there, put Wirth in charge and himself gave the orders how the camp was to be reorganized. (Suchomel, too, told me that "Eberl was gone by the time Stangl arrived".) Oberhauser also testified that it was at Treblinka, "leaning against a door [of a barrack] in the square", that Globocnik decided on Stangl as the replacement for Eberl, and said he would "organize all that from his office the next day" – also Stangl's replacement (Reichleitner) for Sobibor. It is probable that Stangl altered the sequence of these events for my benefit so as to convey as much as possible the impression that his reassignment to Treblinka had been "a surprise" to him and that, once again, he "didn't really know" what his function was to be, a myth he kept up throughout his trial and only relinquished in his conversations with me at the very end.

"What were you doing during the time Wirth was 'reorganizing the camp'?" I asked him.

"Well, of course I had my specific orders: to find out about the valuables and the money. On the fifth day I was there, a courier – Felke was his name, I think – came from Sobibor and Lublin. He said that Michel sent his best regards and that my family had left. After that I felt better. I'd got a funny feeling that something fishy had been going on between Wirth and Eberl" – he now spoke with the animation and interest characteristic of the dedicated police officer. "It seemed to me, the chaos – the complete break-down in security – might almost have been deliberate, so as to make control impossible and enable somebody to by-pass HQ in Poland [Globocnik] and send things straight to the Führer Chancellery in Berlin." He sounded secretive about this even now, indeed to such a degree that what he said became believable. He went on, in this same secretive manner, to mention names of people such as Blankenburg whom he claimed always to have suspected of illegal dealings in Jewish property.

"But wasn't there a common interest involved here?"

"Oh, you have no idea of the rivalries and intrigues between different departments, sections, ministries and individuals. There were enormous – fantastic – sums involved and everybody wanted a piece of it, and everybody wanted control."

Although the booty from the extermination camps was not, as I have said, so enormous as Stangl seemed to think it, this last claim of his is borne out by the record, which provides a wealth of documentary proof of the greed and jealousies between different departments of the Nazi administration regarding the spoils of the "Final Solution". One interesting account – later confirmed to me by Suchomel – speaks of a messenger arriving from Berlin with "a suitcase" and orders, from Blankenburg, to return with one million marks. "We crammed a million into it," said Suchomel, "and he went off with it to Berlin." Equally, the record speaks on many occasions of Globocnik's financial unreliability because of which, after being involved in currency speculations, he was originally removed from his job as Gauleiter of Vienna, reduced in rank and only reassigned to his position in Lublin because of his well-known virulent anti-Semitism and his friendship with Himmler (who called him 'Globus' – Globe in English).

Stangl, however, quite clearly admired Globocnik and was soon to become "his man". He had moved into Eberl's quarters and Wirth, for the two weeks which, according to Stangl, he spent there, had the guest room next to him. One evening during those two weeks in September, Wirth told Stangl that Kurt Franz, whose reputation for ruthlessness had preceded him, was going to arrive shortly "to get this heap moving". "I went back to see Globocnik," Stangl said, "and told him that I believed Eberl and Wirth to have conspired about routing the Treblinka valuables to Berlin instead of to the HQ in Poland. Globocnik said, 'Ah, the villains', as if this had finally explained something that had puzzled him all along. I told him that I was prepared to see that all material as of now would be safely delivered to his office."

Here again the dates are wrong; for it is known that both Stangl and Kurt Franz (and not Wirth) were in Treblinka on September 11 when an SS man (whose name is variously reported as Max Biala or Bielas) was killed by a prisoner – an event rare and heroic enough to be remembered very precisely by a number of people. But dates are only marginally relevant. What the court considered important in the Stangl trial was motivation; and the prosecution later contended that Stangl's offer to Globocnik was not motivated – as he was attempting to establish – by his desire to limit his function in the camp, but rather, when he learned that Kurt Franz was to arrive (whenever that was), by a wish to protect his superior position in the hierarchy. And this contention seems supported by Stangl's own confirmation to me, during our second series of conversations nine weeks after the first, that it was from then on that Globocnik considered him "one of his men", on whose loyalty he relied completely.

"But if you made this offer to Globocnik," I said, *"it means that you actually volunteered your collaboration, doesn't it?"*

"All I was doing," he replied sharply, his face once again undergoing that now familiar change, "was to confirm to him that I would be carrying out this *assignment* as a police officer under his command."

"But you and Michel, months before, had acknowledged to your-

selves that what was being committed here was a crime. How could you, in all conscience, volunteer, as you were doing now, to take any part in this crime?"

"It was a matter of survival – always of survival. What I had to do, while I continued my efforts to get out, was to limit my own actions to what I – in my own conscience – could answer for. At police training school they taught us – I remember, it was Rittmeister Leitner who always said it – that the definition of a crime must meet four requirements: there has to be a subject, an object, an action and intent. If any of these four elements are missing, then we are not dealing with a punishable offence."

"I can't see how you could possibly apply this concept to this situation?"

"That's what I am trying to explain to you; the only way I could live was by compartmentalizing my thinking. By doing this I *could* apply it to my own situation; if the 'subject' was the government, the 'object' the Jews, and the 'action' the gassings, then I could tell myself that for me the fourth element, 'intent' [he called it 'free will'] was missing."

"Except as far as administering the valuables was concerned?"

"Yes. But having established the possibility of illegal trafficking this had become a legitimate police activity."

"But these valuables which you were proposing – or agreeing – to administer wouldn't have been there but for the gassings. How could you isolate one from the other? Even in your own thinking?"

"I could, because my specific assignment from the start had been the responsibility for these effects."

"What if you had been specifically assigned to carry out the actual gassings?"

"I wasn't," he said drily, and added in a reasonable and explanatory tone: "That was done by two Russians – Ivan and Nicolau, under the command of a sub [Gustav Münzberger]."

3

THE CAMP was between forty and fifty acres (six hundred metres by four hundred) and was divided into two main sections and four subsections. The "upper camp" – or Camp II – included the gas chambers, the installations for the disposal of the corpses (lime-

164

pits at first, then huge iron racks for burning, known as "roasts"), and the barracks for the *Totenjuden*, the Jewish work-groups. One of the barracks was for males, another, later, for females. The men carried and burned the bodies; the twelve girls cooked and washed.

The "lower camp" or Camp I was subdivided into three sections, rigidly separated by barbed-wire fences, which, like the outer fences, were interwoven with pine branches for camouflage. The first section contained the unloading ramp and the square – *Sortierungsplatz* – where the first selections were made; the fake hospital (the *Lazarett*) where the old and sick were shot instead of gassed; the undressing barracks where the victims stripped, left their clothes, had their hair cut off if they were women, and were internally searched for hidden valuables; and finally the "Road to Heaven". This, starting at the exit from the women's and children's undressing barrack, was a path ten feet wide with ten-foot fences of barbed wire on each side (again thickly camouflaged with branches, constantly renewed, through which one could neither see out nor in), through which the naked prisoners, in rows of five, had to run the hundred metres up the hill to the "baths" – the gas chambers – and where, when, as happened frequently, the gassing mechanism broke down, they had to stand waiting their turn for hours at a time.

To the left of this part of the camp, separated from it by barbed wire, were the living and working quarters of the *Arbeitsjuden* – the Jewish workers who staffed this lower part of the camp: the joiners, carpenters, shoe-makers, tailors and goldsmiths, doctors in the clinic, laundry workers, kitchen hands and the *Kapos* – the ghetto administrators and police. To the right of this so-called ghetto complex was the *Appelplatz* – the yard where roll-call was taken twice a day. The yard was also used for other purposes, such as concerts, Kurt Franz's ideas of "sport" (running races and boxing matches which ended when the losers were dead), punishments (the whipping-block was in almost daily use at the evening roll-call) and executions (usually by hanging, frequently upside down). *"Did the workers have any kind of social life?"* I asked Stangl. "Of course, of course," he replied. "At the end of the working day they went for walks." – *"Walks? Where?"* – "On the *Appelplatz*; or they sat about in groups and chatted." (Another subtle idea of ss-fun was the ghetto-latrine which the work-Jews could only visit for a precise number of minutes controlled by a prisoner guard with a big clock, whom the Germans dressed comically as a rabbi and called the "shit-master". "He was a quiet gentle man, I think an engineer or designer from Warsaw," one of the survivors told me. "He used to lie on his bunk at night and cry.")

To the left again of this central area, beyond yet another fence, were the quarters of the eighty Ukrainian guards. Forty yards or so west began a small side-street which led into the "Kurt-Seidel Strasse", a two-lane cement road built on Stangl's orders and named after the ss officer in charge of its construction. South-east of this road, along which in the spring of 1943 flowers and ever-green shrubs 'had been planted, were Stangl's quarters containing his bedroom, a guest room, his office and the offices of his two senior administrative assistants, the orderly Stadie, and the book-keeper Mätzig. There was also a clinic for the staff, a dentist, barbers – and a zoo. "We had any number of marvellous birds there," Stangl said, "and benches and flowers. An expert from Vienna designed it for us – of course, we were able to have experts for anything."

Finally, across the street were the ss living quarters; forty ss men were assigned to Treblinka at one time or another, but only twenty were stationed there at any time. The cleaning of the ss quarters was done by Jewish girls, the cooking however, by Polish – non-Jewish – women. I have not seen this fact mentioned in any of the histories of the period. "Oh yes," said Suchomel, "there were three Polish girls working in the German mess; and they lived there too. Of course they had their days off and could go and see their families. Their names were Janina, Sofia and Genjia – that's short for Eugenia. Oh yes, they all survived."

If the mind boggles at the idea of people having a "job" at Treblinka from which they had "days off" to go and see their families in the surrounding villages, this is perhaps a deficiency in our imagination. For the car-entrance to the camp, and the section where the Germans – and Ukrainians too – lived was, it would appear, anything but forbidding. The street, the mess, the barracks, Stangl's house, the munition depot, the garage and petrol "station" – all of it was banked with flowers. "It is difficult," said Stangl, "to describe it adequately now, but it became really beautiful."

* * *

In this exploration of how the weaknesses and fears of men such as
Stangl can be exploited to operate a death-machine like Treblinka,
his own account of his daily life there, and the way he deliberately
manipulated and repressed his moral scruples (which unquestionably existed) is particularly illuminating.

Throughout the three days of this part of his story he manifested
an intense desire to seek and tell the truth. This need, strangely
enough, was emphasized rather than belied by the extraordinary
callousness of many of his explanations and tales. He was telling the
truth as he had seen it twenty-nine years ago and still saw it in 1971,
and in so doing he voluntarily but unwittingly told more than the
truth: he revealed the *two* men he had become in order to survive.

"I got up at dawn," he began. "The men used to be livid
because I made my first round at 5 a.m. It kept them on their toes.
I first checked the guards – the British were supposed to have
dropped parachutists in the region and I had had to secure the
camp against the outside; we had put up a second outer fence of
steel anti-tank obstacles. And then I went up to the *Totenlager*."

Franz Suchomel would have none of this, although in fact he
ended by confirming Stangl's description. "Five o'clock?" he
said. "Nonsense. Why *should* he get up that early? He had other
people who could do that for him. At least, *I* never saw him at that
hour and I was often around then. Yes – he probably came to
breakfast some time around 7; anyway, that's when breakfast was
served. I don't think he often started work at 8. If he really got up
early, it was only to check that everything was properly prepared in
the gas chambers. That was his main concern, because, after all,
he had to reckon with new transports every hour."

"Stangl?" said ss man Otto Horn, who worked for a year in the
upper camp supervising the burning of the bodies. "I only saw him
in the upper camp twice in all the time I was at Treblinka. He told
you he came there twice a day?" He laughed. "Impossible. Of
course," he then added quickly, "I shirked as much as possible – I
always volunteered for night-duty so as to avoid the other things, so
he may have come when I was off. But *I* only saw him there twice.
When I was on duty at night I used to go and just sit behind one of
the barracks and snooze. I didn't *want* to see anything. Yes, I think
several people felt like I did. But that was the most positive thing
one could do – you know, play possum. . . ."

"*What were you doing at the* Totenlager *at 6 a.m.?*" I asked Stangl. "It was a *round*; I went everywhere. At 7 I went in to breakfast. After a while I had them build our own bakery. We had a wonderful Viennese baker. He made delicious cakes, very good bread. After that we gave our army-issue bread to the work-Jews. Of course."

"*Of course? Did everybody?*"

"I don't know. I did. Why not – they could use it."

This bakery is a good example of how variously things are remembered by different people, something I was to find time and again while researching this book. Suchomel and Richard Glazar both remembered the baker and his name (Reinhard Siegfried – "Lovely name for a Jew, isn't it?" said Glazar). And both said he came from Frankfurt, not Vienna. But Glazar thought that although he was supposed to start work in the SS bakery, the bakery never actually materialized because "this was only just before the uprising" (August 2, 1943). Suchomel, on the other hand, had, so to speak, two versions of the baker, which he gave me on two different occasions. In the first story Siegfried worked in the SS bakery, "but there was no question of giving army-issue bread to the work-Jews," he said. When, however, in reply to a question, he wrote about it a few months later, he wrote, "Kapo Siegfried . . . baked *only* for the Jews."

"I tried other ways to get them food too," said Stangl. "You know the Poles had ration books which allowed them an egg a week, so much fat, so much meat. Well, it occurred to me that if everybody in Poland had the right to ration tickets – if that was the law – then our work-Jews were in Poland too and also had the right to ration tickets. So I told Mätzig the book-keeper to go to the town council and request a thousand ration books for our worker-Jews."

"*What happened?*"

He laughed. "Well, in the surprise of the moment they gave him a thousand rations for that week. But afterwards the Poles – the town council – complained to somebody at HQ and I was hauled over the coals for it. Still, it was a good try and we did get something out of it; they had a thousand eggs that week." ("Oh yes, certainly," said Suchomel. "Mätzig got out of the Polish authorities what he could; he was a decent bloke. He got the Jews cereal and marmalade – that I remember clearly. A thousand eggs? Well, I don't know anything about that – but it's possible.")

"Getting back to your daily routine, what did you do after breakfast?"

"At about 8 I'd go to my office."

"What time did the transports arrive?"

"Usually about that time."

"Didn't you attend their arrival?"

"Not necessarily. Sometimes I went."

According to Suchomel, Stangl was usually there, "though he always avoided any transports from Germany or Austria, which were accompanied by German police. When that happened, the police officers were quickly taken to the mess so that they couldn't see anything, and then they were pushed off again on the same train when it went out (after it was cleaned)." According to Treblinka survivor Joe Siedlecki, Stangl was "often, always on the ramp in his white suit, often on horseback, very elegant". (But Siedlecki's account is another example of how misleading memory can be, because although Stangl didn't arrive at Treblinka until September, at the earliest late August he said, "He was there when I arrived. . . . I arrived in July. He *must* have been there – he was the Kommandant.")

"How many people would arrive on a transport?" I asked Stangl.

"Usually about five thousand. Sometimes more."

"Did you ever talk to any of the people who arrived?"

"Talk? No. But I remember one occasion – they were standing there just after they'd arrived, and one Jew came up to me and said he wanted to make a complaint. So I said yes, certainly, what was it. He said that one of the Lithuanian guards (who were only used for transport duties) had promised to give him water if he gave him his watch. But he had taken the watch and not given him any water. Well, that wasn't right, was it? Anyway, I didn't permit pilfering. I asked the Lithuanians then and there who it was who had taken the watch, but nobody came forward. Franz – you know, Kurt Franz – whispered to me that the man involved could be one of the Lithuanian officers – they had so-called officers – and that I couldn't embarrass an officer in front of his men. Well, I said, 'I am not interested what sort of uniform a man wears. I am only interested in what is inside a man.' Don't think *that* didn't get back to Warsaw in a hurry. But what's right is right, isn't it? I made them all line up and turn out their pockets."

"In front of the prisoners?"

"Yes, what else? Once a complaint is made it has to be investigated. Of course we didn't find the watch – whoever it was had got rid of it."

"What happened to the complainant?"

"Who?"

"The man who lodged the complaint?"

"I don't know," he said vaguely. "Of course, as I said, usually I'd be working in my office – there was a great deal of paper work – till about 11. Then I made my next round, starting up at the *Totenlager*. By that time they were well ahead with the work up there." He meant that by this time the 5,000 to 6,000 people who had arrived that morning were dead: the "work" was the disposal of the bodies which took most of the rest of the day and during some months continued during the night. I knew this, but I wanted to get him to speak more directly about the *people*, and asked where the people were who had come on the transport. His answer continued to be evasive; he still avoided referring to them as "people".

"Oh, by that time of the morning everything was pretty much finished in the lower camp. A transport was normally dealt with in two or three hours. At 12 I had lunch – yes, we usually had meat, potatoes, some fresh vegetables such as cauliflowers – we grew them ourselves quite soon – and after lunch I had about half an hour's rest. Then another round and more work in the office."

"What did you do in the evenings?"

"After supper people sat around and talked. When I came first they used to drink for hours in the mess. But I put a stop to that. Afterwards they drank in their rooms."

"What did you *do? Did you have any friends there? Anyone you felt you had something in common with?"*

"Nobody. Nobody with whom I could really talk. I knew none of them."

"Even after a while? A month?"

He shrugged his shoulders. "What's a month? I never found anybody there – like Michel – with whom I felt I could speak freely of what I felt about this *Schweinerei*. I usually went to my room and went to bed."

"Did you read?"

"Oh no. I couldn't have read there. I was too unquiet. . . . The electricity went off at 10 – after that everything was quiet.

Except of course when the transports were so big that the work had to continue in the night. . . ."

"I can't think what he was talking about when he said the lights went out at ten," said Suchomel. "That's nonsense. They stayed on all night; after all, we had to guard the place – how could we have done that without light? People went to bed anyway – they were so *tired*. It's quite true," he said, "there was a great deal of drinking in the rooms. The decent ones among the men liked Stangl – because he wasn't such a swine as most of the others. But he boozed too, but not so much in the camp – outside. Most of us never went out; I remember, about three of the men had women somewhere, but on the whole going out was not encouraged. It was too dangerous anyway, with all the partisans there were around. But Stangl had this friend, Greuer he was called – he was political officer in Kossov; that's where he drank. I remember, once they brought him back to the camp totally, speechlessly drunk. There *were* books," he said. "In fact it was Stangl himself who told me once that several books for the staff had arrived from Berlin, sent by Reichsleiter Bouhler. And those could be borrowed any time."

One of the most extraordinary things about delving into this period now is the different interpretation given to individual events by different people. This is less the result of failing memories or deliberate manipulation, than because most people now represent these events and their part in them with a view to seeming – to themselves even more than to others – what they would have *liked* to have been, rather than what they were. And this applies to Germans as well as Poles, Christians as well as Jews, West as well as East Europeans. A few – a *very* few – of those I met showed no wish to hide, embellish or change the past in any way: Franz Suchomel, for example. Even fewer – and for very different reasons – had no need to do so.

4

A MAN of Richard Glazar's integrity is rare anywhere. That he should have survived Treblinka and be in a position to chronicle it for us is hardly less than a miracle.

He lives with his wife and their children in a sixteenth-century farmhouse in the tiny village near Berne, in Switzerland, where Emmenthaler cheese is made. Their house stands on a path in a meadow, and has gables, dormer windows with geraniums in window-boxes, small warm rooms and a wide view over fields and mountains. "This is how we chose – how we want to live," said Richard when I went to stay with him and his family in the late autumn of 1972.

He was then fifty-three years old, a slender man of medium height with long, tapering hands, brown hair and perceptive brown eyes. He has the kind of face that doesn't alter much over the years; give and take a bit of hair, he probably looked very much as he does now when he was a boy. His Czech wife who, incidentally, is not Jewish, is an attractive woman with a quick smile and a firm mind who works in an office in Berne. Their pretty twenty-year-old daughter, who recently married a nice young Austrian who also works in Berne, is a computer programmer; the young couple live with the Glazars. Their twenty-one-year-old son is studying in Germany.

Richard Glazar was born in Prague. His father, a financial consultant who worked first for a bank and later on his own, had served in the Austrian army during the First World War, and had been wounded. In 1932, when Richard was twelve, his parents were divorced. Four years later, his mother remarried. Her second husband was a wealthy leather-merchant, Adolf Bergmann. Richard loved his stepfather and his two stepbrothers, Karl (who was to be killed in the concentration camp Mauthausen) and a younger boy (who was to be saved by the Danish Red Cross evacuation scheme for Czech-Jewish children under fourteen). "It was a marvellous time," he said. "I spent my holidays with my maternal grandparents in the country; that's where I learnt how to make things, how a wheel is made, how a calf is delivered, how one works the land." He matriculated in March 1939 and was accepted at the University of Prague in June. "I wanted to study philosophy," he said, "but by that time there was already an unofficial quota* and I couldn't get into that course; but they did offer me a place to read economics. My stepfather was very aware of the dangers around the corner. At Christmas 1938, after the annexation of the Sudetenland, he had managed to get a permit

* Limiting the number of Jews.

172

to travel to England to see friends. And he had arranged that we would all emigrate to England. When I think that we might have done that – but we didn't. In the end he didn't have the courage to leave everything he had built up at home and start again, abroad.

"But in Czechoslovakia the measures against Jews started very gradually; first it was just signs on shops – 'Jews Unwelcome', or sometimes a bit sharper 'Forbidden to Jews', but otherwise not much happened for a while."

There was no real anti-Semitism in Czechoslovakia, compared to other Central and Eastern European countries, partly because of a young but very strong democratic tradition, and more perhaps because most Czech Jews were assimilated middle-class people in business or the professions, with a distinct German-Austrian orientation. The men had often served as officers in the Austrian army; the children went to German or Czech schools; and segregation or taunting of Jewish children, common in Poland and Rumania for instance, was unknown. To envisage in this atmosphere the full or even partial extent of the future horrors was all but impossible, even when the first signs of it were apparent.

"On November 17, 1939," Richard went on, "after several students had been executed,* the students demonstrated and all universities were closed. After this I worked for my stepfather until, in 1940, my family sent me to the country near Prague to work for a farmer – safer, they thought. In 1941, Jews were ordered to wear the Star of David on their clothes, but I didn't register as a Jew and nobody bothered me."

Some time during 1940 Richard's father, who had fled the Nazis to Russia, died there – of pneumonia, so they were told. In the autumn of 1941 his mother telephoned him from Prague to say they were being "moved" to Lodz in Poland. "She cried," Richard said, "and she said to hold on as long as I could and however I could. My stepfather – we were not religious, but he blessed me in Hebrew. I learned later that in Lodz Mother went to work in a laundry and my stepfather fell very ill and was taken away. Later my mother was sent to Auschwitz and later still to Bergen Belsen where she worked in a munition factory – and, thank God, survived.

"The farmer where I stayed was nice enough in the beginning – later a bit less, but his wife was always nice. They had two very nice daughters; I became great friends with the older one. The

* For anti-German activities.

173

younger one was small. Later, after I escaped from Treblinka, I wrote to the peasant's wife, you know, from Germany, under my assumed name. I had to let somebody know that I was alive. I addressed them in my letter as 'Dear aunt and uncle' – it was a risk for her, a real risk. But she answered at once and sent me clothes and other things I had left there."

On September 2, 1942, Richard, in spite of not having registered as a Jew, received a notification to report to the *Mustermesse* – a huge exhibition hall in Prague. "When I left the farm they were both upset – she cried," he said. "I had no idea at all what to expect or what was expected of me." None of them knew, but Richard in particular had been isolated from rumours and for that matter from other Jews for more than a year. "Not far away from the farm there was a pub where the farm labourers went and I too had gone there sometimes," he said. "Not long after my parents were deported they were talking at the bar and a man who worked at 'our' farm said that he'd heard it was pretty bad in Lodz. I remember saying sort of flippantly, 'Well, they can't cut their heads off,' and he answered, 'I heard they shoot people there.' I said, 'Nonsense.' That's how little I knew."

When he left the farm, he carried a knapsack and two bags. "I wore boots, two pairs of trousers – dungarees or jeans and over them flannels – a sweater and a sports coat. In my rucksack I carried a suit, some shirts, a pair of flannel pyjamas, sport shoes and black shoes, underclothes, handkerchiefs and towels. And in the bags I had food: lard with onion, biscuits, and tins of this and that.

"By the time I got to Prague it was already 'Jew-free' as they called it. We stayed at the *Mustermesse* two or three days and waited; they distributed food and there were sinks to wash in. We slept on the ground. Of course there were a great many rumours of every kind and there was this fear of uncertainty, but there was no physical fear.

"One morning they counted us and we went to a nearby station and travelled to Theresienstadt, a village around a fortress north of Prague built in the time of Maria Theresa, which had been turned into a huge internment camp."

Theresienstadt was intended to be the Nazis' "model" internment camp for Jews, housing Czechs, Germans and Austrians who had served in the armed forces and been wounded, and elderly people of means and influence. Quite a few of them had important connections abroad, able to make large payments for them in US currency. This camp, under Eichmann's personal supervision, was later to be exhibited on three different occasions to Red Cross delegations, one from Germany, one from Denmark and one from the International Red Cross, and convinced several of the delegates that it was indeed, as Himmler was to say: "Not a camp in the ordinary sense of the word, but a town inhabited and governed by Jews, in which every manner of work . . . is done. This type of camp was conceived by me and my friend Heydrich, and this is what we had intended all camps to be." None the less, between November 1941 and 1942, 110,000 people were crammed into this "town" which formerly housed 7,000, and by the end of 1942 there were only 49,392 left. Sixteen thousand had died of illness and starvation, and 43,879 had been "shipped East" in that one year.

"I was assigned quarters in a stable," Richard Glazar said. "Two cousins found me there; they were in an attic."

Richard stayed in Theresienstadt for a month working in a garbage disposal unit. He found his maternal grandfather and his paternal grandmother – they had been there for several months. His grandmother lived in a room with a dozen other old women, sleeping on blankets on the floor. "She seemed very small," said Richard. "I used to bring her chocolate, whenever I could scrounge some, but she always said 'No, thank you, keep it for yourself'. But then one day I brought her a pot of lard and she accepted that. My grandfather was in an old people's ward: that was really terrible. He was almost blind; he had tried to cut his veins."

After a few days in the stable, Richard had moved into a large hall, with friends. This is where he met another Czech, Karel Unger, who was to become his closest friend, and who survived and escaped from Treblinka with him and now lives in the US.

"After a month in Theresienstadt I was notified that I was to leave the next day for another camp, in the East. I ran to see Hannah, my cousin – she said grandfather had just died; it was that day too.

"We, our Czech transport, travelled on a passenger train; later I was to find out how rare that was; only transports from the 'West' – Germany, Austria, Holland, etc – travelled on passenger trains with their comparative comfort; everybody else went in cattle trucks. The people supervising our transport were police – in

175

green police uniform. They appointed some of the young men as monitors and gave them armbands. It wasn't particularly rough, or frightening. True enough, the police officer in charge expressed himself rather oddly. 'I am to bring a thousand pieces,' he said, 'and a thousand pieces I am going to bring. So anybody who puts his head out of the window is going to have it blown off; we shoot.' We thought he was being unnecessarily crude; no need, we thought, to frighten the women and children that way; but we didn't really give it a second thought. We left Theresienstadt on October 8 and we travelled two days. First we thought we were going in the direction of Dresden, but then the train turned and we went East. During the nights it stood more than it moved. The last morning we saw in the distance the outline of a city; it must have been Warsaw. We got to Treblinka at 3.30 p.m. We all crowded to look out of the windows. I saw a green fence, barracks and I heard what sounded like a farm tractor at work. I was delighted. The place looked like a farm. I thought, 'This is *prima* [marvellous]; it's going to be work I know something about.'

"The transport we had come on was numbered BG 417 – Karel Unger, who was travelling with his whole family, had been assigned to a different set of numbers, BU. But we had arranged that I'd keep a lookout for him the day after or whenever, and reserve bunk-space for him next to me and all that, so that we could continue to stick together.

"I saw men with blue armbands on the platform, but without insignia. One of them carried a leather whip – not like any whip I'd ever seen, but like something for big animals. These men spoke very strange German. There were loud announcements, but it was all fairly restrained: nobody did anything to us [the prescribed pattern for transports arriving from the West]. I followed the crowd: 'Men to the right, women and children to the left', we had been told. The women and children disappeared into a barrack further to the left and we were told to undress. One of the SS men – later I knew his name, Küttner – told us in a chatty sort of tone that we were going into a disinfection bath and afterwards would be assigned work. Clothes, he said, could be left in a heap on the floor, and we'd find them again later. We were to keep documents, identity cards, money, watches and jewellery with us.

"The queue began to move and I suddenly noticed several men fully dressed standing near another barrack further back, and I was wondering who they were. And just then another SS man (Miete was his name) came by me and said, 'Come on, you, get back into your clothes, quick, special work.' That was the first time I was frightened. Everything was very quiet, you know. And when he said that to me, the others turned around and looked at me – and I thought, my God, why me, why does he pick on me? When I had got back into my clothes, the line had moved on and I noticed that several other young men had also been picked out and were dressing. We were taken through to the 'work-barrack', most of which was filled from floor to ceiling with clothes, stacked up in layers. Many of the clothes were filthy – we had to tear them apart by force, they stuck together with dirt and sweat. The foreman showed me how to tie the things together into bundles, wrapped up in sheets or big cloths. You understand, there was no time, not a moment between the instant we were taken in there and put to work, to talk to anyone, to take stock of what was happening ... and of course, never forget that we had no idea at all what this whole installation was for. One saw these stacks of clothing – I suppose the thought must have entered our minds, where do they come from, what are they? We *must* have connected them with the clothes all of us had just taken off outside ... but I cannot remember doing that. I only remember starting work at once making bundles, I *thought* as the foreman had told me, but then he shouted, 'More, more, put more in if you want to stay around.' Even then I didn't know what he meant; I just put more in. Even though stuff was being carried in from outside, the very clothes the people who had arrived with me had taken off minutes before, I think I still didn't think; it seems impossible now, but that's how it was. I too went outside to pick up clothes and suddenly something hit me on the back – it was like being struck by a tree-trunk: it was a Ukrainian guard hitting me with one of these awful huge whips. ["Yes," said Stangl, "I think there may have been umbrella wire in the whips." – "No," said Suchomel, "there was nothing in the whips except leather – they just say that now."] 'Run,' he screamed, 'run' – and I understood from that moment on that all work in Treblinka was done at a run."

Later somebody whispered the truth about Treblinka, "But carefully, carefully," Richard said.

Life in Treblinka was always incredibly dangerous, always hung on a thread, but perhaps the most dangerous time was each morning, after the arrival of the transports, while the queues were moving up through the tube towards the death-camp and while the gas chambers were in operation.

"There was an incredible rivalry amongst the SS men," Richard said. "You see, they weren't just an amorphous mass, as people now like to imagine them; they were, after all, individual men, with individual personalities. Some were worse, some better. Almost every one of them had their protégés amongst the prisoners, whom they played off against each other. Of course, one can't look at this in the same way one might consider other 'organizations' where heads of sections have their favourites. Obviously, no ordinary standards of emotion or behaviour can apply; because all of existence, for us especially, and up to a point, at least by reflection, also for them, was reduced to a primeval level: life and death. Consequently all ordinary reactions became special, or at least very different. Perhaps some SS men developed a kind of 'loyalty' to one prisoner or another – though one hesitates to call it that; there really was almost invariably another, and usually nefarious, reason for any act of kindness or charity. One must always measure whatever they did against the deep fundamental indifference they felt towards all of us. It was of course more than indifference, but I call it that for want of a better word. Really, when one wants to evaluate how they behaved and what they were, one must not forget their incredible power, their autonomy within their narrow and yet, as far as we were concerned, unlimited field; but also the isolation created by their unique situation and by what *they* – and hardly anyone else even within the German or Nazi community – had in common. Perhaps if this isolation had been the result of good rather than evil deeds, their own relationships towards each other would have been different. As it was, most of them seemed to hate and despise each other and do anything – almost anything – to 'get at' each other. Thus, if one of them selected a man out of a new transport for work, in other words to stay alive at least for a while, it could perfectly easily happen – and often did – that one of his rivals, and make no mistake about it, in one sense or another they were all rivals, would come along and kill that man just to spite him [send him into the queue to be killed] or else 'mark' him, which was tantamount to death [anybody 'marked' went with the next transport]. All this created a virtually indescribable atmosphere of fear. The most important thing for a prisoner in Treblinka, you see, was not to make himself conspicuous. To this, too, there were degrees – which I will tell you about later. But basically it meant, first of all, not to do anything 'wrong' – the 'wrongest' thing being to work at anything remotely less than one's top capacity. And there were a hundred and one other arbitrary 'wrong' things, depending only on who saw you. Of course, I am not talking about any kind of insubordination; I mean in the context of our lives that would have been impossible – simply unthinkable. What one had to do was to develop to a fine art one's understanding of how to remain alive.

"All this applied much more during the first six months than the second. The whole Treblinka time needs to be divided into four phases. The first one was the months under Dr Eberl [before Glazar himself – or Stangl – arrived]. The second one, already under Stangl, but in the beginning of his rule, was still a period of utter arbitrariness where one SS might select a man for work and an hour later, he might be dead, sent 'up' by another. Phase three – after the beginning of 1943 – was one of comparative stability: there were less transports; the SS by then knew their comparatively safe jobs far from the shooting war *depended* on their proving themselves indispensable by running efficient camps, so they began to value useful workers. And by that time, too, the prisoners had become individuals of sorts to them. They had, so to speak, 'tenure' in their jobs; there was a terrible kind of communality of basic purpose between the murderers and the victims – the purpose of staying alive.

"Finally phase four was the two, three months before the uprising in August 1943 – a period of increasing insecurity for the Germans when the Russians were approaching and the SS had begun to realize what it would mean if the war was lost and the outside world learned of what had been done in Treblinka, and that they were in fact individual men, individually accountable. And that it followed that they might, eventually, be able to make use of individual prisoners [to speak in their defence].

"However, these are generalizations; the reason why, the morning of our arrival, it was fifteen or thirty minutes before somebody managed to whisper to us what Treblinka was for, was that this was phase two of the camp's existence and fear dictated every move."

Richard Glazar, as I had learned to understand by then, has

an extraordinary capacity for recall, and for relative detachment – essential if this particular story is to be bearable – and, in a wider sense, of value.

"How can one say how one reacted?" he said. "What I remember best about that first night is that I decided not to move; to . . . how can I say it . . . stand, sit, lie very very still. Was it already an unconscious realization that the main thing was not to be noticed? Did I instinctively connect being 'noticed' with 'movement'? I don't know. I told myself, 'Swim along with the current . . . let yourself be carried . . . if you move too much, you'll go under. . . .'

"That night I wasn't hungry. I mean, there *was* food – there was always food after the arrival of 'rich' [Western] transports – but I couldn't eat. I was terribly terribly thirsty, a thirst that continued all evening, all night. . . .

"I remember, that evening in the barrack, the others watching us new ones. 'How are you going to behave?' they wondered. 'Are you going to scream, shout, sob? Are you going to go mad, hysterical, melancholy?' All these things happened; and from the next night on, when I myself was one of the 'old' ones, I watched the 'new' ones in exactly the same way. It was not curiosity – nor was it compassion. Already we were beyond such simple feelings; we did it in response to a need within ourselves; we needed to prove to ourselves, over and over, that everyone was the same as oneself, with the same fears, the same aggressions – perhaps not quite the same capacities. There was a kind of reassurance in both these things, and watching the new arrivals became a kind of rhythm, every night. . . ."

Richard spoke a great deal about "relationships" and how important they were to survival. "My friend Karel arrived in a transport the day after I had come. His whole family were killed at once but he was twenty-one years old and strong like me, so he too was among the lucky ones to be selected for work. From that moment we were never apart until 1945 when we returned to Prague together – they used to call us the twins." (Karel Unger now lives in the state of Washington and refused to come to Germany to testify at the Treblinka trial, and later at Stangl's trials.) "He cannot understand how I can send my boy to Germany to study," said Richard sadly. "Our feelings about some things may be very different now." (A year later Richard told me that

Karel and his wife had come to stay with them in Switzerland a few months earlier, "and our feelings *weren't* different," he said happily. "It was as if we had said goodbye a week before; we are still twins.")

The small Czech contingent of which Glazar was a part, so important in the life of the camp, is even today spoken of by other survivors, and by former SS men too, with a kind of awe. "They were special," said Samuel Rajzman, who lives in Montreal and is, in terms of wisdom and achievement, a rather "special" man himself. "They had a special kind of strength, a special life force." "The Czechs?" said Suchomel. "Oh yes, I remember them very well. They *were* a special group: Masarek, Willie Fürst – they worked in the tailor shop under me. And then there was Glazar. Those lads slept on and under feather comforters. They were tidy – really tidy." And Berek Rojzman in Poland, also mentioned the Czechs. "I slept next to them. They were – they were a sort of élite group. Masarek," he said with awe, "and of course Glazar. I knew them all." It is gratifying to him to speak of them.

Richard says they were aware of this feeling in the other prisoners. "At the time," he said, "it was shaming for us. They seemed to feel we were superior to them. One of the Poles, David Bart, said once, '*You* must survive; it is more important than that we should.' But there were very few of us. At the 'peak period' of the camp – autumn and winter of 1942 – there were a thousand work-Jews, eighteen of them us Czechs. Two of us survived, that's all." (Altogether about 250,000 Czech Jews were killed during the "Final Solution".)

At the beginning of what Glazar called phase two, the SS (Stangl, no doubt, with his talent for organization) decided they could use certain professionals and people with qualities of leadership to improve efficiency. With few exceptions (one of them a woman, and an informer who was later "executed" by the revolt committee) the members of this "élite" were Warsaw Poles over forty; doctors, engineers, architects and financiers. They were given the best, and slightly segregated accommodation, and arm-bands with the word *Hofjude* – "Court Jew" (derision even in privilege) – the main purpose of which was to protect them from some SS man's murderous whim. (Of the Czechs, only Rudolf Masarek – much younger than the others – was eventually to be appointed a "Court Jew".)

"Later, when we were in phase three," said Richard, "the arm-bands became unnecessary; they took them off then because they found it embarrassing to flaunt them before the rest of the slaves when they came back at night, half dead from exhaustion."

Six of the young Czechs, all arriving within days of each other, became close friends; but even within the six, they paired off in twos. "There was Karel and me," said Richard. "We worked from October until March in the warehouse, more specifically in 'men's clothing' – they called us 'Karel and Richard from Men's Better Overcoats'. The one who arrived next was Robert Altschuh, a twenty-seven-year-old medical student, and after him thirty-two-year-old Hans Freund; he'd worked in textiles in Prague. Five days after us Rudi Masarek arrived; he was twenty-eight, tall, blond, blue-eyed; his family had owned one of the most exclusive men's shirt shops in Prague...." (When Suchomel first saw Masarek, he said, "What the hell are *you* doing here? You aren't a Jew, are you?")

"Rudi was a sort of 'golden youth'," said Richard. "You know what I mean? His had been the world of sports-cars, tennis, country-house weekends, summers on the Riviera. He was a half-Jew; there really was no reason for him to be there.* Except that in 1938, after the Austrian Anschluss, he had fallen in love with a girl from Vienna who was Jewish. He married her the day before the regulation came into effect that Jews had to wear Stars of David on their clothes. Of course, he didn't have to wear it, but the day after his wedding he had the Star sewn on all his suits and coats. When she (though not he) was ordered to Theresien-stadt, he went with her. And when she (not he) was ordered to Treblinka, he came with her there too. She was killed immediately. Rudi was an officer, a lieutenant in the Czech army, and he was later of decisive importance in the planning and execution of the revolt. But after his wife was killed it was three weeks before he would speak to anyone; he had been assigned to work in the tailor shop under Suchomel, who, by comparison to some, was relatively decent," Richard shrugged his shoulders. "That doesn't mean Suchomel didn't beat us; all of them beat us.

"The last arrival of our particular group, ten days or so later, was Zhelo Bloch – a photographer in ordinary life. He too was a

* Western European half-Jews were often able to escape the rigorous laws applied far more relentlessly to half-Jews in the East.

Czech officer, also good-looking, with brown hair, a strong square sort of face and a muscular body. He was the military brain behind the planning for the uprising – for a long time. Both he and Rudi – and Robert too in other ways – were immensely important to us and to the camp as a whole. Zhelo and Robert became inseparable; and Rudi Masarek and Hans Freund. All of us had great respect for Galewski, the Polish camp-elder; he was an engineer of note, in his forties I think, tall, slim, with dark hair. He looked and behaved like a Polish aristocrat, a very remarkable man.

"Our daily life? It was in a way very directed, very specific. There were various things which were absolutely essential to survival: it was essential to fill oneself completely with a determination to survive; it was essential to create in oneself a capacity for dissociating oneself to some extent from Treblinka; it was important *not* to adapt completely to it. Complete adaptation, you see, meant acceptance. And the moment one accepted, one was morally and physically lost.

"There were, of course, many who did succumb: I have read more or less everything that has been written about this subject. But somehow no one appears to have understood: it wasn't *ruthlessness* that enabled an individual to survive – it was an intangible quality, not peculiar to educated or sophisticated individuals. Anyone might have it. It is perhaps best described as an overriding thirst – perhaps, too, a *talent* for life, and a faith in life. . . ."

I understood what Richard had meant when I met Berek Rojzman who came to Treblinka with me when I visited the camp.

5

LIKE HIS father and his grandfather before him, Berek Rojzman was brought up to be a butcher. Nowadays he works in a factory in a Warsaw suburb; a solidly built man, six foot two, married to a widow – a gentile – with two children.

His family, in which there were six children, lived in Ejrodzisk Maz, a medium-sized town in Eastern Poland. He was the second eldest and went to a Jewish school. "But they taught us Polish," he said. Yes, he was aware of anti-Semitism. "The Polish children called us 'Jew-Jew'," he said. (The present government in Poland is – rightly – determined to obliterate this use of "Polish" for "Christian"; it is arguable that this use of language may have originated quite as much with the Jews themselves as with the Christians in Poland, where Jews, particularly in Eastern Poland, always felt themselves to be – and appeared to wish, or had to remain – a separate ethnic entity within the country.)

"Nationalists came and stood in front of our shop and said, 'Don't buy. Jews, go to Palestine.' There were often fights between Jewish and non-Jewish boys. Our parents said, 'Pretend not to see, pretend not to hear.' " And if the same situation arose now, he says, he would do the same. "The best way with hooligans is to ignore them."

Berek Rojzman finished school at fifteen and started working in his father's shop. He met his first wife when he was seventeen, and married her when he was twenty-eight. People in Poland, perhaps unused to this kind of journalism in connection with these events, were usually puzzled if I asked about anything other than the horrors they had lived through, and when I asked Berek Rojzman what their relationship had been all those years, he smiled shyly and answered with a joke. But he finally gave me to understand that it was near-platonic. The engagement was so long because "my mother died, and I had to help my father with my smaller brothers and sisters."

When I remarked at one point during our conversations that his family sounded very strong, he agreed. "My grandmother," he said, "lived fifteen kilometres away from us, on her own. When she was 115 years old, she came to see us, on foot, for a drink. And when she'd had her drink she refused to be driven home in the cart – she said she'd walk, just as she had come. We had suggested repeatedly that she should come and live with us. But Babka said, no, she wouldn't, she might disturb us. She was about 120 or 121 when she died, still living fifteen kilometres away, still on her own."

When Berek finally married in 1938, he continued working for his father for a year and then bought his own shop in a Warsaw suburb. In pre-war Poland it was rare for any but upper-class, artistic or academic Jews to make friends with non-Jews, but the young Rojzmans made friends with – as he put it again – a "Polish" couple.

"This couple," said Berek Rojzman, "were enlightened people.

184

They felt, as we did, that they believed in God and that God is God however one happens to pray to him. My wife," he said, "was killed by the Germans in Treblinka. The husband of this friend was killed by the Germans in Warsaw. After the war she and I met again and we married."

Berek had joined the army on August 24, 1939, and for the short time he was a soldier, before he was captured by the Germans, he worked as a medical orderly. Clearly he was one of those soldiers who are never at a loss, a born fixer, using his enormous physical strength and his cunning to improve the lot of his comrades, his officers and obviously – his own. He likes to crack jokes. "When they sent me on patrol," he said, "I always took food and vodka along with me, and I always managed to find some treat to take back to the officers. I was giving them the strength to fight!"

When he got home after escaping from a POW camp, the Germans wouldn't let him reopen his shop. "I butchered secretly," he said.

At the end of 1939, when the Germans decreed that all the Jews of Warsaw were to move into the ghetto, the Rojzman family decided that there would be safety in numbers; that in this city within a city life could be made reasonably normal, with homes, work, clinics, help for the old and, above all, schools for the children. They bought a flat in the ghetto and the whole family moved into it. Berek and his father opened shop again as butchers.

There was an interlude of a few months when they were given a cottage on his estate by a Polish landowner, Janusz Rogulski ("I had a lot of connections in the countryside, of course," said Berek, "but he was good; he wanted to help us. We just lived there. We didn't even have to work.") By the spring of 1942, back again in Warsaw, they had decided that they would be safer in a smaller place. They got away by train (which Jews were not entitled to use) and on foot to Biota Rawska, where again they bought a place to live in the ghetto. Other Jews in Poland at that time – hundreds of thousands of them – were creeping into the nearest hole to hide: the Rojzmans bought houses and flats. Others accepted whatever work they were given and starved on ghetto rations: the Rojzmans practised their trade, fought, bartered, sold this and that, and none of them lacked food, clothes or shelter. Others who escaped from the Warsaw ghetto lived rough in the forests or were sheltered by heroic Christians: the Rojzmans took a scheduled train to the town of their choice.

But for all the vitality and ingenuity, in November 1942 they were shipped to Treblinka. Berek was selected for work, all the others died within the hour.

"My older son had died as a baby; but they killed all the rest of my family, including my wife, of course, and my two-year-old boy.

"I got selected for work because one of the men in the 'Red Command' [who worked in the undressing barracks] was a former friend. When he saw me – and two other young men he knew – he told us to stay in the undressing barrack and if necessary hide under clothes – there were mountains of them on the floor – and he ran to see the Jewish camp chief, Galewski, and told him that he knew us, that we were strong young men and could work. First Galewski said only I could stay – but finally he said all right for all three of us. I worked in the Red Command all that winter. After that I was assigned to agricultural work – gardening and the planting of vegetables."

It emerged very clearly that Berek Rojzman continued in Treblinka the same survival techniques which had already proved themselves outside. "I traded," he said, with a smile. "Mostly with the Ukrainians. They were *in business*: they wanted gold, clothes, objects and food. On the other hand, when we were short, they could get food from the peasants for gold and money and bring it to us. It worked," he said. "It worked well. They were just like anybody; they traded."

"If I speak of a thirst, a talent for life as the qualities most needed for survival," said Richard Glazar, "I don't mean to say that these were deliberate acts, or even feelings. They were, in fact, largely unconscious qualities. Another talent one needed was a gift for relationships. Of course, there *were* people who survived who were loners. They will tell you now they survived *because* they relied on no one but themselves. But the truth is probably – and they may either not know it, or not be willing to admit it to themselves or others – that they survived because they were carried by *someone*, someone who cared for them as much, or almost as much as for themselves. They are now the ones who feel the guiltiest. Not for anything they did – but for what they didn't do – for what . . . and this cannot be any reflection on them . . . for what simply wasn't in them to be."

186

It was quite clear that Richard did not mean to say that people died because they didn't have these qualities. To be chosen to live even for an extra day was nothing but luck, one chance in a thousand: it was only that if they had this incredible luck, then these qualities, he thought, gave them a chance to survive longer.

Joe Siedlecki, who is now a *maître d'hôtel* at Grossinger's Hotel in Upper New York state, is a strikingly good-looking man of six foot three, who looks eminently capable of taking care of himself, and others. He was a soldier in the Polish army at the start of the war – "in some of the worst battles," he said – and then a prisoner of war. His wife is a lovely thirty-two-year-old German, Erika, who converted to the Jewish faith in order to marry him. She comes from Kiel where her family still lives. "My father and mother said I must take his religion," she said. "A wife must be the same religion as her husband, they said. And I wanted to anyway. My family, they love Joe. No, they were never religious; my father left the Church forty-six years ago to become a *Gottgläubiger* – no, I don't know why, but," she laughed, "perhaps the fact that in Germany we have to pay a church tax had something to do with it."

The Siedleckis have an enchantingly pretty daughter, five when I met them – an almost classic example of a much-loved child growing up in freedom and security – and live in a particularly nice modern flat in a Grossinger staff-house; a sunny, golden place, flower-filled and beautifully equipped, almost like something out of an American ad-man's dream. Its atmosphere is Erika's creation and represents very vividly her personality. "Some people ask Joe how he could marry a German," she said when Joe had gone off on an errand. "After all he's been through – they just can't understand. He gets very angry sometimes. It happened at the hotel just the other night, when one of the guests had the temerity to ask him. He told him it was none of his business. But on the other hand, he himself often used to tell people I was Italian or something, and he doesn't want me to speak German to the little one. But in that I think he is wrong. I think I owe it to her to teach her. Later, when she goes to college, she'll get credits for it; it'll help her get on. And anyway, I can't help it, I *am* German you see; if something nice happens like Willie Brandt getting the Nobel Prize or something – I feel proud. I do speak German to her – I sing German songs and read German fairy tales to her. First in German and then I translate them for her. I do that every evening for an hour, from 7 to 8 . . . when Joe is not here."

"The Germans?" said Joe. "What shall I tell you? When I was over there to testify, they treated me like a king; a king I tell you. And my wife's family, they respect me. In Treblinka, some of them were animals, but some of them were good too. I tell you, the Poles were worse, much worse than the Germans, and so were the Ukrainians. There was one SS, if I saw him today, if there was anything he needed, I'd give it to him; Karl Ludwig. He was a good good man. The number of times he brought me things, the number of times he helped me, the number of people he probably saved, I can hardly tell you. I don't know where he is now, but I wish I did.

"Then of course there were terrible ones; Kurt Franz, Küttner, Miete, Mentz; animals, sadists. But there were such people amongst the Jews too: the *Judenrath* in Warsaw, the Jewish Gestapo; and then in Treblinka, the Kapos, the squealers, some of them again better than others, but on the whole I was as scared of them as of the Germans.

"My parents and my twenty-year-old sister were sent to Treblinka a week before me. I had got married six weeks earlier. Not a love match – a sort of 'arrangement'; she had money – our families arranged it. Her mother, sisters and brothers – she no longer had a father – were also shipped to Treblinka a week before us. But she and I had been sent to the SS HQ to work – we were both young and strong. The day we were ordered to the *Umschlagplatz* [the square from which the transports departed], the HQ officers said they didn't want to lose their workers. There was a lot of discussion and finally it was decided that all bachelors could stay but married couples had to go. An announcement was made that 'anyone who wants a divorce could have one, right away'. Well, it was a choice between life and death. [Earlier he had said that they had no idea where the trains were going; a little later, "Perhaps we didn't know for certain, but we had a good idea what it was"; this was in July 1942, at the very beginning of the camp.] I saw men who had been married for thirty-four years ask for a divorce then and there. My wife – well, I told you, it wasn't love between us but – she said, 'I am going to be soap anyway, so ask for a divorce, save yourself.' But I thought to myself, 'I have no family, nobody left. She has nobody. We'll stay together.' So both of us went.

"As soon as we got to Treblinka I was selected to work. They called me *Langer* [long one] because I was so big and tall. I said to the ss who picked me out, that she was my wife and could she work too. And he – I can't remember who it was, Miete or Küttner – he said, 'Don't worry, she is going to work in the laundry in Camp II.' But of course, it wasn't true; they killed her right away. I never saw her again.

"They put me first in the Red Command – we had to superintend the undressing in the undressing barracks. We had to call out, '*Ganz nackt, Schuhe zusammenbinden, Geld und Dokumente mitnehmen.*' [He called it out for me, to show me how: 'Strip, tie your shoes together, take along money and documents.'] That's how they fooled people. They thought they were going to bathe and be disinfected and that they were being allowed to keep their valuables and documents with them for their own protection. It reassured them. Some German Jews – you know, they were more German than the Germans – were very authoritarian, very much the *Herren* [the gentlemen – or masters]. 'Keep an eye on my shoes will you, till I come back,' they'd say condescendingly, you know, to us of the Red Command. Of course, ten minutes later they were dead.

"Later I was appointed to the disinfection room, probably one of the worst places to be in; it was between the hairdressers who chopped off the women's hair, and the 'tube' which led up to the gas chambers. We would have to disinfect the hair, you see, right away, before it was packed up to ship – they used it in Germany to make mattresses.

"Stangl?" he said. "I never saw him kill or hurt anyone. But why should he have? He didn't have to. He was no sadist like some of the others, and he was the Kommandant. Why should he dirty his own hands? It's like me now in my job; if I have to fire somebody, *I* don't do it – why should I? I tell somebody else to tell the person he is fired. Why should I do the dirty job myself? Stangl never beat anybody either," he said. "Why should he? Oh, he was there when it was done of course . . . well . . ." – he retracted, as he was to do in almost every instance when he mentioned Stangl's being present at or taking part in anything – "He *must*

189

have been there; they were all there. And he was the Kommandant. I tell you exactly the way it was; *I* was there for a year, and I
know. Anyone tells you differently, anyone tells you Stangl beat
or killed anyone, or anyone tells you Stangl *talked* to them – they
are lying. He didn't talk to any Jews – why should he?

"Did I have friends? Yes, of course I had friends. All right, yes,
I had friends. But how could one have friends there? I never did
any harm to anyone. I kept myself to myself – it was better. But
they liked me – the others. On my birthday, I remember, I was
going to have a bit of a party and I managed to buy some ham off
a Ukrainian and the Germans found it. They lined us up and
asked whose it was . . . nobody budged . . . but then one of my
pals said it was his. So I said no, it was mine. They marched us to
the *Lazarett** and told us to undress. Only shortly before, we had
taken a friend of mine who was very ill there – to be killed; nobody went there for any other reason. But when we were carrying
him, on the stretcher, he asked me and I told him that no, we
weren't taking him to the *Lazarett* – he was going to the *Revier* –
the sick room. Anyway, when we were pushed in there ourselves,
Hansbert, this friend, was still burning in the pit. And then they
began to shoot our group. One, then the next, the third, the fourth –
I was fifth and last, and by that time I was lying on top of the
others [he must have fallen forward] waiting to be shot. I turned
around, looked up and said, 'Hurry up, why don't you. Shoot, for
God's sake.' And then, whoever it was . . . I think it was Miete
who had come . . . said for me to get up and get dressed. Well,
they must have liked me – otherwise they would have killed me
too." (It was probably Miete who had originally picked him out
for work, in which case he was possibly now seeing him to some
extent as his protégé.)

---

* The *Lazarett* was nothing but a shell of a small building – about twelve metres
by twelve, with a Red Cross painted on the front. There was no roof. Immediately
inside the door was a weather-shelter for the ss guard, and a small table and bench.
Just beyond was an earthen wall running almost the length of the building with a pit
on its other side. Victims were helped to undress, then had to sit on that wall, were shot
in the neck and dropped into the permanently burning pit.

Franz Stangl in the Remand Prison at Düsseldorf,
having prepared himself for the photographer

Left The photograph of Franz Stangl issued by the Jewish Documentation Centre at Vienna at the time of his arrest in Brazil

right Franz Stangl in conversation with the author

Three of the photographs of a transport bound for Treblinka, taken secretly at Siedlce Station, on August 22, 1942, by an Austrian soldier, Hubert Pfoch

Franz Stangl at Treblinka, talking to his adjutant Kurt Franz.
He is wearing the white jacket often referred to at his trial

The grab used to transfer bodies from the burial pits to the "roasts".
Photograph from Kurt Franz's album, its title-page inscribed "Happy Days"

The house built at Treblinka after the camp had been demolished, in which
a Ukrainian farmer was to be installed. If questioned, he would claim
that he and his family had lived there for years

Treblinka
now

6

"IN OUR group," said Richard Glazar, "we shared everything; and the moment one of the group ate something without sharing it, we knew it was the beginning of the end for him. *Food* was uppermost in our minds; for a long time eating was an end in itself; we'd be given tin plates of soup at lunchtime, and bread and coffee. While the Western transports went on, there was so much food around, we used to throw the soup and bread away. There was a huge mountain of mouldy camp bread around [confirming what Suchomel had already told me, and contradicting Stangl's story]. We only drank the coffee. No, they didn't mind our taking food from the transports [presumably as long as they didn't know] – there was so much, you see. Of course, the SS and the Ukrainians had first choice, but there was much much more than that. We stole it, and we bought it too. That is, the Ukrainians would help themselves to most of it and then sell it back to us for gold, American dollars or jewellery. They had no means of getting at the valuables – they guarded the outside work details and the camp itself, but the work camp, inside, was worked by Jews, and guarded by the SS. The group who actually worked on registering the valuables – millions in money and stones – were called the 'gold-Jews'. SS-man Suchomel supervised them too; he did that and the tailor-shop."

To be given several SS assignments was a proof of efficiency. "It was Wirth who originally appointed me as chief of the gold-Jews," said Suchomel, "not Stangl. But Stangl was very careful about the valuables. I remember the day Eichmann came. . . ." For some reason hard to fathom, when I asked Stangl about this he always denied that Himmler or Eichmann visited either of the camps under his command. "Oh, he lied about that," said Suchomel. "It was most certainly Eichmann who came that day with an SS group from Berlin. He told me himself; he said Eichmann and Globocnik were coming and to put everything in order, first in the tailoring shop and then I had to run over and make sure about the gold-Jews' shop too. 'Mark all the trunks and cases exactly as to content and description,' he told me. 'He is going to want to see it looking exactly right. And when they are here, you come up to us and make a report in proper military style.'

"Of course," he said, "one was able to help sometimes, too. One morning one of the young Poles who worked under me came, distraught. He said, 'Chief, please help me. My sister Broncha has arrived; she is already in the undressing barrack . . . please save her.' I went in there and asked which was Broncha. There she was, naked, trembling from head to foot and crying. I said, 'Stop trembling. You are a seamstress, are you?' And she – would you believe it, she said, trembling, 'No, I can't sew.' So I said, 'Don't be stupid, you *are* a seamstress; just remember that and I'll get you out.' Then I told the barrack Kommando to hold her back – not to let her get into the tube or they'd have to answer to me for it. And I went over to see Stangl and told him that I just didn't have enough workers in my shop – I had to have more. He said Wirth had ordered there was to be no more recruiting. 'Everything has to go,' he said. But I said I just had to have at least one more girl; so finally he said, 'Well, in God's name then,' and gave me a chit for her – to show Küttner. If there wasn't an official chit from Stangl, then, although Küttner might have agreed to let somebody stay if we asked him, Franz was almost bound to push them in again, just because they hated each other. Anyway, that's how Broncha got out. She survived, you know; she is in Israel."

"Later in the autumn," Richard Glazar went on, "we were allowed a thirty-minute lunch break when we could talk, and everybody would ask each other, 'What have you "organized" today?' And that always referred to gold, money and food. After a while we did begin to think that we must *do* something; plan something, resist. But the work and the unremitting tension made us fearfully tired, just tired you know, and one used to say to oneself, or to close friends, 'We *must* think – we *must* plan,' but then we'd add, 'We'll think tomorrow, not today.'

"Did we become hardened, callous to the suffering, the horror around us? Well, one can't generalize; as with everything in life, people reacted differently. One did, I think, develop a kind of dullness, a numbness where the daily nightmarish events became a kind of routine, and only special horrors aroused us, reminded us of normal feelings; sometimes this would be connected with specific and special people, sometimes with special events.

"There was the day when Edek arrived – he was a small fourteen-year-old boy. Perhaps he arrived with his family, perhaps alone, I don't know; when he got off the train and stood on the ramp, all one could see of him was his head and his shoes; in between was the accordion he'd brought, and that was all he brought. An SS saw him and said right away, 'Come, come,' and from that day on he played for them. They made a kind of mascot of him; he played everywhere, at all hours, and almost nightly in their mess. And just about the same time a famous opera singer arrived – a young one, from Warsaw – and somebody drew him to the attention of the SS and he too was pulled out. It wasn't long after that that they started the fires; we saw them for the first time in December, one night, through the barred window of the barrack; the flames rose high, high above the camp, flames in all colours: red, orange, blue, green, purple. And in the silence of the camp, and the terrible brightness of the flames, one heard nothing except little Edek playing his accordion and the young singer singing *Eli Eli*.

"Robert Altschuh said later that night – and that was the first time we had thought of it that way – 'They are trying to find ways to hide the traces; they are burning the corpses. But they aren't going to find it so easy – even one corpse doesn't burn easily, and hundreds of thousands of corpses. . . ?'

"So you see, that night, on the one hand we had allowed ourselves to be emotionally overwhelmed by this 'special event' – the fires. But then, only minutes afterwards, it was in a way cancelled out – and perhaps, although we may not have realized it, deliberately so – by Robert's scientific consideration of the problem of how to burn hundreds of thousands of corpses. He had a lot of ideas on it; he analysed the human body for us, what burned and what didn't burn; who would be easier and who more difficult to burn. And we listened, you know – with interest.

"Secrecy? Good heavens, there was no secrecy about Treblinka; all the Poles between there and Warsaw must have known about it, and lived off the proceeds. All the peasants came to barter, the Warsaw whores did business with the Ukrainians – it was a circus for all of them." (Both Zabecki and Berek Rojzman had already spoken of the peasants who tended their fields which adjoined the camp. "And many others," said Rojzman, "came to the fence to barter, mostly with the Ukrainians, but with us too." Stangl was to talk about this too.)

Suchomel, in this context, also spoke about the "whores" Stangl had said were grouped about the camp. "They weren't 'whores' in that sense," he said. "We called them *Spekulantinnen*. They were women who came from all over – Warsaw too, I expect – to do business with the Ukrainians. They may have fucked with them – I suppose they did – but mainly they were around to 'shop'. After Wirth came, he had twelve of them picked up at random, brought into the camp and had them whipped. Afterwards he shipped them to the labour camp . . . " (the Polish labour camp near a stone quarry about two kilometres above the extermination camp, which Zabecki had described as having been built first). Suchomel paused. "Did you know," he said then, in a tone signifying scientific interest, "that all Jewesses have dimples in their buttocks? This was confirmed by the racial scientists."

"No I didn't," I said. "But what has this to do with your *Spekulantinnen* story anyway? *They* weren't Jewish, were they?"

"No," he said, not understanding my meaning, or his own *non sequitur*.

"You can't really believe this nonsense anyway, can you?" I asked. "Have you ever seen the backside of a fat Christian woman? A German for instance?"

He didn't answer.

I asked Richard Glazar whether there were girls among the "work-Jews" and he said "Yes, there were girls. They worked in the kitchen and the laundry, in both the lower and upper camps. Of course, anyone who was sent to work in the upper camp, girls or men, knew they'd never come down again." (There is one single case on record – the carpenter Yankiel Wiernik – of someone moving back and forth between both parts of Treblinka. And although several people from the "upper camp" survived the August uprising, an authentic escape from there before then is unknown and considered impossible.)

"Yes," said Richard, "of course most of the – few – girls who were there paired off with somebody. Love? It's hard to say; relationships, strong friendships, yes – and yes, perhaps love; Kapo Kuba was in love – or lived with, if you like, a girl called Sabina. All the girls who were there were young and attractive; they only picked young and attractive ones, many of them blondes or redheads. Anyway, Sabina was found in bed, I think, with

Kuba once, or something like that, and Küttner, one of the very bad SS men, said, 'We can't have all this whoring about,' and sent her up to work in the laundry at the death camp. Well, Kapo Kuba volunteered to go up too, to be with her. They didn't let him. But what would you call that? Not love? [Kuba is dead; "Sabina" is one of the two girls who survived, and lives in Israel.*]

"Then there was Tchechia. She was in love with Rakowski, the former camp elder. And he, they said, was in love with her. Stadie shot him when he discovered (through an informer) that he had planned an escape for himself and Tchechia, and found gold on him. Perhaps Tchechia slept with other men afterwards. But can you wonder? Did it really matter?"

("Tchechia Mandel was the only real red-blonde in the camp," said Suchomel, whose assiduous memory of individuals and events is remarkable. "She was a really intelligent distinguished girl, very proud and courageous. She was one of the few Jews all of us Germans addressed as '*Sie*' rather than '*Du*'. Steiner [Jean-François Steiner, author of the controversial book *Treblinka*] in his book said she slept with Germans – but never never did she do that. She was Kapo Rakowski's girl friend – he was the chief Jew of the camp and she became pregnant by him and had an abortion. Tchechia was the daughter of an industrialist in Galicia – she was extremely well educated. I was told later how she died; I didn't see it myself; it happened after I left Treblinka. It was quite a while after the revolt; only a few girls were still there waiting on the remnant of the German personnel who were liquidating the camp. The Unterscharführer who was in charge – he got up after lunch that day and apparently said to the three girls, 'Well girls, it's your turn now' [*jetzt muss es ja einmal dran' gehen*].† And Tchechia laughed and said, 'Aha, I never did believe your fairy-tale promises, you pigs. Go ahead, kill us. Just do me a favour and don't ask us to undress.' One of the girls, she was also called Tchechia – 'little Tchechia' they called her – she cried, and Tchechia said, 'Don't cry, don't do them the favour. Remember, you are a Jewess.' She was really something – *somebody*, you know." The position Suchomel has adopted as an admirer of the Jews is as remarkable as his memory, and psychologically interesting.)

"Escapes?" said Richard Glazar. "Yes, there were a few, three

---

* This is not now her name.
† The shocking callousness of this phrase is untranslatable.

I think which were successful, all in phase two; afterwards it became impossible.

He was to tell me later that two young men – "they were twenty-four and twenty-five, I think," he said – were smuggled out of the camp in the very first train to be sent out of Treblinka with the victims' clothes and other belongings. "It was the last two days of October or the very first of November. We helped to hide them; it was all very carefully organized to get the news out to Warsaw.

"At the end of November, beginning of December, seven men from the Blue Command tried and were caught. Kurt Franz shot them in the *Lazarett* and then called a special roll-call and said that if anybody else tried, particularly if they succeeded, ten would be shot for each one who escaped."

"I wouldn't have cared if any of them had run away," said former ss male nurse Otto Horn, who was in charge of the "roasts" in the upper camp but, generally described as "inoffensive", was acquitted at the Treblinka trial. "I sometimes wondered why they didn't. Once Matthes (who commanded the upper camp) sent me to take a detail out to look for branches: six men and a Ukrainian guard. We were no sooner out of the camp than the Ukrainian was off; they were always foraging in the villages for food and drink. Never a day passed that they didn't come back with roast chicken, *slivovitz*, etc. . . . Anyway, here I was with the six men. I thought to myself, 'This is their chance. All they have to do is caper off.' There wasn't anything I could have done and, as I say, I wouldn't have cared. No, I don't think anything would have happened to me. It wouldn't have been my fault. They were looking for branches all over the woods – that's what they were supposed to be doing and I was alone with them and they were out of my sight for long periods – how could I have kept count of them? It was impossible. But – in the end they all came back." He shook his head. "I couldn't understand why."

And Suchomel says, "A few days before the revolt I advised Masarek and Glazar to break out, but I said they should do it in small groups. And they said they couldn't do that, because if they did, there would be terrible reprisals. That's really something, if you come to think of it, isn't it? And then they say the Jews aren't courageous. I tell you, I got to know the most extraordinary Jews."

"I know nothing about advice from Suchomel to break out," said Richard. "But the revolt was being planned from November 1942. Very very few people knew about it, and even fewer were actually on the planning committee. It was headed of course by the camp elder, Galewski, and until March, when catastrophe struck us, Zhelo Bloch was the military expert on it.

"The period between late October and the beginning of January was the peak period – that was when most of the transports arrived, sometimes six of them – 20,000 people a day. At first mostly Jews from Warsaw and the West, with their riches – above all enormous quantities of food, money and jewels. It was really incredible how much and what we ate; I remember a sixteen-year-old boy who, a few weeks after his arrival, said one night he'd never lived as well as here in Treblinka. It was – you know – very very different from the way people have written about it.

"You see, we weren't dressed in striped uniforms, filthy, lice-ridden, or, for much of the time, starving, as the concentration camp inmates mostly were. My own group – the Czechs – and the 'court-Jews' dressed extremely well. After all, there was no shortage of clothes. I usually wore jodhpurs, a velvet jacket, brown boots, a shirt, a silk cravat and, when it was cool, a sweater. In hot months I wore light trousers, shirt and a jacket at night. I shone my boots once or twice every day until you could see yourself in them, like in a mirror. I changed shirts every day and of course underclothes. *We* had no body-lice ourselves, but there were of course vermin all over the barracks – it was inevitable with all that was brought in by the transports. I'd wear a pair of pyjamas for two nights or so and then they'd be full of bloodspots where I had killed bugs that crawled up on us in the night, and I'd think to myself, 'Tomorrow I must get new ones; hope they are nice silk ones; they are still on the way now.' That sounds terrible, doesn't it? Well, that is how one became. One was very concerned with the way one *looked*; it was immensely important to look clean on roll-call. One thought of small things all the time, like, 'I must shave; if I shave again, I have won another round.' I always had a little shaving kit on me. I still have it. I shaved up to seven times a day. And yet, this was one of the most torturing uncertainties; one never knew how the mood of the Germans 'ran' – whether, if one was *seen* shaving or cleaning one's boots, that wouldn't get one killed. It was an incredible daily roulette;

you see, one ss might consider a man looking after himself in this way as making himself 'conspicuous' – the cardinal sin – and then another might not. The *effect* of being clean always helped – it even created a *kind* of respect in them. But to be seen doing it might be considered showing off, or toadying, and provoke punishment, or death. We finally understood that the maximum safety lay in looking much – but not *too* much – like the ss themselves and the significance of this went even beyond the question of 'safety'.

"At the beginning of winter the huge transports from the East started coming," Richard said. "The [Eastern] Polish Jews; they were people from a different world. They were filthy. They knew nothing. It was impossible to feel any compassion, any solidarity with them. Of course, I am not talking about the Warsaw or Cracow intellectuals; they were no different from us. I am talking about the Byelorussian Jews, or those from the extreme east of Poland."

7

THE WORK-JEW slaves hated their jailer-masters from the depth of their souls. And yet – and this is probably the most complex aspect of these awful events – as time went on, a terrifying kind of link developed between them. The origin of this link which, I believe, the Nazis recognized and used to the utmost extent, was the incompatibility between the two worlds of European Jewry; the Eastern and the Western. The generally highly educated, sophisticated Western Jews found themselves confronted by an appalling moral and emotional conflict on not only being identified by the Germans with the Jews from Eastern Poland and Russia, but even more on realizing *in themselves* a moral obligation – and a moral and emotional pressure – to accept this identification. But for many of them this was impossible; being Jewish had become a matter of religion, not race; their allegiance was to the country of their birth, be it Czechoslovakia, Hungary, Austria, Holland, France or for that matter, Germany. And it was thus, tragically, almost easier for them to identify with the Germans, whose way of life had been so like their own, than with the vast numbers of "different" Jews whom many of them encountered now for the first time in their lives.

The hundreds of thousands of Eastern Jews, who had always, by choice as well as by necessity, lived apart from the mainstream of the population, felt themselves exclusively as Jews. Their religious, racial and national feelings were all combined in this one identity. It determined their way of life and all their allegiances, and outside it there was nothing except fear: the traditional and ingrained fear of pogroms which had been their lot for centuries.

It is this fear, combined with a measure of fatalism about the fact of racial persecution, that represented the widest gap between them and Western or assimilated Jews who knew, theoretically, about vicious pogroms but had never experienced them. It was the retrospective misunderstanding of this fatalism – its interpretation as some kind of mystical death wish – which allowed the victims of the "Final Solution" to be seen by some, in shocking distortion, as "sheep who allowed themselves to be led to slaughter".

The fact is that at the time neither the Eastern nor the Western Jews could conceive that what they appeared to be facing was true, and the Nazis displayed terrifying astuteness in their understanding of the essential differences between the personality of the two groups; an "achievement" which can hardly be attributed to men like Stangl and Wirth, but probably originated either with Heydrich or the "medical" chiefs of T4 – the psychiatrists Professors Heyde and Nitsche. They recognized the capacity of the Western Jews individually to grasp the monstrous truth and individually to resist it, and therefore ordered that great pains be taken to mislead and calm them until, naked, in rows of five and running under the whiplash, they had been made incapable of resistance.

By the same token they realized that these precautions were unnecessary with the Eastern Jews who – up to a point – expected terror. All that was needed here was to create mass hysteria. "They arrived, and they were dead within two hours," Stangl said. And these two hours were filled with such an infinity of carefully devised mass violence that it robbed these hundred thousands of any chance to pause, or think.

8

AT CHRISTMAS 1942 Stangl ordered the construction of the fake railway station. A clock (with painted numerals and hands which never moved, but no one was thought likely to notice this), ticket-windows, various timetables and arrows indicating train connections "To Warsaw", "To Wolwonoce" and "To Bialystock" were painted on to the façade of the "sorting barracks"; all for the purpose of lulling the arriving transports – an increasing number of whom were to be from the West – into a belief that they had arrived in a genuine transit camp. "It is possible," Stangl agreed at his trial, "that I ordered the construction of the fake station."

"You've been telling me about your routines," I said to him. *"But how did you feel? Was there anything you enjoyed, you felt good about?"*

"It was interesting to me to find out who was cheating," he said. "As I told you, I didn't care who it was; my professional ethos was that if something wrong was going on, it had to be found out. That was my profession; I enjoyed it. It fulfilled me. And yes, I was ambitious about that; I won't deny that."

"Would it be true to say that you got used to the liquidations?"

He thought for a moment. "To tell the truth," he then said, slowly and thoughtfully, "one did become used to it."

"In days? Weeks? Months?"

"Months. It was months before I could look one of them in the eye. I repressed it all by trying to create a special place: gardens, new barracks, new kitchens, new everything; barbers, tailors, shoemakers, carpenters. There were hundreds of ways to take one's mind off it; I used them all."

"Even so, if you felt that strongly, there had to be times, perhaps at night, in the dark, when you couldn't avoid thinking about it?"

"In the end, the only way to deal with it was to drink. I took a large glass of brandy to bed with me each night and I drank."

"I think you are evading my question."

"No, I don't mean to; of course, thoughts came. But I forced them away. I made myself concentrate on work, work and again work."

"Would it be true to say that you finally felt they weren't really human beings?"

"When I was on a trip once, years later in Brazil," he said, his face deeply concentrated, and obviously reliving the experience, "my train stopped next to a slaughterhouse. The cattle in the pens, hearing the noise of the train, trotted up to the fence and stared at the train. They were very close to my window, one crowding the other, looking at me through that fence. I thought then, 'Look at this; this reminds me of Poland; that's just how the people looked, trustingly, just before they went into the tins. . . .'"

"You said 'tins'," I interrupted. *"What do you mean?"* But he went on without hearing, or answering me.

" . . . I couldn't eat tinned meat after that. Those big eyes . . . which looked at me . . . not knowing that in no time at all they'd all be dead." He paused. His face was drawn. At this moment he looked old and worn and real.

"So you didn't feel they were human beings?"

"Cargo," he said tonelessly. "They were cargo." He raised and dropped his hand in a gesture of despair. Both our voices had dropped. It was one of the few times in those weeks of talks that he made no effort to cloak his despair, and his hopeless grief allowed a moment of sympathy.

"When do you think you began to think of them as cargo? The way you spoke earlier, of the day when you first came to Treblinka, the horror you felt seeing the dead bodies everywhere – they weren't 'cargo' to you then, were they?"

"I think it started the day I first saw the *Totenlager* in Treblinka. I remember Wirth standing there, next to the pits full of blue-black corpses. It had nothing to do with humanity – it couldn't have; it was a mass – a mass of rotting flesh. Wirth said, 'What shall we do with this garbage?' I think unconsciously that started me thinking of them as cargo."

"There were so many children, did they ever make you think of your children, of how you would feel in the position of those parents?"

"No," he said slowly, "I can't say I ever thought that way." He paused. "You see," he then continued, still speaking with this extreme seriousness and obviously intent on finding a new truth within himself, "I rarely saw them as individuals. It was always a huge mass. I sometimes stood on the wall and saw them in the tube. But – how can I explain it – they were naked, packed together, running, being driven with whips like . . ." the sentence trailed off. ("Stangl often stood on the earthen wall between the

201

[two] camps," said Samuel Rajzman in Montreal. "He stood there like a Napoleon surveying his domain.")

"Could you not have changed that?" I asked. *"In your position, could you not have stopped the nakedness, the whips, the horror of the cattle pens?"*

"No, no, no. This was the system. Wirth had invented it. It worked. And because it worked, it was irreversible."

Suchomel remembered Stangl telling the SS personnel that an order had come from Hitler that nobody was to be beaten or tortured. "But then he said, 'It's impossible. But when the bigwigs come from Berlin you must hide the whips.' "

At the Treblinka trial Richard Glazar testified that the beatings often had distinctly sexual overtones and Suchomel's account seems to confirm this, if confirmation were needed. "When Kurt Franz beat them," Suchomel recounted, "it was on their bare buttocks [the crasser German word he used was *Hintern*]. They had to drop their trousers and count the blows of the whip. The others didn't insist on that, though."

Joe Siedlecki too talked about Kurt Franz's beatings. "He'd give them fifty strokes," he said. "They'd be dead at the end. He'd be half dead himself, but he'd beat and beat. Oh, some of the others, they were just weaklings – two strokes and *they'd* collapse; but Franz and Miete and some of them – they could go on and on."

"Stangl did improve things," Suchomel said later. "He alleviated it a bit for people, but he could have done more, especially from Christmas 1942; he could have stopped the whipping post, the 'races', 'sport', and what Franz did with that dog, Bari – he was Stangl's dog originally. He could have stopped all that without any trouble for himself. [The dog, originally harmless, had been trained to attack people, and specifically their genital regions, on command.] He had the power to do that – and he didn't. I don't think he cared – all he did was look after the death camp, the burning and all that; there everything had to run just so because the whole camp organization depended on it. I think what he really cared about was to have the place run like clockwork."

Gustav Münzberger, who was more incriminated than Suchomel, put it differently. "Do I think that Stangl could have done something to change things at Treblinka?" he said. "No. Well, perhaps a little, the whipping post and all that; but, on the other hand, if he had, then Franz would have told Wirth, and he would just have countermanded it. So what was the use?"

"What was the worst place in the camp for you?" I asked Stangl.

"The undressing barracks," he said at once. "I avoided it from my innermost being; I couldn't confront them; I couldn't lie to them; I avoided at any price talking to those who were about to die: I couldn't stand it."

It became clear that as soon as the people were in the undressing barracks – that is, as soon as they were naked – they were no longer human beings for him. What he was "avoiding at any price" was witnessing the transition. And when he cited instances of human relations with prisoners, it was never with any of those who were about to die.

"But were there never moments when this wall you built around yourself was breached? When the sight of a beautiful child perhaps, or a girl, brought you up against the knowledge that these were human beings?"

"There was a beautiful red-blonde girl," he said. "She usually worked in the clinic but when one of the maids in our living quarters was ill, she replaced her for a time . . . It was just around the time when I had put up new barracks with single rooms for quite a few of the work-Jews," he said (a claim confirmed by Suchomel but put in doubt by Richard Glazar who says that only just before the revolt were two couples, both stooges for the ss, given single rooms).

"This girl – I knew one of the Kapos was her boy friend . . . one always knew about things like that. . . ."

"What nationality was she?"

"Polish, I think. But she spoke German well. She was a – you know – a well-educated girl. Well, she came to my office that day to dust or something. I suppose I thought to myself, 'What a pretty girl she is and now she can have some privacy with her boy friend.' So I asked her – just to say something nice, you know – 'Have you chosen a room for yourself yet?' I remember she stopped dusting and stood very still looking at me. And then she said, very quietly you know, 'Why do you ask?' "

His tone of voice even now reflected the astonishment he felt twenty-nine years ago when this young girl responded to him not as a slave to her master, but as a free human being to a man she rejected. Not only that; she responded as to a social inferior, and the wording and tone of his reply confirm that he was immediately aware of this. "I said, 'Why shouldn't I ask? I can ask, can't I?' And again she just stood there, very straight, not moving, just looking right at me. And then she said, 'Can I go?' And I said, 'Yes, of course.' She went. I felt so ashamed. I realized she thought I'd asked because – well, you know, because I wanted her myself. I so admired her for facing up to me, for saying 'Can I go?' I felt ashamed for days because of the way she had misunderstood."

"Do you know what happened to her?" I asked this question each time he spoke of any of the prisoners in individual terms. But each time the answer was precisely the same, in the same tone of detachment, with the same politely aloof expression in his face.

"I don't know."

In this case I persisted. *"But here was a girl who had enormously impressed you. Didn't you ever want to find out what happened to her?"*

He looked uncomfortable. "I heard something about her having been transferred to the *Totenlager*." (The life expectancy of prisoners working in that part of the camp rarely exceeded two months.)

"How did that happen?"

"I am not really sure. You see, when our usual maid returned – I was on leave at that time – this girl went back to her work at the clinic. The doctor – I can't remember his name – had a run-in with Kurt Franz. It was never very clear what had happened. But the doctor killed himself – he took poison. And the girl was there when this happened and Franz sent her up to the *Totenlager*."

Later, when I tried to identify the girl Stangl had talked about, no one could say for certain who she was.

"Why don't you ask Otto Horn?" said Gustav Münzberger. "He was always larking about with the girls in the laundry in Camp II."

"Yes, I sometimes went into the laundry and talked to the girls," said Horn. "But I don't know of any red-blonde girl who was sent up to the upper camp by Franz. There was one amongst the six in the laundry who had red hair. But I don't know what her name was. All the girls spoke German. What did they do when they weren't working? I don't know. They had their own barracks and were locked in there at night. Later on, I sometimes let them out on a Sunday to go for a walk in the wood behind the camp; it was fenced in, you know. . . ."

But the last word, as often, was Suchomel's, for whom recalling the details of Treblinka has become something of a passion.

"The only red-blonde was Tchechia who had been Kapo Rakowski's girl friend," he said, "a very proud and courageous girl. It would certainly have been her who would have said no to Stangl. But she was never sent up to the *Totenlager*. Otherwise, there was Sabina – but she was sent 'up' much earlier on, by Küttner, not by Franz – after her affair with Kapo Kuba; it can't have been her. And it can't have been Irka, the doctor's assistant; she was dark. No, it was Tchechia Mandel from Lemberg. But she never worked at the clinic; she always worked in the kitchen. . . ."

It has been generally agreed that although Stangl drank heavily at Treblinka, women, other than his wife, played no part in his life. Therefore, although we will never know for sure who this exceptionally brave and proud young girl was, it is probable, and corresponds with the overall impression he gave me, that his description of his impulsive attempt to communicate with her was accurate.

"Couldn't you have ordered her to be brought back?" I asked him. He shook his head. "No."

I spent a good deal of time investigating this sequence of events, interesting for several reasons but particularly as this was the first instance of Stangl reacting personally or emotionally to any of the Treblinka inmates. As often happened, each of the people I questioned gave a different version of what happened.

The circumstances surrounding the death of the doctor, Dr Choronzycki, sadly misrepresented in at least one much-discussed book on Treblinka, are in general agreed on by all those who were in Treblinka at the time – prisoners or guards – though there is a curious difference of opinion concerning Dr Choronzycki's medical speciality (not to speak of the spelling of his name). Stangl told me that this physician had been a "famous Warsaw internist". In Steiner's book *Treblinka* Dr Choronzycki is described as "the doctor of the Germans". Suchomel says: "Of course, I remember him well; he was a nose and throat specialist. I talked with him many times; my son was physically handicapped you know, and Dr Choronzycki often advised me about him. He was a converted Jew, you know. He wore a golden necklace with a cross. He said his Polish colleagues in the hospital in Warsaw had given him away. . . ." Richard Glazar says: "Choronzycki was a dentist, or at least that is what he claimed to be in Treblinka. That is why the ss picked him out of the transport for their own so-called ss *Revierstube*. This ss dental clinic was almost exactly opposite the room of the gold-Jews. The money for the revolt was to go from one of the gold-Jews via Choronzycki. . . ."

All the survivors I spoke to agreed on the essential part the doctor was playing in the preparations for the revolt. But Suchomel said, "Dr Choronzycki had nothing to do with the revolt. That was just invention, like the book by Jean-François Steiner."

On the other hand, Suchomel agrees that Kurt Franz surprised the doctor in possession of gold, and that after the doctor attacked Franz with a surgical knife (surely an extraordinary act of courage) and the latter fled out of the window, he had time to take poison before being apprehended.

"Stangl was away," Suchomel says. "Franz sent for me and said, 'Get that woman doctor on the double.' " The woman doctor, Dr Choronzycki's assistant, was Dr Irena (Irka) Lewkowski.

"I ran," said Suchomel. "The old bitch pretended she couldn't walk quickly. Anyway, when we got there, the doctor's eyes were still open – he was still alive – she pumped his stomach out. Then Franz told me to assemble all the gold-Jews. The doctor could no longer speak. Franz was wild. . . ."

"Kurt Franz kept beating him with his whip even when Choronzycki was quite obviously dead," said Glazar. "He had him dragged to the *Lazarett* – all the gold-Jews had been brought there; he told them they'd be shot, one after the other, unless they told where the doctor got the gold. I remember, Willie Fürst was there – he was a hotel owner from Slovakia; and little Edek, the accordion player – they'd picked him up too. After a while Edek – I was told – cried and begged the others to tell what they knew. 'I don't want to die,' he is supposed to have cried. Well, none of them told anything – the doctor was dead – and in the end Franz let them all go; he knew perfectly that they were the most valuable specialists they had, more important to them than anyone else in the camp."

"I didn't actually hear the end," said Suchomel. "I went out.

Though before leaving the *Lazarett* I called out in Czech telling the gold-Jews that Franz was faking, he wasn't going to kill them, and for them not to tell. . . ."

"I have never heard *anything* about Suchomel calling out something like that to the gold-Jews," said Glazar.

"I *did* have contact with the work-Jews," Stangl said. "You know, quite friendly relations. You asked me a while ago whether there was anything I enjoyed. Beyond my specific assignment, that's what I enjoyed; human relations. Especially with people like Singer and Blau. They were both Viennese: I always tried to give as many jobs as possible to Vienna Jews. It made for a lot of talk at the time, I know. But after all, I *was* Austrian. . . . Singer I had made the chief of the *Totenjuden*; I saw a lot of him. I think he was a dentist in Vienna. Or perhaps an engineer," he reflected. "He was killed during the revolt; it started in the upper camp you know." (He was wrong about Singer, who was a German, not a Viennese, and a businessman, not a dentist; and also about the revolt, which started in the lower camp.)

"Blau was the one I talked to most; he and his wife. No, I don't know what his profession had been; business I think. I'd made him the cook in the lower camp. He knew I'd help whenever I could.

"There was one day when he knocked at the door of my office about mid-morning and stood to attention and asked permission to speak to me. He looked very worried. I said, 'Of course, Blau, come on in. What's worrying you?' He said it was his eighty-year-old father; he'd arrived on that morning's transport. Was there anything I could do. I said, 'Really, Blau, you must understand, it's impossible. A man of eighty. . . .' He said quickly that yes, he understood, of course. But could he ask me for permission to take his father to the *Lazarett* rather than the gas chambers. And could he take his father first to the kitchen and give him a meal. I said, 'You go and do what you think best, Blau. Officially I don't know anything, but unofficially you can tell the Kapo I said it was all right.' In the afternoon, when I came back to my office, he was waiting for me. He had tears in his eyes. He stood to attention and said, 'Herr Hauptsturmführer, I want to thank you. I gave my father a meal. And I've just taken him to the *Lazarett* – it's all over. Thank you very much.' I said, 'Well, Blau, there's no need to thank me, but of course if you *want* to thank me, you may.'"

"*What happened to Blau and his wife?*"

That same vagueness – "I don't know."

This story and the way it was told represented to me the starkest example of a corrupted personality I had ever encountered and came very near to making me stop these conversations. I broke off early that lunchtime and went to sit for nearly two hours in a pub across the street, wrestling with the most intense *malaise* I'd ever felt at the thought of listening further to these disclosures.

I think the reason I finally did return to the little room in the prison was because I came to realize – perhaps as a result of the intensity of my own reaction – that for a man whose view was so distorted that he *could* tell that story in that way, the relatively simple terms "guilt" or "innocence", "good" or "bad" no longer applied; what was important was that he had found in himself the need – or strength – to speak. Even as I acknowledged my own apprehension at continuing with these talks, I also knew for certain, at that moment, that if I did he would end by telling me the truth.

All the Treblinka survivors I talked to affirmed – with the fatalistic lack of vehemence of those who have come to terms with the inevitability of human failings in everyone, themselves included – that "Blau" was an informer. But it was Suchomel, in his chosen role of an objective observer, who put this into cogent words.

"Oh, Blau," he said. "He was *Oberkapo* at first. You see, he had known Stangl in Austria; he told me himself. No, I don't think he was lying. Stangl made no secret of having known him previously. He was Austrian, but by origin I think Polish and I think he had been sent from Vienna to a Polish ghetto. He told me about his arrival in Treblinka; apparently he got off the train and saw Stangl standing there. He said, 'I threw my arms around him.' In Austria he had been a cattle- or horse-trader. He said Stangl had said to him, 'Listen, I am going to appoint you Chief Kapo; you help me now and I'll see that you survive this. And after the war I'll get you a farm in Poland.' That's how Blau became *Oberkapo*. When he arrived he had a big stomach – he was a big fat man; in two weeks he had shrunk by half. Yes, he was hated, of course he was; he certainly 'collaborated', so naturally they feared and hated him. He didn't just carry an ordinary whip – he had one of the long ones and he'd stand there swinging it and shouting in his broad Viennese, 'You pigs, you shit sows, get on with it, let's see how quick you can learn to be.' He behaved as if he wanted to outdo the worst of the Ukrainians. I suppose he did it to survive; who am *I* to accuse or blame him? He stayed Kapo till early spring, I think. Then he asked Stangl to relieve him on medical grounds. He complained of heart flutters or something and Stangl made him and his wife cooks for the Jews. Old Frau Blau, she was a good cook; she cooked many a meal for me. I hated the food in our mess, so quite often she'd cook me something special. After the revolt, they were amongst the hundred or so who were left over, and who were evacuated to Sobibor – I went there too.

"One day I heard they were going to shoot these hundred the next day. So I went to see old Blau and warned him. I just asked him whether he had some poison and he understood. He and his wife took poison and so did a doctor and his wife who had been in this group; they had helped to put out the fire in the Ukrainian barracks after the revolt. Well, they too died that day. It was better that way than being shot."

"In the midst of all the horror that surrounded you," I said to Stangl the afternoon of the day he told me the story about Blau, *"and of which you were so aware that you drank yourself to sleep each night, what kept you going? What was there for you to hold on to?"*

"I don't know. Perhaps my wife. My love for my wife?"

"How often did you see her?"

"After that first time in Poland they let me go on leave quite regularly – every three or four months."

"Did you feel close to your wife – when so much had to remain hidden, remain unsaid between you?"

"The little time we had together, we usually talked about the children and ordinary everyday things. But it is true, things changed between us after that time when Ludwig told her about Sobibor. There was tension. And I knew she was terribly worried about me. . . ."

"The first time I saw Paul again after Sobibor," said Frau Stangl, "was five months later when he came home for Christmas. It was so wonderful to see him, and at Christmas too. In Austria, at home, what with Christmas and everything, what I knew was happening in Poland seemed utterly unreal. I asked about Treblinka of course, but he said he was only responsible for the valuables, construction and discipline. No, he didn't pretend then that it wasn't the same sort of place as Sobibor, but he said that he was doing everything he could to get out. He stayed home for eight or ten days, but he'd only been there a couple of days when he said he'd run over and see Fräulein Hintersteiner [in Linz] who had been a secretary at Hartheim and who afterwards worked for a man called Kaufmann who went out to the Crimea as police chief. Paul wanted her to help him get a transfer to the Crimea. When he came back from seeing her, he was very happy and said it was all right – all he had to do now was wait to be notified of the transfer. So we had a good Christmas after all: I can still see his happy, relieved face. . . ."

9

"THINGS CHANGED very much towards the middle of January," said Richard Glazar. "That was the beginning of phase three: fewer and fewer transports; less food and of course no new clothes. This was when the plans for the uprising were being worked on very intensely. And then, in the very beginning of March 1943, real catastrophe struck us.

"Küttner smelled something – there is no other way of putting it. He sensed that something was going on, and with perfect instinct he picked on the one person who was almost irreplaceable for us: Zhelo Bloch, the revolt committee's military expert. What Küttner took as a pretext was that some men's coats had disappeared, and Zhelo was in charge of them. He came to our barracks and raged; two men were shot on the spot, several were beaten. And Zhelo was sent up to Camp II.

"It was the most terrible blow to our morale, an anti-climax which is indescribable now. It wasn't only, you see, that he was so necessary, in a planning sense; it was that he was loved. Contrary perhaps to some of us, he was very much one of the people. Don't misunderstand me, I only mean that, of all of us, he was the one person who could talk to anybody, give anybody a sense of faith in himself and his capacities; he was a born leader, of the best kind.

"The evening he went was the end of hope for us – for a long time. I remember that night so clearly; it was the one time in all those months that we nearly lost control; that we gave way to emotion. It could have been the end for us.

"Robert Altschuh cried like a child. Of course, he had been closest to Zhelo; they needed each other. Zhelo was essential to Robert because he was a *doer*, but Robert was just as essential to Zhelo because he was an intellectual; they complemented and reassured each other. Zhelo had relied utterly on Robert intellectually. It was Robert who was the 'psychological' planner; who would explain the Nazis' psychology to us; he who advised us when to lie low and when to make ourselves noticed. He had an unfailing instinct for what was the right approach, and when. On the other hand, he was physically frail, and Zhelo of course was very strong. Without Zhelo's physical strength, Robert collapsed. Hans Freund, too, despite his closeness to Rudi Masarek, somehow couldn't recover from the psychological blow of Zhelo's going. It took some weeks before Rudi came into his own as a leader – by that time much of Hans's effectiveness had gone." ("Freund and Altschuh," he was to write later, "were still alive at the time of the revolt. But in all probability they died in the course of it.")*

"The evening of the day Zhelo was sent up to Camp II, I remember we were lying on our bunks; it was not quite dark. It was very very quiet. And suddenly Hans Freund said, 'We aren't human beings any more. . . .' It was something we had ceased to – or never did – think about. Certainly we had never talked about it; regret for the loss of one's sensitivity and compassion was something one just couldn't afford, just as one couldn't afford remembering those we had loved. But that night was different. . . .

" 'I can only think of my wife and boy,' said Hans, who had never, with a word, spoken of his young wife and small boy from the day he arrived. 'I never felt anything that first night after we had come. There they were – on the other side of the wall – dead, but I felt nothing. Only the next morning, my brain and stomach began to burn, like acid; I remember hearing about people who could feel everything inside but couldn't move; that was what I felt. My little boy had curly hair and soft skin – soft on his cheeks like on his bottom – that same smooth soft skin. When we got off the

---

* Although the lists of survivors of Treblinka and Sobibor are believed to be complete, it is impossible to place accurately the circumstances of the deaths of those who perished during or after the revolts.

train, he said he was cold, and I said to his mother, "I hope he won't catch a cold." A cold. When they separated us he waved to me. . . .' "

During the many many hours Richard and I talked, he never faltered; this was the only time. It was late at night, his family had gone to bed; his house is so deep in the country, there wasn't a sound except the occasional shuffle or wheezing from a cow in a nearby field. We sat in his living room which was dark except for a lamp on his desk. He hid his face in his hands for long minutes. I poured some coffee his wife had made before she went to bed. We drank it without talking. "Did you see this?" he asked then after a while, pointing to something behind me. I turned around. In a cabinet, on a shelf by itself, a beautiful small Bristol-blue glass jar. "How lovely," I said. He shook his head, stood up, walked over, picked it up and handed it to me. "What do you think it is?" There was half an inch or so of something in the bottom of the jar. I didn't know. "Earth," he said. "Treblinka earth."

"Things went from bad to worse that month of March," he went on. "There were no transports – in February just a few, remnants from here and there, then a few hundred gypsies – *they* were really poor; they brought nothing. In the storehouses everything had been packed up and shipped – we had never before seen all the space because it had always been so full. And suddenly everything – clothes, watches, spectacles, shoes, walking-sticks, cooking-pots, linen, not to speak of food – everything went, and one day there was nothing left. You can't imagine what we felt when there was nothing there. You see, the *things* were our justification for being alive. If there were no *things* to administer, why would they let us stay alive? On top of that we were, for the first time, hungry. We were eating the camp food now, and it was terrible and, of course, totally inadequate [300 grammes of coarse black bread and one plate of thin soup a day]. In the six weeks of almost no transports, all of us had lost an incredible amount of weight and energy. And many had already succumbed to all kinds of illness -- especially typhus. It was the strain of anxiety which increased with every day, the lack of food, and the constant fear of the Germans who appeared to us to be getting as panic-stricken as we were.

"It was just about when we had reached the lowest ebb in our morale that, one day towards the end of March, Kurt Franz walked into our barracks, a wide grin on his face. 'As of tomorrow,' he said, 'transports will be rolling in again.' And do you know what we did? We shouted, 'Hurrah, hurrah.' It seems impossible now. Every time I think of it I die a small death; but it's the truth. That is what we did; that is where we had got to. And sure enough, the next morning they arrived. We had spent all of the preceding evening in an excited, expectant mood; it meant life – you see, don't you? – safety and life. The fact that it was their death, whoever they were, which meant our life, was no longer relevant; we had been through this over and over and over. The main question in our minds was, where were they from? Would they be rich or poor? Would there be food or not?

"That morning, all of us stood around everywhere, waiting. The ss did too; for once they didn't care whether we worked or not. Everybody was discussing where they would be from; if only it were from somewhere rich like Holland.

"When the first train pulled in, we were looking out through the cracks in the wall of our barrack, and when they got out, David Bart called to one of the Blue Command, 'Where are they from?' and he answered, 'The Balkans.' I remember them getting off the train, and I remember Hans Freund saying, 'Ah yes, you can see they are rich. But they won't burn well, they are too fat.' This was a very, very special transport of rich Bulgarians who had lived in Salonika – 24,000 of them. They had already spent some time in a camp together; they were organized and disciplined, and they had equipped themselves with a special supply-car for the long journey. When the Blue Command opened those doors, we nearly fainted at the sight of huge pieces of meat, thousands of tins with vegetables, fats and fish, jars of fruit and jams, and cakes – the black earth of the ramp was yellow and white with cakes. Later, after the Bulgarians had been taken away, the Ukrainians fought us for the food; we managed 'accidentally-on-purpose' to drop some of the big wooden chests in which the jams were packed. They burst open, the Ukrainians beat us with their horrible whips, and we bled into the jam. But that was later; oh, the ss were very, very careful with this transport; if the Bulgarians had had the slightest idea what awaited them, they wouldn't have stood still for it. It would have been a bloodbath. But they hadn't a clue; even then, in March, almost April, 1943 – with nearly a million already killed in

Treblinka [so Richard thought, and Zabecki agreed], three million or so by then in all the extermination and other camps in Poland – they were as full of illusions as we Czechs had been six months before. They still didn't know. The mind just boggles – with all the hundreds, the thousands of people who by then knew – how could they not have known? Marvellous-looking people they were; beautiful women, lovely children; stocky and strong-looking men; marvellous specimens. It took three days to kill them all. And ten days later we had processed all their belongings. Imagine, at fifty kilograms a person – that's what each was 'allowed' to bring for this 'resettlement' – there were 720,000 kilograms of *things*; incredible, how the machine proved itself in those ten days.

"This is something, you know, the world has never understood; how perfect the machine was. It was only lack of transport because of the Germans' war requirements that prevented them from dealing with far vaster numbers than they did; Treblinka alone could have dealt with the 6,000,000 Jews and more besides. Given adequate rail transport, the German extermination camps in Poland could have killed all the Poles, Russians and other East Europeans the Nazis planned eventually to kill."

10

IN APRIL–MAY 1943 a new wave of transports began which would continue throughout the summer. Some brought survivors of the desperate rebellion of the Warsaw ghetto. Others were from the Russian and Polish ghettos which were being cleared of the remnants of their populations as the Germans began the long retreat from Stalingrad. Others came from Holland, from Vienna, and even from Germany.

The threat of "practical measures" announced by the Allies in their combined statement of December 17, 1942, had turned out as time went by to mean not rescue projects but the pursuit of Allied victory. This, both the British and the American governments had become persuaded, was the only real solution to the catastrophe of the Jews in Europe. In retrospect it can, of course, be appreciated that the magnitude of the events seemed at the time to defy any large-scale solution; yet it is impossible not to think that there were things which could have been done if the will had existed more generally, up to the highest level.

In America, Britain, Switzerland, Sweden and some of the Latin American countries there were certainly individuals, and some newspapers, who tried their utmost to pressurize or to inspire governments into action; but for reasons outside the scope of this book they were unable to fire a sufficiently strong general will.

To take first some cases where this will did, in particular instances, exist. Early in 1943, when the Germans had ordered that the 25,000 Jews of Sofia be deported to Poland, one man – Monsignor Angelo Roncalli, Apostolic Delegate to Turkey, later Pope John XXIII – acted without thought of political expediency or of what the Nazis might do. "When Monsignor Roncalli found out about this," said Luigi Brescani, a confidential servant of Roncalli's, "he wrote immediately a personal letter to King Boris. I had never before seen Monsignor Roncalli so disturbed. Before I carried this missive to a certain person able to put it personally into the hands of King Boris, Monsignor Roncalli read it to me. Even though calm and gentle as St Francis de Sales come to life, he did not spare himself from saying that King Boris should on no account agree to that dishonourable action ... threatening him among other things with the punishment of God."*

As we know from Richard Glazar's story, 24,000 Bulgarians – those who had been in Salonika – did die in Treblinka in the spring of 1943; but there can be little doubt that the 25,000 Jews of Sofia were saved by the intervention of the future Pope and the courage of a king.

There is also the action taken by the Danish underground when, with the official sanction of the Swedish Minister for Foreign Affairs, Christian Günther, they spirited 7,000 people (seven-eighths of the country's Jews) from Denmark to Sweden, where they lived safely till the end of the war. By that time Sweden had already admitted approximately 35,000 Jewish refugees; and after the war the Swedish government waived the repayment of a thirty-million kroner loan which they had made to Denmark and Norway for the support of their Jewish co-citizens in Sweden.

Later, in 1944, there were to be other successes. Ira Hirschmann, President Roosevelt's appointee on the War Refugee Board (finally formed in January 1944) managed to persuade the

* Quoted from *While Six Million Died*, Arthur D. Morse.

Rumanians that the war was lost and that it was in their interest to stop the Germans from killing those who remained of the 185,000 Rumanian Jews. In March 48,000 people were returned to their homes.

And in June 1944, after hundreds of thousands had been deported from Hungary, there was the action of the heroic Swede, Raoul Wallenberg, who went to Budapest with stacks of so-called "protective Swedish passports" and issued them to anyone who could provide any semblance of a family or business connection with Sweden. Moreover he persuaded the Hungarian authorities to lease him apartment houses in Budapest which were then put under the protection of the Swedish embassy and where these people were housed. This crash programme is said to have saved some ten thousand people. (By this time, of course, the situation had changed somewhat in that Himmler, aware that the war was lost, had begun to co-operate with certain Jewish agencies. In addition to those saved by Wallenberg's initiative, and others who were hidden by non-Jewish compatriots, many with the connivance of German officials, a further 20,000 were taken out of Hungary, some to a "tolerable" camp in Vienna and some to Switzerland.)

But for 1942–3 the figures tell their own story. It was all but impossible to escape, certainly from anywhere in Eastern Europe. The hope of both the Western and the Eastern Jews was focused chiefly on America – traditional haven of the oppressed – and Great Britain, because of Palestine. But even if these countries had opened their borders – and although this step was urged by many liberals in both countries, there was no question of either government's agreeing to it – a refugee's first step had to be an attempt to escape to one of the neutral countries: Spain, Portugal, Sweden or Switzerland.

In November 1942 it was announced over the Swiss radio that 14,000 refugees had managed to make their way into Switzerland.* In August 1942 the Swiss government had invoked an emergency law which had been passed in October 1939, under which anyone crossing the frontier illegally was to be expelled. "About 100,000 people," said Councillor von Steiger, Minister of Justice at the time, "were trying to escape to Switzerland from France, sometimes a hundred a day." The traditional right to sanctuary, he said,

* According to *Encyclopedia Judaica 1972*, page 907, 11,000 Jewish refugees entered Switzerland between 1942 and 1944.

was not a right in the juridical sense. The mass entry of refugees represented a danger to the security of the State. To which a pastor in Basle replied: "If these people clamouring for admission were politically oppressed, prisoners of war or deserters they would and could be accommodated. It is the fact that they are Jews that excludes them from receiving the traditional sanctuary of our country."

From 1939 to 1941 30,000 European Jews reached the United States by way of Italy, Spain and Portugal. In 1940 4,400 Polish Jews escaped from Lithuania to Japan, the United States and – a few hundred of them – Palestine. Between 1940 and 1944 from 31,000 to 41,000 Jews escaped from France to Spain and Portugal. In 1942 a number of Polish Jews managed to leave the USSR with the Polish Anders Army, including 850 children, mostly orphans. These children were admitted into Palestine in 1943.

In May 1939 a British White Paper on Palestine had restricted Jewish immigration to 75,000 over the next five years. From September 1939 to the spring of 1941 about 12,000 were, in fact, brought in illegally. Immigration to Palestine in late 1942 and 1943 was limited to 350 Jews from Europe. One of the blackest memories for many of the people in Britain who were struggling to help the Jews was the government's refusal in January 1942 to admit to Palestine 769 refugees without British permits who had come from Rumania on the freighter *Struma*. This vessel, which was not seaworthy, was towed out to sea by the Turks on February 24, and sank with the loss of all on board: 70 children, 269 women and 428 men.

On April 19, 1943, began the British-US conference on refugees, in Bermuda. It ended on April 30 and was described by Myron Taylor in a memorandum to Cordell Hull as "wholly ineffective [as] we knew it would be". On May 19 a debate on refugee problems in the British House of Commons laid bare both the despair of concerned individuals and the position taken by the government.

Eleanor F. Rathbone, MP for the English universities, who had recently produced a heartrending pamphlet entitled *Rescue the Perishing*, advocated passionately a twelve-point programme for immediate rescue measures. These included the supply of blocks of unnamed visas to British consuls in neutral European countries; the offer of guarantees and financial aid to neutral countries, to encourage them to admit more refugees; the provision of transport facilities; admission to Palestine by cancelling the conditions set out in the White Paper of May 1939; pressure on German satellites and appeals to the people of enemy and enemy-occupied countries; the examination of the possibility of exchanging civilian internees with Axis sympathies for Jewish and other potential victims of the Nazis; and the setting up of refugee camps in distant places. Point Twelve was the adoption of the principle that, whatever other nations might do or leave undone, "the British contribution to the work of rescue should be the speediest and most generous possible without delaying victory."

It was to this last point that the government mainly addressed itself in its reply, given by Mr Peake, Under-Secretary for the Home Department, and by Anthony Eden, Secretary of State for Foreign Affairs. In the prevailing circumstances, they said, nothing but the most minimal rescue attempts was possible. Almost everything the government had tried – including saving a number of children for whom visas to Palestine were available – had failed as a result of German determination to block such attempts. The only solution – the one thing to be aimed for – was military victory by the Allies.

A week before that day the Swedish government had agreed to ask Germany to release 20,000 Jewish children who would be cared for in Sweden until the end of the war, provided the United States and Great Britain agreed to share the cost of their food and medical supplies, and would place them in Palestine or some other haven when the war was over. The British Foreign Office indicated its approval of this imaginative proposal on May 19, the day of the above-mentioned debate, and transmitted it to the State Department.

Almost precisely the same argument as had taken place in the House of Commons that day, had raged in America for months. Here too the desperate requests of innumerable public figures, Christians and Jews, left unmoved the State Department which controlled the issuing of life-saving visas. For a variety of political and emotional reasons, the American government – perhaps even more than the British – was wary of seeming to fight "a war for the Jews". In 1940, when France fell and Britain stood alone, it took the State Department only eight days, from July 6 to July 14, to decide to admit 10,000 English children to the US on visitors' visas, waiving all regulations. The Swedish proposal, on the other hand, received no reply from Washington for five months. Then, on

October 11, the State Department suggested that the project should not be limited to Jewish children, and that it should be channelled through the Intergovernmental Committee on Refugees (a thoroughly ineffectual body). The British hastily revamped the project to include some Norwegian children. But by the time the changed plan reached the Swedes in January 1944, Sweden had more or less burnt its boats with Germany by welcoming many Danes and Norwegians, and the plan was dropped.

It is, of course, questionable whether the Germans would have entertained such a project – they had already refused to allow Norwegian children into Sweden. But Sweden's position was undeniably "special" ("That's where they got their steel from," Stangl was to say); it is unlikely that as many as 20,000 children would have been let go, and probably none from the East. But at least some might have been saved, from some of the Western countries. As it was, in the eight months it took to kill this plan, many more than 20,000 children had been slaughtered in Treblinka and elsewhere.

On May 12, 1943, in London, Smul Zygielbojm had committed suicide in protest. "By my death," he wrote in a farewell note addressed to the President and Prime Minister of the Polish government in exile, "I wish to make my final protest against the passivity with which the world is looking on and permitting the extermination of the Jewish people."

II

"THAT APRIL," said Richard Glazar, "the main preoccupation of the SS was to keep the camp going, to keep us occupied, to justify their own positions there. This is when, with again almost no transports arriving, Stangl ordered the camp 'street' to be built, new fences to be put up, the forest cleared, a zoo installed, the famous railway station made to look totally genuine; with a false clock, everything painted in beautiful, garishly bright colours; the 'petrol station', again with flowers around it; wooden benches dotting the landscape like a luxury spa – it was not to be believed. And during all those weeks, the preparations for the uprising continued, the military part now firmly in Rudi Masarek's hands.

In the course of that month there was the business with Dr Choronzycki, a very popular man; another blow when he died. . . . But, there were other doctors. . . ."

It was also in the spring that a new method was evolved for the burning of the dead. Two enormous iron racks were constructed (the second one only after the first had proved itself efficient). "They sent us out into the countryside to forage for disused rails," said Glazar. These racks, called "the roasts", each held several hundred stacked-up bodies, and were used from then on not only for the incoming transports, but also to burn thousands of partly decomposed corpses dug up by excavators and either thrown into "the roasts" by the machine or carried on stretchers by two men at the double. "We always had to run," said one of the very few survivors of this death-camp detail, in trial evidence in Germany (and also in Poland), "and we had to be careful never to carry just one adult corpse, but always to add a couple of children – otherwise it would have looked as though we were shirking."

In the upper camp – the death-camp – there was no whipping-post or roll-call, but equally there was no possibility of stealing food to supplement the camp rations, and the least infringement of the rules meant being shot on the spot. And the rules became ever more stringent as the SS, with the inexorable advance of the Russians, became increasingly desperate to hide the evidence of the slaughter.

"In May," said Richard Glazar, "Karel and I were transferred to a special 'camouflage' unit: our job was to bring in huge branches from the forest to camouflage the new fences. Our foreman was Heinrich Kleinmann, a former Czech civil servant – a quiet, polite, bespectacled man, a curious choice of foreman for our tough little gang of dare-devils.

"We were called the 'smugglers' because, being the only people who were ever allowed out of the camp, we made full use of our many opportunities to smuggle things in. As weeks went by and transports were a rarity, it was increasingly important to bring in food for those who were particularly essential to us, some of whom were ill and dangerously weak. Of course, we had nearly unlimited supplies of money; the Ukrainians we paid and paid and paid. And the Poles – well, in May 1943 the going rate for two white rolls, three-quarters of an ounce of sausage and two-thirds of a litre of vodka was between ten and twenty dollars – often more.

"We knew that Zhelo was still alive, because some time in the late spring, one of the SS, a man called Poltzinger who worked up at Camp II, came to our shop and asked which were 'Karel and Richard', and when we said it was us, he said he'd brought a message from Zhelo: he was OK and would we like to send a message back to him. We always thought the SS up there were better than ours, probably because, after all, they had to live through the same unspeakable horrors as the slaves up there. If our latrines smelled pretty bad, this was nothing by comparison to the ever-present sweetly sick smell of the burnings. If we found it hard to bear it down where we were – imagine what it was like for the people who lived up there. . . ."

12

AS IT happened, two of the former SS men I met had worked "up there": Otto Horn, in charge of the incineration of the bodies, and Gustav Münzberger, in charge of the gas chambers. "Münzberger?" said Otto Horn (who had also testified to this effect at the Treblinka trial in 1965). "One of his jobs was to stand at the door to the gas chambers and drive them in. He had a whip of course. He did that, day after day. He was drunk most of the time. What else could he do? Could he have got out of that job? I don't know. I think finally he no longer cared – he drank."

Oberammergau, famous for its passion-play festival every ten years, lies two hours south of Munich, deep in a lovely valley surrounded by pine-clad hills and friendly rather than forbidding mountains. Unterammergau, one station – four minutes – earlier on the single-track railway line, is tiny by comparison: the station, a road, two streets, a general store, an inn, and perhaps fifty houses, all of them brilliantly white, with brilliantly green or striped shutters, window-boxes, scrubbed children who smile and say "*Grüss Gott*", and the smell of tar, manure, meadows, pine trees and freshly cut timber.

Gustav Münzberger, sixty-eight when I met him in the spring of 1972, is a big man who often looks ten or fifteen years older. He sits at the kitchen table, his body slack, his head bowed. He is clean-shaven but looks stubbly; he is immaculately dressed, but looks as if he cannot button his own shirt.

Sentenced to twelve years in prison in 1965, he came out, with the usual remission for good behaviour, in July 1971. His son Horst – a master cabinet-maker – and Horst's wife, had meanwhile built up a workshop in Unterammergau and divided their house into two self-contained flats, downstairs for themselves and their three children, upstairs a kitchen/living room, bedroom and bathroom for Horst's parents.

"What else could we do?" said Horst. "They are my parents; he is my father." His wife's father, an old socialist, really *was* a known anti-Nazi during the Third Reich and the family had a rough time of it. Even so she agrees. "We had to have them. There was no other way."

The Münzbergers came originally from a town in the Sudetenland, the border of Saxony.

"Where we lived in 1938," said Horst's mother, "we knew nothing, we heard nothing about politics." She is a big woman, with a flowered dress, an apron, and big bare arms. "Of course, we were Germans in Czechoslovakia, that's true. But no, we never heard any of their propaganda. My husband – he was just interested in the gym society, that's all."

"I don't like contradicting you, Mother," said Horst gently, "but young as I was, I remember that time. I remember on my way to music school when I was eight, I had to pass the synagogue. And I remember that, after the *Kristallnacht* it was destroyed. So we weren't all that untouched by their 'propaganda', were we?"

Later, when we were alone, Horst said thoughtfully: "At home, in the Sudetenland, my father was ... well ... a joiner, neither very good, nor bad – you know. But I can remember when he got that black ss uniform: that's when he began to be 'somebody' I suppose, rather than just anybody. And then, in Treblinka – it is inconceivable, isn't it, what he suddenly was: the scope, the power, the uniqueness, the difference between himself and all those others – imagine. ... No, it is unimaginable.

"I wish he would speak to you. For me it was like lightning when they came to arrest him. Oh, I had an idea that everything hadn't been as it should have been. And when he was arrested, of course, the wildest rumours went about. But I didn't know anything. I wish he had prepared me, talked to me, told me the truth. ... Yes,

I know now what he was accused of and sentenced for; I read the indictment. But I don't know it from *him*. Now I just wish, for his sake, that he could ease his mind by talking about it. . . ."

Münzberger, a non-commissioned officer in the SS, came to Treblinka after having served in the euthanasia institute at Schloss Sonnenstein in Pirna – also called *Die Sonne*.

"After he was called up," said Horst, "he often came on leave, very often. But never in uniform. I never saw him in uniform again – always in civvies. We had very good holidays, yes, we had it very good, I remember. Yes, I think people at home knew about him. I remember the father of a school friend saying to me once, 'You wait. Your father – we'll get him one day.' He was a Czech. At the time, of course, I didn't know what he meant, but I think he knew. But my mother didn't say anything. . . ."

"Well, I knew after a while what he was doing," said the old Frau Münzberger. "He wasn't supposed to say of course, but you know what women are. I probed and probed and finally he told me. It was awful of course, but what could *we* do?"

"My mother and I visited him in Pirna," said Horst. "There was a special building, with 'common rooms', you know, for the staff, where we saw him. I remember, there were a lot of Balts around in the grounds, women and children too."

"The Balts," said the old man as if he was only just coming to. "Oh, they were just *Umsiedler* [resettlers] – they had nothing to do with what was being done at Pirna. It was so big you see – they just used part of the grounds as a reception centre for these Baltic-Germans. Did I think what they were doing at Pirna wrong? I don't know," he said wearily. "Some of them, the people who were brought there were so . . . it was so dreadful – it really was a mercy for them to die. Did I try to get out of it? Away from Treblinka later? When they sent me to Treblinka there was some administrative mix-up I think, and they gave me two different postings you know, two different pieces of paper. So I went to Wirth when I got to Treblinka and showed them to him and said could I please request permission to go to the other posting. But he sent me packing in no uncertain terms. He said the posting to Treblinka was more important than anything else – it overrode any other orders.

"We up at the *Totenlager*," he said, "we didn't have any whipping-posts or anything like that. I was just glad every night when I could go down to my room and have peace. Oh yes, our quarters were down in the lower camp. What did I do at night?" He shrugged his shoulders and made the gesture of lifting a bottle to his lips. His wife smiled sympathetically. "I worked for years for the Steins," she volunteered. "Jews in our home town. And Gustav, he had many Jewish customers."

"Anyway, before the war a quarter of the population were Jews," he interposed.

"We had nothing against them," his wife continued. "In my school I sat cheek by jowl with I don't know how many Jewish girls. What did we know, what did we care? They went to the synagogue, we went to church, that's all. . . ."

Gustav Münzberger's face changes from moment to moment, from an old man's ever-present, ever-running tears, to resignation and to weariness. And then – as if by some sleight of hand – there is a sudden momentary glimpse of force, of what he may have been like in the past. This is physical, not moral or spiritual strength. He was, no doubt, a tall broad-shouldered man, with a fine head and blue eyes, the sort of man a woman like Horst's mother, in that small Sudetenland town, would have fallen in love with. But, even though there sat a man who by the very fact of still being alive sullied all he touched – he was a "small man", one of the proverbial cogs in the wheel.

"Did I have any personal contact – relationships you ask, with the people at Treblinka?" he said in his broad Bavarian-Sudeten accent and in a slightly quavering voice. "With those naked ones? How? Oh . . . you mean the work-Jews? No, they had their Kapos, *they* organized them. . . ."

"And then there were your Ukrainians, weren't there, didn't you say?" his wife prompted quickly.

"Yes, the Ukrainians too. *We* didn't have to do anything. There wasn't really anything for us to do. Yes, we just had to be there; that's right; that's all."

"When they informed us that he was to be released from prison," said his wife, "I said I'd take the train to Münster to get him. But Horst, he said, 'Stay home, get things ready for Father – I'll get him.' Without Horst, I don't know what we would have done. He has given us everything. Built us our rooms here, given his father work – that's what's keeping him going now – working. The nights are hard for him: no sleep before two or three, and even then, never without pills."

Horst Münzberger is thirty-eight but looks thirty. His wife, although they have three young children, the oldest – when I met them – eight, the youngest three, looks like a young girl. Their house, at the end of the road from the village, is a gem of traditional Bavarian craftsmanship, inside and out.

"I think", said Horst later, downstairs in their living room, "one can make someone weaker than he is, by telling him all the time he is weak and tired. That is what my mother does. I think my father is much stronger than he seems. You know, these tears he sheds, they are not all that new. I remember when I was a boy and he spanked me; he cried more than I did; he really did. I remember it well.

"Of course, he was always a very thorough man; thorough in his work and in his habits. Did they *select* people because of special qualities, or perhaps special vulnerabilities? I don't know. I wish I did. I can't really imagine that they chose them at random. In our village, for instance, they took two for this awful thing – my father and a neighbour. Two out of – I think there were twenty of that age and of the same status. Why just them? Why, too, did so many of the men who worked these terrible places come not from Germany proper, but from one of the annexed states – Austria, the Sudetenland, Ukrainians, Lithuanians?

"My father – I can quite imagine that he would have approached Treblinka with the same thoroughness with which he approached his carpentry at home: it was his principal quality as a craftsman."

The fact that many of these men were not from the *Altreich* was also emphasized by Dieter Allers, former administrative director of T4, who continues to insist that the men had not been deliberately picked for these jobs, that the majority of them had not been drafted into T4, but had volunteered. *His* purpose – conscious or unconscious – was to convey that it was these morally inferior semi-outsiders who competed for these assignments, not "real" Germans. I am inclined to take a different view. Although, at least as far as the original recruitment for the Euthanasia Programme was concerned, I think he may be telling the truth in claiming that many of the people who joined did so voluntarily, for the additional benefits and the chance of not having to go to the front; and although the number of Austrians who occupied leading positions in just this area of Third Reich policies cannot be ignored; nevertheless I believe that accepting so many "volunteers" from outside the *Altreich* was a deliberate part of the system. Psychologically, these were men who could be expected to feel less secure and therefore could be made to feel more dependent, more anxious to prove their new national allegiance. In a practical sense, therefore, they were more vulnerable to pressure. And when it came to the selection of the ninety-six ss who were to run the *Aktion Reinhard* in Poland, these men, I am convinced, were chosen very carefully from the ranks of the original four hundred T4 personnel, for specific qualities observed during their "apprenticeship" in the Euthanasia Programme. It is of considerable significance here that while the files of German army personnel in general, and most of the ss in particular, did survive the war, the files *(Kartei-Karten* as Dieter Allers described them) of these ninety-six men which were kept in the offices of T4, as well as other T4 files have disappeared.

Earlier I had asked Horst's father whether, when he was first ordered to report to T4 in Berlin, he too (like Stangl) had signed a paper renouncing the Church and stating that he was a *Gottgläubiger*. "No," he had replied at once.

Had they ever asked him to do that?

"No."

Supposing they *had* asked, and had said they'd shoot his family if he didn't, would he have signed?

"No," he persisted. "I wouldn't give up my faith."

"Gustl," his wife nudged him. "If they threatened your family? Your children?"

"I would have given up my faith," he said obediently.

"I don't want to say much," said Horst later, "but about this business of the Church: it's only here, in Unterammergau, that he went back to going to church. After he ... after he rejoined the Church."

"Rejoined?"

"There was a ceremony. After being a *Gottgläubiger* he was officially received back into the Church." (A priest was to tell me later that this was *not* an officially prescribed – or required – ceremony. "It would be at the discretion of the local priest," he said. "Ordinarily, all a Catholic who had become a *Gottgläubiger* would have to do, would be to go to confession, receive absolution

226

and then take communion. It is a matter of choice whether or not it is also made into a festive occasion.")

I asked Horst Münzberger and his wife whether they spent a lot of time with the old people? Did the grandparents have a lot of contact with the children? Was there tension, or did they all get on all right?

"All right?" Horst laughed bitterly. "How can it be all right? We manage, that's all, because we have to manage."

His wife nodded sadly. "What can we do? They are old."

"Of course there is tension; it is in us all the time," said Horst. "It is especially difficult for my wife."

"Do the old people have any money of their own?" I asked, and he shook his head.

"I can't say whether he ever had any money after Treblinka – I couldn't say yes or no. But certainly he had none at the time of the trial and afterwards. I even went to try to get some help for him. . . ."

"Help? From whom? Odessa?"*

"No, I don't know 'Odessa'. But somebody told me there was an organization who helped people like him, so I went to them – HIAG I think they were called."

"How did you get their address?"

"It was all very hush-hush. I was sent from one place to another – this one knew and that one too. Anyway, finally I got to this office and they asked all about my father. I asked them for money for my mother – you know, he was going to prison for twelve years; we hadn't got anywhere much yet with the business; we had so little money. So I thought perhaps they'd want to help look after my mother. But not at all. They said he had no right to their help. . . ."

As HIAG is the SS equivalent of the British Legion or of American veterans' organizations, an organization primarily designed to keep up contact with, and give assistance to, members of former SS *fighting units* (of whom there were many more than those who have become so familiar to the world through films and novels, as concentration camp personnel) it is a little puzzling why so much mystery should have been made of HIAG's whereabouts. They advertise their existence quite openly in the SS magazine *Der Freiwillige*, published by the Munin Verlag, in Osnabrück. It is true that this paper is obtained by subscription and is sent out

* The name of a possible Nazi escape network, much discussed in recent years.

under plain cover; but it is not by any means a clandestine publication. What is more understandable is that they refused Horst's request. They are very anxious to establish the SS, in retrospect, as a purely fighting unit and are therefore, no doubt, loth to contribute financial assistance to those members of the SS who they are most anxious to repudiate.

"But now it's not a question of money, of course," said Horst. "The business is doing well. It isn't that. And I am glad to let him work here – he does small simple things; it helps him. . . . Yes, I still love him – I suppose. I suppose loving one's father is like living – one just does. About what he has done . . . I could not even tell you – I could not find the words to tell you how terrible, how beyond everything terrible I think it is. And that it should be *my* father. . . ."

There was silence in the beautiful small sitting room full of beautifully made things – all made by Horst himself. Next door, in the big kitchen, the children played and laughed. They are very attractive with that gay and clear-voiced beauty of small German children.

"The worst of it," Horst continued, "is the children. You see, my wife and I, we know very well that one day, not long from now, Christian [the oldest boy] will ask us questions; he is eight now. When he is ten or so, they'll be getting modern history at school. I don't know how much that school teaches them – but they can't just not tell them about these horrors. And then – you know what villages are – some other child is bound to say to him, 'Yeah Christian, your grandpa was in this.' And he'll come home and say to us, 'What did Grandpa have to do with that?'

"That's what my wife and I wanted to talk to you about. That's what we wanted to ask: How shall I tell my son?"

13

"At the trial," I said to Stangl, *"it was said over and over that you had the reputation of being superb at your job. The prisoners called you a* Burgherr *'Napoleon'. When you appeared, they said, everyone, including your own staff, worked harder, faster. And, in fact, you received an official commendation as the 'best camp commander in*

Poland', didn't you? Would it not have been possible for you, in order to register some protest, if only to yourself, to do your work a little less 'superbly'?"

One couldn't help but remember the evidence at his trial given by three survivors who were described by the prosecutor, Herr Alfred Spiess, as "particularly unemotional, balanced and reliable". They affirmed that he was present at floggings and hangings, although he denied that he ever had been. Four of the witnesses, Glazar, Unger, Strawczynski and Samuel Rajzman, and five of the SS men, Rum, Matthes, Münzberger, Miete and Horn, confirmed that at least seven hangings took place at Treblinka during Stangl's tenure – several of them hanging men upside down – and that Stangl, if he did not attend them, as was claimed by some of the prisoners, must "at least" have known about these events, which were, of course, noted in the official camp reports – the logbooks. One of the survivors testified that he particularly remembered a hanging which took place in the presence of the Kommandant on May 8, "because that happened to be my birthday".

This question about his dedication to his work was one of the few during our meetings that made Stangl angry. "Everything I did out of my own free will," he answered sharply, "I had to do as well as I could. That is how I am."

Frau Stangl, with good reason, had very definite memories about the month of May 1943. "That's when I saw him again for the first time since Christmas," she said, "when he came on his way through from Cracow to Linz on an official trip; but he only stayed one night. It was the only time I saw him until July, so that was when we started our youngest, Isolde. She was an eight-month baby, born on January 5, 1944. Later, at the trial, a witness said Paul had attended an execution – a hanging – on May 8; he said he remembered it was May 8 because it was his birthday. I thought and thought about that; for a while I wasn't absolutely sure whether he had been home on May 3 or May 8, but then later I realized it couldn't have been May 3 because I had my period that day. So he was home on May 8; so he couldn't have attended an execution in Treblinka that day, could he?"

It was never quite clear why it couldn't have been on May 5 or 6 he was at home; equally, it was never quite clear why – considering that he was involved in the death of hundreds of thousands, his wife thought it so vital to prove that he had not "attended" *one* execution, except of course that to her, disproving any horror he was accused of, must be a comfort. "That day in May," said Frau Stangl, "I hardly asked him about anything. He did tell me that he was still trying to get out; to get a transfer to an anti-partisan unit in the East. But of course that night I was only happy – it was such overwhelming happiness just to be together for these few unexpected hours. But even on that brief stop-over I remember he went again to see Fräulein Hintersteiner in Linz."

Fräulein Hintersteiner had worked as a bookkeeper-secretary at the Schloss Hartheim euthanasia institute and her testimony at Stangl's trial, like that of other witnesses called by his defence, bore out the old saying about sinking ships. She said she had met Stangl at Hartheim; that the work there was under the seal of secrecy on the penalty of death; that she had been a member of the Nazi Party only since the Anschluss but, yes, that she had "sympathized with them" before the Anschluss. She said she knew what was happening at Hartheim but couldn't remember whether she had ever discussed this with Stangl, though it was possible. There were ten to fifteen people working in the office there – a community bound by secrecy – who lived, worked and took their recreation together. Was she an intimate friend of Stangl's? No, just "colleagues" as with all the others. She knew "Kaufmann and his wife" through her brother; they were neighbours of theirs at home. She could not recall whether or not she had told Stangl that Kaufmann was being posted to the Crimea, but it was possible; Kaufmann had told her after the beginning of the war against Russia that he was being posted there, though she couldn't remember in what capacity. She didn't know whether Stangl and Kaufmann knew each other. She could not recall that Stangl had asked her to use her influence with Kaufmann to obtain a posting for him as Kaufmann's aide. She could not remember whether or not she had "put in a good word for Stangl" but she rather thought not, as her acquaintance with Kaufmann was not "this close". Nor could she remember whether Stangl had reminded her of such a request and consequently she couldn't remember either whether she had transmitted such a request. In short, Fräulein Hintersteiner's memory – like that of many others – was so impaired that all she could remember precisely were details of what so conveniently she didn't remember. It is quite extraordinary how the the memories of the people who lived through hell – and this applies in different ways to men like Glazar as well as to Stangl – remained intact, while those so infinitely less imperilled broke down.

"We were now going into phase four," said Richard Glazar, "and life did become somewhat better. Partly I suppose it was that we were completely conditioned to it. Partly because we were more secure. Robert Altschuh had heard an ss tell Suchomel in the tailor-shop that Stangl had said 'too many Jews had been sieved through': if the transports increased again, he said, and the camp was reactivated, there were no longer sufficient workers to operate it efficiently. That sounded to us as if they were unlikely to kill any of us experienced personnel. But, it was also because, with our minds focused on the revolt, we were by now almost hysterically alive; we were reckless to the point of insanity.

"In June the remnant of the Warsaw ghetto arrived; they were a terrible sight, more dead than alive. And in July there were a few more very poor transports. . . ."

From what Richard Glazar and the other survivors say, the enormous importance that was attached by the prisoners to every word and every move of Stangl's emerges very clearly; and equally the extent to which whatever he said or did affected their spirit – their spirit being what kept them alive.

"You have said all along, you hated what was happening," I had asked Stangl. *"Would it not have been possible, I ask you again, to show some evidence of your inner conflict?"*

"But that would have been the end," he said. "That is precisely why I *was* so alone."

"Supposing for a moment it would have been the end, as you say. There were people in Germany who stood up for their principles; not many, it is true, but some. Yours was a very special position; there were less than a dozen men like you in all of the Third Reich. Don't you think that if you had found that extraordinary courage, it would have had an effect on the people who served under you?"

He shook his head. "If I had sacrificed myself," he said slowly, "if I had made public what I felt, and had died . . . it would have made no difference. Not an iota. It would all have gone on just the same, as if it and I had never happened."

"I believe that. But even so, don't you think somewhere, underneath, it would have affected the atmosphere in the camp, would have given some others courage?"

"Not even that. It would have caused a tiny ripple, for a fraction of an instant – that's all."

"What did you think at the time was the reason for the exterminations?"

His answer came at once: "They wanted the Jews' money."

"You can't be serious?"

He was bewildered by my reaction of disbelief. "But of course. Have you any idea of the fantastic sums that were involved? That's how the steel in Sweden was bought."

"But . . . they weren't all rich. At least 900,000 Jews were killed in Treblinka – more than 3 million altogether on Polish soil during the existence of the extermination and concentration camps. There were hundreds of thousands of them from ghettos in the East, who had nothing. . . ."

"Nobody had nothing," he said. "Everybody had *something*."

("Even those from the extreme East of Poland, the poorest, brought something," said Richard Glazar. "I remember working on their clothes: they wore padded tunics, very much like coolies', in China. They were awful to handle, full of lice – *white* with lice along the seams. One time I was just about to put one of them into a bundle I was making up and somebody said, 'Wait.' He ripped it open and there, glued together inside the padding, were dozens and dozens of hundred dollar bills. Another day, one of the ss came in with a basket full of food. 'Pull up your sleeve,' he said to me, 'and put your hand in all the way.' I did. It was full – elbow deep – of gold dollars.")

"That racial business," said Stangl, "was just secondary. Otherwise, how could they have had all those 'honorary Aryans'? They used to say General Milch was a Jew, you know."

"If the racial business was so secondary, then why all that hate propaganda?"

"To condition those who actually had to carry out these policies; to make it possible for them to do what they did."

"Well, you were part of this: did you hate?"

"Never. I wouldn't let anybody dictate to me who to hate. Anyway, the only people I could ever hate would be those who were out to destroy me – like Prohaska."

"What is the difference to you between hate, and a contempt which results in considering people as 'cargo'?"

"It has nothing to do with hate. They were so weak; they allowed everything to happen – to be done to them. They were people with whom there was no common ground, no possibility of communication – that is how contempt is born. I could never understand how they could just give in as they did. Quite recently I read a book about lemmings, who every five or six years just wander into the sea and die; that made me think of Treblinka."

"If you didn't feel an overriding sense of loyalty to the Party or its ideas, what did you believe in during that time in Poland?"

"Survival," he said immediately. "In the midst of all that death – life. And what sustained me most was my fundamental faith in the existence of just retribution."

"But you knew your own position. You were so afraid of a few men like Globocnik, Wirth, Prohaska. How is it that you were not as afraid of this 'just retribution' you were certain existed and which, when it came, was bound to include you?"

"It was all part of the way I construed it for myself; I am responsible only to myself and my God. Only *I* know what I did of my own free will. And for that I can answer to my God. What I did without, or against my free will, for that I need not answer. . . . Yes, I knew the day would come when the Nazis would go under and that I'd probably go under with them. If it did happen, it just couldn't be helped. At the time of the worst degradations in the East," he said (wording it rather ambiguously, I thought, leaving me in some doubt as to whether he was referring to his own sentiments in connection with Treblinka, or to the rout of the German army in Russia), "I went on leave and we spent it at a priest's house: Pfarrhof Klaus in the Steyrthal, with Father Mario, a friend of my wife's family. We went to Mass every morning. . . ."

14

"I DIDN'T see Paul again until July," Frau Stangl said. "And that was a terrible time – he stayed almost a month. By that time I had thought more about Treblinka. Of course I was pregnant, that probably also influenced my state of mind. At Christmas, you see, he had told me again that he was the 'highest ranking' officer in Treblinka and I had asked him – again – what that meant. Because he'd never mentioned being Kommandant – never. He answered that it meant everyone had to defer to him, and do what he said. I said, 'But then . . . my God, Paul, then you are *in charge*?' But he answered, 'No, Wirth is *in charge*.' And again I had believed him, I suppose because I needed to – I *had* to believe. How could I have gone on otherwise? As it was, I often looked at him and thought to myself, 'Who are you? Oh my God, what are you that you can bear even to *see* this? What – oh God, *what* are you seeing with these eyes which look at me?' Still, that Christmas I had still believed him: he said so often, so firmly that he wanted only to get out, that he could ask for nothing better. And even when *I* said, 'If you are really doing only administrative things and nothing bad, well, at least you are not at the front' – because, yes, I did say that – he answered, 'No, no, I must get out of it.'

"It is true, you know, although I cried, oh so many times when I thought of those people they were killing, I never never knew there were children too, or even women. I, too, rationalized it I suppose; I told myself, I suppose, that we were at war and that they were killing the men; men, you know: enemies. I suppose I thought – or told myself – that the women and children were being left at home. I know it isn't logical, but I suppose I just didn't dare to think further. What I did know and did think was already more than I could bear. But it's true, I also said to myself many times: if he did refuse, if he did just run away, throw away his life and ours, it would still go on. There would not be just hundreds, there would be thousands only too happy to take his place. Well, that's how I thought until July. Because until then I still kept believing that he was trying to get out, as he told me, and that he would succeed in getting a transfer.

"But by the time he came on leave in July I had ceased to believe; it had been too long. And now I began to see the terrible change in him. No one else saw this. And I too had only glimpses; occasional glimpses of another man, somebody with a different, a totally changed face; someone I didn't know; that face that you too saw later, in the prison – red, suffused, swollen, protruding veins, coarse – he who was never coarse or vulgar, who was always loving and kind. That was when I began to nag him – at least he called it that. I asked him again and again, 'Paul, why are you still there? It's a year now, more than a year. All the time you said you'd manage it, you'd wangle a transfer. Paul,' I'd say, 'I'm afraid for you. I am afraid for your soul. You *must* leave. Run away if must be. We will come with you, anywhere.' – 'How?' he said. 'They'd catch me. They catch everybody. And that would be the end for all of us. I in a concentration camp, you in *Sippenhaft* [detention for compromised relatives of unreliables] – perhaps the children too; it's unthinkable.' That's what he said. Well, you understand, I wasn't thinking of Germany's victory or defeat, I was only thinking of him, my man, and what was happening to him inside, and I went on nagging him. He'd get terribly angry, quite out of character for him. 'Is this what my whole leave is going to be like?' he'd shout. 'Aren't you ever going to stop pestering me?'

"I ... I could no longer be with him ... you know ... near him. It was quite terrible, for both of us. We were staying in the mountains with this friend of my mother's, a priest, Father Mario; she had arranged for us to stay there, for our holiday. And one day I couldn't stand it any longer; I no longer knew where to turn, I *had* to talk to somebody. So I went to see Father Mario. I said, 'Father, I must talk to you. I want to talk to you under the seal of the confessional.' He is dead now. I can tell you about it. And I told him about Treblinka. I said, 'I know you won't believe it but there is this terrible place in Poland and they are killing people there – they are killing the Jews there. And my Paul,' I said, 'my Paul is there. He is working there. What shall I do?' I asked him. 'Please tell me. Please help us. Please advise us.'

"You see, I thought – I suppose – the priests had ways; there were convents up in the mountains where one could disappear, hide – I had heard things.

"He gave me such a terrible shock. I remember, he brushed his face with his hand and then he said, 'We are living through terrible times, my child. Before God and my conscience, if I had been in Paul's place, I would have done the same. I absolve him from all guilt.'

"I walked away like a zombie, in a dream, in a nightmare. How could he? Then I told myself, he is old, perhaps he is senile; it was the only explanation. But afterwards ... I don't know ... after all, he was a priest ... I had carried this awful thing around with me for a year, I had thought and thought and cried and worried myself sick over what would happen to my Paul, if not on earth, then after his death ... and then he, a priest, had taken it so ... not calmly, but, well, matter-of-factly. I don't know. I could no longer think at all. And that night, I told Paul that I had told Father Mario and what he had answered. All Paul said was, 'You took a terrible risk telling him.' He wasn't angry, he didn't rave at me like I thought he might. I think I was grateful for that. I had been so lonely and so frightened. . . . Well, his leave came to an end soon after that. And then, of course, as you know, it was all over within a few days after his return to Treblinka. . . ."

15

IT IS very difficult to assess now to what extent the prisoners at Treblinka (or later at Sobibor) really believed an uprising could succeed. What is mostly likely is that although it was carefully planned, the most intelligent amongst them – in fact the planners themselves – in the final analysis believed least in the possibility of success. It was, however, they who were most determined to see that at least *some* would escape, even if not they themselves; that a maximum of damage would be done to the installations, and that – and this was part of the plan they failed to bring off – the three worst murderers amongst the SS, Kurt Franz, Miete and Mentz (significantly enough *not* Stangl), would be "executed" by the insurgents. The details of the uprising vary greatly in the memories of different survivors, which may explain why there is hardly any reliable record of what must be one of the most heroic efforts of the war-time years in East or West: a revolt undertaken by people who had virtually no contact with any underground movement "outside", no hope of help from the Poles or the Western Allies, virtually no arms except what they might hope to capture at the moment of the uprising, and who bore the responsibility for a large group of men and women only a very small minority of whom were considered capable of being "active insurgents".

"The revolt was planned for the late afternoon of August 2," said Richard Glazar, "so as to give people the maximum chance to escape in the dark. The Saturday before, we of the camouflage unit were ordered out to gather juniper branches; light and good for camouflage. There were twenty-five of us in this unit, all terrifically disciplined, and organized into three groups each with its own foreman; he held the money – the gold – with which we bribed the Ukrainians to bribe the Poles to allow us to pay them for food! And when food was obtained, only he, the foreman, could distribute it. One of our lot, a Pole, did all the talking to the Ukrainians. That day he told them that he wanted enough food for everybody to eat their fill. Oh yes, there was an SS with us – there always was. But he didn't care – he was all right. The Ukrainians said, for forty dollars in gold they'd get us all the food we could eat. So we gave them forty dollars in gold. And they came back with a peasant who was leading a horse and cart, and it was full, absolutely chock-a-block full with food – ham and sausage, salami, bread – all kinds of bread; cream and vodka. The Poles tell you now there was no food; but of course there was, in the country. And there was nothing you couldn't buy for gold. That peasant with his horse and cart; the field and the woods; and the multi-coloured food – it looked like a Breughel, you know; anyway, we ate ourselves stupid. The SS didn't say anything much; he got some ham and vodka and ate too. Only at the end he called one of the three foremen over and said he had no objection to our eating, but not this amount, ever again. It didn't mean anything, he just said it to show how good he was being to us. Of course by then the SS had changed; they saw the writing on the wall.

"Of course the Ukrainians hadn't always been so accommodating either. Ordinarily, on these forages all they did was get drunk and even meaner than usual. I remember once – long before that day – one of them brought a whore into the forest and told Kuba – there were three Kubas at Treblinka; this one was a big chap – to ... well, you know what. Kuba couldn't make it and they laughed themselves sick. That's the kind of joke they appreciated. Many of us young men ceased to have any sexual feelings whatever; Karel and I, during all the time we were in Treblinka, and for long afterwards, were men in name only."

(By the same token, many women in camps ceased to menstruate. The rumour was that in *concentration camps* something was put in the food. But it is unlikely that this happened in places such as Treblinka; the number of girls kept alive didn't warrant such precautions, and anyway this particular aspect of life only afforded the Ukrainians and the SS one more opportunity for sadistic humour. There were, of course, no sanitary napkins, or even newspapers, and the girls used large leaves – burdock leaves if they could find them – to protect themselves. But any blood showing on a dress meant death; it was unaesthetic, and the SS were very keen on aesthetics.)

"August 2," said Stangl, "was a very hot day. A Monday. Mondays were always days of rest – because of course on Sundays nobody worked in Warsaw, so they didn't load transports.* Kurt Franz had taken a swimming party of twenty down to the River Bug straight after lunch; four Germans and the rest Ukrainians. I had a visitor, a Viennese. He was an army political officer who was temporarily stationed in Kossov, six kilometres away. He had rung to say hello and ask whether he could drop by."

("On the day of the revolt," says Suchomel, "drinking had been going on in Stangl's quarters since mid-morning. Mätzig was in on it too. Stangl's guest was his old friend Greuer, the lieutenant from a Vlassov unit in Kossov. Franz was not in Treblinka that day – that's true enough – but neither was he swimming, though perhaps Stangl thought he was. In fact he was with his tart in Ostrow. By the time the revolt started in the afternoon, Stangl and his friend were both drunk as lords and didn't know which end was up. I remember seeing him stand there, just stand and look at the burning buildings . . .")

"Was it usual for you and the other officers," I asked Stangl, *"to receive visitors in the camp?"*

"Not while I was there. I would never have permitted it. Of course, even I wouldn't take a visitor into the camp; just my quarters, or the SS mess."

"Even so – it meant he saw what was going on, didn't it?"

"In the lower camp – which is what he could see through the barbed wire – as I told you, after eleven or so in the morning, nothing really went on except routine work in the work-shops. Of course up in the top camp they'd have their fires – they'd burn what was left over; there was always something going on there," he shrugged his shoulder. "But anyway, by this time everybody knew what was going on."

"Did they? Even during your trial any number of people denied having known anything at all about these things."

* A curious slip, because by that time there *were* no more Jewish transports from Warsaw; there were no more Jews.

238

"I know," he said bitterly. "None of them knew anything, saw anything, guessed anything. But hundreds of soldiers and civilians used to come up to our gate, stand along the fences, gawk, and try to buy things off us because it was known that there was all this stuff around. For a while we even had planes circling around overhead and flying low so that they could watch what was going on. I rang through to HQ about that finally and they told us to shoot at them. So we did, and that stopped that. But we never could stop the others – not quite, ever. They saw dead Jews on the ground and being carried away from the station. They photographed them. The whole place stank to high heaven from kilometres away. For two weeks after coming through there – or 'visiting' there – many used to say they couldn't eat. But no, they saw nothing and knew nothing. Of course. . . .

"Anyway, this officer from Kossov was sitting in my room with me that Monday after lunch. My windows looked out on to the street – that's the street I had them build you know, 800 metres, all bordered with flowers. And to the right was the guards' house we built, in Tyrolean style. I tell you, I had the best carpenters in the world – everybody envied me. It was all done in wood – stylistically perfect. Of course we built all these things to create work," he said, without undue emphasis. "The more people we could legitimately employ at useful work, the more survived, at least for a while. Anyway, that's where the shooting began, at 2 p.m., at this blockhouse. My batman, Sacha, he was Ukrainian, he came running. Looking out of my window I could see some Jews on the other side of the inner fence – they must have jumped down from the roof of the SS billets and they were shooting. I told the fellow from Kossov to stay put and took my pistol and ran out. By that time the guards had begun to shoot back but there were already fires all over the camp. . . ."

"At 2 p.m.," said Richard Glazar, "an order came through from the committee that from that moment no Jew would be allowed to die; if there was any threat from anyone, the balloon would have to go up earlier than planned. At ten minutes to four Kuba said something to Küttner and shortly afterwards Küttner started to beat a young boy. That was what started it – at three minutes to four, probably about two hours early. . . ."

In a subsequent letter Richard confirmed these timings and

239

– replying to my question what it was that had prematurely triggered off the revolt – said, "Probably none of us can know what Kuba said to Küttner. But", he added, "this Kuba was the 'barrack-elder' of Barrack II and an informer like Blau, and that was quite enough to convince us [that something wrong was going on]."

Suchomel has another idea about what started the uprising prematurely. "There was a man called Salzberg," he said. "He had two sons. Both the boys were cleaners in our barracks. Father Salzberg was storekeeper in the tailor-shop, therefore under me. He was very intelligent and worried about his boys. He told me his wife had died in Kielce before he came to Treblinka. Salzberg was on the so-called 'committee', and it was upon his urging that the revolt began an hour earlier than planned, and thus insufficiently prepared. The reason why Salzberg insisted on this may be because his older boy, two days before the revolt, had done something – I don't know what – that annoyed Küttner. I had pleaded with Kurt Franz for the boy's life and it seemed all right, but Salzberg was still afraid that Küttner would take him. That boy was fifteen – that's what his father told me – the younger one was twelve and his name was Heinrich. He was a nice boy. The older one I didn't know because he worked in the other barrack."

Richard Glazar too had written to me about Salzberg, but spoke of him as only having one son, sixteen years old. "The only case," he said, "where father and son were selected together from a transport. The young Salzberg", he said, "worked as a cleaner in the ss barracks with Edek, the accordion player. I hear he is supposed to have survived and be living somewhere in Spain."

"My main memory of the revolt", Richard said, "is one of utter confusion; the first moments were of course madly exciting; grenades and bottles of petrol exploding, fires almost at once, shooting everywhere. Everything was just that much different from the way it had been planned, so that we were thrown into utter confusion. . . ."

"Of course, we were on the telephone," Stangl said, "and in an emergency like that my first duty was to inform the chief of the external security police. By the time I'd done that, our petrol station blew up – that too had been built just like a real service station, with flower-beds round it. Next thing the whole ghetto camp was burning, and then Matthes, the German in charge of the *Totenlager*, arrived at a run and said everything was burning up there too. Later we found out that they'd begun earlier than planned – probably because Franz and twenty men were out of the camp and they thought it was the best moment to get at our munition dump. But actually the shooting lasted only about another ten minutes – perhaps half an hour altogether. By that time there was hardly anybody left. . . ."

(Kurt Franz, by all accounts the most viciously sadistic killer of the lot and now serving a life sentence in West Germany, had *his* say at Stangl's trial about his own part in these events and made a most extraordinary and ludicrous claim. "On August 2," he said, "I arranged that, as a result of the absence of two-thirds of the guards – who with the permission of the accused [Stangl] had gone swimming – the revolt could take place at all. I sensed what the work-Jews were planning and what was ahead of us, and it is for this reason that I left my submachine-gun in my quarters. . . .")

"Within minutes," Glazar said, "it was more or less each man for himself. There were groups who escaped together as planned, but of each group only a few made it. Of the twenty-five of us in the camouflage unit who had planned to stay together, six, possibly eight, got out. Only four of us are alive today. . . ."

16

"OH YES," said Berek Rojzman during our visit to Treblinka, "I knew the revolt was being planned, but I wasn't one of the planners. There were just a few [and he used the word for 'gentlemen'] on the committee. I was assigned to get rid of the Ukrainian guard on one of the watch-towers near where I worked."

He showed it to me; it was at the extreme eastern end of the camp (adjoining the fields, some of which were worked by Polish peasants, others by prisoners like himself, for the SS staff) and overlooking the *Totenlager*.

"The man on duty on that watch-tower that day was called Mira," he said. "He was sitting on the tower dressed only in his shorts, getting the sun. When he heard the first shots from the lower camp and realized there was trouble, he jumped down, in his shorts. I ran up to him and said, 'Mira, run, the Russians are coming.' I took his gun away from him and he didn't make a move to stop me. 'You run,' I said, 'but I must have the gun.' He ran."

Rojzman had made an arrangement with a cousin for the escape – all the prisoners had made individual arrangements like this; the cousin was to carry their funds. He had been given a large sum; he was not to participate in the fighting so as not to jeopardize these funds. They had arranged a meeting-place just inside the perimeter of the camp, and until they met there at a prearranged time just after the revolt had started, the cousin was to remain in hiding. In fact the cousin never appeared; Rojzman still thinks he went off with the money, although he admits he's never heard of him being seen since. (This is highly unlikely as all the survivors are known to the Polish and West German judicial authorities – and of course, to each other. No doubt the cousin died in the revolt.)

Rojzman finally left with several other men, one of them a young prisoner called Leon who said he knew "a Pole" who lived in a cottage deep in a forest; he wanted to get to this man because he trusted him and he thought he would be willing to take a message to his wife in Warsaw who was a gentile and who would bring him clothes and perhaps false papers.

Before they reached the cottage, they were several days in the woods, hiding first from the security police and their dogs, then from Ukrainians and Poles who continued the chase even after the Germans had given up. The man, Staszek, when they got to him, *was* willing to help. "When we asked him to go and get Leon's wife," said Rojzman, "some of our group weren't all that sure of him. Of course, we had a *lot* of money. Staszek had a little distillery going next to his cottage. I asked him how much his distillery was netting him and told him I'd double that sum if he would really go to Warsaw and bring Leon's wife. Some of the others still thought he wouldn't, but Leon trusted him and so did I. I'd given him half the money and said he would get the other half when he came back. I bet the others he'd be back by the next day, Saturday. And he was, and brought Leon's wife who had the suit, hat and papers for Leon. They went and that left just six of us in the forest."

They stayed in the forest for a year. "We built a very nice shelter underground, not far from Staszek's cottage," he said. "Staszek was cooking for us – in the evenings we'd often go and drink with him in the cottage. One night I got drunk and said something silly like 'I could kill you all'. The youngest of our group got scared and ran away into the woods. He came back late that night and asked the others whether I was asleep before he dared come in."

Berek Rojzman's story about this year in the forest is full of such examples of tension within the group and of his dominance, and their fear of him. "We often argued about money," he said. "We were buying food and clothes through Staszek. Two of the group didn't have money; I didn't mind, but the others said they weren't going to feed them if they couldn't contribute, and told them to get out.

"We used to go to the village to buy things. I had grown a long moustache and looked like a Polish farmer. One day we were stopped by a group of young boys; they wanted our guns, but we didn't let them take them; we said we were partisans. There was a lot of curiosity about us."

He said Staszek, too, had become "too curious", always asking where their shelter was. "But we didn't think he should know. After that we cooked for ourselves. We had serious arguments about who should do the cooking. In the end I assigned the duties; there would be those who would cook and those who would stand guard and I was going to decide who would do what, when.

"We got to know from people around that the Germans were sending Ukrainians who pretended to be partisans, into the woods to look for Jews. No, we didn't actually *do* anything as partisans – our purpose was to survive. After about a year we learned from people in the village that the Russians were approaching. That day, while we were foraging around for food, Janiek [one of the group] had been left to guard the shelter, and when we got back we found he had taken it apart searching for money. He didn't find it. I gave him a good beating."

Shortly after this they left the shelter and made their way to the town of Otwock. Rojzman said no more about the man Staszek, thanks to whom they had survived. The implication was that he was paid for what he did. (He probably was, but considering the risk he had taken, one did wonder whether *that* degree of help could ever be paid for in money.)

"When we got to Otwock," Rojzman said, "we'd been walking for a long time and my feet hurt. I asked Janiek to help me take my shoes off. But he said, 'In the woods I *had* to do it. Now I don't.'

243

So I said, 'In the woods we *had* to live together – here we don't. So get out.'

"We had 400 dollars left amongst the four of us and we divided them equally and parted. In Otwock I met again the wife of that Polish couple who had been our friends in Warsaw. The Germans had killed her husband and she was left with two children. She was trading a little and I was trading too, so we became good friends and later I married her. . . ."

Richard Glazar broke out of Treblinka in what he described as a frenzy of elation, carrying nothing except his old shaving kit, a soap-box with two small remnants of soap (he still has it, and the soap, all cracked and mouldy), money and a few pieces of jewellery: some gold rings and two small diamonds. "Two of the Czech gold-Jews gave Karel and me these things the evening before the uprising – in case we got out. Both of us still have the diamonds; we held on to them throughout our escape and until now."

Joe Siedlecki told me that although he was not on the committee, he too knew about the revolt. "I had arranged to go with another man and a bag full of diamonds," he said.

I asked him about a girl friend I had heard he had in the camp.

"Well, girl friend in a manner of speaking," he said. "There were nine girls for fifteen hundred men [actually the work force consisted of a thousand men, but by the time of the revolt it had been reduced to about eight hundred]. The one you mean, I talked with her, but I didn't sleep with her. No, she didn't escape with me, she escaped with Samuel Rajzman. I saw her later in the forest, though. No, I don't know what happened to her."

(Samuel Rajzman, who also spent a year hiding in the forest, told me that one day, when he returned from a nearby village where he had gone to get food for his group, he found them all dead, including Joe Siedlecki's "girl friend", killed – he said – by Polish partisans.)

"There were two men who wanted to go with me," Joe continued, "but one of them looked very Jewish. Like a rabbi, he looked. I said, 'What do you want of my life? Do me a favour, you go that way, I this.' He had diamonds and gold and offered me a share if I let him go with me – the other one too. In the end we did go together, and only separated when we reached Warsaw."

Like several of the Treblinka and Sobibor survivors – those whose appearance made it possible – Joe Siedlecki spent the rest of the war passing as a gentile. "I got into a Polish construction unit attached to the German army," he said. "We got army rations, billets, travel passes." He spent a year with this unit, in Wehrmacht uniform (presumably in Germany). "Finally everybody was going on leave. I had passed it up several times, but people were becoming suspicious, so in the end I too had to go to Poland on leave."

When he got back to Poland, a Polish woman let him bunk in her kitchen. "Then I found out that she was hiding four Jews," Joe said. "They'd been there for two years, and were paying her. She, her children and I slept in the kitchen, the hidden Jews in the bedroom. Not long after I came, their money ran out. And then she sold them to the Gestapo, for 100 zloty each." After the liberation, he told the authorities that she had turned Poles over to the Gestapo. "I just said 'Poles'; if I had said Jews, they probably wouldn't have cared. But that way they took care of her," he said. "*I* had nothing to do with it."

It had all been planned so carefully, said Richard Glazar, "but all the plans came to nothing in this fantastic, really indescribable confusion when none of us finally knew where or in which direction to go. All we knew was that we had to run. . . ." ("We climbed the anti-tank barriers round the camp," said Charles [Karel] Unger in his statement for the trial, "and got to a pond. We waded in and stayed there for hours with only our heads above water. While we were standing in the water, we could hear the posses and the dogs, jeeps and cars. . . .")

Richard and Karel were to spend two years as foreign workers in Germany. They worked their way across Poland into Czechoslovakia, then to Mannheim where they lived among Germans and worked in a German factory. Richard remembered "sitting in a bloody German cinema, seeing *Baron Münchhausen* with Hans Albers – it was ridiculous, just ridiculous after Treblinka. We went quite mad."

Their madness manifested itself in recklessness, "cocking a snook at the Germans", he said, making "a sport out of challenging them", laughing aloud in public at the reports of military defeats, walking through the streets and smiling broadly during air-raid alerts. Once, by a truly shattering irony, the Mannheim welfare service offered them coats which were unwrapped in front of their eyes from appallingly familiar "bundles tied up in sheets". "We thought we were going mad," Richard said again, but in a different way.

But there is a great deal more to the story of Richard Glazar's escape, and I feel it should be left to him to tell it in print one day. Equally, he may perhaps publish the "Open Letter" he wrote to Jean-François Steiner after the publication of *Treblinka*, in which he expressed the "profound dismay felt by all the survivors at the politically or personally motivated misrepresentations [in that book] of real events and real people, most of them now dead and unable to defend themselves."

"No one at all could have got out of Treblinka," Richard said to me, "if it hadn't been for the real heroes: those who, having lost their wives and children there, elected to fight it out so as to give the others a chance. Galewski – the 'camp elder'; Kapo Kurland who had worked in one of the most tragic places in this tragic place – the *Lazarett* – an extraordinary man and the senior member of the revolutionary committee, to whom we prisoners swore an oath on the eve of the uprising; Sidowicz and Simcha from the carpentry shop; Standa Lichtblau, one of our Czech group, a mechanic by profession who worked in the garage and blew it up with the petrol tanks – the biggest, most important fire of the uprising; he died in it. And of course Zhelo Bloch who survived four hellish months to lead the revolt in the upper camp and who died in it. And finally Rudi Masarek; tall blond Rudi who of all the men in Treblinka would have had the best chance of getting away; he looked more German than the most 'Aryan' of the ss; he was better looking than their most carefully selected élite soldiers. He had his mother in Czechoslovakia and could have gone back, eventually, to a life of ease and plenty. He had come to Treblinka, deliberately, because he loved someone else more than himself. He died, deliberately, for us."

17

WHEN STANGL described the steps he took to put down the revolt, he spoke without animosity and only in terms of strategy; one could in fact, detect in him, and in several of the former SS men I spoke with a measure of admiration for the insurgents.

"At the moment of the revolt," he said, "we had about 840 Jews in the upper and lower camp. When the shooting stopped, after about ten minutes, we called out that those who wanted our protection were to assemble outside my quarters."

("When it started," said Suchomel, "Tchechia – you remember, the good-looking red-blonde – was working in the kitchen. SS, cleaners and kitchen-girls were all lying together on the floor in the passageways because they were shooting in, from outside. Tchechia was lying quite near me. I don't know whether she had known about the revolt in advance. I know that Wirth sometimes boasted that he had even got the Jews to kill each other. Well, I was there and I have never heard or seen one single instance of such a thing happening. Except, of course, there were Jewish informers, employed by Küttner, and Jews died because of them – that is true. But perhaps even there not many. But I do know that the notorious 'Kappowa' Paulinka gave away at least six Jews to Küttner. After the revolt she was found, with her head shattered, on the path where she had tried to escape to the upper camp. And they dealt with one other informer too; but those were the only cases I know of. . . .")

"More than a hundred reported to us when we called them," said Stangl. "Meanwhile the security troops had surrounded the camp at a distance of five kilometres. And of course, they caught most of them."

"Did they bring in the ones they caught?"

"Oh no, they shot them. Towards the end of the afternoon the figures began coming in. I had somebody sitting by the telephone taking them down and adding them up. By 5 or 6 o'clock it looked as if they had already caught forty more than ever escaped. I thought, 'My God, they are going to start shooting down Polskis next' – they were shooting at anything that moved. . . ."

Franciszek Zabecki, the traffic controller at Treblinka station, was, of course, a witness of the uprising. He says that it began exactly at 3 p.m.

"I heard shooting and almost at the same time saw the fires. They burned till 6 p.m. The SS came to the mayor and told him that anyone who helped escapees would be shot at once. There were hundreds of troops around, almost immediately; people were so afraid to be taken for Jews, almost everybody stayed locked up in their houses. The troops shot on sight at anything that moved. One woman, Helen Sucha, hid a Jew: they took her up to the labour camp and she was never heard of again."

"Did Poles join German posses, as all the survivors have claimed they did?"

"I think," said Zabecki, "that people were far too afraid to be mistaken for Jews to venture out at all, but of course there may have been some; I myself didn't know any. I only know how happy we of the 'Conspiracy' were that the Jews were at last rebelling. . . ."

"I gave the order to stop shooting as soon as I realized they were shooting wildly at anything that moved," said Stangl. "Yes, I remember exactly now: we had 105 left – that's right. I also gave the order at once that none of these 105 were to be killed. We had to stop these reprisal measures; they were what had made us hated by everybody. So nobody else was killed in Treblinka – certainly not while I was there. . . ."

"The record appears to claim that the exterminations continued after the revolt? Perhaps after you left?"

"I don't think so. How could they have? Everything – all the facilities – had been burned down. . . ."

("After the revolt and all the fires, of all things the gas chambers remained intact," said Suchomel. "They were of brick. And Stangl said to me, 'The fools, why didn't they burn those down?' You know," he said, a little regretfully, "Stangl was going to put the work-Jews to work outside the camp, in the peat bog; the new programme was to start on August 3, one day after the revolt. He intended to rebuild Treblinka, better than ever; he was going to have brick houses for the work-Jews. He already had building material lying there all ready when the order came to obliterate the camp – and then of course the decision to reassign most of the staff. . . .")

"They left me stewing for three weeks," said Stangl, "before Globocnik sent for me. It was my hardest time. I was sure I'd get all the blame. But as soon as I entered the office, Globocnik said, 'You are transferred as of immediately to Trieste for anti-partisan combat.' I thought my bones would melt. I had been so sure they'd say I had done something wrong, and now I had on the contrary what I had always wanted; I was going to get out. And to Trieste too – near home.

"I went back to Treblinka, but I only stayed three or four days, just long enough to organize transport. The last day I had all the work-Jews who were left fall in, because I wanted to say goodbye to them. I shook hands with some of them. I heard about *that* later too. . . ."

("He assembled everybody", said Suchomel, "and told us that we were to go to Italy. He was overjoyed. You could see it. . . .")

"Paul wrote me right after the uprising," said Frau Stangl, "although he didn't tell me there had been a revolt; he just said it was all over now. And later he wrote to say that he'd been transferred to Italy and how happy, how relieved he was to get out of there at last. I only heard about the revolt later. . . ."

Franciszek Zabecki, who continued to make notes of everything that went in and out of Treblinka station, knows exactly what happened after that.

"After the revolt there were still transports from Bialystock. Thus, on August 18, 1943, came 'Pj 202' consisting of thirty-seven cars. The last transport for Treblinka came on August 19: 'Pj 204' from Bialystock with thirty-nine cars . . . " Pj stood for transports of Polish Jews.

This was the point when the *Aktion Reinhard* ended in Treblinka. All the buildings were demolished, lupins and pine trees were planted all over the site and a small farm was built from the bricks of the dismantled gas chambers.

"A Ukrainian called Strebel was put in the farmhouse," said Pan Zabecki. "He received permission to send for his family from the Ukraine and they all lived there until the arrival of the Russians."

Globocnik confirmed the real function of the Ukrainian "farmer" in a report to Himmler dated Trieste, January 5, 1944. "For reasons of surveillance," he wrote, " a small farm has been built on the sites of each of the [former] camps, the farm to be occupied by an expert to whom a regular income must be assured so as to enable him to maintain the farm."

"After the liquidation of the camp," said Pan Zabecki, "five [railway] cars with prisoners [Jews] left Treblinka on October 20, 1943, for Sobibor" (where they were to be killed soon afterwards).* The last twenty-five or thirty work-Jews in Treblinka – amongst them the three girls Suchomel spoke of – were killed a few days later. And shortly afterwards the remaining SS personnel left the camp-site in two lorries.

There have been conflicting reports of the number of people who were killed in Treblinka. The Polish authorities finally adopted the figure of 750,000. The West Germans raised their official estimate in early 1971 when new evidence emerged, to 900,000; and Stangl was sentenced on the basis of this new figure. Franciszek Zabecki has insisted from the very beginning that the numbers were much higher. I myself have always felt that the deeds and the numbers were so monstrous, the figures have become almost irrelevant: however many there were, each individual represents equally the crime, and the loss. But, even so, for the record I feel we should allow the last word to the man who is the only one still amongst us who was there from the very first day to the last.

"*I* know," Franciszek Zabecki said to me, "the others guess. There *were* no German papers on which to base these estimates except those I rescued and hid – and they are inconclusive. But I stood there in that station day after day and counted the figures chalked on each carriage. I have added them up over and over and over. The number of people killed in Treblinka was 1,200,000, and there is no doubt about it whatever."

* The uprising at Sobibor took place on October 14, so there, too, the killing continued after the revolt.

Part IV

I

MY CONVERSATIONS with Franz Stangl were in two parts – the first, seven days during April 1971, and the second, nine weeks later, in June. This gave me time to work on what he had told me in April and to see what else I would need, and allowed him to reflect – and to rest. By the time I left him in April, just before the Easter weekend, promising to return a few weeks later, I knew that in a curious way – and I say this with reflection – I had become his friend. It was, of course, a completely one-sided relationship. He knew nothing about me except my name and would never have dreamed of presuming to ask me any personal question. As he did not know my married name, he never even knew that it was my husband who came with me when I returned to Düsseldorf, to take the photographs for the article that was to appear in the *Daily Telegraph Magazine* (some of which are reproduced in this book).

During the nine weeks that had intervened, I had been as conscious of the possibility that he might choose to withdraw from these conversations, and even disavow what he had already said, as I was of the enormous emotional and physical strain they had put on him. And I had sent him several messages through the prison governor, Herr Eberhard Mies, to say that I would indeed be coming back quite soon. Herr Mies, his wife and, it seemed to me, all the officers of the prison (and many other people in Germany) had become intensely interested in what these conversations would produce, and the governor, who is not ordinarily in personal touch with individual prisoners, had made a point of making sure that Stangl received my messages. None the less, Stangl's first words to me in June – reassuring to me in the context of my interest, but indicative of his state of mind – were, both in wording and tone of voice, a reproach.

"I've been expecting you every day; I've waited for you," he said at once – instead of bowing or saying "*Grüss Gott*", as had been his custom. We needed to make sure that the cell was suitable for photography so it was there that we met at nine o'clock that Monday morning. He was wearing a suit and a meticulously laundered white shirt, but no tie – it was obvious he hadn't quite finished dressing. He bowed. "I'll be ready in five minutes," he said and withdrew into his cell.

"He's been cleaning, tidying his cell since six this morning," said the officer who waited with us in the corridor.

The photography, to which he had of course agreed, and which was essential for the magazine presentation, had worried me a good deal – the relationship I had established between Stangl and myself was both subtle and exclusive, and very vulnerable, I feared, to intrusion.

The photographer would have to photograph him as neutrally – as basically unemotionally – as I was trying to *talk* with him, and would also need the ability to make himself totally unobtrusive.

Stangl, for whom – as for many other people – being photographed had a kind of status significance, was determined to "pose" for these photographs in his well-cared-for grey suit; it was only after a few such photographs had been taken, and with a good deal of persuasion, that he agreed to a less artificial approach, exchanged the coat for a cardigan and – later still – took off his tie.

That day was an important stage within this experience as a whole, not only because the photographs turned out to be extremely revealing, but also because it was to be the only opportunity I had to see Stangl's bearing with and towards his fellow-prisoners.

Confirming the prison officers' opinion that despite his new opportunities to associate with others, he was a "loner", he had already told me that the only other prisoner he sometimes talked with – had anything to say to – was the man in the cell next to his. Like himself, this man was a long-term inmate awaiting appeal, also there because of, as Stangl put it, "*NS-Sachen*" (Nazi-crime things). But he had shown little interest even towards this man (who, when asked the day after Stangl's death whether he would be willing to talk to me about Stangl, sent a message that he "really hardly knew him, had hardly talked to him and felt he had nothing to contribute").

On our way to the interview room, after finishing the photographs in and in front of his cell, we passed several working parties. Some of the men, waving their brooms or whatever implements they carried, made jocular or snide remarks. "Why don't you come and photograph back there in the shithouse where *we* live – that would be edifying for the good citizens" – "How much do you pay for posing? I'll pose for you any time." – "What one obviously has to do to get photographed for the papers," one man murmured darkly under his breath as I passed, "is to murder half a million Jews." Others, with a great show of hilarity, called out to Stangl in a variety of dialects, "You looked *great* – cute – very elegant" – "Make them pay through the nose – these newspaper people are all moguls (*Bonzen*)" – "Going to have caviar and champagne now? Have some for me."

It was interesting to see that the rather lofty attitude he usually displayed towards at least some of the prison officers – the younger ones – gave way to a forced, almost ingratiating kind of camaraderie, born, one felt immediately, of a mixture of fear and need; so much so that when we reached the room there was a set smile on his face, so stiff and determined, it was several minutes before his face returned to normal.

By the end of the seven hours we spent talking that day, we had re-established and indeed deepened our original "contact". He had repeated – in a slightly modified tone – his question why I hadn't come back sooner, and I had explained, and then read to him, translating as I went along, a good deal of the first draft I had already written. Above all – without making any concessions to him – every single thing he had said on the most sensitive subjects: his parents, his wife and children, the Euthanasia Programme, Sobibor and Treblinka. He readily recapitulated many of the points I raised, and although photographs were taken throughout, he became unaware of the photographer's presence.

"There is so much – there are so many more things we need to talk about," he said that afternoon. "I have done nothing but think while I was waiting for you to come back."

My professional interest notwithstanding, it had been important to me not to persuade or fatigue this man into disclosing more about himself than he wished to. If the sum total of what he could tell, and possibly teach us, was to be valid and of real value, I felt he had to offer it freely, and in full possession of all his faculties.

He had brought a book from his cell, and his hands, holding it – for the first time since I knew him – trembled. "This woman came to see me while you were away," he said. "She sent a message that she was from the Red Cross and could she talk to me, so I said, 'Certainly, why not?' She had apparently looked after witnesses who came from abroad to testify at my trial and she brought this book; she wanted me to read it and let her know what I think of it. She said the author, Janusz Korczak, who wrote it when he was twenty-eight – had been a very talented pediatrician in Warsaw. His real name, she said, was Henryk Goldszmidt or something like that. She said that shortly after he had written this book, he gave up his lucrative practice and dedicated the rest of his life to the children of the Warsaw Jewish orphanage. She said he came to Treblinka with the two hundred orphans – he was seventy-five years old then – and died there with them. She asked me, 'What did you feel when you saw these children?' I said I didn't remember any two hundred children. She said, 'You *must* remember them – you can't have forgotten two hundred children. Didn't you *feel* anything – how could you not feel anything?'" he looked distraught. "I thought and thought about it," he said, "but I just don't remember a group of children like that – a school – an orphanage. . . ."

2

SAMUEL RAJZMAN, the Treblinka survivor who lives in Montreal, told me about this visitor who had caused Stangl to question himself about the children. Frau Kramer, a remarkable German woman who has worked for years in Düsseldorf for the Society of Christians and Jews, and for the Red Cross, acting as hostess to the survivors who are brought to Germany for the NS trials, has become a friend to numerous people who never thought they would ever again wish to call a German a friend.

The Rajzmans, obviously prosperous and well established in Canada, live in a quiet residential district of Montreal; a wide tree-shaded street, large cars, nice brownstone houses. Mr Rajzman, who was the only Treblinka survivor to testify at Nuremberg, at the Polish Treblinka trial, and subsequently at the Treblinka and Stangl trials in Düsseldorf, conducts his flourishing lumber business from an office in his Montreal flat. He and his wife are a quiet gentle couple who found each other after the war during which they had both lost everyone they loved. The story he told about his own little girl illustrated hauntingly how utterly helpless parents were to protect their children.

In July 1942, he, his first wife and their twelve-year-old daughter lived in the Warsaw ghetto. "I knew what was happening," he said. "Many people knew, but most of them wanted to pretend they didn't. I knew for certain because, only ten days before I was finally taken [August 27, 1942], a young man called Friedmann came back from Treblinka hidden under rags.* His escape had been carefully arranged so as to have somebody come back to bring us the truth; to warn us. But nobody believed him. It was perfectly extraordinary. But I *did*." (Another source tells how this young man besought the ghetto elders to believe him and how finally they said he was overwrought and needed a rest which they would arrange for him in the ghetto clinic. The President of the Jewish Council in the Warsaw ghetto, Dr Adam Czerniakow, had in fact killed himself one month earlier when the number of Jews he had to make available for "resettlement" was increased from six to seven thousand a day. In view of the terrible posthumous criticism to which the Ghetto Council officials have been subjected, one should, I think, question just what action was open to them apart from rejection of reality.) "My wife and I," said Samuel Rajzman, "had only one thought: to hide our little girl. In the street where both my wife and I worked at a factory, was a cellar. And in that cellar was a coal-bunker. We took about twenty children and hid them in there and locked the door. Even though we were considered essential workers, the Gestapo came the next day and we were all driven to the assembly square." After two days – the transports were frequently kept waiting – Mr Rajzman managed to get away and immediately went to the cellar where they had left the children. "The door was open and the children were gone. A neighbour said the Germans had come the day before and taken them."

His one thought now was to get back to the square. "After all, it was possible the children could still be there." He had a "Polish" friend, he said – obviously a man who held some kind of official position – and this man went with him to help. The miracle

* This was evidently before trains packed with the victims' effects were sent out of Treblinka. The first of these, according to Richard Glazar, left at the end of October. There is no authenticated escape from Treblinka except this young man, in August, and the two others mentioned by Glazar, two months later.

happened – the children were still on the square. "We managed to get my little girl and a boy whose parents were friends of ours out, and we took them back to our factory. They stayed hidden there for some days – but in the end they took them anyway. . . . Since that day", said Mr Rajzman, "I cannot bear to look at a child – above all, I cannot bear to look at German children. It is not their fault – I know – but when I was in Germany to testify, every time I saw a little girl – I thought of mine. I will never go there again. I cannot understand Jews who survived Treblinka," he said, "and then married non-Jewish women . . . even Germans. That is why it is so extraordinary for us to feel as we do about Frau Kramer. When we met her we were as suspicious of her as all the others; but she convinced us; she gave us back something we had lost; we really love her; she is a valuable – a really valuable human being. . . ."

They showed me a letter they had received from Frau Kramer in which, after writing at length about her own family, she reports on the visit she paid to Stangl in prison.

"I went to see him", she wrote, "with this beautiful book by Janusz Korczak. I told him that we'd seen each other so often across the courtroom, I wanted at last to speak to him." She said that she had asked after his health and his family and that she had told him she wanted to talk to him as a human being, to tell him how someone like herself – who had had nothing to do with it, no axe to grind either way – had felt about Treblinka and to ask him to tell her how he could have done what he did. "He said nothing," she wrote, "but his colour changed and he bowed his head. Just then – at a most unfortunate moment – the prison chaplain [who was present because she was not allowed to see Stangl alone] no doubt meaning well, intervened, and this, I think, gave Stangl the opportunity to get a hold of himself and then he recited once again all the justifications we have heard so often. I left," she said. But she thought she had left behind a badly shaken man. . . .

3

THE MAIN reason why Frau Kramer's approach to Stangl failed (although, as we can see, she did succeed in shaking him) was because her information was incorrect. She tackled him not on his general conduct or attitude, but specifically about Janusz Korczak and his orphans, and in fact Stangl was not at Treblinka when they reached the camp on August 4 or 7 1942. (There are so many stories about Dr Korczak and his little orphans – so many of them contradicting each other as far as bare facts are concerned – that the exact date when he and these children were killed cannot be ascertained. What appears certain is that Stangl wasn't there, and therefore couldn't possibly have known about this.)

"There was no specific 'children-transport' after I got to Treblinka," said Suchomel, who arrived there on August 24. "What is true," he said, "is that towards the middle of October Küttner picked out ten or twelve boys from a transport and assigned them as orderlies for the ghetto camp; they had their own Kapo. However, when this boy was caught giving gold coins to a Ukrainian, Küttner sent all the boys into the gas – they weren't in the camp more than three weeks."

The above affair, as well as another involving children, was laid at Stangl's door by two imaginative novelists. One of them described Stangl (by name) as "playing with these children by the hour", dressing them up, getting them special delicacies and, when they "no longer amused him, with total indifference and a wave of the hand" ordering them into the gas chamber. In another novel, a similar situation was invented with similar irresponsibility, although not involving Stangl. This time the passing passion for a group of little boys was ascribed to a homosexual (the previously named Max Biele or Bielas*) who, according to the author, had a special miniature barrack with miniature beds, night-tables and candlesticks built, in a special rustic setting and kept the boys as a personal harem until he, too, got tired of them and had them killed. It does seem extraordinary that novelists find it necessary to invent such tales when the appalling truth is surely far more "dramatic."

Stangl's non-involvement in this particular sort of horror is confirmed by the most credible of witnesses, Richard Glazar, who says, briefly: "Stangl had no boy orderlies."

Stangl claimed that Frau Kramer had told him that people in Germany weren't buying Janusz Korczak's book (with which he

* Who did exist, and – a unique case – was killed by a prisoner on September 11, 1942.

had obviously become fascinated) and that she couldn't understand why not, and would be interested to know what *he* thought the reason was. "I've studied it," he said, opening the big book with its lovely illustrations at a page he had marked with a piece of paper torn out of a notebook. "I know why they don't want to buy it. Now listen to this . . . " and he read aloud from the fairy tale in the book. " . . . 'When a soldier gets an order, he must obey it. He must not ask questions, he must not hesitate, and must not think: he must obey.'" He closed the book. "Of course parents here don't want their children to read this. I told that woman that if I liked the book I might even buy it myself as a present for my grandson in Brazil. But I am not buying it. I don't want my little grandson to read this either. That is exactly the sort of thing they must not read, ever again."

(Interestingly enough – although I was at a loss to find an explanation for it – Frau Kramer told me later that she had never asked him what he thought the reason was for people in Germany not buying the book. Perhaps he had invented her request – possibly, we thought, to justify an intellectual exercise for himself; or else, more likely, he had misunderstood something she said, although she couldn't imagine what it might have been.)

After we had gone over several of the points we had previously discussed, Stangl said he wanted to tell me about Trieste. He had obviously looked forward to recounting this inoffensive part of his story, and during the first forty-eight hours of that week spoke so quickly that at times I had difficulty following the innumerable details. It was as if he wanted to compress the whole time of the war into the time he had spent in Italy and Yugoslavia; as if by crowding ever more words at ever greater speed into this part of his story, he could force out of existence all the other words he had spoken, all the awful scenes he had relived.

"I went there in convoy," he said "with Globocnik, Wirth and 120 other men, ten of them from Treblinka; five non-commissioned officers, and five Ukrainians, and it was to be a very different life.* Also in part, because I had finally managed to get rid of the sword of Damocles that Prohaska and Linz represented to me: in the spring of that year [1943] I had applied to Blankenburg at the Führer Chancellery [significantly enough, no longer to T4],

* All the members of the Aktion Reinhard were transferred to Trieste – their third and last transfer as a group.

requesting that my home station be changed from Linz to Vienna. And in September, very soon after I arrived in Trieste, I heard that this request had been granted and that as of September 1 I was attached to Kripo HQ (CID), Vienna. [One must assume that this manœuvre was *not* to escape from Prohaska, but was a considered, and rather intelligent, move to alter the record which established him as belonging to the Linz Gestapo.]

"My first assignment in Trieste and for the first three months, to December, was 'Transport Security'. I realized quite well," he said, "and so did most of us, that we were an embarrassment to the brass: they wanted to find ways and means to 'incinerate' us. So we were assigned the most dangerous jobs – anything to do with anti-partisan combat in that part of the world was very perilous. Our new baby," he said, "was born the first week of January, and I was granted compassionate leave. Reichleitner, who had been on leave over Christmas, was to take over my functions while I was away. I drove from Udine with Franz Höldl (a name which – again quite significantly – was to crop up later in Frau Stangl's account) and met Reichleitner briefly in Wirth's office in the Via Martine in Trieste, in the afternoon. I was leaving the next morning. But in the middle of the night someone routed me out of bed with the news that Reichleitner had been killed on a patrol that evening and my leave was cancelled.

"I got twenty-five men and we scoured the whole valley all night. There wasn't any sense to it: it poured, it was pitch-dark, there could have been a partisan behind every tree and we wouldn't have known or found them. In fact the next morning we heard that at 8 o'clock the night before, partisans had marched singing through a village; everybody hid them – they were safe as houses."

In February – by this time he was stationed in Fiume – it appears that Globocnik called him to HQ in Trieste and told him that he was approving a two-week home leave for him. "He said, 'I've found the best car for you; go home and look after your wife. But the condition is that you go and visit my fiancée in Klagenfurt.' She was a big blonde," said Stangl, "she worked at the hospital. 'I've already ordered roses and all that for you to take,' said Globocnik. I left at once. It was snowing. . . ."

And it would appear that Globocnik, for this very special private commission, provided Stangl with more than "the best car" and roses.

"Paul came home on leave at the end of February, beginning of March 1944," said Frau Stangl. "It was very cold. My baby had been born in January and I'd had a very difficult time – I was in bed. He came, and he brought along a lorry full of things – from the General, he said: priceless things like blankets, down comforters, linen – it was like Christmas in March.* Paul stayed about a week, I think. I really don't know what his work was in Italy, though he told me they had ordered him to be on the lookout for Jews there, too. But he said to me he wouldn't do it. 'What do they think I am?' he said. 'A headhunter? They can leave me out of this now.' [And Suchomel, who was also by then in Trieste, quotes Stangl as saying the same words to him.] No," said Frau Stangl, "I don't think he had anything more to do with this Jewish business. After that leave, he didn't come back for a year – he was very ill for a while in Trieste – they sent him to hospital. He had big blue spots all over – they didn't know why." (Later it was found that whatever else he had at that time, he had also had a first heart attack.)

During the two full days Stangl talked about his activities in Italy, he only mentioned the death of Wirth in passing. "I saw him dead," he said. "They said partisans killed him but we thought his own men had taken care of him." (All histories of the time refer to Wirth as "presumed dead"; Stangl's statement, therefore, must be considered the only one made by an eye-witness.)

"My biggest and longest assignment in Italy," he said, "was as special supply officer for the *Einsatz Poll*.† I was responsible for getting everything; shoes, clothes, food. I was the only one who went about in civilian clothes. Everybody, army and SS, had to help me. I carried a paper signed by the General stating that 'Hauptsturmführer Stangl is authorized to act in uniform or civvies and all services are requested to give him every assistance in the execution of his command'. Globocnik told me, 'Buy whatever you need; money is no object.' I had a man with me who had nothing to do except carry trunks with cash . . . millions. . . ."

Suchomel confirms all this. The *Einsatz Poll* he says, "was the camouflage-name for the fortification of Istria – the workers were Italians under German command. And the whole thing was under General SS Globocnik whose main job was to provide everything

* Later she was to write denigrating these gifts.
† Strategic construction project in the Po valley involving 500,000 workers.

needed in the way of materials. Whatever couldn't be obtained legally, as for instance petrol, tyres, fabrics for uniforms, etc, was bought on the black market." Suchomel talked about this part of Stangl's activities with particular reference to Stangl's later escape. "Through his activities in Udine and especially in Venice-Mestre and Treviso, Stangl had many contacts amongst Italians," he said. "As I know myself and can testify, he helped a great many people in Italy for which activities in fact a disciplinary action was brought against him [Stangl told me about this]. Stangl and his *Einsatz Poll* staff had a lot of Italian touts, including people from the Italian nobility. In the end practically everything there had to be done through the black market. And he may well have used these connections later to get out. After all, he was aware for a long time before it actually happened that the war was lost. And it's quite possible that he and Gustl Wagner, with whom he was very close, were already looking into possibilities for hiding out or getting away. . . ."

4

IT IS mostly from Frau Stangl that I learnt about their two years following the end of the war. Stangl himself (although I had intended to question him a little further on this subject, the only one I felt we had not sufficiently discussed) was not particularly interested in talking about this period; especially not about the weeks before he was finally imprisoned by the Americans as an SS officer.

"I had moved with the children to the mountains," said Frau Stangl. "To Lembach – that was in August 1944 when the bombings got very bad in Wels. We stayed there with the headmaster of the school – they had been friends of ours. Well, we *thought* they were friends; most of our 'friends' remained our friends only so long as Paul had a 'position' – they changed faces pretty quickly when he was out in the cold.

"Anyway, it was towards the end of the war that Paul had fallen so ill – you remember, I told you, he had fever and these blue or black spots all over his body* and the doctors didn't know what it

* Not unknown as a symptom of intense emotional stress.

was. This illness often hit people who had been in the *Afrika Korps*. He was in the field hospital in Trieste or Fiume and when he recovered was given orders to report to Berlin. When he got there, there was nobody left in the Reichssicherheitshauptamt [Main Reichs Security Office] to report to; things were in an unholy mess. He finally managed to get a lift to Hof [on the border between Germany and Czechoslovakia] and then came on foot to Austria – he got to us in Lembach at the last moment, with the Americans and Russians almost upon us. He said he would try to get himself reassigned to the police in Linz – and he went there. But they didn't want to know – they said his whole section had been trans-ferred to Vienna and that's where he now belonged. So he made his way to Vienna, but there too everybody had gone, fled, everything was in disarray. So – believe it or not – he went back to Berlin; he thought if at least he could get an official paper saying that he belonged to the Vienna police. . . . He didn't go to T4 – he went straight to the CID offices, but there wasn't anybody there either. So he came back to Lembach. . . ."

(It seems unlikely that Stangl would have made such desperate attempts to get some sort of valid document – and would have been so naïvely convinced that such a document could save him – if he had prepared his retreat in advance with the help of some individuals or organization, as has generally been assumed.)

"Our flat in Wels", said Frau Stangl, "had been bombed and afterwards burgled, and we had very little left of our possessions. But I said, 'Get out of this uniform; get into a pair of the head-master's trousers – put on civvies and stay here. Here we can hide you: it would be best.' But he said no, if he took the uniform off, the Gauleiter would find out and he'd be hanged as a deserter even at this late date. Yes, the Gauleiter was still sitting in Linz. Anyway, Paul went off and we stayed in Lembach. Later I found out that he had gone to Ebernsee near Salzburg, to his mother. And from there he went to stay with a man in a village on the Attersee – a police officer we had sometimes stayed with on holidays. It was there he was denounced to the Americans. Perhaps not by that policeman himself – though I thought it was probably him – but he claimed it was one of his underlings who told the Americans that there was an SS officer at the house. And they came to get him right away. But I knew nothing of this at the time. I was just terrified at the thought of what might be happening to him. One night somebody came and said there was an SS officer lying buried down in the valley. There was shooting everywhere, but I slipped out in the night, through the woods, down to the place that had been described, and I dug and dug in the earth until I reached that corpse and I felt his face and hair. It was pitch dark, I had no light, and anyway I wouldn't have dared light even a match. But I knew – my hands knew it wasn't Paul. So I covered him up again and climbed back up to the little house where we were staying. A couple of weeks later I couldn't stand it any more and I decided to go look for him. By that time we knew that the Americans had started to gather people up in camps – some for ordinary soldiers, some for SS; and then others in Polish DP [Displaced Persons] camps. I decided just to go from camp to camp, making my way in the direction of where his mother lived, because I did think he just might be there.

"It was quite something; I left the children with the teachers in Lembach and started out, on foot of course – there wasn't anything else. I walked from camp to camp; some of the Americans were nice, others less. In the end I never did dare to go to the Polish camps, although I had heard that there were soldiers hiding out in those too. Anyway, one day I got to Bad Ischl [near Salzburg] and went to the CIC [US Counter-Intelligence Corps] there; there weren't any Americans in there, only Austrians. I said that I was looking for my husband who had been an SS officer and that his name was Franz Stangl. And the man I was talking to said at once, 'Oh yes, he's here. We'll get him for you' – just like that. I thought I'd faint. Anyway, then he came. We couldn't talk much, but at least he was alive. The prison where he was, was awful. I never saw it, but he told me – it was a real cage. But never mind, at least I knew where he was. I went back to Lembach and not long after that he was transferred to the huge camp at Glasenbach. Then the Russians were getting very close to where we were and I took the children back to Wels. . . ."

"Glasenbach," Stangl told me, "was really a conglomeration of six different camps with different categories of prisoners, 18,000 to 20,000 altogether. Some were housed in barracks, others in former 'boat-houses', still others in temporary buildings. It was pretty rough, for a long time. I was in Barrack XVI, with 2,000 men. [Frau Stangl said Barrack XVIII.] From July 1945 to May 1946 we slept on the floor – there were neither bunks nor blankets. Then in May we got permission to build wooden frames with planks, and we lay on those. In the winter of 1946 we built sort of wooden chests in which we slept; in the spring of 1947 we were able to build a stove and after that it really did get better – we got bunks, blankets and were allowed parcels. . . ."

"It was a long time before I could begin bringing anything to Paul in Glasenbach," said Frau Stangl. "When we first got back to Wels and to our house, our neighbour opened her door and shouted that I wasn't allowed in – the 'Amis' [Americans] she said, had locked it up and requisitioned it. And anyway, they'd taken out everything that was in it. So I took the children to a friend and went right away to the American HQ. They said they certainly had *not* requisitioned our home, nor did they have the key. It was just as I'd suspected. That woman had always wanted my flat. I asked the Americans to send a soldier back with me and they did – in a jeep. The soldier went to the neighbour and all he said was one word, '*Schlüssel*' [key], and off she went to get it.

"It was true enough, there was practically nothing left; bare bedboards, a couple of chairs, that was about all. But we managed. First we slept on the floor, then friends lent us blankets, and then, one day not long after, the neighbour's door happened to be open when I passed by, and I saw my carpet on the floor. Before she had time to shut the door I was in; I went through that flat with a fine-tooth comb; I found our eiderdowns, our bed linen, pots and pans, and all our china. She screamed at me. She said, 'You can't take any of that; the Americans gave it to me.' Well, maybe they did, but I didn't believe it, and anyway, I didn't care. You know, that woman – the day the Nazis marched into Wels, she had run out of her house, knelt on the ground, opened her arms wide towards the soldiers marching past and screamed, 'Oh, my Führer, my Führer.' The whole of Wels had reacted like that. Of all the women I knew, I was the only one who had refused to join the Frauenschaft and the Party. In my situation now, you know, it really makes no difference whether I was or wasn't a Nazi. One way or the other I stand and fall with the man I loved, whatever he did. I don't even want it any other way. But that was the truth. And I wasn't going to let that woman rob me and my children for whom I was now entirely responsible.

"After this we had a very very hard time; we had terribly little money, only the little I had saved. We got very hungry. I used to go out to pick apples and hike around the farms to scrounge what I could from the peasants. But things went from bad to worse, and it was absolutely essential for me to find work. I finally managed to get an office job in a distillery, Bartl & Co. Hinterschweigergasse, in Wels. In fact it was quite interesting – I ended up doing quite a bit of their fruit-buying. I didn't earn vast sums, but at least enough to eat modestly, though even then we were often hungry. The children's health had begun to suffer – they were ten, nine and just under two years old. They'd come every afternoon to pick me up at work and almost every day my heart would sink when I saw them at the gate, looking pale, wan and often freezing cold. Paul tried to help; he made slippers and bags out of old military coats – God knows how he got hold of them, but the finished articles were very good; he'd send them to me in a big package once a month and I sold them. It turned into quite a thriving little business. The wives of other men who were with him in Glasenbach heard from their husbands that Paul was making these things, and they came to me, from as far away as Vienna, to buy them. It really helped.

"As soon as the trains worked again, I went to Glasenbach every week to bring him food parcels; I was so regular with my visits, other wives who couldn't go so often, gave me parcels for their men. [The round trip took about six hours.] But I never saw Paul in the two and a half years he was in that camp. I didn't see him until after he was handed over to the Austrians and sent to prison in Linz. After that I was able to see him every week. At first only in the presence of a guard – the Austrians, as you know, were always more Catholic than the Pope about their attitude towards Nazis – *after* the war; they were frightfully strict in that prison."

5

IT APPEARS that the Americans interned Stangl simply because he had been a member of the ss. The routine examination revealed his anti-partisan activities in Italy and Yugoslavia, and he was asked no questions about any other war or prewar assignments.

Much has been written since then about the American occupation authorities and their investigation of Nazi criminals and crimes, a great deal of it critical in one way or another. And it is true that the political attitude of some of the American *civilian* authorities, reflecting as it did that of important factions in the State Department, was often neither consistent nor, to go even further, morally defensible. It is equally true, however, that the occupation authorities were faced with problems of such magnitude as to be almost insuperable (not unlike those confronting the International Red Cross and, to some extent, the Vatican).

As I saw for myself when working for UNRRA in Germany from the spring of 1945, the American fighting troops who first took over, while naturally inexperienced in the complexities of European history and politics, lacked nothing in moral indignation at what they found in Germany and elsewhere and were determined to "lock 'em up first and ask questions later". They were, however, faced with an incredible medley of potential prisoners of war, many of them disguised as civilians, and of displaced persons of all nationalities. To make sense of the stories they were told, they would have needed literally thousands of meticulously trained investigators fluent in many foreign languages and commanding a wide knowledge of recent European political history. In such an intractable situation, any high degree of efficiency was unobtainable, however strong the will to see justice done.

A few months after the end of the war, additional conflict was introduced by a shift in the situation which had been neither foreseen nor guarded against. The fighting troops were very soon replaced by occupation personnel, men who had not experienced the discoveries made by the armies that had actually entered German-held territories at the end of the war. These men, on the whole, had a different attitude towards the Germans, towards other Europeans, whether in Germany or elsewhere, and towards displaced persons, whether Christians or Jews, former slave-workers or concentration-camp prisoners. There were, of course, some specialists among them – mostly of European origin – who were extremely well informed and dealt fairly with all concerned (or not, depending on the extent of their prejudices), but on the whole the US personnel soon felt considerably more sympathy for the Germans than for their victims. For the latter they often manifested a condescension bordering on insolence, and a distrust in their individual and collective integrity which – not surprisingly

– made many perfectly honourable displaced persons resort to the very behaviour which they knew they were suspected of anyway.

To the demoralization of the displaced persons was added with the passing of time the "amoralization" of the occupation personnel, whose black-market activities in cigarettes, medical supplies, food and transport were soon nothing short of staggering.

The moral quagmire was even more complex in Austria than it was in Germany. There the psychological difficulties of the occupying forces were increased by the fact that Austria, manifestly an "enemy" in the war, had been declared a "liberated country" – a triumph for the Austrian Nazis, which caused bitter disillusionment for those who had suffered at their hands, and total bewilderment for the occupying troops.

In such circumstances anyone who wished to draw a veil over his Nazi activities could do so without the least difficulty, and Stangl's belief that some sort of last-minute documentation from Berlin, Linz or Vienna might save him turned out to be not quite as naïve as it had appeared. Even without such documentation, there was still the touching faith displayed by the occupation forces in questionnaires, which could be filled in with convenient dishonesty by anyone able to put pen to paper.

In a letter to me written after our conversations in Brazil, Frau Stangl says: "I remember now that in the autumn of 1945 two men from the CIC came to see me; one was very ugly with bad teeth, the other was quite nice. The ugly one said, 'I know your husband from Lublin; he was in Sobibor and Treblinka; I have reported it; he is as good as dead.' And then they searched the house and took everything there still was belonging to my husband, and left. They knew my husband was at Glasenbach – I think they were looking for some sort of proof and because they didn't find anything, they just went away and I never heard from them again."
There was, of course, no reason for Frau Stangl to invent this incident, which therefore indicates either that people could pose as CIC officials and get away with it,* or – even worse – that the American authorities, or some individuals working for them, knew in 1945 that they were holding in Glasenbach the former Kommandant of Sobibor and Treblinka.

* A letter from Frau Stangl shortly before this book went to press confirms her story about the CIC. "I examined their papers," she writes. "I have no doubt whatever that they were genuine."

It is quite possible that if Stangl had not originally been posted to Schloss Hartheim, he would never have attracted attention (even though, by 1947, Treblinka had come up repeatedly during the Nuremberg trials). The Austrians began their investigation of the Euthanasia Programme at Schloss Hartheim and discovered, as a result of a circular to Allied prisoner-of-war camps that Stangl was at Glasenbach. In the late summer of 1947 they requested he be handed over to them for trial and he was transferred to a civilian prison in Linz.

6

"BY THIS time our situation in Wels had also somewhat improved," said Frau Stangl. "A young Hungarian girl, Maritza Rubinstein, had been billeted on me a few months before. [Later Frau Stangl corrected this name. "Maritza's name," she wrote, "was Lebovitch or something like that – her mother's maiden name was Rubinstein. I remembered this after you left."]

"First they were going to send me a rabbi, but I went to see the priest and begged him to intercede for me; I was quite prepared to have any number of women, but a man, in that small flat with the four of us, it just seemed impossible. Anyway, they relented and sent me Maritza – and she saved our lives I think. She worked at the US library in Wels and had UNRRA ration tickets; so she gave them to us and herself ate at the US officers' mess; that's how I was able to feed the children that terrible year. Even so, the two older ones got TB; the little one, thank God, sailed through it all healthy as a cricket. Later I got her into a kindergarten. Maritza – I wish I knew where she is now, she used to call me *Muttilein* – she was a wonderful, wonderful girl. Yes, I told her that my husband had been in the SS and in a camp. She had been imprisoned, at Mauthausen I think. When I told her, she said, 'Show me his photograph. Then I'll know whether I've met up with him.' But she hadn't. And we became friends. . . ."

(The fact that Maritza Lebovitch who was billeted on Frau Stangl worked at the US library is incidentally interesting because it throws light on the origin of one item of misinformation concerning Frau Stangl that has appeared in print. On page 313 of Simon Wiesenthal's *The Murderers Are Among Us*, he says, "After her husband's escape, Frau Stangl had found a job – at the local American Library."

"I have never in my life worked in an American library," Frau Stangl commented on this. "How could I have? I can't speak English.")

"But after Maritza had lived with us for a year or so, the arrangement became impossible; if I was to continue working – and I *had* to work – I had to have help with the children. So I found a maid and Maritza moved out.

"It wasn't long after that, that the Hartheim trial began, in Linz. And one day I read in the paper that it was said at the trial that Franz Stangl had been police chief at Hartheim, and of course what had been done there. I went to see Paul, with the paper in my hand. By this time he had been moved to an open prison and was working in a construction gang. In this prison many prisoners – Paul too – had single rooms and they allowed us to be alone for as long as we liked. It really *was* 'open' – we could go for walks and everything. He could have walked out of there any time he chose. Anyway, I showed him the paper and said, 'Is this true? But then, why didn't you tell me? Didn't you know I'd stand by you?' He said, 'I didn't want to burden you with it.'

"Well, I must tell the truth: however really terrible I felt about the people they killed in Treblinka and Sobibor, I didn't feel like that about Hartheim. He told me all about it that day; who they were, how ill they were; how nobody could be killed without the four certificates from the doctors. I never knew exactly how these killings were done – not in Poland either; I somehow thought they assembled people and then exploded a gas-bomb. I thought at Hartheim they had given them injections. But I often imagined how I would have felt if I had had a baby who was so terribly abnormal; I know I would have loved it as much, perhaps even more than my normal children and yet . . . no, I cannot say in all honesty that I felt as badly about Hartheim. . . .

"Not long after this talk with Paul, I asked my boss for a day off and went to the Hartheim trial. I was lucky because just that day they heard testimony from a man – I think his name was Hartl or Höldl who had been a driver at Hartheim [the same Höldl, no doubt, who Stangl said drove him in Trieste]; I remember, he had a finger missing on one hand. And someone, one of the prosecutors I think, asked him, 'And what about Franz Stangl? What

271

did he do at Hartheim?' And he answered, 'He had nothing to do with the killings; he was only responsible for police matters.' I can't tell you how relieved I was. After all, it was only a co-incidence that I was in court that day. Nobody, not even Paul, knew I had gone there. And here this man had exonerated him. I was so happy. . . . "

(It is a further indication of self-protective thinking that Frau Stangl is able – even now – to remember this testimony with such relief, even though in the context of Stangl's later activities, which she honestly deplores and is deeply ashamed of, it is irrelevant whether or not this witness "exonerated" him in court for his actions at Hartheim.)

"But this driver got four years, you know," she said. "That's when I went back to Paul and told him that it couldn't go on like this. 'If this driver gets four years,' I said to him, 'what will you get, having been police superintendent of that place?' I told him that he must get away, at once. 'We've got my savings,' I said, 'my jewellery. . . . ' That, I thought, would at least get him started. I had a cousin in Merano who I knew would help him, and my former employers, the Duca di Corsini in Florence, I thought they would help too. Paul argued and hesitated for a long time – he really thought he should stay. But finally I told him I couldn't take any more; I said if he didn't get out, get himself a job abroad and send us money to live, the children and I would end up dead. I said I was at the end of my strength. So finally he agreed.

"No, I never thought for a moment he was in danger of being sentenced to die – not that. Why should they? He had never killed anybody. In Treblinka? As far as I knew – or at least had rationalized and accepted – in Treblinka too he was never responsible for anything but the valuables. No, it never occurred to me for a moment that he was in that kind of danger."

"What about justice?" I asked. "Do you not feel and did you not feel then that 'crime', or if you like 'sin', requires retribution?"

"All I could think of then was the children. But anyway, you see, in the period between July 1944, after that traumatic experience of confessing to the priest, and the time we are now talking about – 1948 – I had managed to persuade myself that what had happened, what Paul had been involved in was part of the war . . . that awful awful war. And it was over. There was a really horrible institution in my home town, Steyr, a real antideluvian sort of prison; and I had visions of Paul being sent there, languishing perhaps for years and years in that ... that dungeon, because that's what it really was. You see, I never thought about Treblinka at that time – I suppose I ... I had put it – forced it – out of my head. I thought of his being tried for Hartheim, and of his being sent to this dreadful prison – Garsten I think it was called. And so, you see, my only thought was that he had to escape.

"I gave him my savings, not much; I can't remember how much exactly but I think it was less than 500 schillings. And I gave him a watch I had, a ring the Duchessa had given me and a necklace I had inherited from my grandmother.

"He went with another man – I can't remember his name [later she remembered it – Hans Steiner]. They walked out of the prison a few days later carrying a rucksack with provisions; I think they took mostly tinned food. The next day an Austrian police officer came to see me. He asked whether my husband was in the house. I said no, he wasn't and asked him to search the flat and he said, very politely, 'No, no, that isn't at all necessary,' and left, just as quickly as he had come. Aside from this no one ever came to ask me anything; either from the Americans or from any newspapers."

"Of course I only heard the details about Paul's escape much later. But they certainly didn't have much money – they didn't even have enough to take a train – they walked, first to Graz; there he sold the jewellery, for terribly little. And it was also there he met up with Gustav Wagner.... They were walking past a construction site – a house that was being pulled down – when a man ran out and shouted 'Herr Hauptsturmführer' – and it was Wagner who was working on that site. When they told him they were on their way to Italy, Wagner begged them to let him come and he came then and there, more or less as he was; he had no money, nothing. . . ."

Simon Wiesenthal, widely credited with Stangl's "capture" twenty years later in Brazil, was very sceptical of Frau Stangl's statements to me. "I am afraid she led you by the nose," he said. Herr Wiesenthal's theory has always been that the escapes of people such as Stangl were carefully organized and aided by organizations such as the mysterious "Odessa" (often referred to in novels and popular journalism), the existence of which has never yet been proved. The prosecutors at the Ludwigsburg Central Authority for the Investigation into Nazi Crimes who know precisely how the postwar lives of certain individuals now living in South America have been financed, have searched all their thousands of documents from beginning to end, but say they are totally unable to authenticate "Odessa". Not that this matters greatly: there certainly were various kinds of Nazi aid organizations after the war – it would have been astonishing if there hadn't been. But we should not allow the seductiveness of various theories of conspiracy to prevent us from examining with an open mind the identities and motivations of the individuals who – now an established fact–really did help people like Stangl to escape.

I have spent a great deal of time seeking documentary evidence which would support or contradict the Stangls' story of how they, and others like them, escaped from Europe; and the real facts, it turns out, are neither dramatic nor unequivocal; they are complex, ambiguous and merely prove again that in the final analysis, history is not made by organizations, but by individual men, with individual failings, and individual responsibilities.

"What nonsense," Simon Wiesenthal said to me with reference to the Stangls' claim that he "just walked out of Austria". "How could he have, without papers, passport – what about the frontier? It's all lies; he obviously had papers provided for him by Odessa."

"My husband," said Frau Stangl, "had his identity card in four languages. All Austrians had these cards from the end of the war.* He told me later that they were challenged by a policeman in Styria. They showed him their identity cards and asked him directions to the next village and he let them pass. My husband was a very good mountaineer and knew the Tyrolean mountains well from his youth. I think he said he found a way across to Italy behind the Brenner – or did he say Bolzano? – I am not quite certain. But I do remember that he said they crossed in the night and that it was very difficult for the two others, but that he managed to get them across. I don't know myself how far they finally went on foot; I do know that they took a train from Florence

* I queried Frau Stangl later about this card as I finally felt it unlikely that anyone who had been at Glasenbach would have had such an identity paper. "I don't know where he got it from," she replied, "but I vaguely remember something about a comrade who came to the prison later than he did, and who gave him his card. Paul replaced that man's photograph with his own."

to Rome. I had a cousin in Merano whose address I had given
Paul – but I didn't know at the time that he had emigrated to
North America long before. I can of course prove this by my
cousin's letters. . . . "

Stangl had told me a little of this himself, although he did not
mention his companions (he had referred to Wagner, but in another
context).

"I escaped from the Linz prison on May 30, 1948," he said.
"Originally we had intended to ask my wife's former employer, the
Duca di Corsini, to help us. But then I heard of a Bishop Hulda at
the Vatican in Rome who was helping Catholic SS officers, so that's
where we went."

Stangl had the name wrong. He meant Bishop Aloïs Hudal,
Rector of the Santa Maria del Anima, and priest-confessor to the
German Catholic community in Rome (who died there in 1963).

"*Was there any Protestant helping SS officers?*" I asked.

"Oh yes. He was in Rome too; Probst Heinemann." That, too,
was a mistake. There was a Kurator Heinemann at the Anima with
Bishop Hudal, but Pastor Dahlgrün was the Protestant pastor in
Rome who helped escapers. (Like the Catholics, the Protestants
gave legimate aid to all kinds of refugees.)

"*Did you have money?*"

"Very little. Just some my wife had saved. She had a cousin in
Merano – I tried to find him but he wasn't there any more. I got
caught in Merano, by the *carabiniere* – I think just because I was
walking in the street, you know, and I suppose I looked foreign.
Anyway, I talked myself out of it; I told them about my family
and they let me go. . . ."

Frau Stangl enlarged on this incident – and I must emphasize
again that when I saw Stangl, he had no idea that I would visit his
wife in Brazil, and that neither of them knew in advance the questions I would ask. Again she mentioned his companions, while he
didn't, but the discrepancy is in their favour rather than not, under-
lining that this story had not been "prepared".

"They went first to Merano," she said, "where Paul looked for
my cousin while the other two waited for him in the woods. When
he couldn't find my cousin, he went into a church – probably to
have a rest – he wasn't a church-goer otherwise. Anyway, when he
came out, the *carabiniere* arrested him – I am not too sure for

275

what but probably just because he looked like a German and they were supposed to arrest Germans. They put him in a car and were going to take him I don't know where, but he showed' them a picture of me and said how poor I was and how I needed him to earn money for us so that we could survive the next winter – he always *could* talk the hindlegs off a donkey – so finally they let him go. Next he and the two others went to Florence, but the Duca and his family were away on one of their estates, so they went on to Rome. . . ."

7

THE ODYSSES of various "wanted" Germans have been described in dramatic detail in many books. There may, indeed, have been a few adventurous escapes of top Nazis – though reason suggests that since large sums of money, false papers and connections abroad were easily available to such men and it is indeed a known fact that high Nazi administrators were issued with false papers weeks before Germany's defeat, they were probably the ones least likely to be involved in subterfuge and drama. However that may be, examination of published material, together with what is now some years spent discussing this subject with people connected and involved with it, has led me very seriously to doubt that the majority of these men benefited from any sophisticated conspiratorial organization – be it "Odessa", "Die Spinne", "Die Schleuse", "Kreis Rudel", "Stille Hilfe", "Bruderschaft", "Verband Deutscher Soldaten" or "Kamaradschaftswerk".

As defeat approached, the Germans – as did the people of the various countries of Europe they defeated in 1940 – obviously prepared various means of underground resistance, and aid organizations. Some of these were, no doubt, political, others social, others strictly aid organizations. Some – the Ludwigsburg Zentrale Stelle der Landesjustizverwaltungen* has quite precise (though "restricted") information on this – were well supplied with carefully channelled funds. But there is ample – and *real* – evidence that most of the published accounts vastly exaggerate their importance and their practical effectiveness.

* Central Authority for Investigation into Nazi Crimes.

276

It cannot, however, be questioned that escapers such as Stangl (and for that matter Eichmann, certainly a "bigger fish" administratively if not morally) did in the final analysis receive important assistance from two organizations which – to put it very mildly – allowed themselves to be grievously misused in aiding the escapes of individuals so dreadfully implicated: the International Red Cross, and the Vatican.

I believe that as far as the International Red Cross is concerned, it was entirely due to the organization's not being equipped to carry out the rigorous individual screening that would have been required to deal with this complicated problem. This however is an explanation, not an excuse. It was obvious that the problem would present itself, and precisely in the place where it did – the International Red Cross office in Rome. That office ought, therefore, to have been enabled to cope with it.

As far as the Vatican is concerned, the same explanation applies to some extent, but far less convincingly. The Holy See's record in the war years was so questionable that it – above all other organizations – was morally obliged to take a stand as far as escaping Nazi criminals were concerned. As it happened, the Vatican did take a stand, but it would seem that it was the precise opposite from the one that was required.

It is impossible to discuss the matter of the assistance given in Rome to escaping Nazis without devoting some thought to the larger subject of the whole attitude of the Catholic Church towards National Socialism.

When undertaking this project, I had no wish – indeed no thought – of devoting part of it to yet further discussion of the personality and motivations of Pope Pius XII. When Stangl had brought up the details of his escape through Rome, I realized that the matter would have to be touched on, but believed at first that, as he personally had been involved with only one particular cleric in Rome, Bishop Aloïs Hudal, examination could be limited to this one man, who is now dead. Unfortunately this proved impossible. The structure, the special discipline and the essential paternalism of the Catholic Church make it virtually impossible for a Catholic priest (or other religious) to take any action of consequence without the knowledge of his confessor and his superior in the hierarchy. Which is why – to take an example we examined earlier – it would have been highly improbable for the Catholic hierarchy to remain in ignorance of the Nazi plans for euthanasia, once a Catholic theologian had been officially commissioned to present an Opinion on potential Catholic reactions to euthanasia. It is equally improbable – although not, of course, impossible – that individual priests in Rome could help Nazi criminals escape overseas without the knowledge of their superiors.

If we wish to put into perspective the actions of certain individual priests during and after the war, and instead of generalizing, attribute responsibility for attitudes and actions only where it belongs, the consideration of the "Vatican Escape Route", which certainly existed, cannot be divorced from consideration of the Vatican's attitude to the extermination of the Jews and Gypsies, the murder of millions of Russians, the martyrdom of the Polish Catholics – in fact of the whole atmosphere of the Holy See at the time, which if it did not induce the events which have thrown a shadow over the whole of the Catholic Church, certainly allowed them to take place. The resulting self-questionings and accusations may have been out of all proportion to the reality of the situation and the number of priests involved. It is to establish a more accurate perspective that we must again examine the attitude of Pope Pius XII, and of his inner circle.

I believe that there were four reasons for Pope Pius XII's conduct in the fateful years 1939–45.

The first and foremost, as has been established beyond doubt, was his dread of Bolshevism as the arch-enemy of the Church. This rejection was so total that it led him virtually to hold the vast majority of Russians, who supported this system, to be unworthy of concern. (The Pope's attitude was reflected in the reply Monsignor Godfrey, the Apostolic Delegate in Britain, gave to the Foreign Minister, Lord Halifax, when in the spring of 1939 the latter suggested that it seemed regrettable the Russians were not being included in a list of great European powers the Pope was inviting to attend a peace conference. Monsignor Godfrey replied that "in no circumstances would it be possible for the Pope to consider such an approach.")*

We have heard a great deal of the Pope's silence regarding the martyrdom under the Nazis of the Catholic Poles, and of course the

* Telegram from Halifax to Sir Francis d'Arcy Osborne, British Ambassador to the Holy See, May 5, 1939.

extermination of the Jews. But very little has ever been said about his even greater silence. For on several occasions he did in fact address words of comfort, however conventional and ineffectual, to the starving and dying Poles. And on one notable date, December 24, 1942, he actually pronounced seven words which, however obliquely and obscurely, were intended to refer to the Jews (although it is doubtful whether anyone outside professional religious circles noticed them).*

I have thoroughly studied the five volumes of documents, published by the Vatican between 1967 and 1972. In letter after letter, in document after document, the Pope deplores the outrages of war, especially the aerial bombardment of innocent civilians. But not in one single place does he utter a word concerning the murder of millions of Russian civilians.

The editors of the Vatican publication have printed the heart-rending letter to the Pope of August 29–31, 1942, from Archbishop Szeptyckyj of Leopol in Ruthenia (southern Ukraine). Not only does he tell the Pope that 200,000 Jews had already been murdered by then in that small province – and describe in some detail how – but he also speaks of the death of "hundreds of thousands of Christians".

"Liberated by the German army from the Bolshevik yoke," he writes, "we originally felt a certain relief, which however lasted no more than one or two months. Little by little, the government has instituted a truly unbelievable régime of terror and corruption. . . . Today the whole country feels that the German régime is if anything worse, almost diabolically worse, than the Bolshevists."

This saintly man who three years earlier had asked the Pope's permission to take his own life as a gesture of protest against the hardships imposed on the Catholic clergy and faithful by the Communists, thanks the Pope in this letter for having refused his permission. "The last three years," he says, "have persuaded me that I am not worthy of this death which would have had less meaning before God than a prayer spoken by a child."

In another letter, two weeks later, the Archbishop thanks the Pope for two letters he had meanwhile received from him; one sent on July 25, the other on August 26, the first to congratulate the Archbishop on the fiftieth anniversary of his entry into the priesthood; the second to commiserate with him on the suffering of the

* See page 332.

"pastors" in his territory. But in neither letter did the Pope mention with one word the suffering of the Russian people under the Nazi conqueror, nor does he appear to have replied to the Archbishop's letter of August 29–31.

The Pope was certain – as indeed, up to a point, had been his predecessor Pope Pius XI (who was, however, *much* more critical of the Nazis) that the Germans under Hitler represented the main bulwark against Bolshevism in Europe. And this conviction – unshaken by the Russo-German pact which, with his diplomatic experience, he must have recognized as a stop-gap manœuvre – determined the majority of his actions and inactions in the war years.

The second important influence on the Pope's conduct seems to me to have been his fear that the Nazis intended to wipe out Catholicism in Germany. Imposing restrictive measures on Church organizations (both Protestant and Catholic), and constantly attempting to recondition the minds of the young by abolishing Catholic schools and publications, they moved carefully and gradually, but they moved. Although in fact very few German or Austrian priests and *not one Catholic bishop* in all Western Europe was ever arrested or harmed by the Nazis (unlike the great number of Polish clerics imprisoned), the measures the Nazis took from 1934 on were a clear indication of the direction in which they were moving.

The gravity of this threat is vividly illustrated by one of the last of the five hundred-odd books, reports, pamphlets and documents I read in the three years of preparing this book.* It contains a résumé of a letter from Martin Bormann to Gauleiter Dr Meyer of Münster, dated June 6, 1941; a letter that seems to go a long way towards further explaining Pius XII's silence in the face of Nazi horrors, and indeed even towards justifying some of his most deeply felt fears.

It existed in two forms: as Bormann first wrote it, apparently on his own initiative; and as subsequently edited (probably in the autumn of 1941) and sent out as a circular to all Gauleiters. Testimony at the Nuremberg trials indicated that these two versions, which differed slightly in wording, were both finally withdrawn and ordered to be destroyed.

It seems to have been an illegal copy of this letter made when a

* Friedrich Zipfel, *Kirchenkampf in Deutschland 1933–1945* (de Gruyter, Berlin 1965) page 511.

leaflet was being prepared, to be dropped by air, which was accepted in evidence by the court (Nuremberg Document D-75).*

The letter, entitled "Relationship between National Socialism and Christendom", is a careful and clever analysis of all forms of Christian dogma, and a recommendation for the total abolition of all established religions, based on logic, patriotism and a kind of pantheism likely to appeal to many wavering minds. It is – to my knowledge, at least – the most outspoken denunciation of organized Christianity to emanate from any Nazi leader (and indeed, as we have seen, was considered premature and was withdrawn). However secret and restricted this letter was, there can be no doubt that it reached the Vatican. Equally, there can be no doubt that the Vatican already knew, long before it reached them, that the opinions it expressed were current among the Nazi leadership; the letter must therefore have heavily underlined the appalling danger to Catholicism in Germany.

Desperate concern about the very real danger to one of the most important Catholic strongholds in Europe therefore seems to me the second major reason for the Pope's attitude. And fatally connected with this fear for Catholicism in Germany, there was also his evaluation of public opinion and mood among German Catholics.

Jaques Maudaule, in an article for *L'Amitié Judéo-Chrétienne* (December 1949), wrote that " . . . it is almost impossible for the Pope to express an opinion unless he is forced to it by a kind of great *movement* of opinion arising in the masses and communicating itself to the priesthood from the faithful." Because, he says, " . . . (essentially) the Church is a democracy."

This explanation is of crucial importance. If the German and Austrian episcopate were persuaded that Catholic opinion in Greater Germany was predominantly in favour of National Socialism, then according to this thesis the Pope's possibilities of action, determined by this public opinion, would have been limited. We might argue – we would certainly wish to argue – that if this were so, the Pontiff was all the more obliged to influence attitudes tending finally towards the total abandonment of morality – but this argument would be bound to fail.

It would fail because German – Catholic or non-Catholic – sentiment in favour of National Socialism was by no means initially

---

* The Nuremberg document is, of course, on record, but I have been unable to trace such a leaflet through the Imperial War Museum or the RAF Museum.

or primarily dictated by anti-Semitism or any other objectionable motivation. It was essentially the affirmation of a new political and economic system which – the vast majority of Germans believed – offered a "new order" representing integrity, national self-respect, and economic parity. Its pseudo-mystical elements were introduced to the masses only gradually, and primarily for the benefit of the young. The Vatican, theoretically, had no more right to interfere with the internal politics of Germany than it would have to interfere with the political organization of Great Britain, the USA or France.

If we connect this "great movement of opinion" which indicated to the Pope that the German Catholics accepted National Socialism, with his knowledge of the measures taken by the Nazis against the Church and of what these measures portended, then the Pope's refusal to condemn Nazi atrocities becomes not more justifiable or palatable, but easier to understand.

The Pope's attitude was thus determined first by his fear of Bolshevism and secondly by his fear of the Nazis' plans eventually to abolish the Church. He must have felt that in view of the fundamental acceptance of National Socialism by virtually all Germans, and particularly of the unbounded enthusiasm of the young, *anything* he said in criticism of Nazi policies or actions would tend to alienate the Catholic Germans, and would add immeasurably to – and even precipitate – the long-range danger to the Church. (It will be remembered that the Pope waited to issue an encyclical condemning euthanasia until June 1943, by which time he was obviously assured that "the great movement of opinion" amongst German Catholics was definitely against euthanasia.)

These then, were the main reasons for the Pope's attitude. But there were two others. One of them was quite simply that he had come to love Germany. It was in Germany – as he often said – that he had spent his happiest years, and it was with Germans that he had in his youth, and continued to have to his death, the closest emotional ties. Having known so many – and so many excellent – Germans, he must have found it almost impossible to believe the terrible stories he began to hear from the time when the Germans invaded Poland.

But well within a year, it was no longer just "stories"; he was sent detailed reports, painfully authenticated letters and documents, and this is where we have to accept the last – and most obnoxious – reason for his silence.

Anyone who has read Pius XII's letters to the German bishops (and in the original German the phraseology is even more significant) must find it difficult to doubt that the Pope was anti-Semitic. I do not say that this determined his conduct; it is plain enough what his main motivations were. But this perhaps instinctive anti-Semitism must at least have contributed to his passivity on the many occasions when – as he used to say when referring to the Nazi atrocities, and as was no doubt true – he felt "deeply troubled".

Having examined again the reasons for the silence of Pope Pius XII, and disregarding for a moment the indisputable moral obligation, we must ask the tragic question whether, if the Pope from the very beginning had taken a decisive stand against euthanasia, against the systematic debilitation by forced labour, starvation, sterilization and murder of the Eastern European populations, and finally against the extermination of the Jews, this could have affected the conscience of individual Catholics who were directly or indirectly implicated in these matters, enough to force the Nazis to change their policies.

I have deliberately put this question into a chronological sequence, because it can only be answered by considering one development after another.

We have seen in the preceding pages, on the basis of documents and events, how aware Hitler was of the importance of Catholic opinion. And we have seen in the statements of individuals concerned, such as Stangl and his wife, how much the tacit approval of the Church contributed to the pacification of their conscience. I think there is a valid comparison to be made between Stangl's (one individual's) and the Vatican's (fundamentally another individual's) step-by-step acquiescence to increasingly terrible acts. The very first failure to say "No" was fatal, each succeeding step merely confirming the original and basic moral flaw.

It is tragically true that by the time the extermination camps were ready for the murder of the mass of Polish Jews (the great nations of the world, one must not forget, having plainly shown their unwillingness and incapacity to come to grips with this monumental catastrophe) a Papal protest, while still imperative from a moral point of view, could have had no practical effect.

But there can be no doubt that a fully publicized, unequivocal moral stand, beginning with the first whisper of euthanasia, and accompanied by a threat of excommunication for anyone participating in any wilful act of murder, would have established the Vatican as a formidable factor to be reckoned with and would have had at least some – and perhaps a profound – effect on the events to come: the murder of millions of Russian civilians, both Christians and Jews; the martyrdom of the Polish Catholics; and finally of the Polish Jews.

The question of the Pope's attitude unhappily also has a bearing on postwar events. For it is impossible to avoid the thought that it must have influenced the self-justifications and the actions of the priests in Rome who extended substantial aid to escaping Nazis.

I approached with considerable scepticism claims that priests could knowingly have aided men who were accused of such monstrous crimes to escape secular justice. Such conduct was contrary to everything I had seen myself in occupied France, where almost all the clergy, from archbishop down to the humblest village curé and the youngest convent novices, gave constant proof of the highest moral principles and humanity. It was also contrary to what I had learned immediately after the war from many displaced persons, including Jews of all nationalities whose lives were saved by priests and nuns. It is of course true, and often forgotten or minimized, that in the final analysis, everything that is done is done by individual men and women with individual powers of decision. Whatever religious faith a priest, pastor, monk or nun belongs to, he or she remains an individual person and – an essential point – a national of his or her country of origin. It is true that many priests – particularly from Poland – died in concentration camps for their religious convictions, their martyrdom unrelated to their nationality. There have been saintly beings like this throughout the ages. But during the period we are discussing here, many more religious acted against the Germans at least in part for reasons of personal patriotism. Great numbers of the heroic French, Belgian, Italian, Dutch, Norwegian, Danish, Czech, Polish and other priests and pastors who hid Allied airmen, aided underground organizations, operated radio transmitters and helped anti-Nazi Germans to hide amongst the local populations, were acting above all for the sake of their countries, rather than for their Church. Many of them have readily said so. Throughout Europe Jewish children were hidden in convents by nuns. In occupied France I came across several of these noble women, and more than once, when I remarked on their courage, I received the answer: *"Mais je suis Française, à la fin."*

Exceptions that, extraordinarily enough, only prove this rule are those German and Austrian religious who, in time of war, acted *against* the laws of their country. I have talked to some of them, too, and each of these admirable men and women spoke of battles of conscience, and a decision made as an individual who could not accept "that" government and "its" laws as representing the country's true interests. Thus they, too, were acting primarily as morally outraged nationals of their countries who happened to be priests, nuns and pastors.

If, of course, we accept such national loyalties within the Churches as inevitable and right in such circumstances, then it must follow that it was no less right for German and Austrian priests to help Germans and Austrians in general who were in dire straits after the war. So we come back to the central question, the one that appears to raise its head in all these polemics concerning the attitude of the Catholic Church during that period: how much did they know?

We have been told the Church did not know about the Nazis intention to institute euthanasia in 1939, even though a moral theologian, active at the time as Professor at a Catholic university (of which he had previously been Rector), worked for six months on an officially commissioned Opinion.

We have been told the Pope could not protest against the extermination of the Jews in Nazi-occupied Poland, because – although he had heard rumours of these horrors – he didn't really *know*. And we are told that, although it is admitted that after Germany's defeat leading Nazis escaped abroad through Rome, their identities were unknown to those who helped them.

I was open to be convinced on all these claims, but on all of them the proof to the contrary is overwhelming.

As far as the escapes are concerned, even if one discounts all or most of the dramatic stories, and even if one is prepared to ascribe most of the aid given in Rome to perfectly legitimate humanitarian motives,* we are still left with a number of incontrovertible facts which establish that, apart from the genuinely charitable activities of the Roman clergy, there was, on the part of some amongst them

* Before the German defeat such help was extended equally readily to nationals of Allied countries.

(almost all Germans and Austrians), a deliberate effort to aid specific individuals who were particularly implicated in Nazi crimes.

In the interest of fairness, however, one further point needs to be made: in all of wartime Europe, Rome – primarily because of the Vatican – was the city most protected from *overt* acts of terror by the Germans. I do not wish to minimize the deportation of the Roman Jews in 1943–4,* but there was never in Rome the continuous and unabating horror that existed elsewhere. People in Rome, priests included, were to some extent spared the dreadful lessons learnt by those who lived in the midst of terror, so that at least a measure of psychological exoneration may be conceded to those who now plead general – if not specific – ignorance.

Equally – and this again seems to me a crucial element when evaluating these events – much of the initiative and final responsibility for escape and for their subsequent lives overseas rested in the individuals themselves. The best proof of this lies in the comparatively modest lives led in the countries they escaped to, by those men we really know about now (rather than have heard or read dramatic rumours about).

It appears to me that Stangl's escape – and the events preceding it – as described by himself, by his wife, and by a number of other people directly or indirectly involved, provides a significant example against which to measure other, and perhaps less well authenticated reports.

* 2,091 Roman Jews were deported; 102 of them survived. Italy was, throughout the war, in the forefront of the countries who protected their Jewish citizens, and five-sixths of all Italian Jews survived the war, many of them having been hidden in convents and monasteries in the provinces.

Part V

I

"IT WAS too strange, you know," said Stangl. "I had no idea how one went about finding a bishop at the Vatican. I arrived in Rome and walked across a bridge over the Tiber and suddenly found myself face to face with a former comrade: there, in the middle of Rome where there were millions of people. He'd been in the security police in France and they wanted to put him on trial there. He'd been extradited from Glasenbach by the French and escaped in the Tyrol when on the way to France. Anyway, he said at once, 'Are you on your way to see Hulda?'* I said yes, but that I didn't know where to find him. So he told me, but he said not to go until the next day and he told me where I could go for the night. But I didn't see why I shouldn't go at once, so I did – it couldn't have taken me more than half an hour to get there. The Bishop came into the room where I was waiting and he held out both his hands and said, 'You must be Franz Stangl. I was expecting you.' "

"What did Bishop Hudal do for you?"

"Well, first he got me quarters in Rome where I was to stay till my papers came through. And he gave me a bit more money – I had almost nothing left. Then, after a couple of weeks, he called me in and gave me my new passport – a Red Cross passport."

"Did it actually say 'Red Cross Passport'?"

"Yes. It was a whitish booklet and there was a red cross on the cover – it was the same sort of thing, you know, as the old Nansen passports. [He had seen those when he was in the police in Linz.] They'd reversed my name by mistake; it was made out to Paul F. Stangl. I pointed it out to the Bishop. I said, 'They made a mistake, this is incorrect. My name is Franz D. Paul Stangl.' But he patted my shoulder and said, 'Let's let sleeping dogs lie – never mind.' He got me an entrance visa to Syria and a job in a textile mill in Damascus, and he gave me a ticket for the ship. So I went to

* Meaning Bishop Hudal.

Syria. After a while my family joined me and three years later, in 1951, we emigrated to Brazil. . . ."

"Paul wrote me from Rome sounding very depressed," said Frau Stangl. "The other man who had escaped with him – his name was Hans Steiner or something like that – had given up; he returned to Austria and surrendered to the Americans." (Frau Stangl didn't tell me then where Gustav Wagner went – she was always reticent about him – but it seems that he too obtained papers for the Near East, and later for South America.) "Paul was billeted at the Germanikum," she said. "I don't know how long it was before I heard from him again – perhaps not very long, but to me it seemed an eternity. Then suddenly I had a letter from Damascus. He said Bishop Hudal had found him a job in a textile mill and that he had a room in an Arab house and had found friends who had got there ahead of him, and soldiers too – and there were some generals who had come there from Egypt. His letters began to sound quite different: relaxed, calm, liberated. . . ."

I spoke to many people in Rome and elsewhere about Frau Stangl's saying that her husband was billeted at the Germanikum, and they all considered it very unlikely. The Germanikum is the Jesuit hostel for German theological students and is usually full. German priests in Rome said that he might have stayed at one of several monasteries, at a convent, or at Bishop Hudal's own Anima. Stangl himself didn't use the word "Germanikum" but simply said "Bishop Hulda [Hudal] billeted me", which could mean either that the Bishop found him billets elsewhere, or that he put him up at his own House. No one in Rome denies that Catholic institutions sheltered escapers. What they deny is that any of the priests, and particularly the Vatican, knew the real identity of those of the people they harboured who had "something on their conscience". Of course, it still remains odd that Frau Stangl, who doesn't know Rome, should have thought of the "Germanikum". However, just before I finished this book, she wrote to say that she had salvaged another name from her memory: " . . . the 'Salvatorianerkloster' [convent] in or near the Vatican, but I'm not certain in what connection Paul spoke of it," she wrote. "Could *that* be where the men slept?"

"The many many German civilians slept on mats on the floor in their Vatican quarters," she had said in Brazil, "and in the morning they had to get up at dawn and get out, and they weren't allowed back into the building till the evening; there was a priest who supervised it all. They were given meal-tickets for lunch [at a mess run by nuns, according to priests who were in Rome at the time], but otherwise there was nothing for them to do except run around in the streets and do their utmost not to attract attention by sitting on benches in the Pincio Gardens, where they might be picked up by the *carabiniere* who took all German and Austrian nationals without Italian documents to the dreaded concentration camp at Frascatti. He wrote that he had run his feet bloody and that he felt totally hopeless about life and about ever being in a position to help me and the children. And then finally he wrote in another letter that he had volunteered to do masonry work for the nuns and that one of the Sisters was giving him extra food. He spoke of crossing St Peter's Square with her, carrying a mason's bucket, and he described going to Mass in the morning in – I think he said – a Vatican chapel, and I remember he said there was a nun there who sang so loudly and so dreadfully off-key that his ears kept rumbling all day long afterwards. And he wrote – and told me repeatedly later – about his audiences with the good Bishop, who in the end had given him the Red Cross passport. But he never said that anyone questioned him about himself – still less that he had to fill out any sort of questionnaire. . . ."

Frau Stangl's remark about a questionnaire referred to a book I had told her about, *Flucht vor Nürnberg* (Escaping Nuremberg), written in 1964-6 by an unrepentant Nazi, a former chief of the Hitler Youth, Alfred Jarschel, under the pseudonym "Werner Brockdorff".* In this extraordinary and partly autobiographical account of, amongst other things, the so-called "Roman Escape Route", Jarschel describes how escaping Nazis were welcomed to Italy by members of the Catholic clergy, were often accompanied by them to Rome dressed in monks' habits, were given money, sheltered in convents and monasteries, and finally, after writing a kind of extended *curriculum vitae* and submitting to an examination by a "board" of priests, were issued with International Red Cross passports and means for travelling overseas.

While I found some of the more dramatic points impossible to prove – and this book may indeed be a highly coloured account of

* Welsermühl Verlag, Wels and Munich, 1969.

events (the author died in 1967, but I have talked at length with his wife and have seen his publisher) – many other, less vividly written, more factual descriptions, and now my own research, go a long way towards confirming some of the essential details.

2

IN 1966 THE Vatican began the publication of a series of volumes under the collective title *Actes et Documents du Saint Siège relatif à la Seconde Guerre Mondiale*. Breaking with an age-old tradition of not making public papal documents for a hundred years, these volumes – six of which are now in print,* with four more to come – present, in a carefully edited form, many hundreds of reports, memoranda and letters received by and despatched from the Vatican between the years 1939 and 1945.

This project, compiled at the Vatican by four ecclesiastical historians, was obviously undertaken to counter the polemics concerning Pope Pius XII, and particularly concerning his public attitude towards the atrocities committed by the Germans against the Catholics of Eastern Europe and the Jews. Its significance lies at least as much in the *tone* of various letters, from the Pope and others, and in the *omission* of certain documents (some of which I was subsequently enabled to see, and which will be quoted in these pages), as in the material they contain.

Father Burkhart Schneider, SJ, with whom I had two conversations of several hours each at the Gregorian University in Rome where he lives and teaches, has been, for eight years, on the multinational team of Jesuit historians compiling these papers.

Father Schneider made no effort to minimize the importance of the documents as applying to the controversy that has raged since the end of the war about the Pope's attitude towards the extermination of the Jews. He avoided immediate reference to the problem of Pius XII by going back to the Vatican attitude before that Pope's election. "The Holy See," he said, "made its position towards National Socialism clear as early as 1937. Pius XI's encyclical, *Mit Brennender Sorge* ("With Burning Anxiety"), is part

_____
* As of September, 1973.

of the record. By an oversight of the Gestapo, who had been informed that it was to be read from the pulpits in German churches but didn't believe it, this particular protest of the Pope – I assure you, only the first of many – was allowed to be made but didn't in fact receive wide publicity in Germany. But", he said emphatically, "I must call to your attention the fact that, although the Pope gave expression in the clearest possible terms to his profound concern, the 'burning anxiety' with which he had noted the frightening developments in Germany, and although the encyclical was, of course, made public all over the world, his misgivings were evidently not shared by any of the great powers, including France and Poland; they were in fact most pointedly ignored precisely by these two great Catholic nations."

It was Pius XI who concluded the famous Concordat – negotiated by the Papal Nuncio, Eugenio Pacelli, later Pope Pius XII – with Nazi Germany.

In his 1937 encyclical Pius XI did indeed express his concern about National Socialism and its "neo-paganism", and – although in guarded, or somewhat generalized, terms – did touch on the subject of racism. "Whoever takes the race or the people," he wrote, "or the State or the form of the State, or the repositories of power, or any other fundamental value of the human community – all things which occupy a necessary and honourable place in the earthly order – whoever takes these notions and removes them from this scale of values, not excluding even religious values, and deifies them through an idolatrous cult, inverts and falsifies the order of things as created and ordained by God. Such a man is far removed from true belief in God and from a conception of life in keeping with that faith . . . ."

Nonetheless, at that point Pius XI's burning anxiety was still mainly caused by the Nazis' claim to total control over the education of the young, which entailed the abolition of church schools. The encyclical contained one direct reference to the Jews (50,000 of whom had already been forced to leave Germany while the outrageous "Nuremberg Laws" were being applied against those who remained*); they were mentioned in defence of "the sacred

---

* Under these laws the population was divided into two categories, "Reichs Citizens", with full civic rights, and "State Subjects", whose rights were severely curtailed; and marriage between Jews and Germans (and all other so-called Aryans) was prohibited.

books of the Old Testament which are revered in common with the Catholic Church". Unfortunately the sentence ended with an unhappy phrase, in that it referred to the Jews once again as "the people who were to put Him on the cross" (a literal interpretation which, I hasten to add, is becoming less and less common in Catholic teaching).

However, the fact that the Pope, in 1937, was primarily concerned with the Nazis' recently proclaimed educational reforms seemed perfectly legitimate, if hardly relevant in this discussion with Father Schneider to the question of the later attitude of the Holy See towards the extermination of the Jews.

Certainly, in 1937, the indications of events to come concerning the Jews were by no means clear. It has now been amply proved that at that time, and probably until at least the beginning of the war, the Nazi leadership themselves had not decided what to do about the Jewish question and certainly neither the population of Germany, nor any other, could dream of what would develop. What was then happening to the Jews within Germany was still being largely ignored by all the great powers (many of whose statesmen were to refer openly to the anti-Jewish measures of the Nazis as "growing pains") and were not seen as fatally suspicious even by Jews outside Germany – or for that matter many within it. It would therefore have been truly extraordinary if an encyclical of 1937 had taken issue with these aspects of National Socialism.

Furthermore, it is a fact (which only recently came to public knowledge) that Pius XI – far more of a humanitarian than his successor – was to become increasingly concerned with Germany's racist policies. On June 22, 1938 (this would have been just two months after virtually publicly rebuking Cardinal Innitzer for welcoming the Nazis into Austria), he asked the American Jesuit, Father John La Farge, to draft an encyclical, on the basis of principles he had discussed with him in a private audience, denouncing nationalism, racism and anti-Semitism. Father La Farge prepared the draft in collaboration with two other Jesuits, a German, Father Gustav Grundloch, and a Frenchman, Father Gustave Desbuquois, and the paper was delivered (through the Order's customary channels) to the Jesuit Superior General, Wladimir Ledochowski, in Rome, in September 1938. It is believed by many Jesuits that Pius XI was never shown the draft – that it was withheld by Jesuits and members of the Curia more concerned with the threat of Bolshevism than with the Nazis. Father La Farge was to be told after the death of Pius XI that he was free to publish the paper as a private Opinion, on the condition that it remained totally unconnected with the person of the deceased Pope. The paper remained unpublished.

Professor Schneider and I next discussed the public protest, in August 1941, of the Bishop of Münster, Graf Galen; first against anti-Church measures in Germany and then—with what has always been considered spectacular effect – against the Nazis' Euthanasia Programme. But Father Schneider shrugged it off as comparatively irrelevant. "It didn't do much," he said, "and, in some respects anyway, they didn't stop."

When I suggested that, quite apart from the historical record, my own talks with some of those who had taken part in the programme appeared to indicate that the specific – although verbal, not written – Hitler order which finally stopped most of the euthanasia, did in fact result directly from public pressure after Count Galen's sermon, Father Schneider said, "Well, it was almost finished anyway; they had more or less killed all those they had intended to kill."

The fact that the Bishop of Münster, following his sermons, was never either arrested or even stopped from exercising his functions, has always seemed amazing – although the same applies to a number of other men of the Churches, certainly to all the Western European bishops.* As far as Count Galen was concerned, the possibility of arresting him *was* discussed at a meeting of representatives from the Ministries of Justice, Propaganda and Churches, at Himmler's office on October 27, 1941. The unanimous feeling of the participants was that the Bishop *should* be arrested. But while they agreed that he had laid himself open to a charge of treason, they also agreed that as such a charge would involve a formal trial, where the delicate matter of euthanasia would have to be mentioned in public, it would be preferable to send him straight to a concentration camp. The final decision, however, had to be put to Hitler. Hitler replied that he "wished to avoid all controversy with the Catholic Church and would await the end of

* Subsequent to the English publication of this book, the author learned that Bishop Piquet of Clermont-Ferrand, France, was arrested and sent to Dachau by the German occupation authorities. (See: *The Nazi Persecution of the Churches*, John S. Conway, page 297, Weidenfeld & Nicolson, 1968.)

the war to settle [his] account with the Bishop – to the last mark and pfennig".

Albert Hartl, former chief of church information at the Reich's Security Office, told me in addition that he had been informed that Hitler had given Cardinal Faulhaber his promise that no bishop would be arrested. "They shook hands on it," said Herr Hartl.

Father Schneider certainly did not mention any such agreement. His argument, on the contrary, was that all the clerics, high and low – and indeed including the Pope – had been in dire peril.

"Concerning the possibility of later protests by the Pope," he said, "people just don't realize how isolated the Vatican was. It was merely a tiny and comparatively powerless enclave encircled by Fascists and Nazis. Even if the Pope *had* voiced his doubts and horror later on, how do you think anyone would have learned of it? The Vatican radio station was virtually unheard; certainly by the Germans whose 'people's radio sets' were definitely not capable of picking up foreign stations."

I suggested that the Allies – the BBC particularly – would presumably have been very willing to communicate any such protest made by the Pope to the population of Germany, many of whom, it was well known, did in fact listen to BBC broadcasts despite the dangers involved.

"What do you think it did to Galen's reputation," replied Father Schneider, "when the Allies dropped copies of his sermon together with their bombs? Would you call it psychologically apt to present the people of Rhine-Westphalia with this particular double-edged sword? Do you think it was effective? No, if the enemy had used a protest by the Holy See for their own propaganda purposes, and this could undoubtedly have happened, it would have undone any good such a protest might conceivably have done.

"But anyway, the problems the Vatican is faced with in such a situation are not sufficiently appreciated. After all, we have similar situations now, and they have existed all through history. At this moment the Vatican has to choose between condemning publicly certain governments of new nations that are quite manifestly assuming dictatorial powers, or playing along with them in the hope of maintaining sufficiently normal relations to be able to continue to help those in these countries for whom it feels itself responsible. And that was exactly the situation during the Nazi period."

I asked Father Schneider whether the Vatican does not have the wider responsibility of representing certain moral principles before the world of Catholics and others, rather than merely that of trying to protect at any one time any one national group of Catholics.

"The Vatican", he said, "has to be very careful. The Holy See has no bombs, no arms; no 'power' in that sense. If it is to remain effective as the centre and focus of the Church, it must above all remain in touch. Towards that end it must – as far as possible – go along with ruling governments. The Holy Father, Pius XII, wrote very openly about this in his *Letters to the German Bishops*, specifically as I recall [on April 30, 1943] to the Bishop of Berlin, when he spoke about the advisability of leaving to pastors on the spot the decision whether or not it was reasonably safe to lodge protests."*

This often-quoted letter to the brave Bishop Preysing – the first the Pope had written to him in over a year – acknowledged a number of letters and communications the Bishop had sent, too many to enumerate here. Once again the Bishop had delivered a heroically outspoken sermon (on November 15, 1942), which once again has been "forgotten", as far as I can discover, except for another footnote in the Vatican publication.† It was on the equality of all souls in the eyes of God. "This Love", he said, "cannot exclude anyone; above all because he speaks perhaps a different language, or is of foreign blood. Every man has in his soul the image of God. Every man has the right to life and love. . . . It is never permitted to deprive members of foreign races of human rights – the right to freedom, the right to property, the right to an insoluble marriage; never is it permitted to subject anyone to [such] cruelties. . . ."

The Pope thanks him for "the clear and frank words which, on various occasions, you have addressed to your congregation and therefore to the public. We have in mind, among others, your commentaries of June 28, 1942, on the Christian concept of law; of All Souls' Sunday last November on the right of every man to life and love. . . ."

On March 6, 1943, Preysing wrote again to the Pope and begged him to intercede for the Jews. "Here in Berlin we are even more appalled [than about recent bombardments] by the new wave of deportations of Jews, which began just before March 1. Thousands

* *Actes et Documents du Saint Siège Relatif à la Seconde Guerre Mondiale*, vol. II, page 318, "Lettres de Pie XII aux Evêques Allemands, 1939–1944".
† Ibid, vol. II, page 322.

of people, whose probable fate Your Holiness has indicated in Your Christmas message, are involved here. Amongst the deported are many Catholics. Would it not be possible that Your Holiness make another attempt to intercede for these unhappy innocents? Your intervention represents the last hope of so many and the fervent entreaty of all decent men."

" . . . it was a consolation for Us", replied the Pope, "to learn that Catholics, notably in Berlin, had manifested great Christian charity towards the sufferings of so-called non-Aryans. And We would like, in this context, to add a special word of paternal recognition and warm sympathy to the imprisoned Monsignor Lichtenberg. . . .*

"So far as episcopal pronouncements are concerned," the Pope continues, "we leave to the [senior] pastors on the spot the task of assessing whether, and to what extent, the danger of reprisals and pressures and, perhaps, other circumstances due to the length and psychological climate of the war, counsel restraint – despite reasons that might exist for intervention – in order to avoid greater evils. This is one of the motives for the limitations We impose on Ourself in Our proclamations. . . .

"For the Catholic non-Aryans as well as for unconverted Jews," the Pope then writes, "the Holy See has charitably done whatever was in His powers, materially and morally. *It has required, on the part of the executive branches of Our relief organization, a maximum degree of patience and self-effacement, to comply with the expectations – one must really say the demands – of those seeking help, as well as in overcoming the diplomatic difficulties. Of the very great sums which, in American currency, we spent on overseas travel for emigrants, we do not wish to speak; we gave this aid for the love of God and did well not to expect earthly gratitude.*† Still, even Jewish organizations have warmly acknowledged the rescue operation of the Holy See. . . ."

Thus spoke Pius XII in reply to the German Bishop's entreaty for his help for the Jews, and he added that he had said

"a word about the things that are presently being done to non-Aryans in German-controlled territory in our Christmas message. It was short, but it was well understood.‡ It is superfluous to say that Our paternal love and solicitude are greater [than before] towards non-Aryan or semi-Aryan Catholics [whatever that means], children of the Church like the others, when their outward existence

* Monsignor Lichtenberg had been sent to Dachau for publicly praying for the Jews.
† Author's italics.
‡ The Pope's 1942 Christmas message is quoted on page 331.

298

is collapsing and they are in spiritual distress. In the present situation we can unfortunately not offer them any effective help outside Our prayers. We are, however, determined to raise Our voice anew on their behalf as circumstances indicate and permit. . . ."

Returning to the subject of the Pope's threatened position, Father Schneider asked whether I had read General Karl Wolff's recently published claim that he had received orders that, under certain conditions, he was to arrest the Pope and bring him to Germany.* Father Schneider said he had known of this contingency plan for a long time. (Indeed, a statement by Father Robert Graham, one of the three Jesuit historians working with and under Father Schneider on the Vatican documents, had appeared in the press on February 26, 1972, following General Wolff's "disclosure", only a few days prior to this conversation. In this statement Father Graham had said that in 1943 Vatican personnel had been advised to keep a packed bag ready for possible departure.)

Father Schneider obviously intended to emphasize – as did Father Graham in his statement – that the Pope was under tremendous pressure, in constant personal peril, and never free to act as he would have chosen had he been a free agent.

There is, of course, a wealth of published material on Pius XII, his personality, motivation, actions and inactions during the war years. One of the two or three most authoritative books on the subject is Carlo Falconi's *The Silence of Pius XII*† in which reference is made to the plan described by Father Schneider. "But if the Nazis avoided open conflict with the local hierarchies," says Falconi, "still more did they avoid attacking the Church in its central stronghold, however great was their secret desire to do so. Proof of this – besides the evidence of the facts – can be found in Goebbels' *Diary* and Hitler's *Table Talk*. In any case, the only period in which such an attack would have been possible was between July 25, 1943 and June 4, 1944. Directly after Mussolini's arrest on the first of these dates, a project for an attack on the Vatican [held co-responsible with King Victor Emmanuel for the arrest], so as to capture the diplomats in refuge there, make a haul of documents and 'take the Pope into safe custody' in Germany‡

* General Wolff was Himmler's one-time secretary, who has served a prison sentence and is now free.
† Faber and Faber, 1970.
‡ Luxemburg too was briefly considered for such a contingency.

was really entertained. But common sense soon prevailed over such a harmful plan."

The entry in Goebbels' diary for October 1943 provides conclusive proof: he writes about a "momentary idea" – following Mussolini's arrest – to "include the Vatican" in the planned arrests of a number of Romans. He reports that Ribbentrop, Himmler and he himself immediately opposed it. "I don't think it is necessary to break into the Vatican," he writes, "and I also consider that such a step could have fatal effects on world opinion. . . . Everyone, including the Führer, now agrees that the Vatican must be exempted from any measures we will take."*

When the Germans occupied Rome, the Pope was personally informed by the German Ambassador, Baron Weizsäcker, that "the sovereignty and territorial integrity of the Vatican will be respected and . . . that the Germans . . . undertake to conduct themselves in such a way as to protect the Vatican City from the fighting."

The Vatican City was then ringed by German troops, giving rise to broadcast reports by the Allies that the Nazis were holding the Pope prisoner. On October 29 Vatican Radio broadcast a statement (also published in *Osservatore Romano*) to put an end to "unfounded rumours abroad" regarding the conduct of German troops towards the Vatican, which, it was indicated, had in fact been above reproach.

One of the people with whom I discussed this matter was Dr (formerly Standartenführer†) Eugen Dollmann, who was Hitler's interpreter in Italy at the time, and Himmler's representative, and confidant. "Yes," he said, "I did hear of a half-hearted plan to arrest the Pope and take him to Germany. But it was only one of – no doubt – a number of contingency plans. There is not a word of truth in General Wolff's assertion that there were actual orders drawn up to that effect. If there had been, it would have been absolutely impossible that I wouldn't have known about it – I say this categorically. It simply didn't happen. All communications with the Duce or the Holy See, or regarding either, went through me, except for routine matters. I arranged all Hitler's programmes

* Pages 373 and 381. German edition.
† Colonel in the SS.

on all his Italian trips, and attended all official German audiences with the Pope."

I asked Dr Dollmann why he thought General Wolff now claimed that such an order had existed.

"Because he wants to make money," he replied coldly. "I can imagine what the papers paid him for this story."

Father Schneider, like everyone else connected with the Church in Rome, was at pains to point out that religious organizations and individuals in Rome during and after the war helped Jews as much as Christians. We then discussed at great length the matter of help given to the particular group of escapers Stangl belonged to.

Asked if he knew whether the money for aid to refugees – including that particular group – was contributed from a special fund, or had been centrally administered, Father Schneider said: "No money came from the Vatican. The Vatican *has* no money for such purposes. You have no idea how limited the Vatican's resources really are. Whatever was done financially for these people, was done individually, by individual Orders."

I asked him whether he meant to say that it was also done upon individual responsibility.

"Certainly Bishop Hudal had his own convictions and activities," he said dryly, raising the suspicion in my mind that the late Bishop was fated to be thrown to the lions by Vatican officialdom.

I suggested that the idea of the Vatican's being poor was novel.

"Well, of course," said Father Schneider, "if people count paintings by Michelangelo and Raphael as the Vatican wealth . . . but what does that sort of thing really mean in terms of money? It can't be traded – can't be sold." He laughed.

I asked about the Vatican bank.

"Well, one has to have a bank," he replied. "It is in fact because of the bank that the Vatican got into the financial side of refugee aid." He then added, "You mustn't forget that the Vatican bank was the only source of foreign currency – so the refugee funds almost *had* to go through it."

I said that what Father Schneider appeared to be claiming was that individual religious orders paid out of their own funds for people like Stangl – and there were a large number of them – to travel to South America and the Near East; gave them money to restart their lives and, of course, provided for their stay in Rome.

I asked him whether, looking at it realistically, it didn't seem a trifle unlikely. Taking Bishop Hudal and the Anima as an example: supposing he had helped no more than one hundred SS men to go abroad – there were, no doubt, many more, but supposing it had been merely one hundred – what would that have amounted to in actual cash? Did Father Schneider consider $100,000 – one thousand for each man – a likely estimate? I understood that the Anima was one of the poorest religious institutions in Rome and that Bishop Hudal had no private means of any consequence, so how had it been possible for him to pay out such a large sum? Not to mention the fact that keeping the men in Rome before sending them abroad would have been a great additional expense – and that presumably there were in fact many more than a hundred of them. Were there no accounts kept, from which Father Schneider could ascertain these facts for me? Or was it not at least possible to find out how much the Vatican had contributed towards refugee aid *in general* in any one period?

"I don't know," said Father Schneider, and then repeated: "But I think there are no such accounts and there were no such contributions. I can only tell you that the Vatican did not provide any money for this purpose; indeed, again, that the Vatican *has* no money available for such purposes. . . . People are always going on about the enormous wealth of the Vatican," he said a little later. "The Vatican State Secretariat, with all its vast responsibilities, is probably run with about fifty people. And of course by comparison to what men in positions of similar responsibility are paid in lay life, *no one* in the Church earns any money – one must not forget that." He paused for a long moment, then said, as if he had arrived at a decision, "In 1939 three Jewish organizations in New York got together and sent the Vatican $100,000 – no, $125,000," he corrected himself. "If you saw in the account books how *glaringly* conspicuous this huge sum is, and with what minute care it was administered. . . ."

I interrupted to say that $125,000 seemed very little in comparison with what Jewish organizations in the US raised for Polish Jews alone in 1942–3.

"Perhaps," he said. "To the Vatican it was an enormous sum. Proof is that it wasn't just administered by the usual department, but went 'way up to the top'. And every cent of it was considered separately, to be sent to where it could do the most good: $3,000 to the Cardinal of this place; $2,000 to the Archbishop of that; $1,000 to one town; $2,000 to another. . . ."

If, I suggested, that particular sum had been so carefully recorded in the accounts, then the same care would presumably have been taken with other sums. Therefore, if the Vatican had indeed contributed no money for refugee aid in the years following the war, the absence of entries in the books would confirm it. Could this be checked? No, he said, it could not. I suggested that I thought his main reason for maintaining that the Vatican had contributed no such funds was because he wished to establish that it had not contributed towards the escape of the ss personnel we were particularly concerned with. I pointed out that I thoroughly appreciated that these men were very few compared with the huge number of other refugees helped by Catholic institutions, and helped with every justification. No one could question in any way the Vatican's motives in giving money towards helping refugees in general – on the contrary. The controversy lay in the money that appears to have been contributed by the Vatican for the specific benefit of one specific group of men; in the motivations of the priests who distributed these funds; and above all, in the question how much did they know and how much did the Vatican know, about the records of the men on whom such considerable, and it would appear clandestine, efforts were expended, and who received such substantial aid.

"Bishop Hudal," said Father Schneider, "was not at all close to the Vatican. He was very much on the fringes. And certainly not close to the Holy Father. He was . . . how shall I put it . . . even then slightly suspect – not taken seriously. He desperately *wanted* to be taken seriously. . . . Of course, he was not a *Nazi*, you know. As an Austrian, he had lobbied many years for Austria's federation with Germany not an unreasonable proposal, after all. But eventually he went a step further; he thought there was a possibility of collaboration between the Nazis and the Church. And that he might become the means – the liaison man – to achieve this collaboration." An aspiration, Father Schneider's tone implied, which, to say the least, was naïve.

303

3

I HEARD more about Bishop Hudal from Bishop Jakob Weinbacher, now Auxiliary Bishop of Vienna, who took over as Rector of the Anima in 1952, on Hudal's retirement. Bishop Weinbacher, now in his late sixties, was Cardinal Innitzer's private secretary at the time of the Anschluss in 1938, and is deeply loyal to the late Cardinal whose attitude towards the Nazis has been a source of considerable controversy.

He spoke first about Innitzer's appeals to Austrian Catholics; one immediately after the Anschluss in *Die Reichspost** asking for their loyalty to the new government; and another on March 28, 1938, made together with the Austrian bishops, this one addressed to the population in general, asking them to vote for the Anschluss in the coming elections. In this "solemn declaration" in the name of all Austrian bishops (except for the Bishop of Linz, who dissented), and signed by Cardinal Innitzer and Archbishop Waitz (of Salzburg), they said that " . . . the thousand-year-old longing of our people is now fulfilled". Stangl had mentioned the considerable effect these appeals had had on his thinking and that of his colleagues. (On polling day, April 10, Innitzer entered a voting booth saying "Heil Hitler"; on April 16 the Cardinal and some of his bishops were received in audience by the Pope, Pius XI, and his then Secretary of State, Eugenio Pacelli.)

"After that," said Bishop Weinbacher, "the Cardinal was shunned by everybody. They all called him the 'Nazi Cardinal'. In May 1938, there was a convocation in Budapest; bishops from all over the world attended, travelling through Vienna. Not a single one called on Innitzer. And no Austrian cleric was invited to attend."†

This ostracism, said Bishop Weinbacher, continued until October that year when, following the Cardinal's sermon in St Stephen's Cathedral in which he called on young Catholics to oppose the anti-Catholic laws imposed by the Nazi government,

* Church newspaper, equivalent to the British *Catholic Herald*.

† This interpretation was not quite correct: it is true that Pope Pius XI disapproved strongly of Innitzer's attitude, and in fact compelled him to issue a public retraction of his appeal. But according to the official British Catholic magazine, *The Tablet*, of May 21, 1938, the reason why no Austrian – or German – clerics attended the Eucharistic Congress was because the *Nazis* had forbidden them to do so, not the Pope.

the Hitler Youth stormed the Archbishop's Palace. "It was carefully organized," said Bishop Weinbacher. "The Police President sat a few blocks away in a coffee house; he looked at his watch and said, 'We'll let them go to it for one hour'; and only when that hour was past did he start giving instructions to the police. By that time the mob had ruined the palace; all the windows were broken and it was only by the grace of God that the Cardinal wasn't killed."

(Cardinal Innitzer was not the only high Catholic dignitary whose personal experience of violence no doubt had some effect on his future thinking. Eugenio Pacelli described an experience *he* had as Papal Nuncio in Munich in 1919 as follows. "I am one of the few non-German eye-witnesses of the Bolshevik régime that ruled Munich in April 1919. At the head of this 'Soviet' government were native Russians; every idea of justice, freedom and democracy was suppressed; only the Soviet press was available. Even the Nuncio's official residence was part of the battleground between the communists and the troops of the republican government; armed bandits forced their way in here and when I protested energetically against this violation of international law, one of them threatened me with his pistol. I am well aware of the objectionable circumstances under which the hostages were massacred. . . ."*)

"After that," continued Bishop Weinbacher about Cardinal Innitzer, "his situation improved; he received letters from the Vatican and the bishops, sympathizing with him, and he was readmitted into the universal fraternity of the Church."

Bishop Weinbacher, who is an established anti-Nazi and who was consecrated by Pope John in 1962, feels that history has now vindicated Cardinal Innitzer who, he says, no doubt made political errors when the Nazis first took over but retrieved these mistakes later. "They recently did a comprehensive television show about him here," he said (in Vienna), "and it showed very clearly where he stood and that he was fundamentally not at all pro-Nazi."

"Bishop Hudal", he said, "was very close to Pope Pius XII – there is no doubt of that; they were friends. I talked a lot with him and this certainly emerged very clearly. But he never spoke about the things he did after the war. He was . . . well, perhaps 'secretive' is too strong a word, but certainly he was very discreet about it; he didn't like to talk about it at all. One knew his political position, of

---

* In an interview in the French newspaper, *Le Matin*.

course, so one was careful; he was, after all, an older man. In Vienna, a long time before, I remember he came to my office one day, just after he had written two pro-German articles for the *Reichspost* – he wrote them under a pseudonym but everybody knew it was he. He said, 'Well, what did you think of them?' I said, 'Eminence, I think priests don't belong in politics.' And he said, 'Ah, yes, yes, you are right; you are probably right.' He was always like that; always wavering in his opinions, always adapting them to whoever he spoke to last, except that he stuck firmly to his pro-German, his 'nationalistic', attitudes.

"As Rector of the Anima, as you know, he was also Father Confessor to the German community in Rome, and amongst them were certainly Catholics of Jewish descent towards whom he behaved with the utmost correctness. But everybody knew that he later became very involved with getting jobs, passports, visas, etc, for refugees. I *think* he also helped other people, but there is no doubt that among those he eventually assisted were a great many of the Nazi high-ups. He is supposed to have got Bormann out too, I heard. He had his connections with the International Red Cross, I don't know how, and, of course, he disposed of large sums of money. Yes, it is possible that this money came from the Pope – certainly the Pope had such sums at his disposal." I mentioned that Frau Stangl had told me that her husband said Kesselring had transferred army funds to the Pope, thus enabling him "occasionally" to help someone. Bishop Weinbacher had never heard of such funds.

"The Pope was surrounded by German priests," he said. "They were his private group, his friends. Father Leiber, Father Wüstenberg [now Nuncio in Tokyo, and – like Father Leiber – always well known as being anti-Nazi], and Bishop Hudal. He spoke German fluently and in private all the time, with a charming Italian accent. But of course, you know, even if he liked Germans, it didn't necessarily mean that he was pro-Nazi. He had, I believe, spent a very happy time in Germany – this is where the reasons may lie, far more than in any sinister political motivations.

"About Hudal," he said, "there are of course two possibilities – either he helped many people and amongst them some Nazi bigwigs, without knowing who they were. Or, alternatively, he helped *some* other people, which we know he did, but mainly concentrated on the Nazis and in full knowledge of who and what they had been. Of course, if the latter was the case" (he smiled gently) "then one would have to admit that it would seem to have been a bit more than mere neighbourly love.

"He has written his memoirs you know. They are in the hands of the Stocker Verlag in Graz, who haven't published them yet, I don't really know why. I read them, briefly, but he doesn't mention his activities of the postwar years with a single word; it's just as if none of that had ever happened. . . ."

4

MY NEXT talk was with Monsignor Karl Bayer, Jesuit Director of the International Caritas in Vienna, who only recently left the same position in Rome, where he had been since the war.

Monsignor Bayer's connection with Rome dates from his youth. A Silesian by birth, he studied for the priesthood in Rome, staying at the Germanikum. During the war he served as an interpreter, not as a priest, in the Luftwaffe (which had no chaplains, he said), and was based in Italy and imprisoned there when the Allies took over. He was on the general staff in charge of billeting and so on, and was also one of Kesselring's interpreters during the meetings which were to decide whether Florence would be declared an Open City. It was he who translated the announcement to the Italian population that the Florentine bridges were to be destroyed. "I had made friends," he says, "with a family who owned a shop on the Ponte Vecchio – they sold silk fabrics. The night the announcements were posted – it was quite late and I knew that as most people stayed home at night in those days, they wouldn't see the announcements in time – I took a truck and helped that family move their stock out of their shop and into a safe place, in an area which would be under the Open City agreement. They were the only people in the street", he said with obvious pleasure, "who didn't lose their shirts when it was blown up next morning."

Many months later, this family helped him when he was on his way to Rome after an adventurous escape from the US internment camp at Ghedi, where the forty-five priests interned with him had elected him to intercede with the Vatican on their behalf. The

Vatican then appointed him liaison chaplain responsible for the 250,000 German prisoners of war in the north of Italy.

Monsignor Bayer, now about sixty, is tall, slim and fair, and smells agreeably of after-shave lotion. He drives a sporty car with an Italian number-plate, and seems very comfortable in the renovated building not far from Vienna's centre which houses Caritas International. I gathered that he is now mainly concerned with financial administration: he referred often to requests for financial aid from various Catholic communities in the Eastern bloc. Obviously active for refugees from Eastern Europe, he is very knowledgeable about the whole spectrum of refugee aid.

He told me that the help given in Rome to refugees could be divided into four "waves".

"The first wave", he said, "was the Jews [from Germany] in 1933–6. The Raphael Society – Father Weber [about whom more later] and Bishop Hudal were already helping people even then. The second wave came in 1939 when anti-Semitism first raised its head in Italy. It was at the beginning of the war in Europe that the Vatican bank began to handle foreign currency for the benefit of refugees. The third wave came after September 8, 1943, when Italy 'left' the war and Italian fascists began to seek escape. And the fourth wave – no doubt the largest by far – came after April-May 1945. This one included nationals of many countries who were in Italy, in POW camps and elsewhere, at the time, and didn't want to return to their communist-controlled homelands; German POWS, some of whom would eventually go home, but many of whom didn't wish to at the time; the Polish Anders army;* the Russian Vlasov army† (including 10,000 to 15,000 Ukrainians); large numbers of the people fleeing from Yugoslavia, Rumania, Hungary, Austria; and then, of course, the comparatively small group of SS personnel who are the people you are particularly referring to.

"All along", he continued, "there were two 'channels' of help given by the Church or organs of the Church – one financial, the other more indirect. The money most certainly came from the Vatican. But on the other hand, many individual priests and officials helped many people in different ways, and not necessarily with money. I recall hearing about a case – a Frau Muschadek,

* Anti-communist, under the authority of the Polish government in exile.
† Anti-communist, joined the German invading army.

308

whose husband had been a theologian in Germany lecturing on canon law. Being only half-Aryan, he had left Germany in 1936 and had come to Rome for help. Well, they didn't really know what to do for him, but nice Cardinal Mercati,* he discovered that the Muschadeks were quite keen on the idea of emigrating to Brazil. So he gave them a Vatican *laisser-passer* and a letter asking the Brazilian bishops to assist them. I don't know what the bishops did or didn't do for him over there, but anyway, it didn't work out very well, because he died. I gather that after his death Frau Muschadek made a great nuisance of herself and finally the Brazilians, no doubt fed up with her, repatriated her to the only place from which she had an identity paper – the Vatican. She arrived in my office one day with a letter signed by no less than President Vargas of Brazil; it made a great to-do, I remember. Well, she was full of how she was stranded there because of the horrid Nazis and all that. Oh, I can't remember what we did for her. I think we got her some office work or something – anyway, she was looked after. . . ."

Commenting on details I raised from "Brockdorff's" *Flucht vor Nürnberg,* Monsignor Bayer recalled the Croatian theologian Monsignor Krunoslav Draganovic, who was abducted by Tito agents in 1967, taken back to Yugoslavia and executed for collaboration with the enemy. He is said to have been one of the chief administrators of the Genoa branch of the "Vatican Escape Route", which functioned specially for the benefit of members of the Ustaca – the infamous organization which, during the rule of the Nazis' puppet government in Croatia, outdid the Germans in killing not only Jews (although they were rabid anti-Semites) but also, and with even more enthusiasm, many thousands of Orthodox Serbs and Croats (who refused to be converted to Roman Catholicism). "Oh yes," said Monsignor Bayer, "its quite true that after the war various groups set themselves up to help their own nationals. I remember Draganovic very well. He was head of the Croatian Committee. Yes, it's quite likely that he received support from Cardinal Siri who is now Archbishop of Genoa; there again, you see, one's obligation was simply to help people who were in need of help. . . ."

He spoke at length about his own activities for the German

---

* Giovanni Mercati was made a cardinal by Pius XI in 1936 and given the post of librarian and archivist for the Vatican; he died in 1957.

prisoners of war. "The Holy Father opened the Papal Assistance Agency for German POWs and put Sister Pascalena in charge of all the material sent to, or obtained by, the Vatican for refugees."

Sister Pascalena Lehner, a lay sister of eighteen when she first went to work for Eugenio Pacelli in Munich, never left his service thereafter. It has often been claimed that she had considerable influence on the Pope, which she has always denied. Now old and bitter at the allegations and rumours about her, she has said that she will never again leave her Roman convent or speak to anyone but the Sisters there for the rest of her life.

"There were warehouses full of stuff," said Monsignor Bayer. "Everything – clothes, food, toilet articles, cigarettes – especially cigarettes – very important to the POWs because there were certain categories to whom the Allies allowed no privileges whatever. All ranks of SS, for instance, and parachutists, couldn't get cigarettes or anything. I remember, there were two and half million cigarettes in Sister Pascalena's warehouses, left by the Brazilian Corps* – they were called 'Red Birds'. And she gave me the lot for the soldiers. . . ."

It has been claimed by some writers that Sister Pascalena had a say in actually selecting men from the POW camps who were to benefit from the "Vatican Escape Route".

"I think that's nonsense," said Monsignor Bayer. "She wasn't that sort of person at all; I don't think she'd have known who to 'select'. Goodness, everybody knows her type; that type of good German nun; she had no political interest, knowledge or influence."

"Did she have influence on the Pope?"

"Well, she was in charge of the three nuns who looked after the Pope's household – the domestic personnel. But I cannot imagine for a moment that she had any 'influence' on the Pope in the sense you mean. He was a highly cultured man, the most sophisticated pope, certainly, of our time. . . ." (Father Schneider had gone further in his description of Pius XII: "He was the most remarkable pope of modern times," he'd said. "The greatest political mind.")

Inevitably, the subject of Martin Bormann came up in my conversation with Monsignor Bayer – and he, like everyone else, expressed doubt about Bormann's supposed survival, and ignorance about his having come through Rome, or having been helped in

* It has frequently been forgotten that there was a Brazilian Corps attached to the Allied armies.

Rome. (Brockdorff-Jarschel gives a very precise – indeed, disconcertingly exact description of Bormann's alleged escape through Rome in *Flucht vor Nürnberg*. In addition, the author's wife was to tell me that her husband had actually met Bormann in a "conference of international Fascism" that took place in the Middle East in the late 1950s.)

"I was in fact very involved with the whole Bormann business," said Monsignor Bayer, "because of the children. You see, Bormann's wife and children were living in the South Tyrol where, as of course you know, Frau Bormann died in 1945. Theo Schmitz, the POW chaplain in Merano, was with her much of the time; he helped her die. But during all that time we were working on finding solutions for the children; they were very young and homes had to be found for them. Well, to me it seems psychologically very unlikely that, knowing his wife and children to be in Merano and her dying, Bormann would have travelled repeatedly between Genoa and Rome at that time – as the reports claim – and would not have gone to see them."

I said that, assuming he really did survive, I didn't find it all that unlikely; after all, it would have been very dangerous for him; he would have been aware that the Allied intelligence services would have been watching his family day and night in the expectation of just such a move.

"Yes, that *is* true," said Monsignor Bayer, "and it is of course also true that their relationship by this time had deteriorated very sharply; they had serious ideological differences; she had finally heard of some of the things he had been involved in. On the other hand, I really think I would have heard if he had been around anywhere; I really *was* on the lookout for him because of the children. You see, apart from everything selse, there were all kinds of financial problems, all kinds of arrangements needed to be made. You can imagine, had he been available I would have *had* to get to him. No, I don't know whether Hudal would have told me – we weren't that close. But I still think I would have heard. . . ."

When I mentioned that Bormann's children are supposed to have said in 1948 that their father was alive, Monsignor Bayer said he'd never heard of that either. He spoke with contempt of Bormann's oldest son, who, having become a priest, has now left the priesthood – "and married a *nun*", he said.

I asked Monsignor Bayer his opinion of "Brockdorff's" claim

that the SS escapers in Rome had to go through a kind of screening before being allowed to go abroad.

"If there was really a screening," he said, "an attempt at detailed research by examining each of the people concerned, it would have required at least a dozen German-speaking priests. I knew them all. There were of course quite a few, but they were incredibly busy – too busy, I think, for the kind of supervision of the many people he describes in his book."

I asked him what sort of questions were put to people who applied for help.

"Well, of course we asked questions," he said. "But at the same time, we hadn't an earthly chance of checking on the answers. In Rome, at that time, every kind of paper and information could be bought. If a man wanted to tell us he was born in Viareggio – no matter if he was really born in Berlin and couldn't speak a word of Italian – he only had to go down into the street and he'd find dozens of Italians willing to swear on a stack of Bibles that they knew he was born in Viareggio – for a hundred lire."

I told him that Stangl claimed to have stayed in a convent or monastery, to have eaten in a canteen, and later to have obtained work from the nuns.

"There was a special 'Mensa' for foreigners," Monsignor Bayer said. "Each of the National Committees had one; the one in Rome provided lunch and dinner for something like two hundred people. And he may well also have worked there for the nuns. And yes, he may well have stayed in a convent or monastery. As for his story of Hudal knowing he was coming: of course, talking to you he chose to put the emphasis in a certain way; he chose to make it sound as if, when Hudal said, 'You must be Franz Stangl, I've been expecting you,' he meant he had *always* known about him, knew his record and approved of it, and was still – or even because of it – willing to help him. But the emphasis *can* be put in another way. It seems more likely to me that the 'comrade' Stangl met on the Tiber bridge rang Hudal and said, 'A man I know, Franz Stangl, is coming to see you; I know him, he is all right,' or words to that effect. And that would in fact have helped Stangl – it happened all the time, to me too. In the absence, very often, of any proof of identity, this sort of recommendation was valuable, and all of us accepted it *faute de mieux*. . . .

"No, I don't think Hudal could have got him a job, a visa or anything for Syria. Those he'd have had to get for himself." (Information I got later from the International Red Cross, and Frau Stangl's confirmation of Stangl's account to me, both contradict Monsignor Bayer on this point.)

"There were certainly Nazi sympathizers sitting in these Middle Eastern countries preparing the ground for these people, and Hudal may have given him an introduction, or the name of someone in Syria who would be prepared to help him after his arrival in Damascus. We were an aid-committee, you know," he said tersely, "not a labour exchange. And I think it is ridiculous to believe that Hudal handed him the International Red Cross passport. He would certainly have had to queue up for that himself – hundreds did, for hours each. I don't think I remember one single case where the Red Cross gave *me* a passport and I handed it to these fellows. I sometimes went with them to the Red Cross, you know, to tell them that the chap was all right. . . .

"Yes, Stangl would have received money – which came from the Vatican – or a ticket to Syria, but rarely both. Perhaps there were some exceptional cases where they were given a ticket *and* money, but it didn't happen to anyone I helped. . . .

"As far as we were concerned, these were people who had the right to make their own decisions as to where they wanted to live. [He was referring primarily to the former POWs he was in charge of.] For thousands, after all, the choice was whether to live under the Russians or not."

"Do you think", I asked, "that the Pope, Hudal, others who were involved in these aid progammes – you too – ever wondered whether some of these men didn't have serious, very serious things on their conscience?"

"Do you really believe", he replied, "that there were more villains and thieves amongst them than amongst the British and Americans?"

"I am not really talking about stealing – I am talking about murder."

"Look here, there were thousands and thousands of men; how could we possibly know?"

"Well, perhaps *you* in your capacity as POW chaplain took care of thousands of men. But Bishop Hudal seems to have handled specifically these SS men. Do you think *he* wondered what they were fleeing from and whether they should be helped by the Church to escape justice?"

313

"You know, Bishop Hudal helped Jews before he ever helped ss men; he helped more Jews than ss men." (Gustav René Hocke, correspondent in Rome throughout the war and now for the *Arbeitsgemeinschaft Frankfurter Neue Presse* and *Die Tat* of Zürich, told me that to his knowledge Bishop Hudal during the war hid a total of sixteen people in the Anima – Americans, British and Jews.)

"Those others, they came to me too – luckily they weren't within my competence as I was in charge specifically of POWs. Still, one or two tried to slip in; now you tell me, how could we have known what they had done? After all, they didn't *tell* us; they weren't that stupid. And they weren't famous, you know. After all, who knew Eichmann at that time? Stangl? Mengele? Now yes, now we all know their names. But then? I'd never heard Eichmann's name until his trial in Israel." (Others in Rome said the names of people like Eichmann, Mengele, Bormann, Rauff and Müller *were* known at the time, although not Stangl's nor any of the Polish death-camp men.) "Of course we knew that many of them had been in the ss. But the ss were also fighting units; one couldn't identify them only with the horrors – about which, anyway, we knew very little then. . . .

"Even so, we *tried* to question them; we asked everyone questions. And the International Red Cross didn't just give these passports to anyone, without proof of identity. They required *some* assurance of the person's particulars and character. Well yes, it *was* difficult. All we could – and did – do if we suspected a man, was to insist on witnesses, somebody who could vouch for what he said. But of course they all helped each other. I might have phoned the Pastor who was doing the same sort of thing for Protestants, Pastor Dahlgrün, and ask him whether he knew about this and that chap; and if he said, 'Yes, that's the one who comes from Leipzig and I've had two others here who said they knew him there . . . ' well, there you are; that was confirmation.

"Stangl, as his description to you of his months in Italy would indicate, must have known a *lot* of people there. He was in Fiume, Verona, Venice, the Isle of Rab – he may well have earned the hatred of some people, but he probably helped others and made friends – people who then 'owed him a good turn'. So I think myself that the story he told you is quite likely true; obviously he could easily get out of an open prison in Linz – there is nothing startling about that. No, I don't think he'd have needed money to get away. In fact, if he'd had money, he wouldn't have needed to come to us." (Not quite correct; he would still have needed to come for papers – the proof being that other, far higher ranking Nazis, who were presumably well supplied with funds, also went by the Vatican escape route.)

"And of course he wouldn't have needed any papers to cross the Austrian-Italian frontier. Anyone who says a man needed papers for that, at that time, just doesn't know what he is talking about. By that time, all those fellows had told each other which little villages on the Brenner or nearby were the best for crossing, which peasants were old Nazis or just friendly, or to be had for money. But there were enough guides anyway – old hands at smuggling, who took them across for nothing.

"On the whole his story sounds reasonable to me; he could have talked himself out of being taken by the *carabiniere* in Merano if they just stopped him in the street. Of course, once he'd actually been processed into prison, he'd have ended up in a camp – lots of people did. About the passport thing – well, I told you what I think about that – but, perhaps I don't know enough about this; perhaps Hudal *did* get batches of passports for these particular people. And yes, he would certainly have given him money. The Pope did provide money for this; in driblets sometimes, but it did come. . . ."

5

"WE HAD no means at the time of knowing where the money came from for these people," said Madame Gertrude Dupuis, who has held an important position in the International Red Cross in Rome since before World War II. Slim, elegant and quick, Madame Dupuis, within the limits imposed by her position, was sympathetic to the purposes of this book and frank in her replies to my questions. "But certainly", she went on, "we never doubted that the money came from the Vatican who, after all, had quite legitimately been providing financial help for refugees for years. What Monsignor Bayer told you about people having to apply personally, pick up and sign for the Red Cross paper in this office, is perfectly correct. However, if Bishop Hudal asked for some of the *laisser-passers* to be made out according to his specifications (I don't myself know whether he did, but he could or might have done), which then lacked only the holder's signature to make them valid, and if he asked for them to be sent to him ... well, they probably were. It *was* comparatively simple for him to achieve this; he was a bishop, don't forget – that did help. It did have some effect. Certainly, it is highly unlikely that Stangl, or people like him, would have risked ... or perhaps that Hudal would have risked for them, or would have allowed them to risk – formulate it as you wish – coming down here to queue up with hundreds of people. We had dozens of Jewish camp survivors around. Any of them might have been someone who would have recognized an individual like Stangl. This was well known. So how could he have risked it? Yes, of course, if Hudal enabled Stangl and others like him to avoid the necessity of a personal visit to these offices – and they obviously did avoid it – then one is driven to the conclusion that Hudal knew who these people were; or at least knew that they were wanted. ... Hudal was always a very questionable personality," she said. "We had none but the most formal relations with him. I myself *don't* think that he was 'close' to the Pope at all." (This was said by everyone I spoke to in Rome. Bishop Weinbacher, Hudal's successor as Rector of the Anima, was the only person who was convinced that the Bishop had been close to the Pope. Although, as he had probably known Hudal for longer, and better, than any of the others and had taken over his office, personnel, and files, he was, one might think, in a unique position to form such an opinion. It is also possible that it was not from files, but from the Bishop's own claims, that he had gained this – possibly mistaken – opinion.)

"It is certainly a fact", said Madame Dupuis, "that Hudal helped people – different people – before he began to 'specialize'."

Madame Dupuis said that during some of that period they issued as many as 500 *laisser-passers* a day. "They were never meant to be passports; they were intended to provide a means of identification which at the same time would allow the holder to proceed from Italy to his next and, hopefully, permanent place of residence. You see, what was important – no, essential – at the time, was to move the thousands of refugees, to break the bottle-neck Rome had become. Italy had enormous administrative and, of course, economic difficulties of her own at the time, and it was essential to keep this floating population moving. The identity paper usually had a validity of six months. But we know there were people who used them for much longer, particularly in South America where they were accepted as quasi-passports for years; some people are still using them now. . . . There were of course also instances, possibly more than we realized at the time, of people forging them."

She remembered being called in by the police on one occasion when, the Delegate being away on a mission, she was Acting Delegate. "I saw some of them lying on the desk as I entered the room," she said, "and I could see from several feet away that they were forged. Not only were they filled out differently from how we do it ordinarily, but my signature was obviously forged. So you see, even though, as I told you, it was simple for Bishop Hudal to get these documents, it is also possible that for some of the ss people they were forged."

I asked Madame Dupuis whether they were ever suspicious of some of the people to whom they issued the *laisser-passers*.

"Yes, of course we wondered," she said. "But there was literally nothing to be done about it. There were so many who needed help; the practical difficulties we faced almost defy description. We were, after all, an 'aid' organization, not detectives. In the end, the most important thing was to help the many for whom our help was legitimate . . . of course, if one had had proper sources and the time and staff to spend on investigation, or even just on thinking about individual cases, there would have been many doubts – one often talked about it. As it was, we always asked certain questions, but we knew perfectly well that we couldn't really check the replies. So, if there were witnesses, just anybody to corroborate what anybody said, or above all – as happened many times, particularly in the cases of the sort of people you are talking about – if their replies were corroborated or guaranteed by a member of the clergy, then this was accepted. How could we refuse to accept the word of priests?"

6

MOST OF the clerics I approached in the course of this research – and there were more of them than I have found necessary to quote, since several merely confirmed, or duplicated what others had already said – appeared ready to speak frankly. They recognized, I think, that my purpose was to achieve a more balanced view of the involvement of the Catholic church in these controversial matters. On only one of them did I virtually force an interview – reluctantly, and only because I felt it was absolutely essential to the full picture. This was Father Anton Weber, a Palatine priest at the St Raphael Society in Rome, who, in the context of the subject we are concerned with, is probably the most vulnerable cleric still active there. It took me several months before I could communicate with him, and when I met him at last, he was convalescing at his brother's house in southern Germany after a serious illness. There can be little doubt that he was deeply involved in assisting SS escapers. But although he appeared still to be trying to convince himself that he had acted rightly, Father Weber also gave me the impression of being a very troubled man.

Like many of the priests with whom I spoke, he was anxious to bring the conversation round to what the Church had done for the Jews.

"How many Jews did you yourself hide during the war, in your House?" I asked.

"Until September 1943," he said, "it was full of Jews; baptized Jews. And don't forget, the Nazis never bothered us – they bothered none of the monasteries and convents, although they knew perfectly well that we were all hiding refugees."

("Allowing these few Jews who were in hiding in these places, to survive," said another priest who does not wish his name to be quoted, "was a very small price for the Nazis to pay, to keep the Vatican silent. They knew perfectly well there were decent and outraged men amongst the religious community in Rome – indeed at the Vatican too – who were only 'kept at bay' because the convents and monasteries still remained places of safety and could continue to be counted on for hiding people.")

"What do you think would have happened to all these Jews," said Father Weber, "if the Pope had been more explicit in his remonstrations?"

"If you were so certain of Nazi leniency on this point, would it not have been possible to give refuge to Jews who were not baptized, who were, after all, in even graver danger? Did they never ask you for asylum?"

"Oh yes, but I was responsible for baptized Jews only. There was one monsignor in Milan who was very intent upon the argument that in times like that one didn't ask whether a man was baptized or not. He used to compare it to a ship sinking: 'You save whoever you can grab,' he used to say, 'you don't ask him for his identity papers before you pull him out of the water.'" He laughed.

"How did you feel about that?"

He shrugged his shoulders. "It wasn't so simple; the Brazilians, for instance, offered us 3,000 visas for baptized Jews; but they had to have been Catholics for at least two years." He laughed again. "Of course, they were all claiming to be Catholics. . . ."

"But you didn't believe them?"

"I made them recite the Lord's Prayer, and the Ave Maria; that proved in a hurry who was genuine and who wasn't."*

He had told me originally that there were about 20,000 Jews of all nationalities in Rome.

"Of the 20,000 you say were in Rome . . ." I said, and he interrupted: "Only about 3,000 of those were baptized."

"Of the 3,000 or so who were baptized then, how many did you actually get out?"

"Two or three hundred," he said. At the very beginning of our talks, however, he had said that two or three thousand people had left Genoa in sealed trains, and that a ship had sailed illegally from Spezia to Barcelona from where they went on to Lisbon.

Asked about Bishop Hudal, Father Weber said he really didn't know him very well. "Did Bishop Hudal have private means?" I asked.

"I don't think so. Though he did buy a villa after he left the Anima – still, I don't think he had money of his own; not much, anyway."

"About this question of helping ss officers get out of Europe after the war; how was this financed?"

---

* When Father Weber said this I was moved, yet again, to think of Monsignor Angelo Roncalli, later Pope John XXIII. In August 1944, when immense efforts were being made by all of the civilized world to halt the murder of the Hungarian Jews, the field representative of the War Refugee Board, Ira Hirschmann, had gone to see Monsignor Roncalli, who was still Apostolic Delegate in Turkey. Monsignor Roncalli asked Mr Hirschmann whether he thought the Jews of Budapest would be willing to be baptized – "only to save their lives," he said, "not to really convert them, you understand." Mr Hirschmann replied that he thought the Jews would welcome the opportunity to live. And two weeks later Monsignor Roncalli confirmed in a letter to Mr Hirschmann that he had sent "thousands of baptismal certificates" to the Papal Nuncio in Budapest, Monsignor Angelo Rotta.

"Well, there were funds available for aid to refugees."

"Available from the Vatican?"

"That too," he said vaguely. "But of course, we didn't really know who the people were we aided. At least, we knew nothing beyond what they themselves told us."

"I have heard that you are supposed to have got Eichmann out?"

"But if a man called Klement came to me and said that was his name – and had papers to prove it, and you can be certain that *these* people were the first to have legitimate-looking papers – and perhaps someone else came with him to corroborate his story, how on earth could I know that he was someone else?"

I sympathized with that argument. I don't think that – if he didn't know from the outset who the person who came to him was – he *could* have found out. But an hour or so later he mentioned Eichmann again. "Yes," he said, "someone called Richard Klement came to me. He said he came from East Germany and didn't want to go back there to live under the Bolsheviks, so I helped him. . . ."*

"How much did it actually cost to get each of these people to wherever they were going – South America or whatever?"

"They were usually given a hundred dollars to keep going on, and the journeys cost about two to three hundred dollars. Of course, when they got to where they were going they were helped there – or looked after themselves. In Chile, for example," he said, "the Palatines gave guarantees for refugees. I had a liaison man in Lisbon, a Palatine, Father Turowski, and he used to get visas from the Uruguayan [honorary] Consul, and with the Uruguay visas they were able to get Portuguese transit visas. The Spanish Consul in Rome also helped with transit visas." He had mentioned earlier that the Uruguayans had been "very good about the Jews".

A little later, coming back to Bishop Hudal, he suddenly said, "Did you go to the Anima? Did you talk to the porter?"

I said that I had talked about the Anima with the Auxiliary Bishop of Vienna, Weinbacher, but that, no, I had not spoken to the porter.

"Well, how can you expect to find out the truth," he said testily, "if you don't speak to the porter? Of course he is old now. But even so, if Hudal was 'stormed' by thousands of ss people, he would have had to know; he would have let them in."

* Anyone who has heard Eichmann speak in his pronounced Austrian German, might find it difficult to understand how Father Weber could have accepted this story.

I asked him who had claimed that there had been "thousands"?

"That's what is said, isn't it?" he replied. Coming back once more to Eichmann, he said that even if Eichmann–Klement had given him his real name, it wouldn't have meant anything to him. "I never heard that name until much later," he said.

I told him that Stangl had told me that he had reported to Bishop Hudal under his real name and that Bishop Hudal, who had appeared to know about him, had obtained papers for him in that name.

"I can't answer for Hudal," said Father Weber, "though I would doubt that he was aware of the former functions of the people he helped any more than I was." Aside from that however, Father Weber's references to Bishop Hudal were anything but friendly. "He helped Austrians," he said, "not Germans. During the war he had a 'Greater Germany' flag on his car; as soon as the war ended, he was the first to change it – suddenly his flag was Austrian."

But Father Weber, too, said that Hudal was not part of the inner papal circle, nor did he agree for a minute with those who are, he said, now claiming that Pope Pius XII was pro-Nazi.

"Do you remember?" he said, "when Hitler visited Rome, and the Pope ordered all Catholic museums to close for the day and himself retreated to his summer residence in Castelgandolfo? Does that sound like a man who wished to collaborate with the Nazis?" (Dr Eugen Dolmann, in his book *The Interpreter*,* says the Pope retreated to Castelgandolfo out of pique – because he hadn't been asked to receive Hitler.)

"The Pope liked Germans," said Father Weber. "He had been happy in Germany. But that's a far cry from being pro-Nazi. It's true that the Holy Father's private circle, those closest to him, were mostly German, or German-speaking priests. But no one is going to claim that Father Leiber who was the Holy Father's confessor and closest associate, was pro-Nazi. Nor was Monsignor Wüstenberg, who is now Papal Nuncio in Tokyo. . . ."

I asked Father Weber whether he knew anything about Martin Bormann's passing through Rome.

"Nothing," he said. "The only contact I had with Bormann, indirectly, was when I got the Bormann children a special audience with Pius XII in 1950. . . ."

* Hutchinson, 1967.

"What was the routine when people came to ask for your help after the end of the war?"

"The porter would come and say that someone was asking for me. I'd go down into a little reception room we had. Whoever it was would tell me his name – or what he said his name was – and a bit of his story, and in all probability I'd tell him that I wasn't the right person to help him; I'd say he must go and see Hudal, or the Caritas people, or the International Red Cross, to get papers."

"You never helped? You never gave them money if they needed it, or found them a place to stay, or put them up yourself?"

"If it seemed necessary I might have given them a bit of money, just to tide them over a day or two, and I might have indicated where they could stay; the YMCA you know, or some hostel like that: they were of course all putting people up."

"But you yourself didn't help them with papers and lodgings, etc.?"

"I might have helped some of them, if it seemed the right thing to do."

"What was right?"

"Men in need," he replied irritably. "That was our function."

"Did you ever suspect any of them? Did you wonder what their real story – their real past – might have been?"

"Yes, I did sometimes. But there were so many needing help, how *could* we find out more than just the superficial facts they gave us?"

"During the war the Pope entrusted you with assisting baptized Jews, and because you suspected many of those who came of not really belonging in that category, you made them recite the Lord's Prayer and the Ave Maria; and no doubt, if they didn't recite them properly, you didn't help them. Did you ever, after the war, demand similar proof from the men who *then* came to ask you for your help? Did you ever refuse any of *them* because you weren't sure they belonged to a 'proper category'?"

"I may have – I don't remember exactly. It's so long ago."

"Let us put the question theoretically," I said. "If you *had* known, or suspected, about any of the people who came to you for help, that they had been actively involved in the horrors you had by then knowledge of like everybody else; that they themselves had in fact committed or been party to atrocities or murder; that they themselves were wanted by the courts for crimes; would you have felt that the Church had the right, or perhaps obligation, under such circumstances, to save a man from worldly justice? Would you have helped such a man?"

Father Weber didn't answer for many minutes; he thought about the question for a long time before he finally replied softly and sadly: "If I had known – *really* known – I think I would have sent them away. I think I would have said, 'Try somewhere else.' I think that is what I would have done." And I believed him.

Earlier we had talked about the most fundamental question, which everyone, without exception, had brought up during these conversations; the extent of the Pope's knowledge of the true situation concerning the Jews.

"Pius did not know the extent of German measures against Jews," Father Weber said. "He knew they were being put into camps and all that, but he didn't know they were actually killing them. There were of course all kinds of rumours, but it would have been unthinkable for the Pope to have delivered an encyclical because of rumours. As long as he couldn't convince himself of the facts, confirm from his own knowledge that they *were* facts, he couldn't speak.

"As I know the situation," he continued, "one must remember that, whatever they say now, most of Germany was *with* Hitler. I think that if the Pope, with his scant knowledge of the situation, had spoken out and repeated these unconfirmed rumours to Germany's Catholics, fifty per cent of them would have been outraged; it would have resulted in bitter anger against the Pope for allowing himself to be used for enemy propaganda."

"You don't think the German Catholics would have believed the Pope?"

"No, they wouldn't have."

7

DR EUGEN DOLLMANN is one of the rare Germans who has never denied his membership of the Nazi Party – in fact one feels that he makes quite a point of not apologizing for it. He was seventy-two years old when I met him in 1972 at the exclusive Munich residential hotel Das Blaue Haus, where, a very urbane bachelor, he lives with his beautiful dog for company. Dr Dollmann looks a great deal younger than his age, carries himself – although he is not tall – very erect, wears exquisitely well cut clothes, and is well versed in art and antiques.

During his period as Hitler's interpreter in Rome, he also interpreted for all the other important Germans who came there – Himmler, Heydrich, Göring, visiting diplomats and ss generals. He attended every major German-Italian conference, in Rome and Berlin, and repeatedly stayed as Hitler's guest at the Berghof. There is no reason for him to deny his adherence to the Party: he clearly never did anything beyond his glamorous job which – as he appears to have been everybody's confidant – was both gratifying and challenging. He made it quite plain, both in his book, *The Interpreter*, and to me, that he was fascinated with this life. "My book was never published in German," he said. "They didn't dare." Reading it, one doesn't quite understand why they wouldn't have dared, except perhaps that it might interfere with the illusions of those who like to think of the Nazi world as rather more hardy. The picture Dollmann paints – extremely well – of life in war-time Rome, is certainly different from how it has been described by others, and his portrait of Hitler is unusual, to say the least.

"Of course," he said, "my life during those years was not very different from my life in peacetime. I really had nothing to complain of: I had my own delicious flat in Rome; I had innumerable equally delicious Italian friends. And amongst the Germans – well, I *chose* my friends, as one would do. Obviously, one could only really associate with those who had a sense of humour. As you know, that would limit one rather sharply amongst Germans. Still there were some."

It would appear that even after Germany's defeat, Dr Dollmann's life continued fairly agreeably.

"When it became sticky", he said, "I went into hiding. I hid for a year in a monastery in Milan. Of course, I hadn't *done* anything – but, on the other hand, I had worn *that* uniform. So, on paper, after all, I had been in the ss. And you know what *that* meant when the Allies came. So I went to stay with the Cardinal in Milan. It was a nice year. He used to come to my room – my cell – each evening and say, 'Now let us have a glass of wine together,' and we would talk about art and music and people – the things that mattered.

"I am always amused at the nonsense people talk about Hitler," he said. "All that business about his tantrums, his china-throwing and carpet-chewing sessions, you know. When I finally reported to the Americans, after hiding for that first year – undue haste in reporting wouldn't have paid off – they listened to my story and later they wrote out a statement and asked me to sign it. I started reading it over and they said that really wasn't necessary. But I said I was certainly going to read anything I signed. At the very end they had written that I had said I'd seen Hitler have these mad tantrums, throw china about, gnaw carpets and all that nonsense. So I said I wouldn't sign. They said they were prepared to pay me a considerable sum in dollars – but I said I didn't need their dollars, that I had never seen such a thing and that I wouldn't sign. So they said that was certainly to my disadvantage – but they crossed it out.

"You see, I never saw Hitler be anything but totally courteous. In fact, on all the many social occasions I spent with him, indeed on which I was there to advise him as a kind of aide – all heads of state take advice on protocol – I never once saw him make a false move. Extraordinary, really, for a man with his background. He had a very quiet voice, shy and appealing to Germans, with his soft Austrian accent. [Lord Boothby said the same thing: "Soft, hesitant and thoughtful," was how he described Hitler's voice.]

"Of course, Mussolini was very different. He was, you know, a real man; an Italian; full of life, charm – culture too. Yes, he was a warm, a loving sort of man. Hitler was cold," said Dr Dollmann. "The atmosphere around him was ice cold. But he was incredibly receptive to information. He asked, and he listened. He was very clever at social chit-chat, you know. The sort of thing one wouldn't have expected him to enjoy or excel at. You know, when he received Roman socialites, I'd say a few words between each presentation, you know the sort of thing: this is the Principessa something or other, she has a great estate near Florence, husband on the Duce's staff; this is the Contessa x, five children, particularly interested in child welfare, or gardens, or zoology as the case might be. And he'd always catch on at once and converse along those lines. And he had a phenomenal memory – never forgot anything."

"What did you think of the rumours that Hitler was a homosexual?" I asked him.

"Well, I think it's possible," he said. "You know, nobody has ever mentioned, in all the stories and histories of the period, how extraordinarily handsome all the young men in Hitler's immediate circle were. They weren't thugs, you know; they were very well brought up, very well connected young people – and they looked like young gods."

"What about Eva Braun? Do you think there was a normal relationship between them?"

"Certainly not a normal physical relationship. She was nice, you know, but terribly stupid. I used to have to make a programme for her when she came to Rome with him; all she ever wanted to do was see the shops, go and buy clothes and things; she couldn't *wear* anything, with the Italian sort of elegance, but she bought. At the Berghof – yes, I stayed there several times – one could watch her adoring Hitler; she just sat and adored. She had no conversation, no thoughts in her mind, no mind in fact. I expect that's what he liked and sought in her; someone he didn't have to say anything to, who just worshipped at his shrine. He must have needed it more and more as things got worse and worse for him.

"The Jews? No, I never heard Hitler mention the word 'Jew' in private, or even in ordinary conversation. He spoke about '*Staatsfeinde*' [enemies of the State], and with that he meant anyone who was against Germany, including the Allies, Russians, etc. But, as I said, never did he mention the Jews in my hearing. . . . Of course, don't forget that there really was no Jewish problem to speak of in Italy, and of course it was Italian questions that were within my competence as his interpreter. In Italy there were a few people of note who were Jews – industrialists, scientists, writers, to whom, of course, nothing happened; they left in time, that is, before September 1943 when Italy's status changed from ally to occupied nation. Or else they were hidden by Italians, often in convents and monasteries. So of course there really was no call for Hitler and Mussolini to discuss the Jewish question.

"I never heard Pius XII mention the word 'Jew' either. But then, of course, he always spoke in very general terms; he spoke of 'suffering humanity everywhere', 'excesses', etc, but he never specified beyond these generalities. . . . Except once," he said later. "But that was very late, in 1944, on the occasion of the last audience General Wolff had with him; he requested Wolff to arrange at once the release of a young man, the son of a childhood friend – they were Jews. And this was done immediately. During that same last meeting he demanded that 'all excesses' in Italy must cease forthwith, and they did. General Wolff sent out an order that no one was henceforth to be *touched*, and that food, etc, should be improved immediately in prisons and camps. But, of course, he could have made a special point of the Jews – but even then he didn't.

"No, I certainly did not feel the Pope was pro-*Nazi*. But he was certainly pro-German. In a political sense he was primarily anti-Communist, one mustn't forget that. This was certainly so until the end of '43, beginning of '44. Until that time Germany appeared – must have appeared to him – as the main bulwark against Communism. I do think that this was what mainly determined his attitude. Yes, there was – there always has been – latent anti-Semitism within the Vatican. After all, it was inherent in traditional Catholic teaching: you know, Christ-killers and all that. Now that is somewhat outmoded. But I think it quite possibly had influence on Pius XII's thinking and actions – even if only unconsciously. Then, of course, there was fear too; the Vatican, however powerful, was in the middle of Fascist and subsequently Nazi Rome. . . . However, it would have been impossible to touch the Pope at all until after September 1943; the Duce and the Italians would never have stood for interference with the Vatican."

General Wolff's statement to the press about plans to arrest the Pope had been published a couple of weeks before I met Dr Dollmann, and I asked him about it. (At the time I did not know that Father Robert Graham had given a similar statement to the press.) "There was talk, but it never came to an actual order – nothing like that could have been planned without my knowledge. It simply didn't happen."

"How much did *you* know about what was happening to the Jews?"

"Well, there were rumours all over the place about the camps. But of course, again, it hardly applied to Italy with its comparatively few Jews. We never knew that Jews were actually being exterminated in the East, we really didn't. I remember, after the war, when I was preparing my book, I went to see Kesselring. I asked him, in all honesty, for the purpose of historical information: had he known about these horror-camps. And he said, 'I swear to you, I had no idea they existed.' Yes, of course – I know: the army in the East – soldiers, officers, command – they *must* have known;

it was inevitable; how could they avoid it? No, I don't understand myself how it could then have failed to become known everywhere. It is perfectly true; they came on leave; they must have talked about it. But the fact remains: *we* didn't know.

"I always thought – as most people did – that the Pope, like everybody else, didn't have any precise and reliable information on the precise nature of the atrocities against the Jews, or their extent.

"Of course, if the record now shows – as you say – that he did know, if not before, then certainly at the end of 1942, then of course the whole picture changes: then one must really ask oneself what could possibly have stopped him from speaking up. . . ."

8

DID POPE PIUS XII know of the true situation in Poland, and specifically of the extermination of the Jews? We have, of course, discussed this point in various places earlier in this book. But the man best able to inform us fully on this uniquely vital point is Monsieur Kazimierz Papée, Polish Ambassador to the Holy See from July 14, 1939, to December 1958.

Although Poland now no longer has an official representative at the Vatican, Monsieur Papée was still listed in the *Annuario Pontificio* as "Agent of Embassy Affairs", when I visited him in March 1972. A small brass plate on the door of his third-floor flat at 7D Via St Pancrazio in Rome announced "Polish Embassy to the Holy See".*

Kazimierz Papée was eighty-two years old at the time of our meeting and in full possession of his remarkable faculties; a *Grand Seigneur* from the past, small, thin, impeccably elegant, with an exquisite use of language. He spoke with me in French.

(Carlo Falconi, in *The Silence of Pius XII*, describes him as "an outstanding Polish diplomat with a brilliant career behind him at, amongst other places, The Hague, Berlin, Copenhagen, and finally Prague. . . . Active relations between the Holy See and the Polish government [in exile] depended on the Ambassador in Rome, Casimir Papée. It was probably because it had such a trusted man

---

* Monsieur Papée has since moved to a smaller apartment.

in Rome that the Vatican sidestepped [throughout the war] appointing a representative in London [to the Polish government in exile]."

A thin and silent elderly maid, with a face out of a Polish wood carving, dressed in a long creamy-white robe and headcovering, somewhat like a lay nun, opened the door. The large drawing room with its gleaming parquet and furniture, exquisite etchings, signed photographs of statesmen and clerics with household names, and innumerable lovely *objets d'art* on fragile tables was an accurate representation of the man.

Monsieur Papée's memory covers minutely his activities during the war years and afterwards. His very special position now – I soon realized – was delicate: he was, and yet was not, part of the Vatican community. It is unlikely – and it would not have occurred to me to ask – that, after the political upheavals in Poland he had retained any personal wealth. The implications of what he said – and didn't say – and of what I have learned since about his circumstances, are that his position in Rome (not to speak of his personal integrity) requires considerable discretion.

We spoke of many things: life in the distant past; great men he has known; fundamental values which he treasures and the disappearance of which I – much younger than he – found myself regretting with him.

The way Monsieur Papée spoke of his beloved Poland, the war years, his own activities on behalf of all the Poles – Christians and Jews – and Pope Pius xii, was filled not with anger or resignation, but with pain; the pain felt by a man whose long life has been one of service, and whose efforts in the end proved to be in vain.

He recounted in detail the steps he took throughout the tragic years 1940–4 to inform the Holy See of the situation in Poland; his repeated audiences with the Pope, and his continuous communications by letter and in person with the three Cardinals at the Vatican State Secretariat (Secretary of State Cardinal Maglioni; Second Secretary Cardinal Montini – the present Pope Paul vi – and Cardinal Tardini).

Later, as I was about to leave, Monsieur Papée signed and handed me a book. "If you study it carefully," he said, "it will perhaps answer some of your questions better...."

Monsieur Papée's book, *Pius XII a Polski 1939–1949* (Pius xii and Poland 1939–1949), is a compilation of letters, comments, *aide-mémoires* and reports from the Polish government in exile, Polish ecclesiastics in occupied territory and from Monsieur Papée himself, to the Holy See. It was published in Rome in 1954, by Editrice Studium, with the financial help of the Ford Foundation.

While many of the papers are of course of great relevance, the "careful study" Monsieur Papée so kindly – and generously – recommended, revealed that what is perhaps most important to an understanding of that period are not the documents which are published in this volume, but those which – as Monsieur Papée quietly points out in the preface – "remain in the archives until a future date".

With the help of (exiled) Polish sources of various political persuasions, I have been allowed sight of some of these documents which are being kept in Polish archives abroad.

It is essential to mention here that these particular documents, which are of the greatest possible significance in the context of establishing the extent of the Vatican's early awareness of the situation in Poland with particular reference to the extermination of the Jews (and which Monsieur Papée, for very obvious reasons, felt unable to include in his book), have also been excluded from the *Actes et Documents du Saint Siège relatif à la Seconde Guerre Mondiale.** This omission, in view of the purpose of the publication and the nature of these papers – all of which were highly relevant official diplomatic communications – raises the gravest doubts as to the integrity of the Vatican publications.

Considerations of space prevent the reproduction of all three of these documents shown to me; but the most incontrovertible proof of the Vatican's complete knowledge of the methods and extent of the extermination of the Jews in Poland at least as of December 1942, is provided by one of them, the letter the Polish Ambassador personally handed to Cardinal Tardini on December 21, 1942:†

> "The Polish Embassy has the honour of communicating to the State Secretariat of His Holiness the following information emanating from official sources:
> "The Germans are liquidating the entire Jewish population of Poland. The first to be taken are the old, the crippled, the women and children; which proves that these are not deportations to forced

---

* As of 1973 when this book originally went into print. The document reprinted on this page has now (1976) been included in one of the latest volumes.

† Here given in the author's translation from the original French.

labour, and confirms the information that these deported populations are taken to specially prepared installations, there to be put to
death by various means [while] the young and able-bodied are
killed through starvation and forced labour.

"As for the number of Polish Jews exterminated by the Germans,
it is estimated that it has passed a million. In Warsaw alone there
were, in the ghetto in mid-July 1942, approximately 400,000 Jews;
in the course of July and August 250,000 were taken East; on
September 1 only 120,000 ration cards were distributed in this
ghetto, and on October 1 40,000 cards. The 'liquidation' is proceed-
ing at the same rate in the other cities of Poland.

"The Polish Embassy takes this opportunity to assure the State
Secretariat of his Holiness of its highest esteem.

Vatican, 19 December, 1942."

(Here a handwritten remark in Polish: "Handed personally by
the Ambassador to Monsignor Tardini, 21/11.42")

(This was the seventh communication on the subject written by, or
communicated through the offices of, Monsieur Papée. The first
was dated March 30, 1940. Descriptions of other Nazi atrocities
and pleas to the Pope to declare his condemnation of them were,
of course, received by the Holy See; and many of those are included
in the collection of documents published by the Vatican. Apart
from some indicative footnotes, however, none of these refers
specifically to the Jews.)

Three days after receiving this letter, on Christmas Eve, 1942,
Pope Pius XII made public reference to what was happening to the
Jews. In full knowledge of the fact that by that night at least a
million human beings had been methodically put to death in
"specially prepared installations" in occupied Poland – a slaughter
unrelated to any act of war – he made one oblique reference to the
fact, almost at the end of a Christmas message more than 5,000
words long, to the Catholics of the world.* By the time he reached
this sentence he would have spoken for approximately forty-five
minutes, and the sentence itself was part of a repetitive series of
injunctions saying that humanity owed

" . . . a solemn vow not to rest until, in all people and all nations of
the earth a vast legion shall be formed of those handfuls of men
who, bent on bringing back society to its centre of gravity, which is
the Law of God, aspire to the service of the human person and of

* Translated in full in *The Tablet*, January 2, 1943.

his common life ennobled in God. This vow humanity owes to the innumerable dead who lie buried on the battlefields. The sacrifice of their life, the fulfilment of their duty, is an offering to a new and better social order. Humanity owes this vow to the endless, sorrowful army of mothers, widows and orphans, who have been deprived of light, comfort and support. Humanity owes this vow to the innumerable exiles, torn from their motherland by the hurricane of war and scattered on foreign soil, who might join in the lament of the prophet: 'Our inheritance is turned to aliens, our houses to strangers.' Humanity owes this vow to the hundreds of thousands of people who, through no fault of their own, *sometimes only owing to nationality or descent*, are doomed to death or to slow decline.*
Humanity owes this vow to the many thousands of noncombatants, women and children, ailing and old people, whom aerial warfare – whose horrors we have repeatedly denounced since the very beginning – indiscriminately robbed of life, possessions and health, charitable institutions and places of prayer. Humanity owes this vow to the endless stream of tears . . . etc, etc, etc."

Carlo Falconi says, with great precision and presumably with deliberate irony, that the above was "unquestionably the most courageous denunciation of all the acts of violence against civilians that Pius XII dared to pronounce during the whole war. . . ."

In Rome (and in Germany) in 1972 and 1973, priests again and again referred to the Christmas message of 1942 as conclusive proof of the Pope's willingness to take a public stand towards the Nazi horrors.

Did he think, I asked Kazimierz Papée at the end of our talk, that the Pope could have done more to stop the slaughter of the Jews and Christians in Poland?

"He *was* in a very very difficult position," Monsieur Papée said, unhappily. "He was – one must appreciate this – surrounded by Fascism: he had very little freedom of movement."

(A year later I telephoned Monsieur Papée from London to ask him one more question that had troubled me: "Do you think," I said, "that there is a possibility – even the most remote possibility – that the Pope did not *see* the documents you sent or handed to the State Secretariat? Could they have tried to protect him from this knowledge?" There was a long pause while he thought. And then,

* The italics which pick this sentence out are the author's.

332

he answered, in the same anguished voice with which he had replied to some of my original questions, "It is not possible. The Holy Father saw all such communications; it would not have been possible to withhold them from him.")

At our meeting in Rome he followed his remark about the Pope's lack of freedom of movement by raising and then dropping his hands in a gesture of despair, and saying, "It was not only that: I remember when I came to see the Holy Father for . . . perhaps the tenth time, in 1944; he was angry. When he saw me as I entered the room and stood at the door awaiting permission to approach, he raised both his arms in a gesture of exasperation. 'I have listened again and again to your representations about Our unhappy children in Poland,' he said. 'Must I be given the same story yet again?' I knelt before him and I said, 'Holy Father, however often I have already come, I will come again and again to beg you to do more and yet again more for the Poles.' With which", Monsieur Papée added to me, "I meant, of course *all* the Poles, including the Jews, most of whom, of course, by this time, were dead."

Part VI

I

FRAU STANGL'S sister, Helene Eidenböck, has all the qualities we associate nostalgically with the Austria of long ago – charm, gentleness, humour, real goodness . . . it is extraordinary that she of all people, should have lived on the fringes of such infernal events.

She continued her profession as a cook for a large Vienna restaurant throughout and after the war, and met her husband in 1958, when she was forty-nine. "We met at a swimming-pool where I used to go a lot," she said, her face lighting up as it did whenever she spoke of him. "He was a construction engineer, and the gentlest man in the world. We talked a few times, at the pool; then one day he came here to see me, and I suppose he never left again. He surrounded me with care and love. He loved music – he was all music, you know. We went to the opera, to concerts, almost every day. We went to the mountains, the lakes. We stayed with his daughter Hanne and her family on a kibbutz in Israel every year. I love her as if she were my own." She brought out photographs of an attractive young couple and two boys in the flowery garden of a whitewashed house. "I can't talk to the boys," she said. "They only speak Hebrew. But they are wonderful. So clean, so straight, so honest." It was evident that when Heli Eidenböck speaks about Jews she is simply speaking about *people* who happen to be Jews. It would never occur to her to say, "I don't care what they are," because she genuinely doesn't.

Her husband, married to his first wife at the time of the Anschluss, was kept on in his essential job in Vienna until 1939, by which time the United States was no longer issuing visas for Austrian Jews. "The only place he could get a visa for was Shanghai," she said, "and his wife wouldn't go there. She had a friend in England. She said she'd go there, and she did. He went to Shanghai alone, and worked there throughout the war, and then came back to Vienna. His wife wouldn't come back – they had grown apart and she didn't want to live with him again. So he was alone, like me."

They were together when the Stangl affair first reached the newspapers. "No, he'd had no idea," said Heli. "None of us had. He read about it in the papers here in Vienna when it was reported in 1964 that Wiesenthal was looking for him. And then, when it really broke, he hardly spoke for a week. He was totally shattered by it; I suppose it was worse – even worse – for him than me, because here he was, with me, loving me, and this man, accused of these awful, awful things was my brother-in-law. . . . He used to read the papers and then just sit, shaking his head. 'You can't really understand,' he'd say to me. 'Imagine, just imagine it was your child, your baby they took, and slammed against a wall shattering its head. Your child, before your eyes. . . .' Perhaps I didn't understand the way he did," she said softly. "But I felt it; I felt the horror of it all through my body."

Her husband died in 1968. "He lived just long enough to follow the beginning of the trial," she said. "He'd had a heart condition for twelve years but never a tremor since we met. And then – that awful day – he was on his way upstairs and he fell, right down here in the entrance to our house. And was dead. For me, the light went out that day. We had had ten years."

"Only ten years," I said.

"Only?" she repeated. "It was a lifetime, a whole life for me. Now I go to the cemetery every few days. I stay with him a little. I think of our wonderful quiet days, full of music and his goodness. I go to see his daughter in Israel every year. I still can't speak to the boys, but we look at each other and smile, and that is enough. And he has a cousin in Vienna too – and I see her quite often. So you see, he has seen to it that I am no longer alone. . . ."

I asked her what she remembered of the time, in 1947, when Stangl was first imprisoned by the Austrians. "Well," she said, "it was a case of the mighty falling, wasn't it? But again, you see, we'd had no idea that he had done anything special – even about Hartheim, we hardly knew about that. Resl kept a very close mouth about it to the family. She told us later that she was going to him – yes, to Syria – and that she was taking all their furniture. I remember she wrote later from Damascus that the piano had arrived all in pieces. . . ."

"FROM THE moment Paul arrived in Syria," Frau Stangl said, "he lived incredibly frugally; he saved every penny for one year towards paying for our trip out to join him. And finally, in May 1949, he sent us the tickets and we could go. I had got everything ready on our side; I had applied for a passport – the children still travelled on mine – and I had packed up all our things. There was a bit of trouble first about taking the girls to the Middle East; the Austrian authorities were worried that they might fall into the hands of white slavers. It was only when I showed them my husband's letters from Damascus, with his address on them, that they were reassured and believed me that we were really going out to join him. And then they gave us the exit permit." (In Austria, with its long tradition of enlightened laws for the protection of minors, the Court of Guardianship is co-responsible for any child living with a single parent.) "But as you can see," said Frau Stangl, "there was no secret whatever about our leaving; everybody knew we were going to join Paul in Damascus. The packing cases for our household goods stood in the front garden of our house; two men helped me pack – blankets, mattresses, sewing machine, china, chairs, tables, the bedroom furniture, the piano – the whole town could see – and saw – what I was doing, and everybody saw when we nailed the chests shut and I painted on them big and clear (she wrote it for me) FRANZ PAUL STANGL, SCHUHHADER, HELUANIE 14, DAMASKUS. This was also, of course, the address I gave to the police in Wels when they asked me why I wanted to leave Austria; I told them specifically, 'To join my husband who escaped.' "

Austrian law requires anyone arriving or departing to fill in a police certificate; with the assistance of the Ministries of Justice and of the Interior in Vienna, I was able to confirm that Frau Stangl's certificate is on the record in Wels, dated May 6, 1949, with the address she gave me, and the annotation "*Mann geflüchtet*" (husband escaped).

"I applied for the Syrian visa," she continued, "and there was no problem about it at all – though I can't quite remember whether I wrote to Vienna or Linz for it. I know it had to go through a Swiss consulate. Were they representing Syria in Austria at the time? I don't know. Anyway, I was handed it in Wels. And on May 4 or 6, we left by train for Genoa.

"I remember the children were dead tired when we got there and I took a room at the Excelsior, near the station, and put them to bed. The ship was due to leave the following morning, but the line informed me that it was delayed because of repairs and wouldn't leave for four days. I had no money left whatever; you see, all I had was just enough to get us on to the ship; as Paul had prepaid our trip I hadn't expected to need more cash. Now that night at the hotel, dinner and breakfast were going to exhaust everything I had and I needed more. I had to do something. Of course, I spoke fluent Italian – from my time in Florence years before – so I went to the station and offered my services as an interpreter to a group of Germans. I took them to my hotel, got them rooms and spent the next three days showing them around. I earned enough to pay for our stay, and I could even take the children on a boat trip for a day. And finally we got on board and had four really good days crossing – a rest and good food.

"When Paul met us in Damascus, I found him to be the happy sweet man he had been years before all the horror. It was *my* decision not to talk to him again about Treblinka. I felt I had to let him regain his peace of mind; the awful things that had been done were done, and my thoughts now had to be for the children, for our life together, for the future.

"All that year before we came, Paul had worked at this textile mill – the job Bishop Hudal had originally obtained for him. But just after we got there, the owner of this business died, the firm collapsed and Paul found himself without a job. It was very hard. He looked desperately for work but it took a long time before he found some. In the meantime we had to live, so I started to work as a masseuse; it was lucky that my training at the school of social work had included quite a bit of what is now called physiotherapy. Anyway, I got quite a few clients quite soon; fat women, you know; I usually started with their heads; they were always losing their hair, so I first massaged their scalps and then worked my way down to their toes.

"For the first six months we lived in a flat in the rue de Baghdad – with practically no furniture because it took a long time for our things to arrive from Austria."

Several of the books describing the Nazi escape network mention an address in Damascus – 22 rue George Haddat. After our talks in Brazil I wrote to Frau Stangl, asking her if she remembered this address. "I am not sure," she replied, "but that may be the place where we lived for a short time after our arrival in Damascus.* It was a kind of 'pension' where there were other Germans, but I think they used pseudonyms because I can remember them only as 'the Capt'n' or 'Lodz'." (This to some extent bears out the description of 22 rue George Haddat given by "Werner Brockdorff" in *Flucht vor Nürnberg*, who portrays it as a reception centre for refugees arriving from Rome.)

"In the beginning of December 1949, our luck turned," Frau Stangl continued. "Paul got a job as a mechanical engineer with the Imperial Knitting Company; thank God he had qualifications." (He had, apparently, taken a German correspondence course in mechanics in 1935 – when she was in Florence and he working for the police in Linz.)

"His salary – very good for those days – was 500 Syrian pounds a month. Our furniture had arrived and we moved to a bigger flat, in the old part of Damascus, rue de Youssuff. It was a wonderful old house, and with our things we made the flat into a real home." (Later she wrote: "We were the first German family there to have our own home, and *all* the Germans visited us.")†

"I loved the Middle East; I spent every moment I could at museums, and I even managed to get to Mesopotamia to watch excavations. I wouldn't have missed that period for anything.

"It was a good time, but after about a year an extraordinary problem arose. The front of the house we lived in belonged to the Police President of Damascus; he lived there with his harem. Well, he became far too interested in Renate – our middle daughter. She was twelve. . . . [Renate, born February 17, 1937, was actually fourteen. The mistake is insignificant, except that it does point to a slight tendency on Frau Stangl's part, despite her general honesty, to dramatize events.]

"She was very blonde and very pretty and he really had his eyes on her," she continued. "Renate could do anything she liked; she could do no wrong as far as he was concerned. We got into a panic about it. What could we do – foreigners in Syria – if he took it into

* In a recent letter Frau Stangl confirmed that they had definitely stayed at rue Haddat.

† "I remember very many Germans," she wrote even later, "from General Count Strachwitz down to Colonel Rössler." She also said that the flat they rented in the rue Sheik Youssef [*sic*] belonged to people called Husseinis who were relations of the Grand Mufti.

his head he wanted her? What could we possibly hope to achieve against the Police President? Father said we'd have to leave. He said I was to go to Beirut and make the rounds of South American consulates – there weren't any in Damascus – and we'd accept the first visa offer we got. Well, I went off to Beirut at once; I started with the Venezuelans and then the Brazilians. The Venezuelans were very nice too, but they said it would take some time to get a decision from Caracas. The Brazilian consul asked immediately what Paul could do and when I said he was a mechanical engineer, they said they wanted to see him; so Paul went to Beirut as soon as I got back. And we got the visa very quickly – a month later I think.

"When we had it, I went to see the Police President and told him that here we were, offered this great opportunity by the Brazilians, and that we felt we must accept it. We had been afraid of what his reaction might be, but in the end he was really nice about it, and we left very soon afterwards; as soon as Paul's factory found a replacement for him – an Italian it was – two months later.

"I had saved 2,000 dollars; we sold our piano to an Arab for 900-odd Syrian pounds and our bedroom furniture to a German who had brought his girlfriend out from home and got married. And Paul got a leaving-bonus from the firm: he'd done very well there: they gave him a nice reference too."

She showed me the reference, made out to "Paul Adalbert Stangl". She believed that they had muddled his and his father's names, having seen him described on his Red Cross *laisser-passer* as "Paul F. Stangl, son of Adalbert Stangl". "They weren't terribly precise about names over there," she said. She told me that she had often handled her husband's Red Cross paper in Damascus. "It was a white booklet, about six by eight centimetres, with the red cross on the cover and the particulars inside" – the particulars, including his nationality, his parents' names and the birth dates of herself and the children. "I didn't see the Red Cross passport again after he had received or applied for the Syrian *laisser-passer*; maybe he had to hand it in at the *Sûreté*, but I don't remember."

Frau Stangl remembered that their journey to Brazil cost them about 4,000 Syrian pounds, adding, "We had about 5,000 dollars, so we managed quite well." After my conversations with Franz Stangl were first published in the *Daily Telegraph Magazine*, several people were moved to suggest that such an expensive journey must have been paid for with stolen money, or again money from the Vatican, or from "Odessa". The travel agent Thomas Cook confirms, however, that a ticket from Beirut to Santos, Brazil, via Genoa, while it would now cost £173 sterling, or about $432, would have cost considerably less in 1951; and that it would have been perfectly possible for a couple with three children to manage the journey on about £400 or $1,200.

"On the ship from Syria to Genoa," said Frau Stangl, confirming a story her husband had told me, "we met a former British officer who had been imprisoned in Teheran for three years as an agent." Like Stangl, this man had been on the island of Rab during the war. But a far stranger coincidence – one which brought tears to Stangl's eyes when he told me about it – was that the man had once stayed with relations of Frau Stangl in a place called Mürz-zuschlag. When they met him on the ship, he was on his way back to Austria where, it would appear, he had decided to live.

"As soon as we knew we were going to Brazil," said Frau Stangl, "we wrote to a young German engineer who had gone there from Damascus before us. He and his fiancée met us off the ship at Santos, and we stayed our first night in São Paulo with her parents, who were German-Brazilians. The next day we moved into a boarding-house and Paul started at once looking for a job. Of course, again, we had practically no money; in fact, all we had left was forty dollars. But then, we had every reason to think he'd get a job at once. And sure enough, he came back the evening of our first day and said there was hope of one almost immediately, and that meanwhile we'd keep going on our forty dollars. Well, the most awful thing had happened; because of course I had known we'd have to change that money – after all, even though it was a boarding-house, still we couldn't hope to manage without cash. Well, a German woman I had met that very morning said she'd get me a good exchange-rate, so, stupidly, I had given her all our money. And then she came back and said she'd given it to a man who'd said he'd get cruzeiros at a good rate and he'd made off with it. I couldn't *prove* she was lying; after all, it was perfectly possible that she could have been just as stupid as I. Anyway, there was all our money gone and I had to tell Paul.

"No, he wasn't angry; he was never angry with me, or any of us, in that sense; he never raised his voice, or lost his temper – until much, much later – and never never did he strike or spank the children. Anyway, a week later Paul got a job with a Brazilian textile firm. He didn't speak Portuguese but he managed at first with German, Italian and the little English he spoke, and he learned Portuguese fantastically quickly; of course he had this marvellous memory. When they hired him, it was as a 'weaver', but after a very short time he was put in charge of planning – especially everything to do with the machines. It turned into what was an engineering job more than anything else. He earned 3,000 cruzeiros. He stayed with Sutema – that's what they were called – for two years, much of it travelling."

This mention of Stangl's travelling in Brazil reminded me of his story of seeing cattle in pens by a railway, waiting to be slaughtered, and thinking, "This reminds me of Poland; that's just how the people looked – trustingly – just before they went into the tins . . . " and I asked his wife if he had spoken to her about this. She said that he never had. "But you know, he suddenly stopped eating meat at one point; I can't remember exactly when it was, but it was quite soon after we arrived."

She said he changed jobs twice after leaving Sutema, to earn more money. In both his second and third jobs his salary was 8,000 cruzeiros. All the figures given me by Frau Stangl, including these, are confirmed by tax and insurance records she showed me, and which I checked carefully.

"At the end of 1955 Paul fell ill," she said. "It wasn't anything the doctors could put their finger on – nothing we could really understand. Much later – after his coronary in 1966 – we thought it had probably been his heart all along. But that wasn't diagnosable at the time; he felt weak, had rheumatism, was unable to walk or even stand for any length of time. Perhaps it was finally the reaction to all those terrible years; I have always thought that his coronaries were the result of his terrible mental and spiritual stress.

"Anyway, once again a way had to be found for us to survive. We had been building our little house out here in São Bernardo do Campo since two months after our arrival in Brazil; we built every single bit of it, we had no professional help except in the end for the electricity. Paul even did the plumbing, and all the children helped with the building and, of course, the painting. We built room after room, first just camping outside, then moving into one room after another, as the house grew. It was finally completed only in 1960 – it took us nine years to build.

"But when Paul got ill, I got a job at Mercedes-Benz. I started at the bottom of the secretarial ladder, but after a while was given more responsibility until, in the end, for the last two years I worked there, I was in charge of book-keeping, with seventy girls under me. I stayed with them until 1962; they were very very good to me.

"Meanwhile, as he'd got better, Paul had started a small workshop in our house. He had bought old machine parts from second-hand dealers, built several weaving machines, hired a few women and was producing elastic bandages for hospitals. At first he did his own selling, but after a while he had to stop; he became very irritable and used to lose his temper dreadfully if the hospitals didn't buy. Finally I took over the selling in my spare time. I remember a hospital matron saying to me, 'Oh dear, that dreadful man is your husband?' She didn't really mean he was dreadful – I mean, he *wasn't* dreadful; it was just, I think, that he was very concerned over my working so hard, and desperate to make a success of his venture, so when they wouldn't buy, he'd be miserable and get abusive.

"In 1957 Renate [their middle daughter] got married to an Austrian called Herbert Havel; and a year later Gitta [Brigitte, the eldest daughter, born on July 7, 1936] also married an Austrian. Paul continued his work at home through 1958, until the summer of 1959. By that time his health had improved tremendously, and when the little workshop died a natural death, I helped him get a job with Volkswagen. . . ."

A great many writers have either stated outright, or implied, that German firms in Latin America and the Near and Middle East have generally provided employment and "cover" for escaped Nazis. While this is obviously true in some specific cases, it is doubtful whether many or indeed any company ever made it a matter of deliberate policy, or that it happened as a result of pressure by powerful post-war Nazi organizations. Once again, when it did happen, it was probably the result of the initiative of a few individuals. A sober look at the facts in general indicates that as far as Latin America is concerned, most of the "rank and file" escapers had to rely on their own resources, while the majority of those of higher rank who escaped either to very reactionary Latin American countries or to the Middle East were finally employed not by commercial companies but by various governments eager to take advantage of this sudden supply of "talent".

Volkswagen is one of the companies most often mentioned in this connection. Frau Stangl's story – pedestrian rather than dramatic – of how her husband got his job with them, appears to me to represent the kind of thing which very likely happened in the great majority of cases.

I have no particular wish or reason to exonerate Volkswagen (the company was, as it happens, somewhat less than helpful in my attempts to investigate this matter in Brazil), but I would like to separate rumour and gossip from fact. And there are two reasons why Frau Stangl's account appears to make better sense than the kind of stories we have been presented with so often.

The first of these reasons is that it was eight years before Stangl obtained this job at Volkswagen S.A.; eight years of living a more than modest working-class life in a working-class dwelling (just as, incidentally, the Eichmanns did in the Argentine). If he had been able to exploit his Nazi past in order to get a well-paid job with a German firm such as Volkswagen, why did he not do so earlier? And secondly, by October 1959, when he did get the job, it must already have been crystal-clear to anyone that the atmosphere was changing. The old guard in all these companies was nearing retirement age, and the young executives who were arriving from Germany, frequently graduates from American schools of business management, would be unlikely to approve appointments made for reasons of ancient, and now unpopular, political loyalties.

"Through my work at Mercedes-Benz," said Frau Stangl, "I had met a great many people in the car industry. When Paul had to have a job and there was nothing in his line at Mercedes, I asked one of our neighbours who was head of technical management at Volkswagen – his name was Jablonski. It was he who got Paul his job. He started as a mechanic but was soon promoted, and ended up in charge of preventive maintenance for the plant, with a salary of 25,000 cruzeiros a year (a large salary in Brazil at that time).

"Our situation had now really vastly improved, and I thought how nice it would be to move to a different place, and even to have a different and larger house. Where I really wanted to live was 'Brooklin' – one of the best residential districts of São Paulo; a lot of nice Germans lived there, and diplomats and nice Brazilians. I thought it would be so good for the girls. Of course Paul never

had my kind of ... I don't know what to call it ... initiative
perhaps, or cheek if you like, or perhaps just faith, to risk, to plan
things, to bring about a change in our life – actively you know,
rather than just passively. I had asked him what would he think of
our trying to find some place to live in Brooklin. But all he said
was, 'We could never afford that.' Well, I decided to go ahead
anyway. I talked to the people at Mercedes-Benz about it. They
were extraordinarily nice you know, very paternalistic towards
their staff; anyway, they helped me buy a plot of land; it cost 400
cruzeiros (land values were evidently extremely low). I had saved
200 and Mercedes lent me the other 200, and they 'lent' me one of
their architects to design the house."

(Later, having seen this house, I was to tell Frau Stangl that
even so I found it hard to understand how they could have built it
with their limited means. She replied in a letter: "The Mercedes-
Benz solicitor was Dr Jairo. He arranged the contract for the
purchase of the land for me; and a notary public, Senhor Joaquim,
helped me with registering the title. I have all the papers, and all
receipts from builders, etc, and the acknowledgment from Mercedes-Benz on repayment of the loan. All of them are at your
disposal and you can compare them with my salary slips.")

"We built very, very slowly," she said. "It was professionally
done but I got everything quite a bit cheaper because of Mercedes.
But I paid for all of it – Paul didn't even want to move, he disapproved – he finally bought a car when we moved in 1965. I had
done countless hours overtime – whole nights – but when we
moved in, we didn't have one centavos of debts. And I was happier
than I'd ever been because I felt that this was really my creation,
my gift to my family."

(The two-storey house at Frei Gaspar, in Brooklin, stands behind
a wrought iron fence above a small terraced garden full of flowers.
There is a two-car garage at street level, big picture windows and
the whole thing, with its clean Scandinavian-type modern lines
would fit happily into any modern development in Europe or
America. It was here Stangl was to be arrested; after that the
family moved back to the little house in São Bernardo which had
been let. The Brooklin house, now tremendously increased in value,
has since been let advantageously to diplomatic families.)*

* Since the original publication of this book, Frau Stangl has moved back into the
Brooklin house.

"This was a very good time for us; all the children were doing well; Gitta happily married and in her new house in São Bernardo [she was to have a baby soon]; Renate [who later got a divorce] and her younger sister both working at Volkswagen too – everybody had good jobs and was earning good money and I was looking after them and loving it. The new house had everything: a beautiful kitchen, big living room, bedrooms for all of us, a lovely dining room, and of course the garden which Isolde and I had planted. The terrible times were, if not forgotten, then certainly suppressed; we rarely, rarely spoke of them. If I ever very gently touched upon the subject, Paul would say wearily, 'Are you starting on that again?' and I'd stop. After all, I too didn't *want* to think about it any more.

"I was so sorry for the people who had been killed, but I too continued to rationalize: I know this now. I told myself, those men had been killed in those camps like soldiers at the front. They killed them – I said to myself – because of the war. Oh, deep down I knew it wasn't so. But that's how I rationalized it for myself. I never never allowed myself to think that women and children had been killed. I never asked him about that and he never told me. [And she must simply have turned off her mind when these facts were mentioned – as they were, often – in the Brazilian as well as the German press.] If my thinking – as I know now," she said, "was illogical, then it was because that was how I wanted, how I needed, how I *had* to think in order to maintain our life as a family and, if you like – for I know this also now – my sanity.

"Paul was an incredibly good and kind father. He played with the children by the hour. He made them dolls, helped them dress them up. He worked with them; he taught them innumerable things. They adored him – all three of them. He was sacred to them. . . ."

3

"*When the war was over,*" I had asked Franz Stangl in Germany, "*what did you want to do?*"

"All I could think of," he said, "was Knut Hamsun's novel *Segen der Erde* [*Growth of the Soil*]. That was all I wanted; to

348

start from the beginning, cleanly, quietly, with only my family whom I loved, around me."

"You said earlier you always knew that one day you would have to answer questions about that time in Poland. If you knew, why didn't you just face up to it? Why run away?"

"I am an old policeman. I know from experience that the first moments are never the right ones. But you know, in Brazil I never hid. I lived and worked there from the beginning under my own name. I registered at the Austrian consulate – first, because my papers read that way, as Paul Franz Stangl. Later, when I had to get a copy of my birth certificate through them, from Austria, I changed it and it was entered correctly as Franz P. Stangl. Anybody could have found me."

"Did people – friends you made in São Paulo – know about your past?"

"It never came up."

"But in all these years, have you never talked it out with someone? Your wife? Your priest? A special friend?"

"My wife and I talked sometimes about some of it; but not like this. I never talked to anyone like this."

"Did your children know?"

His face went scarlet; it was the second time he showed real anger at a question (the first time had been when I had asked him, with reference to his conduct in Treblinka, whether it wouldn't have been possible for him, in order to register his protest, to do his work a little less well. "Everything I did out of my own free will," he had answered, "I had to do as best as I could. That is how I am.")

"My children believe in me," he said now.

"The young all over the world question their parents' attitudes. Are you saying that your children knew what you had been involved in, but never asked questions?"

"They . . . they . . . my children believe in me," he said again. "My family stands by me." And he cried.

Renate – the Stangl's middle daughter, and the younger of the two small girls who had spent a holiday five kilometres from Sobibor in 1942 – is slim, blonde, with a delicate and vulnerable face that looked, when I met her, much younger than her thirty-three years. "He was the best father, the best friend anyone could

349

ever have had," she said. She was driving me back into São Paulo from São Bernardo do Campo, late on a rainy night.

I knew that none of the Stangl daughters really wanted to talk about these things and – as I feel very strongly that none of the young can be held in any way accountable for their parents' actions (or inactions) – I did not intend to press them. The little Renate said, with great effort, she volunteered.

"All I can say", she told me that night in the car, almost in a whisper, "is that I have read what has been written about my father. But nothing – nothing on earth – will make me believe that he has ever done anything wrong. I know it is illogical; I know about the trial and the witnesses; and now I know what he himself said to you. But he was my father. He understood me. He stuck to me through thick and thin and he saved me when I thought my life was in ruins. 'Remember, remember always,' he once said to me, 'if you need help, I'll go to the end of the moon for you.' Well, when he died in Düsseldorf I had just had an operation; but I decided I would be the one to fly over to bring him back here to Brazil – to us – for burial. I too would go to the end of the moon for him – that's what going back to Germany then was for me. I hope he knows it where he is now. I love him – I will always love him."

The eldest daughter, Gitta, whose health is very fragile, although unfailingly warm and polite on the telephone, was the only member of the Stangl family who felt unable to face the ordeal of talking to me at all. She suffered from one of the debilitating infections common in South America, and became much worse after her father's arrest and trial. The youngest girl, Isolde or Isi, as good-looking as her mother and sisters, is the least oppressed by, or even involved, in these terrible events. Only seven years old when they arrived in Brazil, she has become totally part of this new continent: Portuguese is her language, she has now married a young Brazilian and if she too prefers not to speak of the past, it is not because it worries her, but because, protected by her youth, it is emotionally beyond her; her way of thinking, her concerns are those of a young Brazilian, and she is free of the past.

Renate – for good reason – is the one who feels most involved. Her marriage had broken up some time before Stangl's arrest, for reasons quite unconnected with it. But Stangl believed to the end (despite reassurances I was finally able to give him) that his son-

350

in-law, Herbert Havel, had been involved in his capture. I had asked him in April 1971, when it was he had first realized that he was being looked for.

"In 1964," he said, "when my son-in-law showed me a Viennese newspaper where it said that Wiesenthal was after me."

"You believe, do you, that your son-in-law gave you away to Wiesenthal?"

"Renate had left him. When he came to me in 1964, he said that unless I got Renate to go back to him, he would destroy us all."

At the time this belief of Stangl's did not seem surprising to me, because four months earlier, after his sentence to life imprisonment at Düsseldorf, newspapers all over the world had quoted Simon Wiesenthal to this effect, and I too, meeting Herr Wiesenthal for the first time in Vienna in December 1970, gained a similar impression. To quote the *Daily Express* of December 23, 1970: "Sitting in Düsseldorf High Court today was Simon Wiesenthal, himself a survivor of Nazi camps . . . today he said, 'If I had done nothing else in life but to get this evil man Stangl, then I would not have lived in vain.' [There follows a brief account of Stangl's life since the end of the war] . . . Nazi-hunter Wiesenthal kept on the trail and in 1967 paid Stangl's son-in-law £3,000 for information."

After my first week of talks with Stangl I telephoned Herr Wiesenthal to check once more this particular element in the story of the arrest. Herr Wiesenthal then told me that he had been widely misunderstood; apparently he had just received a letter from Herbert Havel's uncle in Vienna, telling him that Mr Havel intended to sue him for libel. Herr Wiesenthal then said that he was calling a press conference to make it perfectly clear that he had never met or communicated with Havel, had never received any information concerning Stangl from him, and had most certainly never offered him any money or reward. (It should also be pointed out that Herr Wiesenthal states quite plainly in his book *The Murderers Are Among Us** that the £3,000 – or $7,000 – for information about Stangl was paid to "a seedy character" – a former Gestapo man – who came to see him, he says, at his office in Vienna.)

I am glad that these pages offer an opportunity to repeat these assurances, because it was not only Franz Stangl who believed that

* Heinemann, London, 1967.

351

Herbert Havel had been in some way instrumental in delivering him to justice. His family, particularly Renate (Mr Havel's former wife), shared this belief.

When I repeated Herr Wiesenthal's assurances to Frau Stangl six months later, she said that considering the sequence of events, and the many quotes in the newspapers, she still found them difficult to believe.

"You see," she said, "when, some time after Renate's marriage broke up and before we moved to Brooklin, Havel came to the house – it was in February 1964 – and brought this Viennese newspaper which said that Wiesenthal was looking for Paul – he *said* that 'he had sent his Jewish uncle to see Wiesenthal' . . . and we didn't know whether to believe it or not. But seeing how he felt about us, there really wasn't much reason to doubt what he said. A month later, in March 1964, he phoned Paul and summoned him – ordered him – to meet him: there isn't any other way of describing it. Paul went and Havel told him that he had checked a photograph which had subsequently appeared in the Vienna paper and that he now had no doubt: that Paul was the man Wiesenthal was seeking. Paul was fatalistic about it – as he always had been. 'You see,' he said, 'it's unavoidable. But if it comes to it, I want to give myself up – I don't want to run away.' He didn't say that just once, he said it a thousand times. . . ."

(*"You weren't really surprised,"* I had asked Stangl, *"when you were caught?"*

"I wasn't surprised," he said. "I had always expected it.")

"The Eichmann trial?" Frau Stangl said. "Yes, Paul followed it avidly. He sat there [she pointed to an armchair in the little sitting room] and read everything that was said about it in the Brazilian and also in the German papers we got. Yes, he read a great deal about all these things, always: newspaper articles and many of the books that were written. But he never commented on any of them to me – we never spoke about any of it: it was taboo. After that thing with Havel and the Viennese paper, nothing happened for a long time. We moved to the new house in Brooklin, as you know, in early 1965 and there too, as I said before, we rarely talked about it. But he did say, though I don't remember exactly when it was: 'If that clever man Wiesenthal is looking for me, surely all he has to do is ask the police, or the Austrian consulate – he could find me at once – I am not budging.'

"Herr Wiesenthal's account", Frau Stangl said, "of how he found us, as he described it to the press and in his book – I don't believe it. After all, why all the fuss? As Paul said, anyone could have found us, at any time. We were registered at the Austrian consulate in São Paulo since 1954; I was regularly writing home; everybody had our address. There was no call for all that drama. . . ."

4

THERE DOES indeed seem to have been no reason for "all that drama" considering that the Stangls really cannot be described as having "disappeared". What is astonishing is not that Stangl was finally "found", but that he was ever supposed to have been "lost".

The American CIC appears to have known about his position in Sobibor and Treblinka in 1945, yet they handed him over to the Austrians in 1947 and the Austrians put him in an open prison from which – of course – he walked out. When he went to Damascus after being helped in Rome, he immediately informed his wife of his address, keeping up a regular correspondence with her, and when his family joined him there a year later, Frau Stangl gave not only their relatives, but also the Austrian police precise information about their movements, including Franz Stangl's address. When they travelled via Italy to Brazil in 1951, they did so under their own name. When they reached Brazil, they lived and worked under their own name. In 1954 they registered under their own name at the Austrian consulate in São Paulo

The Austrian consul there was Herr Otto Heller, who was still holding the same post when I was there in 1971. It is true that he denied having registered Paul F. Stangl, or having subsequently altered that registration to Franz P. Stangl, or that Stangl had ever, to his knowledge, been inside the consulate. But he agreed that Frau Stangl registered, and that she entered on the form the names of her children, and stated that she was residing with her husband, Franz P. Stangl. He produced two files, one for "Theresa Eidenböck Stangl", the other for "Renate Havel Stangl", and repeated that these were the only Stangls in his records.

Frau Stangl says: "We went together to register at the Austrian consulate in August 1954. Not for any particular reason, but only because we felt it was right and proper to register at one's consulate, and we had so far neglected to do so." ("Registration", said Herr Heller, "is not required by Austrian law. It is in fact accepted by the consulate merely as a courtesy – a service to Austrian residents abroad.")

"We needed nothing from them at that time," said Frau Stangl. "Only much later, in 1957 and '58 when the girls married, they needed a copy of their father's certificate of citizenship or birth certificate – I don't remember which – and we asked for it. The consulate never refused anything to either me or the children. As far as I can remember, when we went to register, the clerk told us he was an auxiliary or provisional clerk. He gave us two papers to fill out. My husband was always much slower and more deliberate than I in writing; and somehow he never remembered dates precisely.* So I remember that he was still writing when I finished and handed in my form. But I saw him fill it in, and I saw the clerk take it from him. I did not see what my husband had written. It was not the custom to be given receipts for registration, so we don't have any proof of this."

"Stangl" is not an uncommon name in Austria, and it is admittedly unlikely that a provisional clerk would have attached any special significance to it. Equally, I thought reasonable Herr Otto Heller's comment to me; "If Herr Wiesenthal thought Stangl was in São Paulo, why didn't he in fact address himself to us? That would have made us look through the files, and then, sure enough, we *would* have found his name – if nowhere else, then on his wife's registration."

However, the fact remains that during my research in Vienna (for which, incidentally, the Austrian authorities readily gave me all the assistance I requested), I found that from 1961 Stangl *was* on the official Austrian list of "Wanted Criminals" (which is circulated to all embassies and consulates abroad), under the number "34/34 Mord: Tatbestand Treblinka."† And in 1964, according to

---

* A fact which had already struck me, considering his extraordinary memory for names.

† His name was thus listed *thirteen years* after he escaped from an Austrian prison where he was held to be tried for – one would presume at least – complicity in the murders at Hartheim; a fact which, one concludes, must have appeared irrelevant to the Austrian authorities between 1948 and 1960. It appears impossible to ascribe this

354

Frau Stangl, his name was conspicuous in the coverage given to the Treblinka trial by the Brazilian and foreign press. So it seems odd, to say the least, that during the six years between the first appearance of his name on the Austrian "Wanted" list, and his dramatic arrest, the fact that he was residing openly in Brazil never emerged.

The very efficient aliens' police (DOPS) must certainly have had his particulars which, on request from Austrian or German government sources, would have been made available; the "Wanted List" appears never to have been checked by the Austrian consulate in São Paulo, although, as said above, his name figured prominently in press reports of the trial; and not a single person at Volkswagen apparently felt moved to ask any questions, though both his co-workers and the management at least knew his name and presumably read the papers. In the light of all this, one can only be amazed that it was left to the private efforts of Herr Wiesenthal to discover the whereabouts of this man who was never hidden.

5

"On the night it happened, February 28, 1967," said Frau Stangl, "I had seen a lot of cars around. Our street was full of them. But it was only in retrospect I realized that I had noticed this. At the time I thought nothing of it. Renate was already home. Isolde came with Paul – they had stopped on the way for a beer in a bar. I heard a commotion outside and went to the window. Police cars were drawn across the street, blocking it off on each side; our car was surrounded by crowds of police. Paul was pulled out of the car – handcuffed – Isi fell to the ground shouting for us; that's what I had heard, and rushed to the window; but the police car with Paul in it, followed by a string of others, was off before I could even get out of the door. Isi was almost incoherent with shock. She said Paul's face went yellow when it happened.

"We phoned Gitta and then we went from police station to police station to look for him, but nobody knew anything. Until

omission to the well-known Austrian *Schlamperei*, an endearing quality which, incidentally, is certainly responsible for the fact that Stangl's name was still listed (Consul Heller showed it to me) in 1971 – when Stangl, after four years' imprisonment in Germany, had already been tried and sentenced, and was dead.

finally we got to the DOPS. And they said we should be glad they had taken him – if they hadn't, the Israelis would have picked him up. After that, all we knew was what we read in the papers.

"In May or so we read that he had been moved to Brasilia, so we went up there. He was in a military prison. He looked – oh, just terrible, very very bad. And he said it was dreadful. He cried. I asked him about Treblinka; by this time, you know, we had read so much. 'I don't know what pictures you saw,' he said, 'perhaps you saw pictures of other camps. . . .' He was so distraught, all I could think of was to console him. All I wanted then was to be for him someone he could be sure of, someone he could lean on.

"The children had come up with me, each driving part of the way. He was so wonderful with them, never gave way, never cried while they were in the room, smiled at them, walked them to the gate and waved goodbye to them. But of course, this was the first time it became real to them; seeing him like this, in prison, was a traumatic experience for them. It was after that Brigitte became ill.

"After that I went up there two or three more times. And on June 22 he was extradited.

"The two years at our Brooklin house had been our happiest in Brazil. We had had friends – mostly the children's friends from Volkswagen, but they were friends for us too: Hungarian, Dutch, Brazilians. No, I don't remember any Germans we were friends with. I don't think Dr Schulz-Wenk even knew we existed then," she said. [Dr Schulz-Wenk, then Director of Volkswagen, SA, was one of the people about whom it was said that he helped former Nazis.]

"After Paul was taken to Germany, we moved back to São Bernardo. It was the only sensible thing to do; we had only the money the two girls were earning, and my small pension – 200 cruzeiros. We knew we were going to need a great deal of money, for Paul's defence. If we sublet the Brooklin house and went back to live modestly in São Bernardo, there was a chance of being able to manage. We moved back in October 1967.

"Everybody drew away from us after this; everybody we knew at Volkswagen and everybody else. Thank God, the girls were allowed to keep their jobs – we were grateful for that. Dr Schulz-Wenk is supposed to have said, 'The girls have nothing to do with it'; that's when he knew about us, you know, but not before."

It was about then that Frau Stangl had a visit from the Austrian Gustav Wagner, who had been at Hartheim and Sobibor with Stangl, and had fled with him from Austria. Suchomel had told me that the two men were "close friends". When Stangl had told me of his distress at Stanislav Szmajzner's "forty-page" attack on him, I had pointed out that in fact only about two pages of the book were devoted to him, whereas Szmajzner wrote with far greater bitterness and horror about Wagner. "Really?" said Stangl. "And yet they live cheek by jowl in Brazil." At first Frau Stangl said that she couldn't understand what he had meant by this remark. Later she said: "Oh, it's because Wagner went for a while with a girl who later married in Goiania [where Stan Szmajzner lives]." But it would appear that Wagner in fact never lived in Goiania, whereas he did live for a long time thirty kilometres away from the Stangls, in São Paulo.

Frau Stangl was somewhat reluctant to discuss Wagner. This, I think (although I felt differently at first) was primarily because she disliked him and didn't want to be associated in my mind with such a person – he is by all accounts a particularly nasty piece of work. Finally, however, she admitted that they knew him quite well and that he "dropped in" on them.

"But I didn't like Paul to associate with him," she said. "He is a vulgar man – we have nothing in common with him."

Gustav Wagner evidently felt otherwise. "He came to see me after Paul had been deported," said Frau Stangl. "He wanted money; he said he was down and out and would I lend him money to bury his wife who had just died. I said I didn't have any to lend him. He said, 'Why don't you and I set up house together? I haven't got anybody any longer and as for Franz – they are going to do him in anyway over there, and you'll be alone too.' " Frau Stangl said she was outraged and threw him out, and never saw him afterwards – but she did in fact lend him money which, she wrote later, he had never returned.

At Stangl's trial she was asked about Gustav Wagner and said that she heard he had gone to Uruguay. Later she wrote to me putting it slightly differently. "He informed me of his intention to emigrate to Uruguay," she wrote. She also told me that she heard, not long before I came to São Paulo in the autumn of 1971, that a woman had seen Wagner in São Bernardo, "looking like a beggar, with torn clothes and shoes".

357

"I didn't see Paul for three years," said Frau Stangl. "He wrote me once a week. All we did – all we could do – was hope. I still didn't believe he had been Kommandant; he denied it to me to the end. I know he admitted it to you – but never to me. To me he always spoke of the gold, the construction work, and Wirth – he did that every time, every single time – in Brasilia too.

"On May 8, 1968, I received a summons to testify at his trial and I flew to Germany on the 12th; I had been ready because I knew it was going to happen.

"I went to see Paul at the prison in Duisburg, where he was then; I went with his lawyer, Herr Enders. I found him enormously changed, depressed, terribly controlled.

"I testified on May 22. I didn't attend the trial because Paul didn't want me to; he was afraid, he said, I'd be attacked or that people – the public you know – would be rude to me. I was only in the court three times: when I testified; when Szmajzner testified; and the day of the sentencing. But even though I didn't attend any other day, I went to the building every day and sat outside, just to be near him. I told him, so that he would know while it was going on, that I was there, just outside the door, and thinking of him. I went there, or I went to church.

"When I first arrived in Düsseldorf they had arranged for me to stay at a kind of hostel, but it was horribly depressing – no, not that anyone was unkind to me, it wasn't that: nobody ever was. It was just that it was a kind of institution and I couldn't stand it. But then I went to stay with a wonderfully kind woman in her house and it saved my sanity. In the evenings we talked and she became a friend." Frau Stangl also said, in another conversation, that she went to museums and theatres.

Frau Stangl's sister Heli commented on this period too. "Resl," she said. "Yes, I've seen her, she stayed with me when she came over last [in 1970]. She went to see all the others in the family. We got closer this time than we had ever been. Still, I never could understand how she could bear to go back to Steyr where everybody knew her." She shrugged. "Well, she felt she could – it is her business. Last time she was here she was quite gay, chipper. . . .

"Do I think she could have stopped him?" She shrugged again. "I think she was ambitious too. You see, my life was good too, even though I was alone for so long. But it was so different – so very, very different – it's difficult for me to understand. But Resl always wanted to get to the top. Well, I suppose in a way she did get there. . . ."

"My own testimony took two hours," Frau Stangl said about the trial. "I had never been in a court before and I was horribly nervous. Of course I didn't tell them that I hadn't believed Paul's story about the illegal Party membership and how disappointed I was. How could I have told them? If Paul hadn't told you about this himself, perhaps I wouldn't have told you either. They didn't believe that I hadn't known about Hartheim, and yet it was true. Yes, they asked me whether I knew what Sobibor was when I was there. I told them that a drunken ss man told me about it. . . .

"When I first arrived," she said, "they only allowed me to see Paul twice a week, for fifteen minutes with a guard. Later – although the guards were always there – they became much nicer; I could stay longer and sometimes they even allowed me to bring him some beer. What was strange", she said, "was that often he would hardly talk to me. He'd sit opposite me at the table in that little interview cell, but he'd chat with the guards, not with me; he'd talk to them about their leaves, their excursions, places he knew, had been to. It hurt me, and sometimes I'd say, 'Don't you want to talk to *me*?'"

There was good reason for this: Stangl knew that by this time she had read everything about the trial and him. He desperately wanted her there – she was allowed to kiss and hug him – but he dreaded her questions and, by this nervous chatter with the guards, was avoiding them at all cost. In my conversations with him it emerged very clearly that in the end the only thing that mattered to him was her and his children's continued loyalty and love; and equally, how aware he was of his wife's profound aversion to what he had done. He was not sufficiently perceptive to realize how thin the line was – for her too – between rationalization of what he had done and accepting it, and living up to her own fundamental principles – and condemning him. He could only think, with real dread, of the possibility – or, as by that time, he probably knew, the probability – of her rejecting him.

Basically, it was when he came to terms with the realization that she knew – that after what had happened, even if he ever got out of prison, life with his family would be impossible – that he decided to talk to me. I came to understand this in the course of the conversations with him; and he, in a way, confirmed it in letters he

359

wrote to his wife until shortly before he died, about his feelings about these talks.

6

THE LAST time I saw Frau Stangl we talked about causes and effects, reasons beyond reasons.

"The day he was sentenced," she said, "I know you won't agree with me about this, as you haven't agreed about other things, but I must go on being honest with you: those other Germans who sat in judgment over him, what do you think they would have done in his place? One of the jury-men came up to me later and said, 'I don't want you to think that it was unanimous – it wasn't.'

"You see, I can't help thinking that there has to be a reason for everything, even this terrible thing that happened. The universe isn't without reason – nothing is. My sister goes to Israel every year, to a kibbutz – she has told me so much about it. I really ask myself, these people who died – they were heroes, martyrs, wasn't there a reason, a sense in their sacrifice? Could that extraordinary country have been built if it hadn't been for this catastrophe?"

I could not help but suspect that she and her husband had come to this consoling conclusion together, for he had said something very similar to me. *"In retrospect,"* I had asked him, *"do you think there was any conceivable sense to this horror?"*

"Yes, I am sure there was," he replied. "Perhaps the Jews were meant to have this enormous jolt to pull them together, to create a people, to identify themselves with each other."

It is impossible not to feel a sense of outrage at hearing either of these two people, so horrifyingly involved, say this. And yet, the way they both said it, they were, if not honourable, certainly trying – and meaning – to search for honesty.

At the very end of our conversations I told Frau Stangl that I needed to ask her an extremely difficult question which I wanted her to think about deeply before attempting to answer. "It is the most important question as far as my talks with you are concerned," I said, "and to me, the reply you give me will determine your own position; the degree, if you like, of your own guilt." I suggested that, before replying, she should leave me for a while, lie down, think about it.

"Would you tell me", I asked, "what you think would have happened if at any time you had faced your husband with an absolute choice; if you had said to him: 'Here it is; I know it's terribly dangerous, but either you get out of this terrible thing, or else the children and I will leave you.' What I would like to know," I said, "is: if you had confronted him with these alternatives, which do you think he would have chosen?"

She went to her room and lay down; I could hear the bedsprings creak as she lowered herself on to the bed. The little house was silent. It was very hot outside and the sun shone into the living room where I sat waiting, for more than an hour. When she came back she was very pale; she had been crying, had then washed her face and combed her hair and, I think, put on some powder. She was composed; she had made a decision – the same decision her husband had made six months earlier in the prison in Düsseldorf; to speak the truth.

"I have thought very hard," she said. "I know what you want to know. I know what I am doing when I answer your question. I am answering it because I think I owe it to you, to others, to myself; I believe that if I had ever confronted Paul with the alternatives: Treblinka – or me; he would . . . yes, he would in the final analysis have chosen me."

I felt strongly that this was the truth. I believe that Stangl's love for his wife was greater than his ambition, and greater than his fear. If she had commanded the courage and the moral conviction to force him to make a choice, it is true they might all have perished, but in the most fundamental sense, she would have saved him.

This was not, however, the last word to be spoken between Frau Stangl and me on this trip to Brazil. The next morning I had to leave my hotel at 6 a.m. to fly to the interior, and only returned late in the evening. At the desk they handed me a letter. "A lady brought it," the clerk said, "early this morning."

"Dear Doña Gitta, I want to beg to correct an answer to a question you asked me where I had, at the time of our talk, too little time to ponder my reply.

"The question was whether my husband, in the end, would have found the courage to get away from Treblinka had I put before him the alternative 'me, or Treblinka'. I answered your question – hesitatingly – with, 'He would have chosen me.'

"This is not so, because as I know him – so well – he would never have destroyed himself or the family. And that is what I learned to understand in the critical month of July 1943.

"I can therefore in all truthfulness say that, from the beginning of my life to now, I have always lived honourably.

"I wish you, dear Doña Gitta, once more all the best,
your
Thea Stangl"*

I telephoned Frau Stangl late that night.

"When did you write this letter?" I asked her. "It sounds like something written in the middle of the night. This isn't really what you want to say, is it?"

She cried. "I thought and thought . . . " she said. "I didn't know what to do. So finally I wrote it at 3 o'clock in the morning and brought it in on the first bus."

"What would you like me to do?" I asked.

"I don't know. I just don't know."

I told Frau Stangl that I would put in my book what she had said to me the previous day – which I thought was the truth. But that I would also add the letter, which only showed what we all know, which is that the truth can be a terrible thing, sometimes too terrible to live with.

7

PERHAPS IN the end it was easier for her husband to tell the truth because, I think, he knew he would die when he had told it.

The last day I spent with Stangl was Sunday, June 27, 1971. He had felt faintly unwell much of that week with stomach trouble, and that day I had brought him some special soup in a thermos – it was an Austrian soup he had said his wife used to make for him when he didn't feel well. When I came back to the prison after a half-hour lunch break, he looked quite different: elated, his face smooth, his eyes fresh.

"I can't tell you," he said, "how wonderful I suddenly feel. I ate that wonderful soup and then I lay down. And I rested so deeply, somehow like never before. Oh, I feel wonderful," he repeated.

As my time for these talks was running out and I only intended

---

* Author's translation from the German.

coming back once more – the following Tuesday for an hour or two, to recapitulate on anything important before flying back to London – the prison governor had said I could stay later than usual this Sunday. We spent four hours that afternoon, going back over many questions we had discussed before.

He talked again, at length, about the fairy-tale book by Janusz Korczak; he became fascinated with the subject of what children should, and should never again, be taught. He spoke for a long time in a decisive but thoughtful and quiet manner. Then he turned to stupidity in general. As he warmed to the subject and went back to relating it to his own experiences, as often before during these talks, his personality changed brusquely and startlingly; his voice became harder and louder, his accent more provincial and his face coarse. ("It happened," his wife had said to me. "God help me; I saw it again here in Brazil – not for years, but then just in the last two years; it happened most often when he was driving and got angry about other drivers – stupidity, he called it, and it frightened me to see his face like that.")

"In Brazil," he said, his voice harsh, his accent almost vulgar, "at vw, the stupidity of some of the people there had to be seen to be believed. It sometimes drove me wild." He gestured with his hands. "There were idiots amongst them – morons. I often opened my mouth too wide and let them have it. 'My God,' I'd say to them, 'euthanasia passed *you* by, didn't it,' and I'd tell my wife when I got home, 'these morons got overlooked by the euthanasia.'"

"Do you think", I finally asked – it had become very late – *"that that time in Poland taught you anything?"*

"Yes," he said, his voice once again calm and pensive – the increasing abruptness of these repeated metamorphoses becoming ever more disconcerting. "That everything human has its origin in human weakness."

"You said before that you thought perhaps the Jews were 'meant' to have this 'enormous jolt': when you say 'meant to' – are you speaking of God?"

"Yes."

"What is God?"

"God is everything higher which I cannot understand but only believe."

The awful distortion in his thinking had shown up time after

363

time as we had talked. And now here it was again, as we came to the end of these talks.

"*Was God in Treblinka?*"

"Yes," he said. "Otherwise, how could it have happened?"

"*But isn't God good?*"

"No," he said slowly, "I wouldn't say that. He is good and bad. But then, laws are made by men; and faith in God too depends on men – so that doesn't prove much of anything, does it? The only thing is, there *are* things which are inexplicable by science, so there must be something beyond man. Tell me though, if a man has a goal he calls God, what can he do to achieve it? Do you know?"

"*Don't you think it differs for each man? In your case, could it be to seek truth?*"

"Truth?"

"*Well, to face up to yourself? Perhaps as a start, just about what you have been trying to do in these past weeks?*"

His immediate response was automatic, and automatically unyielding. "My conscience is clear about what I did, myself," he said, in the same stiffly spoken words he had used countless times at his trial, and in the past weeks, when we had always come back to this subject, over and over again. But this time I said nothing. He paused and waited, but the room remained silent. "I have never intentionally hurt anyone, myself," he said, with a different, less incisive emphasis, and waited again – for a long time. For the first time, in all these many days, I had given him no help. There was no more time. He gripped the table with both hands as if he was holding on to it. "But I was there," he said then, in a curiously dry and tired tone of resignation. These few sentences had taken almost half an hour to pronounce. "So yes," he said finally, very quietly, "in reality I share the guilt. . . . Because my guilt . . . my guilt . . . only now in these talks . . . now that I have talked about it all for the first time. . . ." He stopped.

He had pronounced the words "my guilt": but more than the words, the finality of it was in the sagging of his body, and on his face.

After more than a minute he started again, a half-hearted attempt, in a dull voice. "My guilt," he said, "is that I am still here. That is my guilt."

"*Still here?*"

"I should have died. That was my guilt."

"Do you mean you should have died, or you should have had the courage to die?"

"You can put it like that," he said, vaguely, sounding tired now.

"Well, you say that now. But then?"

"That *is* true," he said slowly, perhaps deliberately misinterpreting my question. "I did have another twenty years – twenty good years. But believe me, now I would have preferred to die rather than this. . . ." He looked around the little prison room. "I have no more hope," he said then, in a factual tone of voice; and continued, just as quietly: "And anyway – it is enough now. I want to carry through these talks we are having and then – let it be finished. Let there be an end."

It was over. I got up. Usually a prison guard had come to fetch him; this time, because we had continued much later than usual, the instructions were that he was to come downstairs with me to the entrance of the prison block, from where a guard would take him back to his cell. When we stood up he became suddenly very gay, fatigue appeared to have gone; he helped me pick up my papers and insisted on carrying the coffee cups.

When we got downstairs, we stood for a moment near the door which was opened for me to leave the block. He stuck his head out. "Nice air," he said, "let me smell it a moment. I'll be glad to see the lady out," he jested to the officer on duty who smiled and pressed the button that closed the electronic door. When I waved from outside, he smiled and waved back. It was just after 5 o'clock.

Stangl died nineteen hours later, just after noon the next day, Monday, of heart failure. He had seen no one since I left him except a prison officer who had taken the food trolley around. On a piece of paper tacked to his wall he had jotted down a name he had been trying to remember. On his table everything was in perfect order. Inside the book of fairy tales by Janusz Korczak, the sheet of paper with which he had marked a page he wanted to show me was no longer blank as I had seen it, but covered with emphatically underlined quotes from the book, each headed by the appropriate page number. The prison library book he was reading at the time of his death was *Laws and Honour* by Josef Pilsudski.

The possibility was certainly in everybody's mind – including mine – that he might have killed himself, and he was carefully examined at the obligatory *post mortem*.

He had not committed suicide. His heart was weak and he would no doubt have died quite soon anyway. But I think he died when he did because he had finally, however briefly, faced himself and told the truth; it was a monumental effort to reach that fleeting moment when he became the man he should have been.

Epilogue

I DO not believe that all men are equal, for what we are above all other things, is individual and different. But individuality and difference are not only due to the talents we happen to be born with. They depend as much on the extent to which we are allowed to expand in freedom.

There is an as yet ill-defined, little-understood essential core to our being which, given this freedom, comes into its own, almost like birth, and which separates or even liberates us from intrinsic influences, and thereafter determines our moral conduct and growth. A moral monster, I believe, is not born, but is produced by interference with this growth. I do not know what this core is: mind, spirit, or perhaps a moral force as yet unnamed. But I think that, in the most fundamental sense, the individual personality only exists, is only valid from the moment when it emerges; when, at whatever age (in infancy, if we are lucky), we begin to be in charge of and increasingly responsible for our actions.

Social morality is contingent upon the individual's capacity to make responsible decisions, to make the fundamental choice between right and wrong; this capacity derives from this mysterious core – the very essence of the human person.

This essence, however, cannot come into being or exist in a vacuum. It is deeply vulnerable and profoundly dependent on a climate of life; on freedom in the deepest sense: not license, but freedom to grow: within family, within community, within nations, and within human society as a whole. The fact of its existence therefore – the very fact of our existence as valid individuals – is evidence of our interdependence and of our responsibility for each other.

List of Principal Works Consulted

Adolph, Walter: *Hirtenamt und Hitler-Diktatur*, Berlin, 1965.
Allen, William Sheridan: *The Nazi Seizure of Power*, London, 1966.
Arendt, Hannah: *Eichmann in Jerusalem*, New York, 1963.
Bartoszewski, Wladyslaw: *The Blood that Unites Us*, Warsaw, 1970.
Bar-Zohar, Michel: *Les Vengeurs*, Paris, 1968.
Berg, Mary: *Warsaw Ghetto: a Diary*, New York, 1945.
Bernadotte, Count Folke: *The Curtain Falls*, New York, 1945.
Biss, Andreas, *Der Stopp der Endlösung*, Stuttgart, 1966.
Brockdorff, Werner: *Flucht vor Nürnberg*, Munich-Wels, 1969.
Bullock, Alan: *Hitler: a Study in Tyranny*, London, 1964.
Churchill, Sir Winston S.: *The Second World War*, London, 1948–54.
Ciechenowski, Jan: *Defeat in Victory*, New York, 1947.
Cohn, Norman: *Warrant for Genocide*, London, 1967.
Devel, Wallace R.: *People Under Hitler*, New York, 1942.
Dicks, Henry V.: *Licensed Mass Murder: a socio-psychological study of some SS killers*, London, 1972.
Dollmann, Eugen: *The Interpreter*, London, 1967.
Falconi, Carlo: *The Silence of Pius XII*, London, 1970.
Frank, Anna: *The Diary of a Young Girl*, New York, 1952.
Frank, Hans: *Dziennik Hansa Franka*, ed. S. Piotrowski, Warsaw, 1957.
Frank, Michael: *Die Letzte Bastion: Nazis in Argentinien*, Hamburg, 1962.
Friedländer, Saul: *Pie XII et le IIIe Reich*, Paris, 1964.
Fry, Varian: *Surrender on Demand*, New York, 1945.
Gallagher, J. P.: *Scarlet Pimpernel of the Vatican: Hugh Joseph O'Flaherty*, London, 1969.
Gilbert, G. M.: *Nuremberg Diary*, New York, 1947
   The Psychology of Dictatorship, New York, 1950.
Goebbels, Josef: *Tagebücher 1942–43*, ed. Louis Lochner, Zurich, 1948.
Gollancz, Victor: *The Case of Adolf Eichmann*, London, 1961.
   Let My People Go, London, 1943.
Gruchmann, Lothar: *Euthanasie und Justiz im Dritten Reich*, Stuttgart, 1972.
Hausner, Gideon: *Justice in Jerusalem*, New York, 1945.
Hill, Mavis M. and Williams, L. Norman: *Auschwitz in England*, London, 1965.
Hirschmann, Ira: *The Embers Still Burn*, New York, 1949.
Hitler, Adolf: *Mein Kampf*, Munich, 1933.
Hochhuth, Rolf: *Der Stellvertreter*, Hamburg, 1963.
Hohne, Heinz: *The Order of the Death's Head*, London, 1969.
Holmes, J. Derek: *The Church in Nazi Germany*.
Höss, Rudolf: *Kommandant in Auschwitz*, Stuttgart, 1958.

Hudal, Aloïs: *Schönere Zukunft – Gedanken zur Judenfrage*, June, 1936.

Rom, Christentum und deutsches Volk, Innsbruck, 1935.

Joffroy, Pierre: *A Spy for God: the Ordeal of Kurt Gerstein*, London, 1970.

Karski, Jan: *The Story of a Secret State*, New York, 1944.

Kastner, Rezso: *Der Bericht des jüdischen Rettungskommitees aus Budapest, 1942–3*, Germany, 1958.

Katz, Robert: *Death in Rome*, London, 1967.

Kempner, Robert M. W.: *Das dritte Reich im Kreuzverhör*, Munich, 1969.

Der Kampf gegen die Kirche, aus unveröffentlichten Tagebüchern.

Kogon, Eugen: *The Theory and Practice of Hell*, London, 1951.

Der SS Staat, Berlin, 1947.

Kosdorff, Ursula von: *Berliner Aufzeichnungen 1942–45*, Munich, 1962.

Laval, Pierre: *Laval parle (Notes et Memoires redigés à Fresnes, d'Août à Octobre 1945)*, Paris, 1948.

Le Chene, Evelyn: *Mauthausen, the History of a Death Camp*, London, 1971.

Leiber, Robert, SJ: *Pius XII und die Juden in Rom, 1943–44*, Freiburg, 1960–61.

Levi, Primo: *If This is a Man*, London, 1959.

Levy, Alan: *Wanted: Nazi Criminals at Large*, New York, 1962.

Lewi, Guenter: *The Catholic Church and Nazi Germany*, New York, 1964.

Malaparte, Curzio: *Kaputt*, New York, 1946.

Mann, Thomas: *Deutscher Hörer! 25 Radiosendung nach Deutschland*, Stockholm, 1942.

Marshall, Bruce: *The White Rabbit: the Story of Wing-Commander F. F. E. Yeo-Thomas*, London, 1952.

Mitscherlich, Alexander, and Mielke, Fred: *Wissenschaft ohne Menschlichkeit*, Heidelberg, 1949.

Morse, Arthur D.: *While 6,000,000 Died*, London, 1968.

Muszkat, Marian: *Polish Charges against German War Criminals*, Warsaw, 1948.

Nalkowska, Zofia: *Medaillons*, East Berlin, 1968.

Neuhäusler, Johann: *Kreuz und Hakenkreuz*, Munich, 1946.

Niemöller, Martin: *Die Evangelische Kirche im dritten Reich*, Bielefeld, 1956.

Herr ist Jesus Christ – Hitler und die Evangelischen Kirchenführer, Bielefeld, 1959.

Niemöller, Wilhelm: *Macht geht vor Recht: der Prozess Martin Niemöller*, Munich, 1952.

Novitch, Miriam: *La verité sur Treblinka*, Paris, 1967.

Nyiszli, Miklos: *Auschwitz: a Doctor's Eye-witness Account*, New York, 1960.

Papée, Kazimierz: *Pius XII a Polska, 1939–49*, Rome, 1954.

Papen, Franz von: *Memoirs*, London, 1952.

Picker, Henry: *Hitlers Tischgespräche im Führerhauptquartier, 1941–42*, Bonn, 1951.

Poliakov, Léon: *La bréviaire de la haine*, Paris, 1951.

Rathbone, Eleanor F.: *Rescue the Perishing*, Parliamentary Debates, House of Commons, May 19, 1943.

Reitlinger, Gerald: *The Final Solution*, London, 1961.

The SS: the Alibi of a Nation, London. 1956.

Ringelblum, Emmanuel: *Notes from the Warsaw Ghetto*, New York, 1958.

Roches, Georges, and St Germain, Philippe: *Pius XII devant l'histoire*, Paris, 1972.

Roosevelt, Eleanor: *This I Remember*, New York, 1949.

Rosenberg, Alfred: *Der Mythus des 20 Jahrhunderts*, Munich, 1934.

Rothkirchen, Livia: *The Destruction of Slovak Jewry*, Jerusalem, 1961.

Rückerl, Adalbert: *NS–Prozesse*, Karlsruhe, 1971.

Russell of Liverpool, Lord: *The Scourge of the Swastika*, London, 1954.

Schlabrendorf, Fabian von: *Offiziere gegen Hitler*, Zurich, 1946.

Schoenberner, Gerhard: *The Yellow Star*, London, 1969.

Shirer, William L.: *Berlin Diary*, New York, 1943.
    The Rise and Fall of the Third Reich, London, 1960.

Speer, Albert: *Erinnerungen*, Berlin, 1969.

Stephenson, William: *The Bormann Brotherhood*, New York, 1973.

Suhl, Yuri: *They Fought Back*, New York, 1967.

Szmajzner, Stanislaw: *Inferno cm Sobibor*, Rio de Janeiro, 1968.

Tenenbaum, Josef: *In Search of a Lost People*, New York, 1949.
    Underground: the Story of a People, New York, 1952.

Thalmann, Rita, and Feinermann, Emmanuel: *La Nuit de Cristal*, Paris, 1972.

Toynbee, Arnold and Veronica (ed.): *Hitler's Europe*, London, 1954.

Trevor-Roper, H. R.: *The Last Days of Hitler*, London, 1947.

Volk, Ludwig, SJ: *Das Reichkonkordat vom 20 Juli 1933*, Mainz, 1972.
    'Der Bayerische Episcopat und Nationalsozialismus', Essay in *Stimmen der Zeit* 1964–65, Heft 7, Katholische Akadamie in Bayern, Aktionpublicationen Vol. II., 1965.

Wiernik, Yankel: *A Year in Treblinka*, New York, 1945.

Wiesenthal, Simon: *The Murderers Are Among Us*, London, 1967.

Weissberg, Alex: *Advocate for the Dead: the Story of Joel Brand*, London, 1958.

Weiszäcker, Ernst von: *Erinnerungen*, Munich, 1950.

Wronski, S., and Zwalakowa, M.: *Polacy Zyszi 1939–45*, Warsaw, 1971.

Yahil, Leni: *The Rescue of Danish Jewry*, Philadelphia, 1969.

Zipfel, Friedrich: *Kirchenkampf in Deutschland*, Berlin, 1956.

Many compilations of records and documents were also consulted, amongst them the following:

Transcripts of the Treblinka trial and the Stangl trial, by courtesy of the State Prosecutors and Administrators of the West German Court at Düsseldorf.

Unpublished documents of the former Polish Government in Exile, by courtesy of the Administrators of the Polish Archives Outside Poland.

Polish Government and trial documents, by courtesy of the Ministry of Justice, Warsaw.

Les Actes et Documents du Saint Siège relatif à la Seconde Guerre Mondiale, ed. Pierre Blet, Robert A. Graham, Angelo Martini and Burkhart Schneider, Libreria Editrice Vaticana, Vatican City. Five volumes had been published by the spring of 1973.

Ritter, Julian: "Hochland", *Nachruf über Pius XII*

Documenty i Materialy, Central Jewish Historical Commission of Poland, Lodz, 1946.

German Crimes in Poland, ed. Central Commission for War Crimes, Warsaw, 1946–7.

War Years in Poland, 1939–45: Scenes of Fighting and Martyrdom, a guide by the Council for the Preservation of Monuments to Resistance and Martyrdom, Warsaw, 1964 (English translation 1968).

Roy Publishers: *The Black Book: the Nazi Crimes against the Jewish People*, New York, 1946.

Leo Baeck Institute: *Yearbook XI, The Jewish Question and Anti-Semitism*, London, 1966.

Encyclopedia Judaica, Vol. 4B, pages 905–10, Jerusalem, 1971.

Frankfurter Rundschau: Sobibor, August 22, 24, 26, 1950; Hirtreiter, November 11, 1950.

Trial Records on microfilm, consulted by courtesy of the Institute for Contemporary History, Munich, and the Central Judiciary Authority for NS Crimes in Ludwigsburg: Case I, no. 205 (Victor Brack to Himmler, Trials of War Criminals I, page 721); Case I, no. 470, no. 3010, affadavits (Dr Gorgass, Trials of War Criminals I, page 803); Case IX, no. 3197 (affadavit, Paul Blobel); Case IX, no. 5384 (affadavit Albert Hartl, cross-examination, Transcript 2898–2900); Case I, no. 2635 (Mennecke's examination before Landgericht, Frankfurt); Case I, Transcript 2481 (examination Karl Brandt, Mischerlich 118).

Index

Aktion Reinhard, 86, 88, 101, 226, 249, 260

Allers, Dieter, 17, 52, 54, 57, 75, 104, 225; and euthanasia, 63–4, 70, 76, 79–81, 83–4, 88; and Jews, 89–90, 93

Allers, Frau, 80–1, 83, 89

Altschuh, Robert, 182, 183, 193, 211

American occupation authorities, 267–269

Anima, 290, 302, 304, 306, 314, 316, 320

Anti-semitism: in Czechoslovakia, 173; in Poland, 89–90, 100, 117, 121, 153, 183–4, 199; *see also* Pius XII

Arbeitsjuden, see Work-Jews

Auschwitz, 100, 151, 173

Austria: Nazi activities in, 28–9; police force of, 28–9; political events, 28, 30–1; socialist uprisings, 27, 30

Babi Yar, 97

Bart, David, 181, 213

Bartoszewski, Wladyslaw, *History of Help to the Jews in Occupied Poland*, 117

Bayer, Dr, 30, 31

Bayer, Monsignor Karl, 18, 307–15

Belsec, 54, 100, 111–13, 141, 151

Bernburg, 77, 78, 86

Berning, Bishop, 68, 73

Bertram, Cardinal, 72, 74

Bielas, Max, 163, 259

Birkenau, 100

Blankenburg, Werner, 49, 76, 79, 162, 260

Blau, 207–9

Blobel, 97

Bloch, Zhelo, 182–3, 210–11, 221, 246

Bodelschwingh, Pastor of, 69

Boothby, Lord, 325

Boris III, King of Bulgaria, 215

Bormann, Martin, 280, 306, 310–11, 321

Bornewasser, Bishop, 72

Bouhler, Philip, 49, 59, 63, 105, 171

Brack, Viktor, 49, 52, 65, 66, 68–70 *passim*, 76, 81, 85, 104, 105

Brandt, Dr Karl, 59, 62, 63

Braun, Eva, 326

Braune, Pastor, 69

Brazil, 140, 319

Brescani, Luigi, 215

British-US conference on refugees, Bermuda 1943, 217

"Brockdorff, Werner" (Alfred Jarschel), *Flucht vor Nürnberg*, 291, 309, 311, 341

Bulgarian Jews, *see* Jews

Bundesarchiv, Koblenz, 71

Caritas International, 307, 308, 322

Catholic Church: and euthanasia, 63, 65–9, 72–6, 278, 282, 283–4, 285, 295; help for Nazi escapers, 277–8, 285–6; and National Socialism, 277, 280–2, 299–300; in Poland, 117, 278, 279, 284; and sterilization, 61–2, 72; *see also* Vatican

Chelm, 107, 108

Chelmicki, Count and Countess, 132, 137, 138

Chelmno (Kulmhof), 54, 85, 99, 111, 139

Child-euthanasia, 54–5, 56, 73–4; and Catholic Church, 58, 59; protests against, 59

373

survival qualities, 183, 186–7, 197–8; on food, 191, 197, 237; on girls in Treblinka, 194–5; on revolt and escapes, 195, 197, 236–7, 239–41, 244–6; on friends, 210–12; "Open Letter", 246; on Stangl, 259

Globocnik, Odilo, 79, 101, 102–5, 107, 110, 114, 131, 133, 160–3, 249, 260–2

Godfrey, Monsignor, 278

Goebbels, Josef, *Diary*, 299–300

"Gold-Jews", 191, 206–7, 244

Gottgläubiger, 37, 226

Grafeneck, 73, 81

Graham, Father Robert, 299, 327

Grauss, Ernst, 150

Great Britain, 112–13, 139–40, 216–19

Greiser, Artur, Gauleiter, 85n

Gröber, Archbishop, 72

Gruchmann, Lothar, *Euthanasia and Justice in the Third Reich*, 60, 69

Grundloch, Father Gustav, 294

Günther, Christian, 215

Gürtner, Dr Franz, 58, 60

Gypsies, extermination of, 93, 99, 100, 278

Hadamar, 56, 58–9, 81, 85

Halifax, Lord, 278

Hamsun, Knut, *Segen der Erde*, 348

Hartheim, Schloss, 53–6, 59, 73, 77, 78, 81, 83, 108, 230, 338, 354n, 357, 359; trial, 270, 271–2

Hartl, Albert, 17, 64–71, 97, 295–6; on beginnings of euthanasia, 65–9

Havel, Herbert, 345, 351–2

Heller, Otto, 353, 354

Hengst, August, 161

Heyde, Prof Werner, 49, 57, 69, 77, 78, 84, 199

Heydrich, Reinhard, 65, 100, 101, 111, 175, 199

HIAG, 227–8

Himmler, Heinrich, 48, 66, 85n, 98, 127, 163, 175, 191, 216, 249, 295, 300

Hintersteiner, Frl, 210, 230

Hirschfeld, Max, 35–6, 48

Hirschmann, Ira, 215, 319n

Hitler, Adolf, 49, 50, 324–6; and Catholic opinion, 283, 295; and compulsory sterilization, 61; and euthanasia, 59, 62–3, 65, 66, 68, 73, 76; *Mein Kampf*, 98–9; *Table Talk*, 299

Hocke, Gustav René, 314

Hofjude, 181, 197

Höfle, Hans, 110, 114, 131

Höldl, Franz, 261, 271–2

Horn, Otto, 16, 86–8, 167, 196, 204–5, 221, 229

Hudal, Bishop Aloïs, 275, 277, 289–290, 301–8, 311, 312–16, 319, 321, 340

Hull, Cordell, 142, 217

Hungary, 216

"Inferior races", 93, 96, 99

Innitzer, Cardinal, 30, 294, 304–5

Institute for Contemporary History, Munich, 71

International Red Cross, 268, 277, 306, 313; passports, 289, 291, 313, 314–17, 342

Invasion of Russia 1941, 96

Jakubiuk, Wanda, 148–9

Japan, 217

Jarschel, Alfred, *see* "Brockdorff, Werner"

Jewish Agency for Palestine, 141

Jewish police, 158–9

Jewish Socialist Bund, 139

Jewish *Sonderkommandos*, 111

Jews: Bulgarian, 213–14, 215; Danish, 215, 219; Eastern and Western, 198–199; executions of, 97; extermination of, *see* Part II and III *passim*; Hungarian, 216, 319; Italian, 318–319, 326; Norwegian, 215, 219; and Poles, 116–17, *see also* anti-semitism; Polish, 181, 198, 217, *see also* Warsaw ghetto; Rumanian, 215–16

John XXIII, Pope, 305, 319n; *see also* Roncalli

Judenrath, Warsaw, 188

375

377

Stadie, Stangl's orderly, 166

Stangl, Brigitte, 345, 348, 350, 355, 356

Stangl, Franz: 16; first meeting with author, 21-4; trial and conviction of, 21, 117, 119, 228-9, 357-9; prison life of, 21-2, 254-5; and prison officers, 24, 253-4; childhood, 25-6; as weaver, 26-7; joining police force, 27; posting to CID, 28-9; his marriage, his wife, 29-30, 33, 45; language of, 29; at the time of Anschluss, 30, 38-9; as "illegal Nazi", 31-4; first contact with Jews, 35-6; transfer to Gestapo, 36-7; and Prohaska, *see* Prohaska; break with Church, 37, 48; disciplinary action against, 37-8, 52; acknowledgment of guilt, 39, 364-5; transfer to Euthanasia Programme, 48-58, 77; and Wirth, 53-4; and extermination of Jews, 101, 200-2, 232-3, 360, 363; in Poland, 101-5; in Sobibor, 106-10, 113-19; in Belsec, 111-13; his white riding clothes, 117-18, 122; and Szmajzner, 119, 122-31; with his wife in Poland, 131-9; leaving Sobibor, 138-9; in Treblinka, 155, 156-7, 160-4, 165-71, 189-92 *passim*, 199-205; and work-Jews, 207-8; floggings and hangings under, 229; leave July 1943, 233-6; in Treblinka uprising, 238, 240-1, 247-9; second part of meetings with author, Part IV; and children, 259; in Italy, 260-2, 267, 314; illnesses and heart attacks, 262, 263-4, 344; arrest in Austria, 264; in Glasenbach, 265-6, 269-70; escape, 273-6, 314-15; in Rome, 289, 321; in Syria, 289-90, 338-42; emigration to Brazil, 290, 342-3; work in Brazil, 344-5, 363; marriage of daughters, 345, 348; building of houses, 344-5, 346-7; arrest in Brazil, 350-3, 355-6; registration in Brazil, 353-4; transfer to Germany, 356; last meeting with author, 362-5; death, 365

Stangl, Isolde, 229, 350, 355

Stangl, Renate, 345, 348, 349-50, 352, 355

Stangl, Theresa, née Eidenböck, 16; on Stangl being illegal Nazi, 33, 46-47; on Prohaska, 38; life in Brazil, 40-1, 343-5, 346-8, 353-4; childhood and education, 41-3; meeting with Franz Stangl, 44; as governess in Florence, 44; attitude to husband, 45; marriage, 45; and euthanasia, 59, 78; and Jews, 119, 360; and Szmajzner, 119, 130; in Poland, 131, 134-9, 359; Christmas 1942, 209-10; on Stangl's leave May 1943, 229-30; on Stangl's leave July 1943, 233-6; on Stangl's leave February 1944, 262; on the years following end of war, 263-265, 266-7, 270-5, 290-1; in Syria, 338-42; on Stangl's arrest, 355-6; at trial, 358-9; last meeting with author, 360-2; on responsibility, 361-2

Staszek, Polish woodcutter, 242-3

Steiner, Hans, 273

Steiner, Jean-François, 195, 205, 206, 246

Sterilization, 60-2, 66

Strawczynski, 229

Struma incident, 217

Suchomel, Franz, 16, 53, 104-5, 123, 262, 357; on Stangl being illegal Nazi, 34; in Euthanasia Programme, 56-7, 77, 80, 82-3; and Otto Horn, 87; on Sobibor, 115; on Treblinka, 157-8, 160-1, 166-8 *passim*, 171, 177, 191-2, 194, 202, 259; and Czech Jews, 181-2; on girls in camps, 195, 205; on escapes, 196; on Dr Choronzycki, 205-6; on uprising in Treblinka, 238, 240, 247, 248; on Stangl in Italy, 262-3

Sumner Welles, 140

"Superior races", 99

Sweden, 215, 218-19

Switzerland, 216-17

Szeptyckyj, Archbishop, 279

Szmajzner, Stanislaw, 16, 119–31, 357, 358; *Hell in Sobibor*, 119

T4, description, 49–50, *see also* Euthanasia Programme and "Final Solution"
Tardini, Cardinal, 329, 330
Taylor, Myron, 140–1, 217
Theresienstadt, 174–5, 182
Thomas, Max, 97
Thomas Aquinas, 61, 67
Thomas Cook, 343
Tittman, Harold, 141, 142
Totenjuden, 165, 207
Trawniki, 109
Treblinka, 54, 86, 100, 133; Part III; arrivals as described by Zabecki and Glazar, 151–6, 175–7; bakery, 168; barter, 191, 193; Blue Command, 196, 213; burning of corpses, 193, 220; camouflage, 219, 220; description of camp, 164–6; end of, 249; escapes, 195–7; fake railway station, 200, 219; floggings, 201–2, 229; gas chambers, 221, 248; hangings, 229; *Lazarett*, 165, 190, 206; rations and food, 168, 191, 197, 213, 220; Red Command, 186, 189; today, 145–9; *Totenlager*, 167, 168, 170, 201, 204, 220–1, 241; uprising in, 119, 236–50; women and girls in, 194–5, 203–5, 237–8
Turowski, Father, 320

Ukrainians, 112, 115, 122–6 *passim*, 150, 153, 155 6, 166, 177, 188–94 *passim*, 213, 220, 224, 237
Unger, Karel, 175, 176, 180–1, 182, 220–1, 229, 244, 245–6
US, 112–13, 139–42, 216–19
US Counter-Intelligence Corps, 265, 269, 353
US State Department, 140, 218–19
Ustaca, 309

Vansittart, Robert, 61n
Vatican: *Actes et Documents du Saint Siège etc.*, 75n, 292, 297, 330; and Bolshevism, 295; and enthanasia, 72, 74; and extermination of Jews, 112, 140–2, 278, 330–3; and governments, 296–7; help to Nazi escapers, 268, 277–8, 285–6, 301–3; help to refugees, 308–15, 319–20, 343; and Nazi government, 60, 282; "White Books", 72
"Vatican (Roman) Escape Route", 278, 291, 309–10
Victor Emmanuel III, King of Italy, 299
Volkswagen, 345–6, 348, 355, 356, 363

Wagner, Gerhard, 62
Wagner, Gustav, 124–6 *passim*, 129, 130, 138, 263, 273, 275, 357
Waitz, Archbishop, 304
Wallenberg, Raoul, 216
Wannsee Conference 1942, 100
"Wanted Criminals" Austrian List, 354–5
War Crimes Commission, 142
"War crimes" and "Nazi crimes", 98
War Refugee Board, 215, 319n
Warsaw ghetto, 140, 185, 214, 231, 257
Weber, Father Anton, 18, 308, 318–23
Weinbacher, Bishop Jakob, 18, 304–7, 316
Weizsäcker, Baron, 300
Werner, Ludwig, 30–3, 38, 46–7, 55
Werner, Paul, 48–9, 50–1, 81
Wienken, Bishop, 68, 73
Wiesenthal, Simon, 21, 273–4, 338, 351–3, 354–5; *The Murderers are Among Us*, 81–2, 270
Wille, Dr Bruno, 31, 33, 46–7
Wirth, Christian, 53, 80–1, 85, 88, 103, 110–14 *passim*, 131, 138, 199, 234, 247, 358; in Treblinka, 160–3, 191, 201, 202, 223; in Trieste, 260, 262
Wise, Rabbi, 140
Wolff, General Karl, 299, 300–1, 326–7